THE HUMAN RIGHT TO RESIST IN INTERNATIONAL AND CONSTITUTIONAL LAW

The human right to resist is a contemporary legal concept with an ancient pedigree. Although it has received recognition in constitutions, customary international law and human rights treaties, and acknowledgment by leading publicists of international law, it remains obscure compared to other human rights. In this innovative and comprehensive book, Shannonbrooke Murphy addresses the perennial question of who has a 'right' to resist – and what, when, why and how, from a legal perspective. Using a systematic and comparative approach to analyzing both the theoretical concept and the provisions in positive law, this study aims to establish that a 'right to resist' can be recognized and codified as an enforceable 'human right', proposing a common conceptual language and an analytical framework for evaluating the legal basis of claims. Murphy makes a strong and detailed case for a firmer place for the 'right to resist' in the human rights lexicon.

Shannonbrooke Murphy is Endowed Chair in Human Rights and Associate Professor in the Human Rights Department of St Thomas University in Canada. She was appointed as a Human Rights Commissioner with the provincial New Brunswick Human Rights Commission in 2023, and as Director of the Atlantic Human Rights Centre in 2024.

The Human Right to Resist in International and Constitutional Law

SHANNONBROOKE MURPHY
St Thomas University

CAMBRIDGE
UNIVERSITY PRESS

CAMBRIDGE
UNIVERSITY PRESS

Shaftesbury Road, Cambridge CB2 8EA, United Kingdom

One Liberty Plaza, 20th Floor, New York, NY 10006, USA

477 Williamstown Road, Port Melbourne, VIC 3207, Australia

314–321, 3rd Floor, Plot 3, Splendor Forum, Jasola District Centre, New Delhi – 110025, India

103 Penang Road, #05–06/07, Visioncrest Commercial, Singapore 238467

Cambridge University Press is part of Cambridge University Press & Assessment, a department of the University of Cambridge.

We share the University's mission to contribute to society through the pursuit of education, learning and research at the highest international levels of excellence.

www.cambridge.org
Information on this title: www.cambridge.org/9781108838214

DOI: 10.1017/9781108974134

When citing this work, please include a reference to the DOI 10.1017/9781108974134

First published 2025

A catalogue record for this publication is available from the British Library

A Cataloging-in-Publication data record for this book is available from the Library of Congress

ISBN 978-1-108-83821-4 Hardback

This work is dedicated to all those throughout history, both renowned and unknown, who, despite the risks and against the odds, have asserted the right to resist and through their actions changed our world for the better.

And in loving memory of my Ukrainian maternal grandparents, Mykhaylo (Mike) Chojcan and Maryna (Mary) Chojcan née Kowtun. Now more than ever, this is for you.

Contents

Foreword

As I read this jurisprudentially fascinating and exceptionally learned book, the media was consumed by its daily accounts of the massive military operation conducted by Israel against the Palestinian civilian population of Gaza. It was a gruesome story rationalized on one side as self-defence against Hamas, cast as a terrorist organization that carried out a barbaric attack on 7 October 2023 and, as such, could be legitimately situated outside the protection that international law provides by setting limits on the violence of warfare, although compliance is often problematic. On the other side, criticism mounted that what was being called self-defence would be better understood if interpreted as a deliberate and unabashed recourse to genocide by Israel, whose slaughter of Gazans amounted to a humanitarian catastrophe affecting the whole of the Palestinian people. By and large, political leaders in the West endorsed Israel's shocking response to the horrific Hamas attack on 22 villages in southern Israel, which resulted in the death of an estimated 1,400 Jewish civilians and soldiers, as well as the seizure of an estimated 240 hostages, severe war crimes committed by Hamas that seemed to qualify as crimes against humanity.

In contrast were exceptionally large and aggressive public demonstrations in cities around the world, including in the United States, United Kingdom, and other states whose governments were giving unconditional support to Israel. These street protests were denouncing the scope, targeting, intensity, and severity of Israel's response as amounting to the crime of crimes, genocide, although the milder events in the West tended to confine their demands to calls for an immediate ceasefire, which Israel and the United States opposed at the UN and in their diplomatic stance. Both views, however contradictory their political outlooks seem, were connected by invoking law to justify and explain their impassioned partisanship.

A reading of Shannonbrooke Murphy's timely and conceptually brilliant book, while itself demanding a reader's sophisticated and dedicated attention, is the most illuminating treatment of these and kindred issues, of how law can be used in good faith to uphold a politics of armed resistance while at the same time putting strict limits on the legally grounded human right of people to resist various forms of oppressive conditions. It is an unusual situation, but far from unprecedented, for law to exist in certain respects but still lack sufficient clarity to offer definitive guidance to parties in conflict as to what is behaviourally permitted and what is not, enabling the more powerful actors to engage in lawfare as part of their strategic approach.

Murphy does not examine specific cases of conflicts between the forces of order and the rights of resistance in trying to depict and improve upon the *conceptual* landscape that throughout history has surrounded this inherently controversial set of issues. Instead, she considers resistance from the perspective of human rights law as it currently functions in international law and constitutional law, while presenting a learned and relevant account of historical antecedents in the work of past celebrated jurists and other normative sources of reflection on the dual role of law in prohibiting and permitting resistance. A prominent feature of the human right to resist is that it functions as a *right of exception* to the normal *duty to obey*. It is a matter of varying circumstances that give rise to resistance in a variety of contexts because existing arrangements of governance are harming individuals, groups, and peoples in socially unacceptable ways, often reflecting changing or evolving societal values. Such a potential role for positive law affirms that the contested behaviour, in addition to being morally and politically deplorable, can be further stigmatized as sufficiently *legally* deplorable as to vindicate the existence and exercise of the human right of resistance. Domestic law typically wrestles with such issues at the level of the individual or group. These issues may be features of governance (for instance, colonialism, apartheid) of characteristics of civil society (for instance, homophobia, racial and religious prejudice, patriarchy).

Such a human right to resist became prominent in the United States in the 1960s due to the refusal of individuals to comply with the legal obligation to serve for a limited period of time in the US armed forces during the Vietnam War. Western democracies had previously wrestled with this issue during World War II, generally granting individuals and groups such a right if it derived from religious convictions and was directed against all wars, or warfare as such. During the Vietnam War an increasing number of secularly motivated young Americans developed a legal argument that became known as 'selective conscientious objection' in which justification for the refusal to join the armed forces was based on moral/legal/political objections to this *particular* war in Vietnam. Revealingly, as the Vietnam War became more unpopular with the citizenry over time, courts in the United States looked with greater favour on this once novel secular rationale for conscientious objection. To be more attuned to Murphy's conceptual clarity, this set of issues of political propriety is addressed as a 'cognate' notion that influences but is distinct from the penumbra of the 'human right of resistance'. In such a spirit, Murphy subtly balances positivist concerns with achieving as much conceptual precision as possible against the importance of retaining enough flexibility to enable law to evolve as societal values and circumstances change. Her jurisprudential stance favours codification efforts that take sensitive account of changing conditions and societal values while recognizing the benefits of achieving maximum conceptual precision and stability with regard to prevailing expectations about the content of the human right to resist.

The originality of this learned discussion of the human right to resist, which should be of particular interest to common law countries such as the United States, is the decision of the author not to address specific cases of collective resistance such as the Irish or Palestinian struggle for human rights including some form of self-rule, or even the radical forms of opposition to Nazi genocide. In this sense, Murphy's jurisprudentially impressive study can be fruitfully read as a complement to Noura Erakat's fine *Justice for Some: Law and the Question of Palestine* (Stanford University Press 2019). What Erakat gains by way of readability and context is somewhat offset by her fully acknowledged substantive sympathies that become part of the policy analysis that underpins her critique of the ways international law has failed the Palestinian people. In this same sense, what Murphy, despite the lucidity of her prose, loses by way of readability is fully redeemed by a fundamental rethinking, with partisan undertones, of what is at stake when a right of exception is given to individuals, groups, and peoples to violate the law *legally*, but within a secondary framework of more or less authoritative *legal* limits.

I am a great admirer of both works, but for different, yet interlinked reasons. In Erakat's case because I share her compelling concern for delegitimizing Palestinian victimization via lawfare, while in Murphy's case because I am made far more aware of the complexity of the issues involved in legalizing resistance, taking account of its continuing evolution and persisting conceptual gaps, and explicating and exploring linkages to other kindred issues that bear centrally on limiting the power of the state. These linkages pertain both to incorporating the right to resist authority into domestic constitutional texts and by way of applicable international human rights standards that have evolved from being moral aspirations to become legal obligations. In this latter instance, for example, such crimes as apartheid and genocide are not conceptually insulated from legal accountability by invoking claims of unlimited sovereignty over territorial governance or by constitutional provisions that accord superiority to domestic sources of law whenever clashes with international law are present.

In one important respect, Murphy's positivist presentation of issues associated with resistance legality takes our attention away from the political contexts of enforcement. We could end up with an admirably coherent conceptual framework but with a useless or even regressively opportunistically legalistic approach to various categories of grievances emanating from those who are deemed as class adversaries or international rivals. The authority of law has radically uneven limits in its functioning within and among sovereign states. For instance, such 'legal' developments as the Nuremberg and Tokyo war crimes trials accepted the taint of 'victors' justice' because of foreclosing inquiry, much less accountability, into the crimes of the victors. Even more consequential for evolving a humane global rule of law was the right of veto inserted into the UN Charter, thereby both hampering and tainting the operations of the United Nations. International law is weak when it comes to vital issues because its implementation tends to be disrupted by and subordinated to the primacy of geopolitics, which rests protection of rights on such unreliable restraints as imposed by deterrence threats and prudence, if at all. This results in major resistance claims being manipulated to reflect the interests and policy priorities of powerful states and domestic elites. What is evident is that the selective implementation of human rights law in general creates images of moral hypocrisy and double standards as diluting the authority of and respect for international legal discourse. True, some creative tension has emerged internationally due to the collapse of European colonialism, although Israel is a reminder of what colonialism has meant for oppressed native peoples. This is expressed by the establishment of counter-hegemonic legal arenas, including among jurists as exemplified by TWAIL (Third World Approach to International Law) scholarship, reflecting the Global South's experience of the hegemonic uses of international law relied on by colonial Europe in exploiting native resources while dehumanizing non-Western peoples. Resistance to colonialism has, in the post-colonial era of international relations, inspired the determined effort to generate support for a counter-hegemonic approach to international and constitutional law, which is expressed by the transnational inclusion of Global South jurists in the TWAIL enterprise.

Shannonbrooke Murphy is fully aware of the incompleteness of a purely positivist focus on the human right to resist, while here setting for herself this already Herculean challenge of conceptual clarification. Her contributions to contemporary jurisprudence are profound, and rendered in ways that permit and encourage diverse inquiries into other bodies of human rights pertaining to a range of topics, including rights of self-defence, freedom of expression, and freedom of religion, in relation to such sensitive policy questions as recourse to war, rights of secession by ethnic or religious minorities, as well as the more sensitive personal issues of gender parity and identity.

Fifty or so years ago a British graduate student at the Yale Law School, Rosalyn Higgins, who like me fell under the charismatic influence of Myres McDougal, was troubled by the subjectivity and seeming ideological bias of a jurisprudential approach that gave legal hegemony to the Cold War values prevalent in the West. I was also troubled, but on different grounds. I questioned the jurisprudential necessity for such an ideological bias and instead sought a contextually sensitive approach to law that was guided by the type of secular humanism that infuses the Universal Declaration of Human Rights.

Professor Higgins, who later became a distinguished judge at the International Court of Justice, organized a conference in London to explore these rifts between the British and American approaches to law. Without the benefit of Murphy's conceptual mapping, I found the conference most intriguing because of the gathering of fine legal scholars for such an unusual conversation, yet intellectually unrewarding as it merely reproduced the tensions between a British insistence that the subjectivity of the New Haven School of International Law undermined the authority of law and the American claim that law without a political and ethical context is artificially cut off from reality. If we were to arrange such a meeting in 2024, I would insist that Shannonbrooke Murphy's book be required background reading, believing that both sides could valuably learn from it. Also, I cannot imagine a better beginning for an advanced course in human rights, resistance claims, or the interplay of international and constitutional law than by assigning this demanding yet remarkably imaginative and profound contribution to an improved understanding of the interactions between law, resistance, and human rights in a variety of substantive contexts.

Richard Falk

Acknowledgments

This book started out as an LLM thesis, then a doctoral thesis. First and foremost, therefore, I am fundamentally grateful for the guidance and general inspiration provided by Professor William A Schabas, my LLM and PhD supervisor at the Irish Centre for Human Rights at the National University of Ireland Galway School of Law and later Middlesex University School of Law. His emphasis on legal history has been particularly influential on my work. I am also fortunate to have benefited from the input and encouragement given at various points by the other members of my supervision team at Middlesex – Professor Joshua Castellino at the earliest stages of the doctoral work, and especially Associate Professor David Keane, whose careful reading and enthusiasm for the project pulled me through this second stage.

For this work to reach its third and final stage of evolution as a book would not have been possible without the support and encouragement of my editors, Finola O'Sullivan, Marianne Nield and Biju Singh, and my anonymous peer reviewers at Cambridge University Press. Likewise, I am deeply grateful for the financial support of St Thomas University, and especially for the unstinting moral and practical support of Professor Amanda DiPaolo, Chair of our Human Rights Department. I proudly acknowledge the sterling research assistance provided by my students Jenicca Jean, Pamela (Graci) Young, Emilia Gutierrez and Elisha Gunaratnam. I thank Professor Richard Falk, not only for his ongoing encouragement and generous Foreword, but also for helping to keep the legal concept of the right to resist alive over the past six decades.

Others made extremely helpful contributions. Professors Ray Murphy and Shane Darcy of the Irish Centre for Human Rights went out of their way to accommodate my research in my two years as a guest of the Centre. My doctoral colleagues there, too numerous to list individually, provided a supportive and lively intellectual and social environment. Special mention goes to Dr Tara Smith, whose positivity never failed to raise my morale, and Dr Nathan Derejko, who believed strongly in the project and provided critical feedback on some of the earliest draft materials. I would be remiss if I did not also acknowledge the consistently thoughtful support of Professor Vinodh Jaichand from my earliest days as an LLM student at the Centre, when I first formed the idea for this project.

Alex Neve, former Secretary-General of Amnesty Canada, and the other dedicated Canadian refugee lawyers Michael Bossin, Kristin Marshall, and Constance Nakatsu, originally encouraged me into the study of human rights law.

Gerry Adams and Mary Lou McDonald TD authorized flexible employment conditions and a sabbatical in order for me to complete both the LLM and PhD stages of the project.

My dear friends Monica Brennan and Tullia Marcolongo generously provided shelter during my final phase of doctoral research at the Robarts Library in Toronto, and my dear cousins Joan Ezesky and Keith Vanderkley selflessly ensured that I had a place to write up my findings in comfortable seclusion.

Finally, my greatest gratitude to the ever-faithful, without whom this work would have been impossible: Brian Murphy (RIP) and Alys Murphy (Lasha Chojcan), my devoted parents; my lifelong friends Kevin Thomas and Dr Rick Lines, who, among other supports provided, have had the greatest overall influence on my thinking and writing; my partner and Socratic gadfly, Ian Ó Maolchraoibhe, for his patience, impatience, and exacting proofing skills – any remaining errors are my own.

And, of course, to Pangur Ruadh.

Table of Cases

[Listed by category, alphabetically]

INTERNATIONAL COURTS, TRIBUNALS AND SIMILAR BODIES

African Commission on Human and Peoples' Rights

African Court of Human and Peoples' Rights

International Court of Justice

International Military Tribunal

Special Tribunal for Lebanon

UN Human Rights Committee

Other UN Treaty Bodies

DOMESTIC COURTS

Australia

Canada

France

Germany

Ghana

South Africa

United Kingdom

USA

Table of Treaties and Legislation

[Listed by category, alphabetically]

INTERNATIONAL TREATIES

REGIONAL TREATIES

Africa

Americas

Arab States

Europe

NATIONAL CONSTITUTIONS, QUASI-CONSTITUTIONAL DECLARATORY INSTRUMENTS, AND OTHER LAWS

[Listed alphabetically and in chronological order]

Algeria

Argentina

Armenia

Azerbaijan

Belgium

Benin

Bolivia

Burkina Faso

Cameroon

Cape Verde

Chad

Cuba

Cyprus

Czechia

Democratic Republic of the Congo

Dominican Republic

Ecuador

El Salvador

Estonia

France

Gambia

Germany

Ghana

Greece

Guatemala

Guinea

Honduras

Hungary

Ireland

Lithuania

Maldives

Mali

Mexico

Mozambique

Netherlands

Niger

Paraguay

Peru

Poland

Portugal

Rwanda

Scotland

Slovakia

South Sudan

Thailand

Timor Leste

Togo

Türkiye

Uganda

UK

Ukraine

Uruguay

USA

Venezuela

Table of Other Authorities

[Listed alphabetically]

INTERNATIONAL COMMISSION OF JURISTS

INTERNATIONAL COMMITTEE OF THE RED CROSS

INTERNATIONAL CRIMINAL COURT

INTERNATIONAL LAW COMMISSION

INTERNATIONAL MILITARY TRIBUNAL

ORGANIZATION OF AMERICAN STATES

UNITED NATIONS AUDIOVISUAL LIBRARY OF INTERNATIONAL LAW

UNITED NATIONS ECONOMIC AND SOCIAL COUNCIL-COMMISSION ON HUMAN RIGHTS AND THIRD COMMITTEE OF THE UNITED NATIONS GENERAL ASSEMBLY

[Listed in chronological order]

UNITED NATIONS EDUCATIONAL, CULTURAL AND SCIENTIFIC ORGANIZATION

UNITED NATIONS GENERAL ASSEMBLY

UNITED NATIONS HIGH COMMISSIONER FOR HUMAN RIGHTS

UNITED NATIONS HIGH COMMISSIONER FOR REFUGEES

UNITED NATIONS HUMAN RIGHTS COUNCIL

UNITED NATIONS OFFICE ON THE PREVENTION OF GENOCIDE AND ON THE RESPONSIBILITY TO PROTECT

UNITED NATIONS SECRETARY-GENERAL

UNITED NATIONS SECURITY COUNCIL

UNITED NATIONS SPECIAL RAPPORTEUR ON THE SITUATION OF HUMAN RIGHTS DEFENDERS

UNITED NATIONS TREATY SECTION

OTHER SOURCES

1

Introduction

In From the Margins

1.1 THE PROBLEM, THE STAKES, AND THE PURPOSE OF THIS BOOK

At any given moment, there will be individuals and groups all around the world, representing a wide variety of causes and using a wide variety of means, that will claim they have the 'right to resist'. Some will have a valid claim. Others will not. How can we tell the difference? Is the 'right to resist' really a human right, and can human rights law provide meaningful guidance when evaluating and distinguishing such claims? The answer to the latter two questions is yes. It is not only possible but crucial to conceptualize the 'right to resist' as a human right.

As this book will show, the 'human right to resist' is a contemporary legal concept with an ancient pedigree. It is domestically codified in constitutions from all regions. It has received recognition in general or customary international law, codification in human rights treaties, and acknowledgment by leading publicists of international law. Despite all of this, it remains obscure compared to many other human rights. It has been neglected by human rights scholarship, and is under-represented in mainstream human rights discourse. One does not find the human right to resist included in standard human rights curricula. The contemporary scholarly literature discussion of it is thin. It is not generally recognized in the standard human rights lexicon. In part because we still lack a common conceptual language and analytical framework by which to evaluate the legal basis of claims, most attributions of a 'right to resist' derive more from intuition than from systematic legal assessment.

Why does this matter? Recognition of this human right, and the ability to evaluate claims based on reasonable, consistent human rights criteria, can make a positive difference for human rights defenders. It can make a difference at domestic level, in the outcomes of certain criminal trials, refugee exclusion or extradition proceedings, and constitutional cases. At international level, it can better inform and potentially make a difference in the outcome of deliberations and decisions at the United Nations Security Council, General Assembly and Human Rights Council, and at international courts and tribunals.

Understanding the right to resist as a human right has three effects. Those effects are exceptional authorization, constraint, and interaction. First, as is well known, most human rights are not unlimited, but rather subject to certain limitations. This means a right to resist will include simultaneous authorization and constraint functions. It is not equivalent to the idea of an unlimited freedom to resist 'by any means necessary'. It does not suggest that all individuals and groups have the right to resist at any time, for any reason, and by any means. Rather, there are conditions that must be fulfilled in order to trigger this extraordinary human right under exceptional circumstances. However, at the same time as it produces these regulatory effects, it also lifts the unreasonable constraints otherwise imposed by ordinary human rights law. That is, ordinary constraints can shift from 'reasonable' to 'unreasonable' when they inadvertently consign individuals and groups to ineffectiveness or martyrdom when faced with serious or grave human rights violations on the part of a state or other powerful entity, or a 'widespread and systematic attack' constituting crimes against humanity, or genocide, or other crimes of an international character such as aggression or war crimes. Because the human right to resist would necessarily interact with other well-established human rights frameworks, standards, and analytical tools such as 'necessity' and 'proportionality', it becomes possible to establish a flexible concept that creates a lawful exception covering a wide spectrum of 'otherwise unlawful acts', expanding and contracting depending on the immediate facts of any individual case.

To fail or refuse to recognize this exceptional right is to accept that human rights must give way when faced with an implacable state, corporation, or other opponent of human rights, or a biased or otherwise paralyzed international system that in any event cannot guarantee human security because its mechanisms for doing so trigger too late in the process of the experience of violations. We need to be able to distinguish between those who may have a sincere but objectively unfounded belief that they have a right to resist, those who consciously co-opt this human rights idea for ends antithetical to human rights, and those who can be determined to have an objectively well-founded basis to a claim to a human right to resist based on lawful exception. As it stands, individuals and groups frequently claim a right they do not have, which can have the effect of degrading the perceived integrity of more well-founded claims. Conversely, categorical denial of the existence of the right, even where a specific claim may be demonstrably well-founded, contributes to greater uncertainty and a cynicism that degrades the credibility of the idea that distinction is possible.

Unfortunately, much of the existing legal scholarship is of limited assistance. Taken as a whole, it lacks conceptual definition and consistent usage. It also lacks the necessary forensic comparative analysis of both the concept and the law. A simplistic and erroneous assumption of obsolescence or relegation to 'sham law' sometimes features, reflecting a general failure to systematically build a coherent knowledge base. This may be the result of a determined liberal orthodox aversion to the idea, which became predominant in the discipline of human rights in the later part of the last century, or it may simply be due to a lack of familiarity with the concept resulting from its progressive marginalization over time. The law itself is equally limited, characterized by uneven recognition and indeed both ambiguity and some apparent ambivalence at international level, as well as uneven human rights compliance in provisions found at domestic constitutional level.

This situation leads to inconsistencies that tend to generate anomalies and sometimes absurd results. For example, by the standards of the United Nations Declaration on Human Rights Defenders, which does not acknowledge an exceptional right to resist under certain conditions, human rights luminary Nelson Mandela himself would not have qualified for recognition as such.[1] That is to say, at present, persons validly exercising the human right to resist in defence of human rights may not always be protected by the formal orthodox international human rights concept of human rights defenders, on the basis that their actions render them 'not deserving of protection'. This creates a situation prejudicial to those most vulnerable and therefore most desperate because they lack the effective remedies or human rights defence options available to those with the least to lose.

[1] See UN General Assembly, 'Declaration on the Right and Responsibility of Individuals, Groups and Organs of Society to Promote and Protect Universally Recognized Human Rights and Fundamental Freedoms' UNGA Res 53/144 (9 December 1998) articles 12 and 13; UN Special Rapporteur on the Situation of Human Rights Defenders, 'Commentary to the Declaration on the Right and Responsibility of Individuals, Groups and Organs of Society to Promote and Protect Universally Recognized Human Rights and Fundamental Freedoms' (July 2011) 5–6, 8–11, 25–26, 31–32, 70–74, 88–90; and an earlier analysis of this particular paradox in Shannonbrooke Murphy, 'The Right to Resist Reconsidered' in David Keane and Yvonne McDermott (eds), *The Challenge of Human Rights: Past, Present and Future* (Edward Elgar 2012) 92–95.

It also leads to uncertainties and gaps that can generate paralysis. That is, the fairly significant certainty gaps remaining in the law of the human right to resist as it stands, when taken as a whole, too often yield insufficient guidance for action or reaction. This is the consequence of an apparent formal asymmetry in the international human rights legal regime, whereby a rule of exception provides a degree of flexibility for states exempting them to a certain extent from certain human rights duties, under certain conditions, but there is no generally recognized analogous exception for the holders of those human rights allowing that, under certain conditions, certain ordinary limitations on the scope of their lawful rights-enforcement action likewise do not apply.

The ensuing legal certainty and uncertainty varies by degree. This can be expressed as categories of claimants according to greatest certainty, reasonable certainty, and uncertainty warranting clarification and confirmation. For example, as of 1970, the greatest certainty is that a 'people as a whole' have the right to resist 'forcible denial of the right to external self-determination', meaning aggression, unlawful occupation, colonization, or apartheid. There is also reasonable certainty that the right to resist 'forcible denial of the right to internal self-determination' is recognized for ethnic minority 'peoples' under 'racist regimes' as defined in international law. What still needs clarification is whether a 'people as a whole' have the right to resist 'forcible denial of the right to internal self-determination' by coup d'état, by 'tyranny or other oppression', or by violations of the right to economic self-determination through economic domination and exploitation. What needs confirmation is that all individuals have the right to resist 'internationally criminal acts' legally constituting aggression, war crimes, genocide, crimes against humanity, or laws and policies leading to these outcomes. Uncertainty remains as to whether individuals and groups have the right to resist 'other violations' of human rights or international law. If so, does this authorize resistance against patterns of only grave or also lesser human rights violations? Does it extend to all unlawful use of force by the state, including individual resistance to police violence or harassment? There is even less certainty regarding the right to resist other violations of economic, social, and cultural rights, including where these amount to interference with the right to internal self-determination as a result of oligarchy, kleptocracy, or corruption. Is there a right to resist violations of environmental rights and related international law, including where grave violations of environmental rights affect the right to life? Do indigenous peoples have the right to resist violations of their particular economic, social, and cultural rights, where these violations may fall short of 'genocide' according to the Genocide Convention, or forcible imposition of a 'racist regime' as legally defined under the Apartheid Convention? All these remaining certainty gaps need further scholarly exploration and legal clarification, whether by new codifications or by new interpretations and applications of the law as it stands. This book shows that there is potentially room for both approaches.

Why is such clarification important? The ambiguity problem in the current law has potentially serious consequences at the international level. It permits inconsistency in UN Security Council decision-making with respect to rebellions or other resistance against oppression, illustrated by its contrasting approaches in comparable contemporaneous cases. It perpetuates a situation whereby there is no clear basis in law for those resisting oppressive or corrupt regimes to request, and thus for the international community to provide, lawful assistance on the basis of a meritorious claim. It also means that there is too much room for disagreement as to the basis upon which a state can be banned from requesting and receiving assistance from other states in suppression of a rebellion or other resistance. Clarification of the right to resist could encourage instead decision-making informed by a transparent legal framework and a consistent regulatory standard. It could help set more appropriate limits on providing UN or UN-authorized assistance to states in suppressing rebellion or other resistance, or in rarer instances provide a sounder legal basis for UN authorization of assistance to those challenging a human rights violator state. Stronger legal recognition of self-help resistance rights of individuals, groups, and peoples under exceptional circumstances, combined with the correlated international obligation to lawfully assist or not obstruct, could thus provide an alternative or complement to the emerging 'responsibility to protect' doctrine. It could provide clearer and firmer guidance to domestic and international courts, tribunals, and quasi-judicial bodies, dealing with relevant cases. It could also provide guidance to international independent experts adjudicating in truth and reconciliation processes. At the level of individual cases, in challenges to exclusion from refugee protection on the basis of alleged criminal conduct, it could provide a clearer and more consistent basis for establishing and distinguishing protected political activity. In challenges to extradition requests, it could provide an international human rights law basis for appropriate political offence exceptions that would not be negated by overbroad counterterrorism clauses. And it could assist criminal defences in appropriate cases.

Ultimately, failure or refusal to recognize the right to resist perpetuates unequal patterns of access to universal human rights and unequal distribution of protections. It does so in a manner prejudicial to those faced with oppressive conditions who do not have legal options available, including those whom

Baxi has identified as the 'human rightless'.[2] Conversely, recognition of the right has 'counter-hegemonic' equalizing potential.[3] This idea is in keeping with Falk's contention that law is a tool – of the powerful certainly, but one also capable of appropriation by the ostensibly powerless, as history has shown. Indeed, this book demonstrates that, upon closer inspection, the ostensible asymmetry in the law is not as absolute as it first appears.

The human right to resist is a concept that deserves a more prominent place in our human rights lexicon. Indeed, reconsideration of the viability of this concept as a human right has become timely and necessary in light of a failed second attempt at United Nations codification in 2016, despite prior endorsement by the UN Human Rights Council's expert Advisory Committee. This book makes the case for reconsideration of the right to resist, its reinstatement in human rights discourse, and firmer recognition in international law. Its theoretical purpose is to establish a sound basis for this reconsideration and reinstatement and for the scholarly dialogue necessary to further develop the legal concept. The book aims to establish why and how a 'right to resist' can be conceptualized as an enforceable 'human right' and positivized as such in law through codification and other recognition. Beyond this, its practical purpose is to offer guidance in utilizing the concept, and to promote greater respect for enforcement of human rights through extrajudicial means 'from below',[4] reflecting what Heyns has called a 'struggle approach' to human rights.[5] That is, in both theoretical and practical ways, this book urges an expanded notion of what constitutes human rights 'defence' or 'enforcement' worthy of recognition and protection. It provides definitional, conceptual, and legal status clarifications, as well as analytical tools to assist both further assessment of theories and application and further development of the existing law. The ultimate purpose of the book, therefore, is to identify an agenda for reconsideration of the right to resist that will enable us to bring this human right in from the margins, to assume its rightful place in the human rights lexicon. In doing so, it invites other scholars, practitioners, and advocates to join this mission.

[2] He defines the 'rightless' as those who are, if not stateless, then 'unclaimed and [treated as] eminently disposable', who 'amidst ... plentiful forms of dehumanization ... somehow eke out their "existence"'. Upendra Baxi, *The Future of Human Rights* (2nd edn, Oxford University Press 2008) 130–134.

[3] On 'counter-hegemonic' human rights see Richard Falk, *Achieving Human Rights* (Routledge 2009) 35–38.

[4] This corresponds to the more general idea developed in Balakrishnan Rajagopal, *International Law from Below* (Cambridge University Press 2003).

[5] Christof Heyns, 'A "Struggle Approach" to Human Rights' in Arend Soeteman (ed), *Pluralism and Law* (Springer 2001).

1.2 THE APPROACH AND METHOD

This book approaches the perennial question of who has a 'right' to resist – and what, when, why, and how – from a legal perspective, intended to complement other scholarship on the subject by philosophers and political theorists. To establish that a 'right to resist' can be recognized and codified as an enforceable 'human right', it uses a systematic and comparative approach to analyzing both the theoretical concept and the provisions in positive law. The findings of this analysis ultimately form the basis of its practical proposals regarding a common conceptual language and an analytical framework for evaluating the legal basis of claims.

Although the right to resist is not a 'new' human right, and indeed predates the concept of 'human rights' as such, due to its relegation to the margins of the discipline it will likely be unfamiliar and therefore 'new' to many readers.[6] With skeptics and those who caution against unnecessary 'rights-inflation' in mind, the book adopts Philip Alston's 'quality control' method for assessing proposed new or otherwise marginalized human rights.[7] This demands first a forensic analysis of the rights concept, followed by a forensic analysis of its status in both constitutional and international law. This Alstonian analytical framework is reflected in the book's two-part structure. Part I on 'The Concept' considers problems of contemporary term usage and legal definition, the right's hypothesized nature and legal function, and identifies the elements that determine its legal content. Part II on 'The Law' examines the right's sources by way of domestic provision in constitutional law, recognition in general or customary international law, provision in treaty law, and other attempts at international codification.

Bringing all these aspects together in an integrated coherent analysis gives this book a distinctive scope. In particular, the positive law examination is wider in scope than other available studies, insofar as it is comparative across international and constitutional sources, and also comparative across historical periods. The conceptual examination emphasizes the excavation of positions

6 On the need to distinguish degree of actual novelty from degree of recognition, acknowledging that a right may be simultaneously considered 'new' and 'not new', see Andreas von Arnauld, Kerstin von der Decken, and Mart Susi (eds), *The Cambridge Handbook of New Human Rights: Recognition, Novelty, Rhetoric* (Cambridge University Press 2020) 1–3.

7 Philip Alston, 'Third Generation of Solidarity Rights: Progressive Development or Obfuscation of International Human Rights Law?' (1982) 29(3) *Netherlands International Law Review* 307; Philip Alston, 'Conjuring Up New Human Rights: A Proposal for Quality Control' (1984) 78 *American Journal of International Law* 607; Philip Alston, 'Peoples' Rights: Their Rise and Fall' in Philip Alston (ed), *Peoples' Rights* (Oxford University Press 2001).

on the right to resist taken by the 'most qualified publicists' – however briefly stated – consolidated with the work of established and emerging legal scholars who have taken up various aspects of this topic or conducted otherwise relevant adjacent research. As such, it provides a comprehensive introduction to this human right for specialist and non-specialist readers, from within or outside the discipline of law.

Another distinctive feature of this book's approach and method is that it deliberately does not use case studies. Rather, it is intended as a general theory of the right. In this regard, the book proposes tests for its practical application that can assist in assessing real-world claims relying on international and/or constitutional law.

One limitation of this study must be acknowledged here. It was not possible to comprehensively treat the separate and no less important literatures on the right to resist in French and Spanish particularly, or those in German, Arabic, Chinese, and Russian. Given its reliance on literature in English, it necessarily focuses on the western origins of the concept of the right to resist, and their subsequent influence on provisions in domestic constitutional law within and beyond the West, as well as on recognitions within international law to whose development states and scholars of all regions now contribute. However, for this reason, it can only tell part of the story. A similar study of the eastern origins of the concept and its analogues in ancient Confucianism, Islamic legal thought of the Middle Ages and since, and the modern advent of Soviet legal theory is necessary to complete the picture of the history and evolution of the right to resist as a human rights concept. Such further study would invite fruitful collaboration with specialists in the preceding disciplines, particularly where a language barrier would otherwise pose access challenges. Systematic comparative treatment of the literatures and case law in other languages would also enable further comparative constitutional research.

1.3 THE STRUCTURE OF THE BOOK

Following Alston's two-part method, the first part of the book examines the legal concept. Responding to the lack of an agreed contemporary legal definition of the 'human right to resist', Chapter 2 compares definitional treatments in ordinary construction with those in legal construction, identifying two related problems of conflation in contemporary term usage. It explains the term's distinction from antecedent concepts such as the *exceptio tyrannoctonos* or exception of lawful tyrannicide, and from corroborative concepts including the *lex generalis* or ordinary 'right of (peaceful) assembly' and 'right to protest' in human rights law, 'resistance movements' in international humanitarian law, and 'insurgent' or 'belligerent' status in customary international law. It also clarifies the conceptual relationship between the 'right to resist' and its cognate terms – the 'right to oppose', 'right to disobey', 'right to rebel', and 'right of revolution' – identifying both points of differentiation and a 'common core'. It finally proposes a consolidated contemporary working definition of the superordinate term 'right to resist'.

Chapter 3 examines the contours of theories and debates about the nature and function of the right to resist as a legal concept. Firstly, it identifies four main approaches to conceptualizing the nature of the right: as moral, legal, both, or other. It then considers three main theories of the concept's relationship to the rule of law. Concerning its other key characteristics, the chapter considers possibilities including that it is: a fundamental 'human right' in the political rights cluster; an 'unenumerated', 'implied', or 'latent' right; an enforceable 'claim' right; a 'right' or 'duty' or hybrid 'right-duty'; a primary or secondary right, or both. Secondly, the chapter identifies possibilities for the legal function of the right, including as: a self-help remedy for enforcement or prevention; an exceptional immunity, justification, or temporary permission by licence; a form of *jus ad bellum*; and a lawful exception and *lex specialis* rule. It concludes non-exclusively that the nature of the contemporary right to resist is a potentially enforceable human right, functioning as a *lex specialis* rule of exception.

Chapter 4 identifies and examines the elements determining the legal content of any given theory of, or positive law provision for, the human right to resist. It reviews the primary triggers or conditions for activation, indicating the 'right to resist *what*', including 'tyranny', 'oppression', and 'other violations'. It reviews the secondary triggers or conditions for activation, indicating the 'right to resist *when*', in particular the necessity condition. It also reviews both aspects of the personal scope, being the rights-holders, indicating '*who* may resist', and also the duty-bearers, indicating '*who* has a corresponding duty'. It identifies a four-fold typology of legitimate 'object and purpose', or 'right to resist *why*', being for human rights enforcement, for self-defence, for self-determination, and for 'peace' or human security. The final element examined is the material scope of application, or 'right to resist *how*', identifying three competing approaches to permissible means, and affirming proportionality limitations and other applicable limitations in international human rights law and international criminal law, as well as grounds for discretionary non-exercise. This general analytical template for identification and comparison of elements and therefore content is then applied to the evidence of legal sources of the right considered in the second part, which examines the positive law.

Chapter 5 assesses the richest source of positive law on the right to resist, domestic constitutional provision in its historical and contemporary iterations. It first considers several examples of antecedent provisions for lawful tyrannicide in 'ancient constitutions' or equivalent law including customary law. It then reviews examples of provisions for a right to resist unlawful exercise of power in Middle Ages 'constitutions' or public law equivalents including customary law, and other quasi-constitutional sources such as coronation oaths, as well as intervention appeals rooted in custom. It concludes consideration of the historical right to resist provisions with a review of key modern revolutionary republican and anti-colonial foundational declarations and constitutions. The remainder of the chapter concerns approximately forty contemporary constitutional provisions for the right to resist in African, Asian, European, and Latin American constitutions. Using the template developed in Chapter 4, it provides comparative analysis of their legal features and content. Finally, the chapter evaluates the provisions' legal meaning by way of a two-fold typology, and their legal value against the question of 'sham law'.

Chapter 6 addresses the status of recognition of the human right to resist in general or customary international law, and the problem of clarifying this absent express provision in material sources. It first considers theories of recognition in customary international law predating the United Nations Charter, followed by theories of implied recognition under the Charter as customary international law or as a general principle of international law, including the generally accepted albeit narrow implied recognition of the right in UN General Assembly Resolution 2625. It then examines the possibility of a broader implied recognition of the right in the Universal Declaration of Human Rights. Applying the analytical template from Chapter 4, it identifies the elements and content of the theorized right in these sources. Finally, it reviews the third material source, the implied recognition of a customary right-duty to resist internationally criminal acts in the Nuremberg Principles. The chapter concludes by reviewing the corroborative sources potentially indicative of customary recognition, including: the customary laws of insurgency and belligerency, recognition, and responsibility; the regulation of 'resistance movements' and 'national liberation movements' by international humanitarian law; the political offence exception in extradition law; and the persistent non-equation of the 'right to resist' with 'terrorism' in international instruments.

Chapter 7 addresses the status of recognition of the human right to resist in conventional international law, and the outcome of recent other international codification efforts. It first considers the universal human rights system, and the theory of implied recognition as an unenumerated right in the

International Covenant on Civil and Political Rights, identifying the theorized elements and content using the analytical template. It also considers the right's corroboration implied by provisions of the Refugee Convention and the Rome Statute of the International Criminal Court. It then considers the right's fragmentation in the regional human rights systems, comparing the elements and content of the express provision in the African Charter on Human and Peoples' Rights and the Arab Charter on Human Rights with its apparent non-recognition in the European and Inter-American systems. Finally, the chapter considers the most recent international 'soft law' codification effort: a proposed provision on the right of 'resistance and opposition to oppression' in the draft UN Declaration on the Right to Peace, identifying its elements and content. After this second failure to codify the right to resist in a UN human rights instrument, it assesses prospects for, and the legal value of, future international codification.

The concluding Chapter 8 summarizes the overall case for reinstatement of the right to resist in the human rights lexicon, and its reconsideration in light of the study's findings. It then sets an agenda for its further reconsideration as a human right by scholars, practitioners, and other advocates with regard to the preceding evidence and analysis, identifying both *lex lata* and *lex ferenda* options for clarification, and suggesting a basic claims analysis template for applying the law as it stands.

Finally, the choice of cover image also warrants brief explanation. The cover depicts a famous scene of Jewish resistance during the Warsaw Ghetto Uprising, known as the 'Captured HeHalutz Fighters' (Małka Zdrojewicz Horenstein, Bluma Wyszogrodzka, Rachela Wyszogrodzka). This image was chosen not only because it is humanizing down to the individual level, but also because it is relevant for two reasons. First, resistance to Nazism was and remains a reference point for the contemporary human right to resist. Second, consistent with the concept elaborated in this book, as archetypical human rights defenders the Warsaw Ghetto Uprising participants did not confine themselves to exclusively peaceful means, or exclusively forceful means, but rather employed the full spectrum of otherwise unlawful means as necessary to resist a genocidal state when lawful means became unavailable. Their example, and similar examples from other contexts, have inspired the study that follows.

PART I

The Concept

2

Advancing a Legal Definition of the Right

2.1 INTRODUCTION

What does it mean to have a 'right to resist'? We are not yet equipped with an agreed legal concept, much less a sufficiently legally precise and commonly accepted definition. The conceptual evolution of the right to resist, from its ancient origins to the present, remains an unfinished business.

Definitional challenges are not uncommon and are not necessarily fatal to the viability of a concept. According to Schabas, even the unquestionably justiciable human right to life remains 'intangible in scope and vexingly difficult to define with precision' due to its 'continuously evolving' content and the relatively recent history of judicial findings.[1] Perhaps then it is not surprising that we are still asking the most basic questions of the comparatively more controversial right to resist: What is the nature of the 'right' in question? What is meant by the words 'to resist'? Who has this right and under what conditions? What are its proper scope and limits? What are the legal and other implications, if any? Indeed, the very idea that such a thing as a 'right to resist' exists is not universally accepted within the discipline of law. It may well be one of the 'great resolved issues' for political theory and philosophy.[2] This is not the case for legal scholarship.

[1] William A Schabas, *The European Convention on Human Rights: A Commentary* (Oxford University Press 2015) 117.

[2] Deborah Baumgold, 'Pacifying Politics: Resistance, Violence and Accountability in Seventeenth-Century Contract Theory' (1993) 21(1) *Political Theory* 6, 6. See also Christopher J Finlay, *Terrorism and the Right to Resist: A Theory of Just Revolutionary War* (Cambridge University Press 2015) 19. Even so, there remain areas of substantial disagreement on what the right actually entails.

What may partially explain this persisting uncertainty is the absence of a distinct and coherent legal literature that systematically builds on, or challenges, the theories and findings of predecessors, creating a firm basis for gradual refinement of the concept. For example, most twentieth- and twenty-first-century theories of the right to resist essentially derive from one of the major historical exemplars.[3] That is, they exhibit either specific features or a general approach that may be described as Ciceronian,[4] Thomasian,[5] Bartolist,[6] Vindiciaen,[7] Grotian,[8] Hobbesian,[9] Lockean,[10] or Vattelian.[11]

[3] There are other historical theories, but those listed here arguably represent the most influential and persistent.

[4] See Cicero, *De Officiis* (Walter Miller tr, GP Putnam's Sons 1913) Book III iv [19] 287, vi [32] 299.

[5] See Thomas Aquinas, 'Commentary on the Sentences of Peter Lombard' in AP Entrèves (ed), *Aquinas: Selected Political Writings* (JG Dawson tr, Oxford University Press 1948) Book II 'The Obedience Owed by Christians to the Secular Power and in particular to Tyrants' di 44, q 2, a 2 181–185; Thomas Aquinas, *De regno ad regum Cypri: On Kingship, To the King of Cyprus* (Gerald B Phelan tr, IT Eschmann rev edn, Pontifical Institute of Medieval Studies 1949) Book I ch 7 'How provision might be made that the king may not fall into tyranny'; Thomas Aquinas, 'Summa Theologiae' in William P Baumgarth and Richard J Regan (eds), *On Law, Morality and Politics* (Richard J Regan tr, 2nd edn, Hackett Publishing 2002) II-II q 40 'On War', a 1 'Is It Always Sinful to Wage War?', q 64 'On Homicide', a 7 'Is it Lawful for a Person to Kill Another in Self-Defense?', q 104 'On Obedience', a 5 'Are Subjects Obliged to Obey Their Superiors in All Things?' and a 6 'Are Christians Obliged to Obey Secular Authorities?, q 42 'On Rebellion', a 2 'Is Rebellion Always a Mortal Sin?'

[6] See Bartolus de Saxoferrato, *On Guelfs and Ghibbellines* (Jonathan Robinson tr, Creative Commons Attribution-Non-Commercial ShareAlike 3.0 Unreported License 2014 rev 1.1a) Book III 4–6; Bartolus de Saxoferrato, *On the Tyrant* (Jonathan Robinson tr, Creative Commons Attribution-Non-Commercial ShareAlike 3.0 Unreported License 2012 (rev 1.0a) 2016 (rev 1.2)).

[7] See *Vindiciae, Contra Tyrannos: or, Concerning the Legitimate Power of a Prince over the People, and of the People over a Prince* (George Garnett ed/tr, 2003 edn, Cambridge University Press 1994) Third Question 67–172, Fourth Question 173–185.

[8] See Hugo Grotius, *The Rights of War and Peace* (Richard Tuck ed, Jean Barbeyrac tr, Liberty Fund 2005) Book I Chapter IV 'Of a War Made by Subjects against Their Sovereigns' 336–383, Book II Chapter I-I 392, III 397, V 309, 401, Chapter XXV 'Of the Causes for Which War Is to Be Undertaken on the Account of Others' I 1151, VI 1156, VII 1158, VIII 1159–1162, Chapter XXVI 'Lawful Reasons Why Subjects of a Ruler May Go to War' III–IV 1167, 1171, 1173, 1176, 1177.

[9] For a synthesis of the Hobbesian position arising from the relevant passages of *Leviathan* 14–15, 21, *Elements of Law* 1.17.2, 2.1.5 and *De Cive* 2.18, 3.1.4, see Susanne Sreedhar, *Hobbes on Resistance: Defying the Leviathan* (Cambridge University Press 2010).

[10] See John Locke, 'The Second Treatise of Government: An Essay Concerning the True Original, Extent and End of Civil Government' in *Two Treatises of Government* (Peter Laslett ed, rev edn, Cambridge University Press 1988) Chapter XVI 'Of Conquest' [175]–[196] 384–397, Chapter XVII 'Of Usurpation' [197]–[198] 397–398, Chapter XVIII 'Of Tyranny' [199]–[210] 398–405, Chapter XIX 'Of the Dissolution of Government' [211]–[243] 406–428.

[11] See Emer de Vattel, *The Law of Nations, or Principles of the Law of Nature, Applied to the Conduct and Affairs of Nations and Sovereigns* (Béla Kapossy and Richard Whatmore eds,

However, contemporary approaches have become disconnected from their origins, which remain largely unacknowledged. The current, admittedly thin, jurisprudential literature on the right to resist mostly consists of discrete theoretical strands clustered around either the right's nature or its scope with regard to means. Other clusters are more like applied theories insofar as they concern either particular objects and purposes of the right or particular case studies. A final smaller cluster concerns theories of the right's sources. While some do cut across several of these, true general legal theories of the right are comparatively scarce. What little discussion there is too often proceeds in isolation from either historical or contemporary preceding work, frequently resulting in counterproductive re-tread or misapprehension.

In the interest of advancing a more systematic and cogent reconsideration of the right to resist as a contemporary legal concept, this chapter and the remainder of Part I on 'The Concept' map the contours of the existing debate within legal theory on its definition and content as a 'human right', bringing these into sharper relief. To counteract the absence of established common points of reference in the contemporary legal theory of the right, Part I aims to help consolidate not only the 'known unknowns' but also the 'unknown knowns' of this nascent sub-field.[12] These chapters therefore focus on the deconstruction of the contemporary theoretical concept and the comparison of competing theories. In doing so they canvass and, where necessary, excavate the sometimes scant or under-elaborated conclusions by some of the 'most highly qualified publicists' expert in the general field of human rights. Because their opinions constitute a recognized source of evidence of international law,[13] this study accords them equal weight to the handful of lesser-known scholars who have published more than one dedicated work on the topic or have otherwise given it more extensive and direct treatment.

Liberty Fund 2008) Book I Chapter IV 'Of the Sovereign, His Obligations and His Rights' [51]–[54] 103–112, Book II Chapter I 'Of the Common Duties of a Nation towards Others or of the Offices of Humanity between Nations' [7] 265, Chapter IV 'Of the Right to Security, and the Effects of Sovereignty and Independence of Nations' [49]–[52] 288–289, [54]–[57] 289–292, Chapter V 'Of the Observance of Justice between Nations' [65]–[70] 296–297, Chapter XII 'Of Treaties of Alliance and other Public Treaties' [168] 344 [196]–[197] 364–365, Book III Chapter XVIII 'Of Civil War' [288]–[289] 641–642, [290]–[293], [295] 642–647.

12 This extension of Luft and Ingham's 'Johari window' to include 'unknown knowns' is borrowed from Slavoj Žižek, 'Philosophy, the "Unknown Knowns" and the Public Use of Reason' (2006) 25(1) *Topoi* 137.

13 See Ian Brownlie, *Principles of Public International Law* (7th edn, Oxford University Press 2008) 24.

In keeping with the Alstonian method described in Chapter 1, the introduction to this book, the ultimate purpose of Part I is to put Part II's examination of contemporary positive law of the human right to resist into its proper context. The present chapter first considers problems associated with contemporary legal definition and term usage. Chapter 3 then identifies the major unresolved conceptual issues and most persistent inherited jurisprudential debates regarding the nature and legal function of the right that bear on its justiciability and enforceability. Finally, Chapter 4 analyzes its elements and legal content as a human right. All three chapters indicate areas of varying degrees of agreement and outstanding disagreement. Since unresolved debates necessitating further scholarly investigations should ideally be grounded in an appreciation of the evolution and current state of the positive law, the conceptual theories of Part I interact with the source theories considered in Part II on 'The Law'.

The general purpose of this chapter is to suggest the basis for a legal definition by consolidating the work of predecessors. Section 2.2 identifies a persistent problem contributing to conceptual confusion, relating to the contemporary interchangeable use of the cognate terms 'right to resist', 'right to oppose', 'right to disobey', 'right to rebel', and 'right of revolution'. Section 2.3 considers possible explanations, comparing the evidence of ordinary construction with legal construction. Section 2.4 proposes a clarification of the conceptual relationships between the cognates for the purpose of legal definition. Sections 2.5 and 2.6, respectively, distinguish these cognate terms from their historical antecedent the *exceptio tyrannoctonos* or 'doctrine' or 'right' of 'tyrannicide', as well as from corroborative concepts such as the *lex generalis* or ordinary 'right of (peaceful) assembly' and 'right to protest'; 'resistance movements' for the purposes of international humanitarian law; and 'insurgent' or 'belligerent' status as understood otherwise in public international law. From this analysis, Section 2.7 extracts standard definitional elements deriving from the 'common core' of the cognate terms. Having taken the preceding into account, the chapter concludes by proposing a consolidated contemporary working definition for the 'human right to resist', with a view to advancing its general conceptual theory.

2.2 CONTEMPORARY TERM USAGE

Given that the 'right to resist' is a legal concept that has been around for centuries, the absence of a widely used definition within the legal literature stands out. Many contemporary scholars use the term and even discuss the right to resist in detail without ever either defining it, or referring to another's definition upon which they rely.[14] Not even Chemillier-Gendreau's encyclopedic entry for the 'right to resistance' defines the term.[15] Lauterpacht also bypasses term definition, proceeding directly to discussion of the usages of Grotius and Vattel,[16] presumed familiar and accurately understood. Yet this may not always be the case, and reliance on second-hand accounts of the historic theories sometimes leads to distorted conclusions.[17] Non-legal definitions provided by philosophers other than jurists, historians other than legal historians, or political scientists can equally pose precision problems for legal scholarship, which must answer somewhat different questions. Even the best of the few existing contemporary legal definitions has important shortcomings,[18] and none fully satisfy the standard for rigour. However, drawing on this previous scholarship and synthesizing areas of significant agreement should yield an improved working definition of the legal concept that, while perhaps not finally conclusive, could better satisfy the precision requirement. This is attempted below, after taking some additional factors into account.

Compounding this definition problem, contemporary theorists in both legal and non-legal literature on the subject often use the term 'right of resistance' and its cognate terms 'right of disobedience', 'right of rebellion', and 'right of revolution' interchangeably. This represents a significant departure from how these separate terms evolved historically, each associated with a

[14] For example, Max Pribilla, *The Right to Resist* (Catholic Social Guild 1952); René Marcic, 'The Persistence of Right-Law: An Inquiry into the Foundations of the Right to Resist' (1973) 59 *Archives for Philosophy of Law and Social Philosophy* 87. Such definitional problems were noted by the 'Meeting of experts on the analysis of the basis and forms of individual and collective action by which violations of human rights can be combated, Freetown, Sierra Leone, 3–7 March 1981: Final Report' in *Violations of Human Rights: Possible Rights of Recourse and Forms of Resistance* (UNESCO 1984) 222, 227.

[15] See Monique Chemillier-Gendreau, 'Resistance, Right to, International Protection of' in Rüdiger Wolfrum (ed), *Max Planck Encyclopedia of Public International Law* (Oxford University Press 2012) vol VIII: PA-SA 954–959.

[16] See Hersch Lauterpacht, 'The Law of Nations, the Law of Nature and the Rights of Man' (1943) 29 *Transactions of the Grotius Society* 1, 23–26; Hersch Lauterpacht, *An International Bill of the Rights of Man* (Columbia University Press 1945) 43–46; Hersch Lauterpacht, *International Law and Human Rights* (Stevens and Sons 1950) 116–119.

[17] See for example Remec's mischaracterization of Vattel's concept of the right to resist as somehow weaker than that of Grotius, contrary to evidence, in Peter Pavel Remec, *The Position of the Individual in International Law According to Grotius and Vattel* (Martinus Nijhoff 1960) 228–234. On Wright having misconstrued Vattel as having abandoned just war theory, which includes the right to resist, see Hans Kelsen, 'Quincy Wright's A Study of War and the *Bellum Justum* Theory' (1943) 53 *Ethics* 208, 209.

[18] See for example Upendra Baxi, 'Otonomic Prowess and Existential Impotence: Reflexions on René Marcic's Sydney Papers' (conference paper for 'René Marcic: Sydney Commemorative Symposium (54)' University of Sydney, Faculty of Law, Department of Jurisprudence and International Law, Institute for Advanced Studies in Jurisprudence, Sydney, 1972) 6 ff.

distinct usage but also related to the 'right to resist'. Yet it is not uncommon for scholars to use several cognate terms in a single work, without clear distinction or further explanation as to why, in their view, these concepts are similar, analogous, or identical.[19] Such usage is not limited to works of dubious quality, or to scholars lacking experience. This lack of precision frequently confuses matters, because while the terms are certainly related, they are not genuinely interchangeable, as closer analysis reveals. Indeed, the contemporary literature suffers from such chronic terminological problems that without inclusion of literature using the other terms this study would be incomplete. While sometimes such interchangeable usage is appropriate and does not obscure the meaning, more often the apparent presumption that it is correct to use these distinct terms generally as synonyms contributes to conceptual obfuscation.[20] This somewhat complicates the task of comparing the conceptual and definitional contributions of the major theorists of the twentieth and twenty-first centuries and is among the significant shortcomings of this body of scholarship.

2.3 CLARIFYING THE CONCEPTUAL RELATIONSHIPS

In the historical theory of the right to resist, starting from its earliest appearance as such in the Middle Ages through its evolution in the modern period,

[19] For example, Lewy uses three terms interchangeably on a single page. Guenter Lewy, 'Resistance to Tyranny: Treason, Right or Duty?' (1960) 13(3) *Western Political Quarterly* 581, 594. See also Raymond E Hayes, 'Revolution as a Constitutional Right' (1938) 13 *Temple Law Quarterly* 18, 20; Philip C Jessup, *A Modern Law of Nations: An Introduction* (Macmillan 1948) 184–186; John D Lewis, 'The Development of the Theory of Tyrannicide to 1660' in Oscar Jászi and John D Lewis (eds), *Against the Tyrant: The Tradition and Theory of Tyrannicide* (The Free Press 1957); Mitsukuni Yazaki, 'Legality and the Right of Resistance' [1957] *Osaka University Law Review* 26, 27; AH Murray, 'The Vindiciae Contra Tyrannos' [1958] *Acta Juridica* 275; Luis Kutner, 'A Philosophical Perspective on Rebellion' in M Cherif Bassiouni (ed), *International Terrorism and Political Crimes* (Charles C Thomas 1975); Gerald Sumida, 'The Right to Revolution: Implications for International Law and Order' in Myres S McDougal and W Michael Reisman (eds), *International Law in Contemporary Perspective: The Public Order of the World Community – Cases and Materials* (Foundation Press 1981) 167–168; Antonio Cassese, 'Human Rights and Humanitarian Law: Terrorism and Human Rights' (1982) 31 *American University Law Review* 945, 946–950; Jordan J Paust, 'The Human Right to Participate in Armed Revolution and Related Forms of Social Violence: Testing the Limits of Permissibility' (1983) 32 *Emory Law Journal* 545, 560–561; Johannes Morsink, 'The Philosophy of the Universal Declaration' (1984) 6(3) *Human Rights Quarterly* 309, 322–325; James L Taulbee, 'Political Crimes, Human Rights and Contemporary International Practice' (1990) 4 *Emory International Law Review* 43, 45–47; Johannes Morsink, *The Universal Declaration of Human Rights: Origins, Drafting and Intent* (University of Pennsylvania Press 1999) 302, 307–312.

[20] See Wolfgang Schwarz, 'The Right of Resistance' (1964) 74(2) *Ethics* 126, 126; Peter Nicholson, 'Kant on the Duty Never to Resist the Sovereign' (1976) 86(3) *Ethics* 214, 215.

the relation and distinction between terms was better understood. It is difficult to determine when and why exactly the conceptual blurring took place, and in particular the point at which the claim of 'rebellion' as a 'right' started to appear in western theory alongside the concepts of a lawful 'right of resistance', 'right of disobedience', and 'right of revolution'.[21] However, by the twentieth century it was at least clearer that the right to resist and the right of tyrannicide were no longer synonymous – if they ever were. The right to resist had become the predominant concept,[22] not specific to a single act but instead referring to a spectrum.[23] On one end of this spectrum was individual 'disobedience' or 'opposition', without force, to specific laws or policies. In the mid-range it included 'resistance', with or without force, to the imposition of sets of laws or policies or practices – either reactively or preventively – or to a particular regime. Such 'resistance' therefore could also include collective acts of 'rebellion', with force, against particular practices such as slavery, or a particular government or regime of usurpation such as a tyranny, but stopping short of constitutional change. At the other end of the spectrum, it included

[21] The extent of terminological confusion results in sometimes garbled accounts. For a prime example, see James C Corson, 'Resistance No Rebellion' (1930) 42 *Juridical Review* 245, 246, 249–251, whose explanation is not consistent with those of other specialists, or with the original authoritative sources from the eighteenth century that continued to distinguish between 'lawful' resistance and 'unlawful' rebellion, or the original anonymous pamphlet 'Resistance No Rebellion: In Answer to Doctor Johnson's Taxation No Tyranny' (J Bell 1775). In his now classic work, even Honoré mislabels Lockean theory as representing the 'right to rebel', contrary to evidence that Locke continued to use the term 'rebellion' in contrast to the right to resist, as denoting unlawful rather than lawful conduct. Honoré then takes the right of resistance, the right of disobedience, the right of rebellion, and the right of revolution, conflates them, and, without explanation for his rejection of the 'right to resist' as the superordinate term, rebrands them collectively as the 'right to rebel'. See Tony Honoré, 'The Right to Rebel' (1988) 8(1) *Oxford Journal of Legal Studies* 34, 38, 40, 42, 45–47, 49, 52–53; compare Locke (n 10) Ch XIX [232] 419. Given Paine's wide influence and reputation for popularization without precision, his passing reference in a 1795 essay that 'when all other rights are taken away the right of rebellion is made perfect' cannot be dismissed as a possible source of this later modern practice of terminological interchangeability. See Thomas Paine, 'Dissertation on First Principles of Government' in William Manley Van der Weyde (ed), *The Life and Works of Thomas Paine* (Thomas Paine National Historical Association 1925) vol V, 225.

[22] See Lewis (n 19) 44, 95. However, compare Mario Turchetti, *Tyrannie et tyrannicide de l'Antiquité a nos jours* (Presses Universitaires de France 2001) 14; Mario Turchetti, '"Despotism" and "Tyranny": Unmasking a Tenacious Confusion' (2008) 7(2) *European Journal of Political Theory* 159, 160.

[23] See Franz L Neumann, 'On the Limits of Justifiable Disobedience' in Franz L Neumann, *The Democratic and Authoritarian State: Essays in Political and Legal Theory* (Free Press 1957) 149–150; Marcic (n 14) 87, 105–106.

'revolution' to effect not only regime change but fundamental constitutional change that could include political, social, and economic aspects.[24]

Given the contemporary phenomenon of term conflation, establishing the precise relationship between the cognate terms – as well as with antecedent terms and corroborative concepts – is necessary to assist definitional and conceptual clarification. It is accepted that many terms are capable of multiple meanings and may not be 'objectively ascertainable'.[25] Therefore, 'ordinary meaning' as divined from standard and specialist dictionary or other expert definition, construction, and parsing of particular words, can constitute a starting point only – albeit one that is 'prerequisite to identifying the content'.[26] It is likewise acknowledged that any resulting 'literal interpretation' is only determinative if the context and object and purpose do not 'contra-indicate' by revealing that an 'absurd result' would follow, and should therefore be relied on with caution.[27]

The evidence suggests that the 'right to resist' may be a 'generic term', meaning one of 'continuing application' capable of 'keeping pace with the development of the law' and that has 'changed over time'.[28] It may also have 'no single or unified ordinary meaning' but rather address multiple criteria.[29] Examination of ordinary and legal construction of the cognate terms should test the conclusion that it is a superordinate term, containing several subordinate cognate concepts. That is, 'superordinate' and 'subordinate' not in the sense of a hierarchy of importance, but rather purely for the sake of legal categorization and understanding the interrelation of the human rights in question. Therefore, the 'superordinate' is broader, the 'subordinate' is narrower.

2.3.1 *Term Relation and Partial Differentiation in Ordinary Construction*

A closer examination of the ordinary construction and comparative usage of the cognate terms sheds some light on the relationship between these cognates and possible reasons for conflation. For example, one authority on the various ordinary constructions lists the terms 'resist' and 'oppose' as directly synonymous. To resist is to '*oppose*, fight against, refuse to accept, object to, defy ...

[24] See Heiner Bielefeldt, 'The Right to Resist' in Wilhelm Heitmeyer and John Hagan (eds), *International Handbook of Violence Research* (Kluwer 2003) 1101–1105.

[25] Richard Gardiner, *Treaty Interpretation* (Oxford University Press 2008) 161.

[26] Ibid 161, 163, 164. While Gardiner discusses 'ordinary meaning' as applied to treaty interpretation specifically, his general observations are applicable here.

[27] Ibid 165–167, 169.

[28] See ibid 172–173.

[29] Ibid 171–172.

obstruct, impede, hinder, block, thwart, frustrate'.[30] 'Resistance' is synonymous with the general terms '*opposition*, fight, stand, struggle' but also with the more specific terms 'freedom fighters, underground, partisans'.[31] While on the one hand to 'oppose' seems like a potentially more passive concept – to 'be against, object to, be hostile to, be in opposition to, disagree with, dislike, disapprove of' – it is also defined in a more active sense as meaning to '*resist*, take a stand against, stand up to, fight, challenge'.[32] 'Opposition' is synonymous with '*resistance*, hostility, antagonism, antipathy, objection, dissent, disapproval; defiance, non-compliance, obstruction'.[33] Both of these terms connote the employment of actions that may or may not involve force, and seem to imply action that may be taken either individually or collectively. Likewise 'disobedience' is the result of 'refusal to obey' or a 'disregard of orders' that includes 'rule-breaking',[34] amounting not only to 'defiance', 'insubordination', 'disruption', 'contravention', and 'mutiny' but also '*rebellion*'.[35]

According to this same source, both 'resist' and 'oppose' are also considered synonymous with 'rebel' – although 'rebel' is not included as a synonym for either term. To 'rebel' is to '*revolt*, mutiny, riot, rise up, take up arms' but also to 'be insubordinate ... defy, *disobey*, refuse to obey, kick against, challenge, *oppose*, *resist*'.[36] On the one hand, 'rebellion' is synonymous with an 'uprising, revolt, insurrection, mutiny, *revolution*, insurgence, insurgency, rioting ... disorder, unrest' but also with 'defiance, *disobedience* ... insubordination, subversion ... *resistance*'.[37] It is noticeable that this term seems to imply

30 Maurice Waite, Sara Hawker, Catherine Bailey, and Chris Cowley (eds), *Concise Oxford Thesaurus* (2nd edn, Oxford University Press 2002) 731–732 [emphasis added]. Likewise, in its ordinary meaning, to 'resist' is to 'withstand the action or effect of', to 'stop the course of progress of', to 'strive against; try to impede; refuse to comply with', or 'offer opposition; refuse to comply'. Judy Pearsall and Bill Trumble (eds), *Oxford English Reference Dictionary* (2nd rev edn, Oxford University Press 2002) 1226–1227.

31 Waite et al (n 30) 732 [emphasis added]. Likewise, 'resistance' is 'the act or an instance of resisting; refusal to comply'. Pearsall and Trumble (n 30) 1227.

32 Waite et al (n 30) 605–606 [emphasis added]. Likewise, in its ordinary meaning, to 'oppose' is to 'set oneself against; resist, argue against'. Pearsall and Trumble (n 30) 1019.

33 Waite et al (n 30) 607 [emphasis added]. Likewise 'opposition' is understood as 'resistance, antagonism', or 'the state of being hostile or in conflict or disagreement'. Pearsall and Trumble (n 30) 1019.

34 Pearsall and Trumble (n 30) 407.

35 Waite et al (n 30) 236 [emphasis added].

36 Ibid 712 [emphasis added]. In its ordinary meaning, to 'rebel' as a verb is to 'act as a rebel', which is one who 'fights against, resists or refuses allegiance to the established government' or 'that resists authority or control'. Pearsall and Trumble (n 30) 1203.

37 Waite et al (n 30) 712. 'Rebellion' in its ordinary meaning is 'open resistance to authority, esp. organized armed resistance to an established government'. Pearsall and Trumble (n 30) 1203.

collective action and greater organization but is also not necessarily limited to the use of force.

Finally 'revolt' is considered synonymous with 'rebel'. To 'revolt' is to '*rebel*, rise (up), take to the streets, riot, mutiny' and 'armed revolt' is defined as '*rebellion*, *revolution*, insurrection, mutiny, uprising, riot ... insurgence, seizure of power, coup (d'état)'.[38] 'Revolution' is likewise synonymous with '*rebellion*, *revolt*, insurrection, mutiny, uprising, riot ... insurgence, seizure of power, coup (d'état)', but also specifying in addition 'dramatic change, radical alteration ... transformation, innovation, reorganization, restructuring'.[39] This term by definition does not include individual action, and is more likely to involve the use of forceful means unless otherwise specified.

It becomes obvious from the above evidence that a degree of term conflation or interchangeable usage likely derives from a pattern established in ordinary contemporary construction. However, it also demonstrates some evidence of differentiation, and a pattern of relationship between the terms that does not amount to straightforward synonymity. It may therefore be that legal construction yields supplemental or better reasons for the incidence of term conflation.

2.3.2 *Term Conflation, Non-definition, and Vagueness in Legal Construction*

In his classic account of legal construction, Levi counsels that 'legal rules are never clear'.[40] Rather, 'rules are discovered through the process of determining similarity or difference'.[41] The intent of this interpretive process of construction is to 'give meaning to ambiguity'.[42] The challenge is that the rules are not static. Yet changing rules are the 'indispensable dynamic quality of law'.[43] He argues that the process of construction must permit the acknowledgment of new situations and the 'infusion of new ideas'.[44] The words of the law 'must come to have new meanings'.[45] Likewise, the meaning of legal concepts continues to change, and legal concepts themselves are fluid and

[38] Waite et al (n 30) 737. In its ordinary meaning, to 'revolt' is to 'rise in rebellion' or 'an act of rebellion' or 'a state of insurrection'. Pearsall and Trumble (n 30) 1234.

[39] Waite et al (n 30) 737. 'Revolution' in its ordinary meaning involves either 'the complete overthrow of an established government or social order by those previously subject to it' or 'any fundamental change or reversal of conditions'. Pearsall and Trumble (n 30) 1234.

[40] Edward H Levi, *An Introduction to Legal Reasoning* (University of Chicago Press 1949) 1.

[41] Ibid 3.

[42] Ibid 104.

[43] Ibid 2.

[44] Ibid 4.

[45] Ibid.

can be cyclical.[46] Legal concepts can eventually break down as the words no longer seem relevant to the cases being compared, yielding entirely new descriptions of similarity or difference through the process of reasoning by example: the old rule will have no meaning and effectively cease to operate.[47] In this process, the differences between those things which are different but eventually treated as similar must be explicitly and thoroughly interrogated.[48] Otherwise, '[e]rroneous ideas' can 'play an enormous part in shaping the law'.[49] This may or may not help explain why the few formal legal definitions of the right to resist and its cognate terms that do exist are sometimes even less helpful than the definitions gleaned from comparing ordinary constructions.

The pattern of relation, partial synonymity but also differentiation between the cognate terms in ordinary construction, is less clearly reflected in the construction found in specialized legal dictionaries and encyclopedic entries. Instead, one finds a general tendency to term conflation and other imprecision in the use of terminology related to the right to resist and its cognates, which is often replicated in the legal literature. The cognate terms are frequently conflated not only with each other, but also with other non-cognate but prima facie related public international law terms such as 'insurgency' or specific domestic law enforcement terms not related to rights, such as 'civil commotion' and 'riot'. More often, the right to resist and its cognate terms do not feature at all.

For example, there is no entry in *Words and Phrases Legally Defined* for 'resistance' or 'rebellion' – much less for the 'right' to these – but the entry for 'revolt', citing *R* v *McGregor* as an authority, seems intended to cover all three by conflating them.[50] While it manages to distinguish these from 'disobedience', there is also no entry for it, or for its more commonly used contemporary synonyms 'civil disobedience' or 'civil resistance'.[51] The entry for the law enforcement term 'civil commotion' drawn from *Halsbury's Laws*, attempting

46 Ibid 8.

47 Ibid 9.

48 Ibid 6, 9.

49 Ibid 6.

50 'By revolt I understand something like rebellion or resistance to lawful authority . . . something more than the disobedience of one man.' *R* v *McGregor* (1844) 1 Car & Kir 429, per Lord Abinger, CB 431, 432 as cited in John Beecroft Saunders (ed), *Words and Phrases Legally Defined* (3rd edn, Butterworths 1990) vol 4: R–Z 338. In the general entry for 'resist'– which when unqualified has much broader legal applications – the dicta cited from *R* v *Hansford* is not much more help as a legal definition: 'the word itself means nothing more than "to oppose" or "strive against" or "put a stop to"'. *R* v *Hansford* [1974] VR 251, 254 per Adam J cited in ibid 84.

51 See John Beecroft Saunders (ed), *Words and Phrases Legally Defined* (3rd edn, Butterworths 1990) vol 1: A–C.

to distinguish it from 'rebellion', also conflates a variety of terms and is equally unhelpful.[52]

The *Dictionary of Modern Legal Usage* does not include a definition for 'resistance' or 'disobedience' or 'opposition' or even 'revolution' – again, much less the right to any of these. Its entry for 'rebellion' refers to the entry for 'insurrection', which does not exist.[53] There is, however, the following entry for 'insurgence/insurgency', which hardly constitutes a definition approaching legal precision: '[t]hese words have undergone [differentiation]. *Insurgence* = a revolt; the action of rising against authority. *Insurgency* = the quality or state of being in revolt; the tendency to rise in revolt (OED)', and the entry for 'insurrectionary/insurrectional' that follows states merely: '[t]he latter is a needless variant'.[54] Similarly, in the *Parry and Grant Encyclopedic Dictionary of International Law*, there is no entry for 'resistance', 'opposition', or 'disobedience', and the terms 'revolt' and 'rebellion' refer to the entries for 'insurgency, insurgent, insurrection'.[55] As such, this gives the impression of both wrongful conflation of the question of the rights of rebellion or revolution with incidental questions of insurgent recognition and state responsibility in international law, and total non-recognition of hundreds of years of legal theory and positive law on the right to resist.

The entry for 'right to resistance' in the *Max Planck Encyclopedia of Public International Law* appears to be the only such entry on this topic in a major

[52] It defines 'civil commotion' as 'an insurrection of the people for general purposes, though not amounting to rebellion . . . a stage intermediate between riot and civil war', while also conceding that 'it is probably not capable of any very precise definition'. 22 *Halsbury's Laws* (3rd edn) 305–306 cited in Saunders (n 50) 261. A supplementary definition drawn from *Langdale* v *Mason*, meant to corroborate the distinction between 'civil commotion' and 'rebellion', is equally confused, managing only to determine that a rebellion is 'something else'. *Langdale* v *Mason* (1780) 2 *Park's Law of Marine Insurance* (8th edn) 965 per Lord Mansfield, CJ 967–968 cited in Saunders (n 50) 261–262.

[53] Bryan A Garner, *A Dictionary of Modern Legal Usage* (Oxford University Press 1987) 463.

[54] Ibid 304.

[55] It defines 'insurgency' and 'insurrection' only as 'some sort of rising or rebellion within a State' with 'no precise meaning in the sense that any distinction can be drawn between a mere revolt or rising and an insurrection. Thus, the use of the expression *recognition of insurgency* is misconceived insofar as it implies any such formal distinction'. John P Grant and J Craig Barker (eds), *Parry and Grant Encyclopaedic Dictionary of International Law* (2nd edn, Oceana Publications 2004) 416, 439 [emphasis original]. The entry continues, citing I *Oppenheim* 550: 'Equally, although responsibility of States for insurgents (but also for rioters) is sometimes spoken of as a distinct category of vicarious responsibility, it is maintained by others that such responsibility "is the same as for acts of other private individuals."' Ibid 416. Citing James Crawford, *The International Law Commission's Articles on State Responsibility* (Cambridge University Press 2002) 116–120, the entry further continues: 'The conduct of an insurrection movement which succeeds in establishing a new government are acts of State for the purpose of State responsibility.'

legal, human rights, or public international law dictionary or encyclopedia. It does not engage in interchangeable usage. However, it replicates the established pattern of failing to define the right, or in the alternative to at least define 'resistance', much less define the relationship between the cognates.[56] As such, it does not counter the imprecision resulting from non-definition and conflation elsewhere.

Given that these terms are the subject matter of contemporary positive law,[57] it is not entirely clear why these legal dictionaries and encyclopedias do not enlist definitional assistance either from authoritative reference sources for ordinary construction or from legal specialists, in lieu of definition from relevant case construction. Nor is it clear why definition of the relevant terms is avoided altogether by many legal reference books. There are a few exceptions, and those definitions are reviewed below. On the whole, however, it would seem that at least some authoritative sources of legal construction reinforce the tendency to conflation, vagueness, and non-definition.

2.4 COGNATE TERMS: RELATION AND DIFFERENTIATION FOR LEGAL DEFINITION

Examining the relationship between these concepts more closely, it is obvious that while they are clearly cognate to one another, they are not merely synonymous and interchangeable and should not be conflated. Each has distinguishable features. These cognate terms set out below are best understood as closely interrelated but nevertheless distinct from one another, particularly as to the objective and to a lesser extent as to means. Their relationship to one another can also be fluid, and in many cases the more specific claims to right would be made sequentially in the event of non-resolution – leading from disobedience to resistance, then rebellion to revolution.[58]

2.4.1 *The 'Right to Resist' or 'Right of Resistance'*

As demonstrated above in its ordinary meaning, and in the historical usage, the 'right to resist' or 'right of resistance'[59] is inherently a general and

[56] See Chemillier-Gendreau (n 15) 954–959.

[57] See Part II, Chapters 5–7.

[58] See Honoré (n 21) 52–53.

[59] Since the Middle Ages the concept has been known by a variety of terms reflecting the regional diversity of its usage, such as *jus resistendi et contradicendi* and *widerstandsrecht*. See Fritz Kern, *Kingship and Law in the Middle Ages: The Divine Right of Kings and the Right of Resistance in the Early Middle Ages* (S Chrimes tr, Basil Blackwell 1939); Murray (n 19) 306; Marcic (n 14) 87.

flexible concept. The resistance could involve either peaceful or forceful means.[60] It could be directed against something as narrow as a specific law, policy, or practice in either a single instance or generally, or something as broad as a whole regime, or a social, political, or economic order. It could be held and exercised by individuals or groups. In this way it is essentially similar to the equally broad and now lesser-used Marxist variant in the doctrine of the 'right to struggle'.[61] While the latter could therefore be considered superfluous, these two terms are so close in meaning that it is probably not incorrect to use them interchangeably in certain instances.

Close comparison confirms that only the 'right to resist' is a broad enough concept to encompass the others, insofar as all other variants involve only an aspect of resistance in its ordinary meaning, in one form or to one degree or another. Since none of the other cognates can be used in this way, it follows that the 'right to resist' is the correct superordinate term.[62] While each individual subordinate 'cognate' right can be discussed individually, when discussing them collectively or generally 'the right to resist' is the most appropriate term to avoid confusion, as it is the most inclusive and moreover was used in this way historically. This also means that the right to resist and its cognates must share an identifiable 'common core' of elements. This possibility is explored below.

While the right to resist is a broad right, it also has discrete aspects to it. That is, in addition to being the correct general term to express all cognates together collectively, the 'right to resist' may have its own distinct application in certain usages. That is – and unlike the other cognates – it is a category of exception that applies to an interregnum where there is a mix of forceful and non-forceful but unlawful action employed, to which the *lex generalis* (ordinary) limitations on political rights do not apply protection and where lawful derogation cannot be established – but where the *lex specialis* (conditional exception) does not yet apply as *jus ad bellum* (the right to make war). Its inclusion of peaceful means distinguishes it from the right to rebellion. Its inclusion of forceful means distinguishes it from the right to disobedience and opposition. Its more limited objectives – unless and until otherwise specified – can also distinguish it from the right of revolution.[63]

60 Historically, these are sometimes alternatively described as 'active' and 'passive' resistance.

61 Compare the general concept in Christof Heyns, 'A "Struggle Approach" to Human Rights' in Arend Soeteman (ed), *Pluralism and Law* (Springer 2001).

62 This finding thus contradicts one particular aspect of Honoré's work. See Honoré (n 21) 34–54.

63 This is a variation on how Kaufmann defines the received 'traditional' right to resist, as comprising five elements: a right to use all proportional means, as a last resort, in conditions of 'emergency' as an exception, for the purpose of self-defence or remedial enforcement of rights,

2.4.2 *The 'Right to Oppose' or 'Right of Opposition'*

As demonstrated above, in its ordinary meaning the concept of 'opposition' is definitionally embedded in the concept of 'resistance', and vice versa to a lesser extent. Arguably, therefore, the now lesser-used term 'right to oppose' or 'right of opposition' is not distinct from the 'right to resist' or 'right of resistance'.[64] Indeed, if there is any substantive difference between 'resistance' and 'opposition' it may be found in the somewhat more passive connotation of the latter term: whereas one may 'oppose' exclusively in one's opinions or entirely through the use of words only, the same cannot be so easily said of 'resistance', which does imply some form of physical action beyond ideas and words alone.[65] One could therefore also argue that the 'right to oppose' is already included in and therefore protected by the *lex generalis* of ordinary political rights, such as the rights to participation, and to freedom of opinion and expression, association, and peaceful assembly.[66] If so, then it is related to but actually distinct from the 'right to resist' and its cognates, and should not be used as a synonym. Either way, it is not a concept that adds value and deserves to fall into desuetude – except perhaps as a superordinate for the ordinary political rights.

2.4.3 *The 'Right to Disobey' or 'Right of Disobedience'*

The 'right to disobey' or 'right of disobedience', with its origin in Thomasian theory,[67] now also includes, in contemporary terms, the 'right of civil disobedience'. It is comparatively narrow and specific. It concerns, according to *Black's Law Dictionary*, '[a] deliberate but nonviolent act of lawbreaking to call attention to a particular law or set of laws of questionable legitimacy or

for the further purpose of upholding the constitutional order in the public interest. Arthur Kaufmann, 'Small Scale Right to Resist' (1985–1986) 21 *New England Law Review* 571, 574–575.

64 Hence their interchangeable or tandem use in Asbjörn Eide, 'The Right to Oppose Violations of Human Rights: Basis, Conditions and Limitations' in *Violations of Human Rights: Possible Rights of Recourse and Forms of Resistance* (UNESCO 1984) 34–66.

65 Similarly, see Kaufmann (n 63) 576–580.

66 Kaufmann, who advocates the 'right of opposition' as a 'small-scale' right to resist, in fact concedes this.

67 See Aquinas, 'Commentary on the Sentences' (n 5) 183; Aquinas, 'Summa Theologiae' (n 5) II-II q 104 'On Obedience', a 5 'Are Subjects Obliged to Obey Their Superiors in All Things?' 183; Thomas Aquinas, *Treatise on Law: The Complete Text (Summa Theologiae I-II, Questions 90–108)* (Alfred J Freddoso tr, St Augustine's Press 2009) q 96 'The Force of Human Law', a 4 'Does human law impose an obligation in conscience on a man?' 63–65, a 5 'Is everyone subject to human law?' 66, a 6 'Is one who is subject to the law permitted to act outside the letter of the law?' 68.

morality'.[68] Arguably, if the modifier 'nonviolent' is removed, the right of disobedience is greatly broadened and made more analogous to the 'right to resist' when directed towards a relatively narrow objective. With the modifier in place, however, it retains its original sense as being related to the right to resist as a subcategory cognate – that is, one involving a specific form of resistance that involves deliberately unlawful conduct that does not include force. It is also generally conceived of as an individual right, albeit one that can also be exercised collectively – this is sometimes known as 'civil resistance'. The right of disobedience is the category of exception that applies to otherwise non-*lex generalis* protected peaceful protest or other activity, that deliberately defies the law in order to change it or to withdraw collaboration with the unlawful.[69]

2.4.4 *The 'Right to Rebel' or 'Right of Rebellion'*

On both ordinary meaning and legal definition, the 'right to rebel' or 'right of rebellion' involves not only law-breaking but also the use or potential use of forceful means. In its most restrictive legal meaning, according to the *Dictionary of International and Comparative Law*, a rebellion is an 'uprising against a government; attempting to change that government. If successful,

68 Bryan A Garner (ed), *Black's Law Dictionary* (7th deluxe edn, West Group 1999) 239.

69 Bielefeldt identifies Bedau and Rawls as the key theorists of the right of 'civil disobedience', having agreed on four main features: 'deliberate breaching of rules' using public acts involving 'strict nonviolence' and a willingness to accept penalty. See Bielefeldt (n 24) 1106–1108; Hugo A Bedau, 'On Civil Disobedience' (1961) 58(21) *Journal of Philosophy* 653, 658–659; John Rawls, A *Theory of Justice* (Harvard University Press 1971) 364, 373. On the 'civil resistance' concept, distinguished not only by non-acceptance of penalty but also because its object is to enforce law not to change it, and to prevent crime, see Francis A Boyle, *Defending Civil Resistance under International Law* (Transnational Publishers 1988) 16–19; Francis A Boyle, *Protesting Power: War, Resistance, and Law* (Rowman and Littlefield 2008) 24–25. Compare the system and process theory of 'justified' or 'legitimated' or 'lawful departures from legal rules' by officials and by citizens in Mortimer R Kadish and Sanford H Kadish, *Discretion to Disobey: A Study of Lawful Departures from Legal Rules* (Stanford University Press 1973, repr Quid Pro Books 2010) xiv, 72, 88–90. See also the theories of an 'international right of non-violent resistance' in Matthew Lippman, 'The Right of Civil Resistance under International Law and the Domestic Necessity Defense' (1990) 8 *Dickinson Journal of International Law* 349, 350, 361; and a right of disobedience to violations of international law in Richard Falk, 'The Adequacy of Contemporary Theories of International Law: Gaps in Legal Thinking' (1964) 50 (2) *Virginia Law Review* 231, 248–249, 255–256, 260; Richard Falk, 'Introduction' in Boyle, *Defending Civil Resistance under International Law* (n 69) xvii–xxii; Frédéric Mégret, 'Civil Disobedience and International Law: Sketch for a Theoretical Argument' (2009) 46 *Canadian Yearbook of International Law* 143–192.

the new government may be recognized'.[70] However, it has a potentially broader meaning also. According to *Black's Law Dictionary*, it is not only an '[o]pen, organized, and armed resistance to an established government or ruler' but may also be an '[o]pen resistance or opposition to an authority or tradition [involving] [d]isobedience of a legal command or summons'.[71] This shows the term's close association with the cognates 'resistance', 'opposition', and 'disobedience' – all of which are embedded in this definition, while the element of force distinguishes it from the latter two. In addition, its objectives are generally broader than disobedience or certain instances of resistance, but more limited than 'revolution'.[72]

As demonstrated above, the term 'rebellion' is often conflated with other terms – not only the evocative but non-legal synonyms 'uprising' and 'insurrection' but also the legal term 'insurgency', as well as the related but distinct cognate 'revolution'.[73] While this may merely reflect the fluidity between these conditions, in fact the terms are not synonymous. Using 'rebellion' in relation to the term 'insurgency' answers an entirely different albeit potentially related legal question, as discussed below. In the case of 'revolution', the distinction becomes clear when both objectives and means are examined. For example, not all rebellions aim at a complete overthrow and replacement of the political-constitutional, social, or economic order, whereas this is definitionally inherent to revolutions.[74] The purpose of a rebellion may merely be to force a change in government policy, but the purpose of a revolution is always to force a change not only in government but also in the system as a whole. In addition, most legal references to rebellion imply an organized use of forceful means.[75] Revolutions, in contrast, however rarely,

70 James R Fox, *Dictionary of International and Comparative Law* (Oceana Publications 1997) 274.

71 Garner (n 68) 1273–1274.

72 Compare the several other points of distinction between the rights of 'resistance' and 'rebellion' asserted in Tran Van Minh, 'Political and Juridical Sanctions against Violations of Human Rights' in *Violations of Human Rights: Possible Rights of Recourse and Forms of Resistance* (UNESCO 1984) 162–166.

73 On the latter usage see Paust (n 19) 560–561; Honoré (n 21) 35–36, 38, 42, 45–53; Jordan J Paust, 'International Law, Dignity, Democracy and the Arab Spring' (2013) 46 *Cornell International Law Journal* 1.

74 Affirming this distinction see Ramon Infiesta, 'The Right to Resist Oppression in Comparative Constitutional Law' in *Cursos Monográficos* (1959) (Academia Interamericana de Derecho Comparado e Internacional 1959) vol VII 303-367, as cited in Robert D Hayton, 'Untitled Review' (1961) 55(1) *American Journal of International Law* 187, 189 fn 6; David C Williams, 'The Constitutional Right to "Conservative" Revolution' (1997) 32 *Harvard Civil Rights-Civil Liberties Law Review* 413, 414, 428–430.

75 See for example Cassese (n 19) 946–950, 958.

can be and have been waged using entirely or primarily peaceful means. This implication is reflected in the customary law of recognition of 'rebels' – rather than 'resisters' or 'revolutionaries' – as insurgents or belligerents.[76]

The right of rebellion applies to the interregnum where force is used but 'belligerency' status based on effectiveness – under which the rebel organization is essentially treated as a de facto state – has not been reached. It is intended as an exception to the *lex generalis* prohibition on use of force, under which providing aid to the incumbent state on request is thereby rendered unlawful and impermissible but providing certain forms of aid to the rebel faction may be permissible, depending on other factors. It is the *jus ad bellum* expression of the *lex specialis*.[77]

2.4.5 *The 'Right to Revolt' or 'Right of Revolution'*

In its ordinary meaning, 'revolt' is construed as entirely synonymous with 'rebel', and this may partially explain the common tendency to conflate the 'right to revolt' or 'right of revolution' with the 'right of rebellion'. However, as indicated above, 'revolution' is both more specific as to aims and potentially more general as to means. Kern makes a sharp distinction between the 'right' of revolution and 'right of resistance'. He demonstrates that, traditionally at least, the right to resist was an absolutely non-revolutionary right. Its object was the opposite – to defend not to alter the constitutional order and to defend the established law.[78] However this particular distinction loosened in the mid-

[76] This is further discussed below in Section 2.6.3 and in Chapter 6, Section 6.6.1.

[77] See Kittrie's concept of a right of 'just resistance' as providing the *jus ad bellum* basis for a 'jurisprudence of domestic conflict' in Nicholas N Kittrie, *Rebels with a Cause* (Westview 2000) 297–350. See also generally Walter Kälin and Jörg Künzli, 'Article 1F(b): Freedom Fighters, Terrorists and the Notion of Serious Non-Political Crime' (2000) 12 supp *International Journal of Refugee Law* 46. Compare the possibility of the development of similar 'common criteria' raised in Richard Falk, 'Janus Tormented: The International Law of Internal War' in James N Rosenau (ed), *International Aspects of Civil Strife* (Princeton University Press 1964) 217 (fn 49); Richard Falk, 'Azmi Bishara, the Right of Resistance, and the Palestinian Ordeal' (2002) XXXI(2) *Journal of Palestine Studies* 19, 28. See also, for example, Paust (n 19) 548–549; Paust (n 73) 12–13; Frédéric Mégret, 'Beyond "Freedom Fighters" and "Terrorists": When, If Ever, Is Non-State Violence Legitimate in International Law?' (SSRN 2009); Frédéric Mégret, 'Causes Worth Fighting For: Is There a Non-State *jus ad bellum*?' in Aristotle Constantinides and Nikos Zaikos (eds), *The Diversity of International Law: Essays in Honour of Professor Kalliopi K Koufa* (Martinus Nijhoff 2009); Frédéric Mégret, 'Should Rebels Be Amnestied?' in Carsten Stahn, Jennifer S Easterday, and Jens Iverson (eds), *Jus Post Bellum: Mapping the Normative Foundations* (Oxford University Press 2014). See also Finlay's 'ethical theory' in Finlay (n 2) 3, 6–7, 9, 11–12, 19–154.

[78] For Kern, therefore, revolution is, in contrast, 'never lawful' but sometimes 'right'. Kern (n 59) 197. Concurring, see Lewis (n 19) 91.

modern period, as the right to revolution concept evolved from the right to resist – as a cognate.[79]

Though some claim that 'revolution' cannot be legally defined,[80] there is evidence to the contrary. For example, the *Dictionary of International and Comparative Law* defines 'revolution' as 'the overthrow or attempted overthrow of a government by some of its citizens, usually by force of arms' and points out that 'the status of revolutionaries usually depends on their success or failure'.[81] For *Black's Law Dictionary*, likewise, 'revolution' involves an 'overthrow of a government, resulting in fundamental political change' and is, by post-hoc definition, a 'successful rebellion'.[82] This view – that a revolution is not a revolution until it is over – may further explain why some legal commentators use the terms 'rebellion' and 'revolution' interchangeably. Depending on the context, this may not always be incorrect.[83]

Black's Law Dictionary provides an adequate definition of the 'right of revolution', as the 'inherent right of a people to cast out their rulers, change their polity, or effect radical reforms in their system of government or institutions, by force or general uprising' where 'legal and constitutional methods of making such changes have proved inadequate or are so obstructed as to be unavailable.'[84] This is quite specific as to objective. It is not the same as 'resistance', 'opposition', or 'disobedience' to, or 'rebellion' against, specific laws or sets of laws or practices, or particular aspects or policies of, or personnel behind, a regime – which therefore seek less profound change. The right to revolution is that category of exception where the object is constitutional replacement and comprehensive change in the basic political, economic, and/or social order.[85] In this regard, the right to revolution is

79 See the contributions in Locke (n 10) Chapter XIX 'Of the Dissolution of Government' [211]–[243] 406–428 and Chapter Ch XIII [149] 367 on popular sovereignty; Vattel (n 11) Book I Chapter II [16] 87, [21] 88–89, Book I Chapter III [32]–[34], [37] 94–96. Compare Honoré (n 21) 35–36, 45–52; Williams (n 74) 413–414, 417–418, 428, 431, 447.

80 See for example the discussion in Josef L Kunz, 'Revolutionary Creation of Norms of International Law' (1947) 41 *American Journal of International Law* 119, 120–121.

81 Fox (n 70) 283.

82 Garner (n 68) 1321.

83 See for example Paust (n 19) 560–562, 569.

84 Garner (n 68) 1326.

85 Wright describes the 'right to revolution' as a right to establish or change a government, including by 'revolutionary methods' except as limited by international obligations, as an 'attribute of state sovereignty' and one of two basic principles implied by the United Nations Charter. He reasons that because the 'sovereign' is the 'state', and not any particular 'government', this is a right of the 'people of a state'. See Quincy Wright, 'International Law and Civil Strife' (1959) 53 *Proceedings of the American Society of International Law at Its Annual Meeting* (1921–1969), 147–148, 152. See also Paust (n 19) 545–546, 550–551, 558, 568–580; Honoré (n 21) 38.

distinct from the other subordinate cognates. It cannot be used interchangeably with them as a direct synonym purely by virtue of its location at the far end of the conceptual spectrum within the same cognate family. Yet if there can be a 'right' to revolution, surely there must be related rights that can fall short of this – particularly if necessity conditions and proportionality limitations apply.[86]

2.5 DISTINCT FROM ANTECEDENT TERMS

Conflation of the right to resist with its antecedent terms by certain scholars presents a similar problem. While the 'doctrine' or 'right' of 'tyrannicide' is the clear ancestor of the right to resist, it is also significantly narrower in scope.[87] 'Tyrannicide' is a specific action involving a particular targeted use of force under particular conditions. In this way it contrasts with the right to resist and its cognates, all of which are to varying degrees more general legal concepts. Therefore, in the contemporary conception it must remain analytically distinct.

Having been eclipsed by the 'right to resist', which has both a broader scope and a potentially lower trigger threshold,[88] the status of the doctrine or right of tyrannicide as a legal concept has become even more uncertain.[89] Yet 'tyrannicide' remains partially analogous insofar as it too is meant to function as a lawful exception immunizing otherwise unlawful conduct. As a specific method used in the course of lawful 'rebellion' or 'revolution' amounting to 'armed conflict' it may be more appropriate for consideration under *jus in bello* (conduct in warfare) rules of international humanitarian law, where necessity and proportionality can be established.[90] Where used as a specific

[86] See also discussions of necessity and proportionality in Chapter 4, Sections 4.3 and 4.7.2 and Chapter 6, Sections 6.3.1.4 and 6.3.1.5.

[87] In general, see Jászi and Lewis (n 19). See also Kaufmann (n 63) 575–576; Bielefeldt (n 24) 1098. Compare Turchetti, *Tyrannie et tyrannicide* (n 22) 14; Turchetti, '"Despotism" and "Tyranny"' (n 22).

[88] See discussion of 'trigger thresholds' in Chapter 4, Sections 4.2 and 4.3.

[89] For an assessment of the status of the doctrine of tyrannicide in contemporary international law, see Shannon Brincat, 'The Legal Philosophy of Internationally Assisted Tyrannicide' (2009) 34 *Australian Journal of Legal Philosophy* 151. Concluding that it is neither specifically prohibited unless an act of a foreign state, nor protected as a right and thus not immune from domestic prosecution, see also Jean D'Aspremont, 'Le tyrannicide en droit international' in Christian Tomuschat, Evelyne Lagrange, and Stefan Oeter (eds), *The Right to Life* (Brill 2010) 288–289, 308–312.

[90] See discussion of corroborative law in Chapter 6, Section 6.6. On the issue of what source of law would supply the conduct regulations, compare for example Andrew Clapham, *Human Rights Obligations of Non-State Actors* (Oxford University Press 2006) 271–298.

method in the course of lawful 'resistance' in conditions short of 'armed conflict', however, it may be another matter – although surely necessity and proportionality would still apply.[91] Used outside a context where resistance, rebellion, or revolution could be established as a right, it is most unlikely that acts claimed as lawful tyrannicide could be immunized from the reach of domestic or international criminal law.[92] As such, while interactions are possible, detailed consideration of the tyrannicide concept in any of these scenarios is beyond the scope of this study. Suffice to conclude that lawful tyrannicide has become at best a concept dependent on a right to resist, whereunder establishing a valid right would be a necessary but not sufficient condition.

2.6 DISTINCT FROM CORROBORATIVE CONCEPTS

While there is not a significant difference between the ordinary meaning and the legal meaning of each term – such as can be established – there may be legally substantive differences between the right to resist cognates and other similar or related terms. Indeed, in certain cases there are differences between these terms as understood in international human rights law, for example, and their 'corroborative' variants as understood in general public international law or in the international humanitarian law or 'law of armed conflict'.

Specifically, the concept of the 'right to resist' in international human rights law is distinct from and should not be confused with the specialized concept of 'resistance movements' for the purposes of application of *jus in bello* rules under international humanitarian law. Likewise, the 'right to resist' and 'right of rebellion' are not entirely unrelated to, but are nevertheless analytically separate from, an assessment of insurgent or belligerent status for the purposes of recognition under the customary rules of public international law. The 'right to resist' including the 'right of disobedience' cognate is moreover distinct from the 'right to protest' in the *lex generalis* of international human rights law. Yet all of these could be considered 'corroborative' concepts.

2.6.1 Lex Generalis *'Right of (Peaceful) Assembly' and 'Right to Protest'*

'Resistance' is not equivalent to 'protest'. 'Protest' is a particular category of public political action, which may also be either peaceful or forceful – but also either lawful or unlawful. 'Resistance', on the other hand, may take forms

[91] On the issue of what source of law would supply the conduct regulations, compare ibid 317–436, 533–566.

[92] Compare D'Aspremont (n 89); Brincat (n 89).

other than public protest, and is not ordinarily considered 'lawful'. Unlike the right to resist which is definitionally excluded from the protection of ordinary political rights under the *lex generalis*, the 'right to protest' is partially protected under the *lex generalis* 'right of assembly' and related political rights, to the extent that said protest conforms with the 'peacefulness requirement' and other lawful limitations under ordinary human rights law.[93] Importantly, however, these are among the rights not protected under the state derogation regimes in international human rights law. Certain assembly and other protest actions can therefore fall into a rather large gap between ordinary lawful limitations and state derogation measures. Thus, on the one hand the 'right to protest' is not only more specific but possibly better protected than the 'right to resist'. On the other hand, under certain circumstances a 'right to protest' beyond that provided for in the *lex generalis* could be derived from a right to resist or from a right to disobedience, as *lex specialis* lawful exceptions – particularly where state derogation is of dubious legality.

These complementary concepts therefore share a symbiotic corroborative function. The exhaustion of ordinary political rights, including the right to protest, may help to determine the trigger point for a right to resist. The right to resist as *lex specialis* may have the effect of extending ordinary protest rights beyond certain ordinary limitations, or offset abuse of a derogation regime.[94]

2.6.2 *'Resistance Movements'*

Crucially, it is necessary to distinguish the concept of the human right to resist in international human rights law from the narrower concept of 'resistance movements' which may be recognized as 'lawful combatants' for the purpose of the application of, and ensuring compliance with, the *jus in bello* rules of international humanitarian law, including in particular but not limited to the Geneva Conventions. Cassese emphasizes this, and cautions against confusion between the regulation of the *jus ad bellum* regarding employment of forceful means on a right to resist basis, and the separate body of international humanitarian law that regulates the *jus in bello*, meaning the use of specific weapons or tactics against particular targets in particular resistance contexts

93 On the 'right to protest' see Susan Marks and Andrew Clapham, *International Human Rights Lexicon* (Oxford University Press 2005) 273–274; David Mead, *The New Law of Peaceful Protest: Rights and Regulation in the Human Rights Act Era* (Hart 2010), 11–12, 63–76, 237–310. See further discussion in Chapter 7, Section 7.2.1.2.

94 The function of the right to resist as *lex specialis* is discussed further in Chapter 3, Sections 3.4.5 and 3.5. The intersection of the *lex specialis* right to resist with the *lex generalis* political rights under treaty law is further discussed in Chapter 7 generally.

and the treatment of qualifying resistance combatants as 'lawful'.[95] The question of lawful combatant status of 'resistance movements' in international humanitarian law is distinct from the question of whether there is a valid claim to a right to resist. The latter does not hinge on the former, but such recognition can be corroborative in certain cases. That is, there can be a right to resist without qualification as a 'resistance movement' for the purposes of international humanitarian law. However, by definition there cannot be a 'resistance movement' that cannot also establish a 'right to resist'.[96]

2.6.3 *'Insurgent' or 'Belligerent' Status*

The designator 'insurgent' or 'belligerent' is another legal category distinct from the question of the 'right to resist' or 'right to rebel'. The recognition of 'insurgent' status for the purposes of regulating third-party relationships with rebels, which is primarily a measure of their legal 'effectiveness', is not dependent on a valid 'right to resist'. Theoretically, that status could equally apply to groups that cannot satisfy right to resist criteria. That is, there can be an 'insurgency' without a 'right to rebel', and likewise a 'right to rebel' or 'right to resist' without recognition of 'insurgency'. Yet in certain circumstances recognition of insurgency can be corroborative, as it can provide evidence of an element of 'representativeness' to the extent that this criterion applies to any particular determination of whether there is a 'right to resist', 'right to rebel', or 'right of revolution'. Though not necessarily determinative, the related public international law questions of legitimacy and recognition of authority are, in some instances, potentially closer to the question of whether a 'right' to resistance, rebellion, or revolution exists for a particular group, than is the question of whether that group qualifies for recognition in order to benefit from belligerent rights.[97] In a context where insurgent or belligerent status could be realistically considered, the right to resist or right to rebel resembles a *jus ad bellum* determination.[98] This point is emphasized by Falk and others.[99]

95 See Cassese (n 19) 946.

96 The corroborative nature of provisions in international humanitarian law is discussed further in Chapter 6, Sections 6.6.2 and 6.6.2.1.

97 The corroborative nature of the recognition regime in international law that guides the behaviour of third parties is discussed further in Chapter 6, Section 6.6.1.

98 The *lex specialis* function of the right to resist as a *jus ad bellum* regime in international law regulating resort to force by non-state actors is discussed further in Chapter 3, Sections 3.4.4, 3.4.5, and 3.5.

99 Though he stops short of using this terminology in his earlier work, the possibility is nevertheless raised in Falk, 'Janus Tormented' (n 77) 188–191, 194, 217 (fn 49), 233, 240–242. Compare his later concept of a *jus ad bellum* doctrine 'as adapted' in Falk, 'Azmi Bishara, the

2.7 IDENTIFYING THE 'COMMON CORE'

In light of the above, and as demonstrated by the further discussion in the following chapters, it is possible to identify definitional and conceptual elements that are not only basic to the broader and more inclusive superordinate 'right to resist' but also constitute 'core' elements common to the subordinate cognates. That 'common core', adapted from Honoré,[100] suggests that each cognate can be conceptualized as a fundamental human right:

- exercised in response to a primary trigger violation or violations;
- exercised against a state or other authority or powerful actor;
- as a self-help remedy of individuals, groups, and peoples;
- to use otherwise unlawful means – as a lawful exception;
- in pursuit of objectives that are consistent with human rights;
- when other means of enforcement or remedies prove unavailable or ineffective – that is, subject to necessity as a secondary trigger condition;
- subject to a proportionality limitation;
- subject to the constraints of international human rights law and international criminal law, and international humanitarian law as applicable;
- correlated with an obligation on state parties and other third parties to either assist within the limits of the law, or not obstruct those exercising a valid right.

These components are examined individually in the following chapters on the right's nature and legal function, elements, and legal content. They suggest the construction of a basic legal test or series of tests for establishing a valid right. However, additional conditions may need to be met for the purposes of a specific cognate, and further tests may also need to be set for a given 'object and purpose', an aspect discussed in Chapter 4. The primary trigger condition, also further examined in Chapter 4 and Part II, to some extent may also be form-dependent. For example, it might involve a test for 'oppression' or 'crimes against humanity' or other human rights violations. It could involve a test for 'aggression' and 'unlawful occupation', or a test for other denial of the

Right of Resistance' (n 77) 28. Compare also Antonio Cassese, *Self-Determination of Peoples: A Legal Reappraisal* (Cambridge University Press 1995) 150–159, 153–154, 197–198; Mégret, 'Beyond "Freedom Fighters"' (n 77); Mégret, 'Causes Worth Fighting For' (n 77); Mégret, 'Should Rebels Be Amnestied?' (n 77).

[100] See Honoré (n 21) 36. Perhaps it is more accurate to say 'inspired by' rather than 'adapted from', since Honoré's definition of the 'right to rebel' and the 'common core' proposed here are expressed quite differently. Nevertheless, most of Honoré's elements are borrowed and incorporated or otherwise adapted.

right to self-determination including by way of 'tyranny' but not limited to this. It could involve a test for 'war crimes', 'genocide', or another test for self-defence against state forces. Meeting such primary trigger tests would be required in addition to meeting the secondary condition of necessity, the threshold for which may be higher or lower per cognate. Specific limits on the exercise of the right may also be cognate- and form-dependent, even if they will always include proportionality, respect for the human rights of others, and general compliance with international criminal law. While recognizing the need for additional tests in particular instances, this 'common core' could nevertheless act as a basic building block for a test of a claim's validity. It updates the historic Bartolist test for a 'right to resist tyranny'.[101]

2.8 CONCLUSION: A CONSOLIDATED CONTEMPORARY WORKING DEFINITION

Taking all the preceding and following into account, it would seem that the contemporary legal concept of the right to resist retains many traditional features of earlier conceptual iterations, though in modified or updated form. At its most basic, it is a right – under certain conditions, for certain generally lawful purposes, and within certain constraints – to commit otherwise unlawful acts or use otherwise unlawful means. It is therefore a form of limited and conditional right to disobey the law. When conceptualized as a human right, this bare definition is modified to suggest a right to resist human rights violations where no other effective remedy is available, in pursuit of objectives that are consistent with human rights and – subject to certain human rights limitations on scope of action already imposed on non-state actors in particular by international criminal law – by using means beyond those permitted under the *lex generalis*. Within this general framework and provided all the elements are met, the right can embrace a full spectrum of objectives from overthrow and replacement of a given political-constitutional, economic, and/or social order, to more modest objectives such as specific grievance redress. It can employ a broad spectrum of appropriate means from the peaceful to the forceful. It can be exercised on one's own behalf, or on behalf of a group including a minority, or by a representative group, mass movement, or majority on behalf of a nation or 'people'.

The proposed contemporary working definition is composited or consolidated from the prior work of the other scholars surveyed. It adds several

[101] See Saxoferrato, *On Guelfs and Ghibbellines* (n 6) 5; Saxoferrato, *On the Tyrant* (n 6) 4 (fn 31), 7–8 (fn 58, 60), 10 (fn 81), 14–15, 18 (fn 173–176, 180–181) 21–24.

missing elements from the 'common core' definition offered for the purpose of demonstrating linkage between the cognate terms. It suggests a provisional definitional theory, as follows:

> *The 'human right to resist' is the exceptional, conditional, and limited secondary self-help right of individuals, groups, and peoples to use otherwise unlawful means, in pursuit of objectives that are consistent with human rights, in response to a trigger violation by a state or other powerful actor, when other means of human rights enforcement or remedies prove unavailable or ineffective. Such exceptional means may be either peaceful or forceful, subject to demonstrated necessity and proportionality, and to the relevant constraints of international human rights law, international criminal law, and international humanitarian law as applicable. The obligation this imposes at domestic level is to make legal allowances for immunity, non-prosecution, and/or exceptional defences or mitigations, and not to extradite or exclude from refugee status those with a valid right to resist where no internationally criminal conduct is shown. The obligation this imposes at international level is to either assist within the limits of the law, or not obstruct those with a valid right to resist.*

This proposed definition of the right to resist as a legal concept is not intended as final and comprehensive. Rather, it is offered as a common point of reference to be improved upon by future scholarship.

In sum, as demonstrated by the cumulative evidence in this and the following chapters, the right to resist is related to, but not wholly interchangeable with, its cognates – the right to disobedience, the right to rebel, and the right to revolution. It is not to be mistaken for the ancient right of tyrannicide, though it did evolve from this legal concept. Nor should it be confused with the narrow definition of 'resistance movements' that is particular to international humanitarian law. It is also distinct from the more familiar *lex generalis* ordinary right to protest. The right to resist and its cognates are understood, on the basis of the definitions above, as being: at least potentially legal as well as moral; possibly 'natural' in origin but also found in positive law; fundamental and inalienable; secondary and remedial and, as such, a form of self-help extrajudicial effective remedy, enforcement, or prevention; conditional as well as limited rather than absolute; mostly procedural but also partly substantive; and finally an exceptional or *lex specialis* form of a political right to action. These are the aspects discussed in the remainder of the book.

3

Clarifying the Nature and Legal Function of the Right

3.1 INTRODUCTION

What is the point of having a 'right to resist'? Is the right 'justiciable' in court, or otherwise enforceable? Though legal scholars often consider this issue determinative, we have not yet managed to produce a consensus. Some argue that this right inherently defies regulation by law – or that its adjudication by a compromised judiciary is pointless and its enforcement hopeless.[1] Others maintain that modern constitutions and mechanisms for judicial review have rendered the right obsolete – that where judicial integrity is maintained, there is no need.[2] This is only one of several jurisprudential debates bearing on the

[1] See for example, Arthur Kaufmann, 'Small Scale Right to Resist' (1985–1986) 21 *New England Law Review* 571, 572–573; Franz L Neumann, 'On the Limits of Justifiable Disobedience' in Franz L Neumann, *The Democratic and Authoritarian State: Essays in Political and Legal Theory* (Free Press 1957) 154. For the origins of such non-absolutist arguments against its viability, see the Kantian and Benthamite theories. Synthesizing the Kantian position from the main sources, 'Doctrine of Right' in *Metaphysics of Morals* VI 320; *Theory and Practice* VIII 297; *Towards Perpetual Peace* VIII 381, and other works, see Katrin Flikschuh, 'Reason, Right and Revolution: Kant and Locke' (2008) 36 *Philosophy and Public Affairs* 375, 380–381. See also Peter Nicholson, 'Kant on the Duty Never to Resist the Sovereign' (1976) 86(3) *Ethics* 214, 214 (fn 1), 215–216, 218, 220–224, 228–230; Lewis W Beck, 'Kant and the Right of Revolution' (1971) 32(3) *Journal of the History of Ideas* 411, 414; Costas Douzinas, 'The "Right to the Event": The Legality and Morality of Revolution and Resistance' (2014) 2(2) *Metodo: International Studies in Phenomenology and Philosophy* 151, 151–154. More straightforward is Jeremy Bentham, 'Anarchical Fallacies; Being an Examination of the Declaration of Rights Issued during the French Revolution', reprinted in Jeremy Waldron (ed), *Nonsense upon Stilts: Bentham, Burke and Marx on the Rights of Man* (Methuen 1987).

[2] See, for example, Neumann (n 1) 154; Heiner Bielefeldt, 'The Right to Resist' in Wilhelm Heitmeyer and John Hagan (eds), *International Handbook of Violence Research* (Kluwer 2003)

question of what a 'right' to resist might mean, particularly as to its nature and legal function, that remain unresolved.

The first debate about its nature starts with the question of whether the right to resist is primarily or exclusively a moral rather than legal right. The second follows on from this: the debate about the relationship of the right to resist to the rule of law itself. For example, in jurisdictions where it is not provided by law, or where its legal status is unclear, do those exercising a claimed right to resist have the right regardless of what the positive law says? If so, is that because the right will always operate outside of law and is unregulatable? Alternatively, is it law's necessary auxiliary, or is it actually intrinsic to the rule of law as an invisible failsafe? These theoretical issues are not only germane to conceptualization of the right but bear on the further question of its enforceability. Because this study focuses on legal right theories, and indeed the existing or theorized or proposed positive legal provisions, the question of moral right is beyond its scope. For the same reason, at least some degree of compatibility with the rule of law is necessarily assumed. This chapter will therefore confine itself to outlining the main contours of these two wider unsettled debates on its nature as background, adopting only pragmatic rather than final conclusions. Detailed consideration is saved for the third debate, on how to classify the right to resist among the various types of legal rights, including with regard to its function – and consequently whether its enforcement is theoretically possible and what that might entail. Firmer conclusions are drawn in this regard and suggestions offered for the purposes of conceptual clarification, particularly where these might bear on how a claim might be made and enforced.

Section 3.2 of this chapter identifies the four main approaches to conceptualizing the nature of the right to resist as a 'right' and the three general conceptions of its relation to the rule of law. Section 3.3 then examines various conceptualizations of the type of legal right it may be: a fundamental

1099. For an argument that the right to resist is a legally primitive self-help method that preceded the development of effective judicial mechanisms, and was ultimately replaced by them, see Barna Horvath, 'Rights of Man: Due Process of Law and Excès de Pouvoir' (1955) 4 (4) *American Journal of Comparative Law* 539, 548. See also Oscar Jászi and John D Lewis (eds), *Against the Tyrant: The Tradition and Theory of Tyrannicide* (The Free Press 1957) 'Preface' v–vi; John D Lewis, 'The Development of the Theory of Tyrannicide to 1660' in Jászi and Lewis (n 2) 94; Edward Rubin, 'Judicial Review and the Right to Resist' (2008) 97 *Georgetown Law Journal* 61, 63, 85ff. Similar obsolescence arguments were made by legal positivism regarding the concept of legality and the constitutional state. See for example, Mitsukuni Yazaki, 'Legality and the Right of Resistance' [1957] *Osaka University Law Review* 28–30; Fritz Kern, *Kingship and Law in the Middle Ages: The Divine Right of Kings and the Right of Resistance in the Early Middle Ages* (S Chrimes tr, Basil Blackwell 1939) 200, 203.

'human right', a 'general principle of law' or '*sui generis*' right; an 'unenumerated', 'implied' or 'latent' right – or simply '*non liquet*'; whether it requires a 'legal fiction' or is in itself an enforceable 'claim' right; whether it is a 'right', 'duty', or hybrid 'right-duty'; whether it is a primary or secondary right; and finally whether it is a superordinate compound right or a subordinate part of another compound right. Section 3.4 considers conceptualizations of the right's function as: a self-help remedy for enforcement or prevention by deterrence; an exceptional immunity, justification defence, or temporary permission by license; a form of *actio popularis*; a form of *jus ad bellum*; and finally, a lawful exception or *lex specialis* rule. Section 3.5 concludes that – whatever other variations may be possible depending on how a given theory, recognition or provision is formulated – today it is predominantly conceptualized as a potentially enforceable human right, theoretically capable of interpretation as such even where unenumerated, and this is the basis for its principal function as a *lex specialis* rule of exception.

3.2 NATURE OF THE RIGHT

Given that over centuries the right to resist has been expressed in positive legal recognitions, whether customary or written,[3] one can assume that the right to resist is capable of expression as a legal right. As such, it must be at least potentially compatible with the rule of law. Its predominant contemporary conceptualization as a human right in constitutional and international law – as shown below and in Part II – reinforces these pragmatic conclusions. Not everyone shares them, however.

3.2.1 *Moral, Legal, Both, or Other? Four Main Approaches*

Unless otherwise specified, this study uses the term 'right' in the positivist sense, as a 'power, privilege, or immunity secured to a person by law' and as a 'legally enforceable claim that another will do or will not do a given act; a recognized and protected interest the violation of which is a wrong'.[4] However *Black's Law Dictionary* also defines 'right' as that 'which is proper under law, morality, or ethics' and something 'due to a person by just claim, legal guarantee, or moral principle'.[5] According to Wacks, a 'moral right is an entitlement which confers moral liberties on those who have them to do

[3] See Part II, Chapters 5–7.

[4] Bryan A Garner (ed), *Black's Law Dictionary* (2nd edn, West Group 2001) 613.

[5] Ibid 613 [emphasis added].

certain things, and the moral constraint on others to abstain from interference', whereas a 'legal right is one recognized by the law'.[6] This illustrates the different ways contemporary legal scholars conceive of the right to resist – whether they consider themselves naturalist, positivist, or critical in orientation. That is, most tend to consider it as a moral right or a legal right, or potentially both. This has further implications for whether one argues that the right is appropriate for positivization and therefore adjudication or other enforcement, or only other – or lesser – forms of recognition.

The debate about whether any given right is moral or legal is not necessarily determinative of whether that purported right is potentially enforceable, but it does shape expectations about how that enforcement might happen – whether judicially, extrajudicially, or both. This equally applies to the debate about the nature of the right to resist, within which there are three main types of argument made, classifying it as inherent, impracticable, or *lex lata/lex ferenda*.

The 'inherence' arguments hold that the right to resist is a moral rather than legal right because its validity does not depend on its recognition in positive law. It is therefore directly self-enforcing, extrajudicially. For example, Lauterpacht views the right to resist as the 'ultimate' and 'supreme' human right, in the form of a natural law 'corrective and the final and inescapable sanction, when all others have failed'.[7] For this reason – and however he may concede its positivization in constitutional law as potentially appropriate – for Lauterpacht its codification in international law is 'not essential' or even 'out of place'.[8] He suggests not only that positivization of the right to resist is irrelevant to its validity, but may even prove detrimental by unnecessarily conceding to the state a regulatory power over it.[9] In contemporary times, such positions are taken by some natural law and some critical theory proponents.[10]

6 Raymond Wacks, *Understanding Jurisprudence: An Introduction to Legal Theory* (2nd edn, Oxford University Press 2009) 298.

7 Hersch Lauterpacht, *International Law and Human Rights* (Stevens and Sons 1950) 325–326.

8 Ibid 325–326. For him, the codification of citizen duties – which would include the duty of resistance – is not appropriate in an instrument for the purpose of securing, through international means, the rights of individuals against their own states.

9 Lauterpacht (n 7) 91–93. This explains why he does not include it in his own draft 'International Bill of the Rights of Man' and does not list it in his 'Subjects Not Included in the Bill of Rights'. Hersch Lauterpacht, *International Bill of the Rights of Man* (Columbia University Press 1945) 69–74, 163–165. It also explains why, despite his 'supreme right' characterization, he expresses no concern at its non-inclusion in the UN draft then under negotiation. See Lauterpacht (n 7).

10 Compare for example Wolfgang Schwarz, 'The Right of Resistance' (1964) 74(2) *Ethics* 126, 128, 130; Max Pribilla, *The Right to Resist* (Catholic Social Guild 1952) 19–21, 25, 29–30;

The 'impracticability' arguments hold that a right to resist can only ever remain a moral right because it is practically unenforceable. Since it cannot be enforced judicially, it remains illusory as a legal right even if codified or otherwise recognized.[11] The more extreme version holds that a 'legal' right to resist is inherently contradictory and thus a nonsense in that law cannot authorize its own violation.[12] Formerly, impracticability arguments were favoured mostly by absolutist opponents of the right to resist, and then by certain positivists.[13] In contemporary times this position tends to be taken variously by legal realists and some positivists,[14] but also by some natural law proponents.[15]

The '*lex lata/lex ferenda*' arguments hold that, whatever its status as a moral right, the right to resist has long been considered customary in some jurisdictions, has proven capable of positivization and codification, and should be recognized in law where it currently is not. It can be directly self-enforcing extrajudicially, but also directly or indirectly enforceable judicially. This position has proponents in the natural law, positivist, and critical camps.[16]

René Marcic, 'The Persistence of Right-Law: An Inquiry into the Foundations of the Right to Resist' (1973) 59 *Archives for Philosophy of Law and Social Philosophy* 87, 88, 105, 112–113; Bielefeldt (n 2) 1102–1104.

11 See for example Kaufmann (n 1) 572, 573.

12 See for example Guenter Lewy, 'Resistance to Tyranny: Treason, Right or Duty?' (1960) 13(3) *Western Political Quarterly* 581, 588, 595–596.

13 See for example the sources in n 1. However, compare HLA Hart, 'Positivism and the Separation of Law and Morals' (1958) 71(4) *Harvard Law Review* 593, 600 fn 21, 616–617.

14 See for example Lewy (n 12) 595–596. See also the account in Yazaki (n 2) 28–30. On other positivist variants, compare for example Hans Kelsen, 'Quincy Wright's A Study of War and the Bellum Justum Theory' (1943) 53 *Ethics* 208, 208–211; Hans Kelsen, 'The Natural Law Doctrine before the Tribunal of Science' (1949) 2 *Western Political Quarterly* 481, 493–494; Hart (n 13) 615–624.

15 See for example Kaufmann (n 1) 572–573, 575–576; Johannes Morsink, 'The Philosophy of the Universal Declaration' (1984) 6(3) *Human Rights Quarterly* 309, 324.

16 See for example Pribilla (n 10) 19–21, 25, 29–30; Marcic (n 10) 88, 105, 112–113; Bielefeldt (n 2) 1102–1104. See also Richard Falk, 'The Adequacy of Contemporary Theories of International Law: Gaps in Legal Thinking' (1964) 50(2) *Virginia Law Review* 231, 248–249, 255–256; Richard Falk, 'The Nuremberg Defense in the Pentagon Papers Case' (1974) 13 *Columbia Journal of Transnational Law* 208; Richard Falk and Burns H Weston, 'The Relevance of International Law to Palestinian Rights in the West Bank and Gaza: In Legal Defense of the Intifada' (1991) 32(1) *Harvard International Law Journal* 129, 155; Antonio Cassese, 'Human Rights and Humanitarian Law: Terrorism and Human Rights' (1982) 31 *American University Law Review* 945, 946–947; Nicholas N Kittrie, *Rebels with a Cause: The Minds and Morality of Political Offenders* (Westview 2000) 193–350, 342–344. See also the theories and international codification efforts discussed further in Chapters 6–7. Those taking such a position follow in the Bartolist tradition and that of the *Vindiciae, Contra Tyrannos* in their attempts not only to advocate but also to locate the right in Roman and civil law. See Bartolus de Saxoferrato, *On Guelfs and Ghibbellines* (Jonathan Robinson tr, Creative

One final major variant worth mentioning is the socialist concept of 'right action', within which 'it is right to resist' on the basis of material interest, regardless of whether there is a 'moral' or 'legal' right to do so, because rights are historically won through mobilization.[17] In this conceptualization, the 'moral' versus 'legal' dichotomy is less relevant than strategic correctness, in keeping with the stages theory of revolution and historical determinism. This is therefore a non-legal concept of a 'right' based not on moral imperative but revolutionary imperative.[18] It parallels the natural law theories insofar as it conceptualizes the right as existing regardless of the positive law and as self-enforcing, but also contrasts insofar as the concept is one of 'necessity' or even 'inevitability' more than 'right'. Therefore, if one category of theories of the right to resist is based on moral right/natural law–natural rights, and another on legal right/positivization of inalienable rights, this constitutes a third category based on right action/socialist objectives. It is not a legal theory and not a moral theory, but a strategic theory of justification. As such, while it relies on self-contained logic, it also borrows legal or moral guises when need be. While the original concept was not human rights-based in today's sense, subsequent theories in the socialist vein have become more harmonized with the human rights concept, if critically so.[19]

Apart from the socialist variant, the three main positions on the nature of the right to resist described above are not always consistent within

Commons Attribution-Non-Commercial ShareAlike 3.0 Unreported License 2014 rev 1.1a) Book III and Bartolus de Saxoferrato, *On the Tyrant* (Jonathan Robinson tr, Creative Commons Attribution-Non-Commercial ShareAlike 3.0 Unreported License 2012 (rev 1.0a) 2016 (rev 1.2); *Vindiciae, Contra Tyrannos: or, Concerning the Legitimate Power of a Prince over the People, and of the People over a Prince* (George Garnett ed/tr, 2003 edn, Cambridge University Press 1994) 188–190.

[17] See for example Vladimir I Lenin, *Critical Remarks on the National Question – The Right of Nations to Self-Determination* (1914, Foreign Languages Publishing House edn 1954) 177, 181–182. While Lenin's is technically an eastern concept, it derives at least in part from pre-existing western theory of the modern period. Lenin admits this, though he distinguishes the Marxist from the republican theories. See also WW Kulski, 'Soviet Comments on International Law' (1951) 45(4) *American Journal of International Law* 762, 765–766. It is relevant to this study as it inspired the formulation of the right as a 'duty' at article 10 of the 'Declaration of Rights of the Working and Exploited People' in the Constitution of the Russian Socialist Federated Socialist Republic (1918), and the socialist bloc representations in later negotiations at the United Nations. Since former colonial states were often as influenced by the Soviet theories as by the more traditional western theories of the right to resist, it also had an impact on subsequent developments in international and constitutional law, discussed in Part II.

[18] See for example Lenin (n 17) 65–68.

[19] For example Issa G Shivji, *The Concept of Human Rights in Africa* (CODESRIA Book Series 1989) 69–87.

philosophical 'schools'. Rather, each supplies both advocates and opponents, who rely on reasoning from within their own framework.[20] What potentially unifies the naturalist, positivist, and critical perspectives on this right is the idea that while law should be instrumental to secure justice, law alone is often insufficient.[21] The question of whether there is or can be a 'right' to resist, and if so what are its enabling conditions and its proper limits, is therefore intrinsically linked to some of the most fundamental questions of jurisprudence, including that of the relationship of law to justice.[22] The position on the right to resist arising from the various schools of jurisprudential thought derives from positions taken on such prior questions.

This study cannot ultimately resolve the nature of the right to resist. Focused instead on investigating the positive legal expressions, it does not interrogate claims of purely moral or strategic right regardless of law. Yet it also does not disavow such claims. While formal legal recognition of the human right to resist may not be determinative of all cases in which resistance can be justified as the 'right' choice for moral or strategic reasons, the main purpose of the present research is to locate the limits of the law's present provision for resistance as a lawful exception. Consequently, the remainder of this chapter focuses mainly on legal right theories.

3.2.2 *Relationship to the Rule of Law: Three Main Conceptions*

In addition to whether one considers the right to resist moral or legal, potentially both or something else, how one conceptualizes it in relationship to the rule of law itself is also relevant to how – and indeed whether – one envisions its enforcement taking place. There are three main conceptions of the relationship of the right to resist to the rule of law apparent from the historical literature and replicated in the contemporary literature. They are that the right to resist: (1) is 'outside' and may also be inimical to the rule of law;[23] (2) whether 'outside' or 'inside', is compatible with the rule of law; (3) is both 'inside' and intrinsic to the rule of law, needed for enforcement or change. While the historical theories of the right to resist are largely associated with the natural law perspective and conform with conceptions (2) or (3) above, in contemporary literature, arguments in each of these three categories

20 See Yazaki (n 2) 26–37, 31–37; Marcic (n 10) 107.

21 See Hart (n 13).

22 Marcic (n 10) 105–108.

23 'Outside' the law is used here in two senses. First, it is used in the sense of unregulated and therefore not illegal, or 'not against the law'. Second, it is used in the sense of outside legality and therefore 'against the law'.

can be found across the spectrum of jurisprudential theory, from naturalism to positivism to critical theory, each employing their particular assumptions and reasoning.[24]

When employed by opponents of the idea of a right to resist, the first position views any such alleged right as inherently contrary to the rule of law: not merely undesirable, but also impossible to regulate much less enforce.[25] When employed by proponents of the right to resist – including by critical theorists wary of law as expression and tool of hegemony – the position concerns itself less with whether the right undermines the rule of law. It holds that the right is a moral or other right 'beyond law' and thus beyond regulation.[26] For some it should remain thus if it is to have any meaning because official recognition, codification, and regulation would render the right immobile and unusable.[27] Indeed, Lewy cautions that such positivizations reflect a 'preoccupation with legalism' that not only 'create[s] a false sense of security' but also a complexity of determination that can impede necessary and effective action against violations, and ultimately make little difference to motivate either those 'of courage' or the 'fainthearted'.[28] While Lewy's conclusion that the right to resist therefore does not exist is questionable, the concern he raises about the relevance of positivization is worthy of consideration.

For those who adopt the second or middle position, whether positivized or not, the right to resist provides protections complementary to the rule of law when the law either fails or provides a cloak of legality to violations. They view it as an 'auxiliary' to law, associated with 'higher law' – meaning natural law, constitutional law, or international law – enforcement, when positive law does

24 Indeed, there is not always a sharp distinction between the three main conceptions. In particular, some contemporary proponent theories appear to blend elements of the 'compatible' and 'intrinsic' positions.

25 To put this argument succinctly, there can be no 'legal right to disobey the law'. David Spitz, 'Democracy and the Problem of Civil Disobedience' (1954) 48 *American Political Science Review* 386, 392–398. Citing 'clear analogies' to the 'state of exception', see also Giorgio Agamben, *State of Exception* (Kevin Attell tr, University of Chicago Press 2005) 10–11, 1.7. Yet compare Mortimer R Kadish and Sanford H Kadish, *Discretion to Disobey: A Study of Lawful Departures from Legal Rules* (Stanford University Press 1973, repr Quid Pro Books 2010) xiv, 72, 88–90.

26 See Monique Chemillier-Gendreau, 'Resistance, Right to, International Protection' in Rüdiger Wolfrum (ed), *Max Planck Encyclopedia of Public International Law* (Oxford University Press 2012) 954 [2], 957–958 [22]–[27].

27 See Kaufmann (n 1) 576.

28 Lewy (n 12) 594, 596.

not comply.[29] This perspective recognizes that judicial review is not the sole, and may not always be the best safeguard of fundamental rights.[30] It positions the right as a compatible extrajudicial and extra-legislative mechanism,[31] supplemental not only to law enforcement but also to the 'process of self-correction' of law – that is, legal change – when ordinary political and judicial means have failed.[32] This conception yields no single position on the question of whether the right, as a means of direct enforcement, can itself be enforced judicially or otherwise.

At the other extreme, the third position views the right to resist as intrinsic to the rule of law, as an element within the lawful enforcement spectrum.[33] For advocates of this position, the right provides a crucial means of restoration of legal equilibrium when the rule of law itself has been usurped or abused. It provides a remedy where enforcement means are absent, have broken down, or otherwise don't work – when the rule of law itself fails. Moreover it fulfills a preventive function, including but not limited to when the rule of law is under active threat.[34] On this basis it can be legitimately recognized as a legal right,

[29] See for example Lauterpacht (n 7) 93, 325–326. For the positivist variant see Yazaki (n 2) 35–37.

[30] For Neumann, the right is compatible because rule of law alone is an 'incomplete guarantor' of human rights. Neumann (n 1) 176–178.

[31] See for example Catharine MacMillan and Charlotte Smith, 'Foreword' in Catharine MacMillan and Charlotte Smith (eds), *Challenges to Authority and the Recognition of Rights – From Magna Carta to Modernity* (Cambridge University Press 2019) 6–7. This conception of a supplementary, extrajudicial mechanism is comparable to the phenomenon of civil society- or social movement-led 'people's tribunals', the quasi-judicial structures developed since the 1960s to address impunity for injustices arising from deficiencies in development or enforcement of international human rights law, international criminal law, and environmental law. See Andrew Byrnes and Gabrielle Simm (eds), *Peoples' Tribunals and International Law* (Cambridge University Press 2018); Regina Menachery Paulose (ed), *People's Tribunals, Human Rights and the Law: Searching for Justice* (Routledge 2020).

[32] See Quincy Wright, 'Towards a Universal Law for Mankind' (1963) 63 *Columbia Law Review* 435, 440; Falk, 'Adequacy of Contemporary Theories' (n 16) 248–249, 255–256. On the right as an intrinsic rather than auxiliary mechanism of self-correction, compare Kadish and Kadish (n 25) 22–23, 50–51, 146–158.

[33] See Marcic (n 10) 104–105.

[34] On the right to resist performing this essential function within democratic systems see discussions in Pierre Rosanvallon, *Counter-Democracy: Politics in an Age of Distrust* (Arthur Goldhammer tr, Cambridge University Press 2008) 121–123, 127; Daniela Bifulco and Angelo Jr Golia, 'The Right of Resistance as a State Law Basis for Transnational Regimes' Self-Contestation' (2018) 45 *Journal of Law and Society* 94. Similarly, see Roberto Gargarella, 'The Right of Resistance in Situations of Severe Deprivation' in Thomas Pogge (ed), *Freedom from Poverty as a Human Right: Who Owes What to the Very Poor?* (Oxford University Press and UNESCO 2007) 373 and fn 20, citing John Rawls, A *Theory of Justice* (Harvard University Press 1999) 336–338.

its exercise regulated, and itself enforced – but only as a rule of exception.[35] For such theorists, the right to resist is not only potentially codifiable and amenable to regulation and enforcement, its recognition provides an essential back-up to the inevitably fallible system. Positions can however differ as to whether such recognition, regulation, and enforcement should be inter- or intra-systemic or both.[36]

Whichever of these three main positions a theorist takes on the relation of the right to resist to the rule of law also derives in part from a stand on prior and related fundamental questions of jurisprudence. That is, the source of sovereignty or ultimate authority under the rule of law, and the consequent limits of obligation. For those supporting the right to resist as consistent with or even necessary to the rule of law, either the law itself is sovereign or the people are sovereign. In the former case, necessary measures to enforce that higher law may include lawful disobedience to law lower in the hierarchy. In the latter, the law must serve the people, otherwise it is not valid and can lawfully be disobeyed. However, the above shows that, no matter what the specific position on its relation to the rule of law, the source of sovereignty, or the precise limits of obligation, for proponents of the right it boils down to a series of positions on positivization and forms of enforcement. For some, the right to resist is a form of direct self-enforcement that does not need to rely on positivization. For others it is a form of direct self-enforcement that cannot or should not be positivized. For a third group, it is a form of direct self-enforcement that not only can and should be positivized but can itself be enforced directly, indirectly, and by third parties.

A definitive answer to the perennial question of the relation of the right to resist to the rule of law is beyond the scope of this book. Instead, it adopts the pragmatic assumptions that, since positive provisions have been promulgated for centuries without demonstrated association with increased lawlessness,[37] the right's recognition must be at least potentially compatible with the rule of law, that positivization is at least possible, and that, in addition to direct

35 Such conditions override both the general duty of obedience and the general obligation to use lawful means of opposition because these are not available. See Pribilla (n 10) 5, 6–7, 28; Kaufmann (n 1) 574.

36 'Intra-systemic' here means that the right would be recognized, exercised, regulated, and enforced entirely within the domestic or international legal system in question. 'Inter-systemic' means that, for example, the right would be exercised within a given domestic system, but if not recognized, regulated, and enforced within that system, this would be done within the international system.

37 See in particular the evidence of quasi-constitutional and constitutional provision in Chapter 5.

self-enforcement, it may itself also be capable of judicial and other third-party enforcement under certain circumstances.

3.3 TYPE OF RIGHT

The third main dispute about the nature of the 'right' to resist is the type of legal right it constitutes. Theorists have attributed a series of characteristics or options, discussed below. Not all but many of these are potentially compatible rather than mutually exclusive. This permits a more nuanced understanding of what the right might entail, and what this potentially means for its enforcement.

3.3.1 *A Fundamental 'Human Right'*

In contemporary terms the right to resist is predominantly conceptualized as a 'human right'.[38] This characterization sometimes takes the form of an

[38] See for example Hersch Lauterpacht, 'Law of Nations, Law of Nature, Rights of Man' (1943) 29 *Transactions of the Grotius Society* 1, 23, 26; Lauterpacht, *International Bill of the Rights of Man* (n 9) 43, 46; Lauterpacht (n 7) 116, 119; Philip C Jessup, *A Modern Law of Nations: An Introduction* (Macmillan 1948) 186; M Cherif Bassiouni, 'Final Document: Conclusions and Recommendations' in M Cherif Bassiouni (ed), *International Terrorism and Political Crimes* (Charles C Thomas 1975) xxi; Marcic (n 10); Upendra Baxi, 'Otonomic Prowess and Existential Impotence: Reflexions on René Marcic's Sydney Papers' (conference paper for 'René Marcic: Sydney Commemorative Symposium (54)' University of Sydney, Faculty of Law, Department of Jurisprudence and International Law, Institute for Advanced Studies in Jurisprudence, Sydney, 1972) 6 ff; Cassese (n 16) 946–950; Jordan J Paust, 'The Human Right to Participate in Armed Revolution and Related Forms of Social Violence: Testing the Limits of Permissibility' (1983) 32 *Emory Law Journal* 545, 560–561; Tony Honoré, 'The Right to Rebel' (1988) 8(1) *Oxford Journal of Legal Studies* 34, 34, 39–40, 42–43; Francis A Boyle et al, 'Citizen Initiatives under International Law' (1988) 82 *Proceedings of the American Society of International Law* 555, 569; Francis A Boyle, *Protesting Power: War, Resistance, and Law* (Rowman and Littlefield 2008) 22; Asbjörn Eide, 'The Right to Oppose Violations of Human Rights: Basis, Conditions and Limitations' in *Violations of Human Rights: Possible Rights of Recourse and Forms of Resistance* (UNESCO 1984) 35, 39; Matthew Lippman, 'The Right of Civil Resistance under International Law and the Domestic Necessity Defense' (1990) 8 *Dickinson Journal of International Law* 349, 353–354; Allan Rosas, 'Internal Self-Determination' in Christian Tomuschat (ed), *Modern Law of Self-Determination* (Martinus Nijhoff 1993) 244–245, 249; Shivji (n 19) 80–87; Walter Kälin and Jorg Künzli, 'Article 1F(b): Freedom Fighters, Terrorists and the Notion of Serious Non-Political Crime' (2000) 12 supp *International Journal of Refugee Law* 46; Kittrie (n 16) 193–350 generally, and in particular his 'Bill of Rights for Just Governance and Just Resistance' 342–344; Bielefeldt (n 2) 1099, 1103–1104; Bertil Dunér, 'Rebellion: The Ultimate Human Right?' (2005) 9(2) *International Journal of Human Rights* 247; David B Kopel, Paul Gallant, and Joanne D Eisen, 'Is Resisting Genocide a Human Right?' (2006) 81(4) *Notre Dame Law Review* 1275; David B Kopel, Paul Gallant, and Joanne D Eisen, 'The Human Right of Self-Defense' (2008) 22 *Brigham Young*

unstated assumption. Even when stated, the claim is often made without regard to whether it is recognized as such by a particular body of law. Indeed, Lauterpacht had sufficient confidence in his reference to the right to resist as the 'supreme' human right that he let it stand without further explanation.[39] Yet the right to resist is not standard in the human rights 'lexicon' in the twenty-first century.[40] That its status in human rights theory has become marginal, at best, is illustrated by its exclusion from almost all legal textbooks on human rights,[41] and other legal reference works.[42] Its standing as a human right therefore cannot be taken for granted.

What does it mean to classify the right to resist as a human right and what does this imply about its nature? As with the right to resist itself, a consensus definition of 'human rights' remains elusive.[43] Nor is there 'complete agreement' about the nature and scope of human rights despite 'widespread acceptance of the principle' among 'the vast majority of legal scholars and philosophers'.[44] Nevertheless, Claude and Weston identify 'five postulates' that command general agreement about the basic conceptual aspects.[45] These postulates also help describe the nature of the 'human right to resist'. They stipulate that human rights imply 'claims against persons and institutions' and 'qualify state sovereignty and power'.[46] These claims are '"fundamental" as distinct from "nonessential"',[47] they range 'from the most justiciable to the most aspirational' and 'partake of both the legal and the

University Journal of Public Law 43; Gargarella (n 34) 359–374; Chemillier-Gendreau (n 26) [5]; Gwilym David Blunt, 'Is There a Human Right to Resistance?' (2017) 39(4) *Human Rights Quarterly* 860.

39 This would indicate that he considered the assertion unlikely to be perceived as far-fetched. See Lauterpacht, 'Law of Nations, Law of Nature, Rights of Man' (n 38) 23, 26; Lauterpacht, *International Bill of the Rights of Man* (n 9) 43, 46; Lauterpacht (n 7) 116, 119.

40 Consequently, the right to resist does not even merit a passing reference, much less its own entry, in Susan Marks and Andrew Clapham, *International Human Rights Lexicon* (Oxford University Press 2005) 61–70, 271–286, 345–358.

41 For a notable exception, see Richard Pierre Claude and Burns H Weston (eds), *Human Rights in the World Community: Issues and Action* (3rd edn, University of Pennsylvania Press 2006) 445–454.

42 For an exception among legal encyclopedias see Chemillier-Gendreau (n 26) 954 [1].

43 This is despite the 'core of reasonable certainty' about its content. Ian Brownlie, *Principles of Public International Law* (7th edn, Oxford University Press 2008) 556.

44 Claude and Weston (n 41) 19–20. Shaw finds this unsurprising given that the 'question of what is meant by a "right" is itself controversial and the subject of intense jurisprudential debate'. Malcolm N Shaw, *International Law* (6th edn, Cambridge University Press 2008) 265.

45 See Claude and Weston (n 41) 20–21. They caution, however, that these five postulates do not satisfy all pertinent questions about 'content and legitimate scope' of human rights.

46 Ibid 20.

47 Ibid.

moral orders, sometimes indistinguishably'.[48] They are 'qualified by the limitation that the rights of individuals or groups in particular instances are restricted as much as is necessary to secure the comparable rights of others and the aggregate common interest'.[49] Finally, they are 'quintessentially general or universal in character', that is 'equally possessed by all human beings everywhere ... simply for being human'.[50]

When conceptualized as belonging to this category, the right to resist is inseparable from the core proposition that governments are instituted to protect human rights.[51] Within a human rights framework, the right to resist therefore activates only in the context of violations of other recognized primary human rights.[52] This updates and enhances the concept from previous vaguer historical iterations whereby the trigger violation was of 'natural law',[53] the theorized governing 'compact' or 'social contract',[54] or the 'public interest' or 'common good'.[55] In addition, the right has limits: it can only be exercised in

48 Ibid.

49 Ibid.

50 Ibid.

51 Paust (n 38) 550. See also for example the approach in Eide (n 38) 43. For the right's characterization as 'inseparable' from the human rights concept overall, see 'Meeting of Experts: Final Report' *in Violations of Human Rights: Possible Rights of Recourse and Forms of Resistance* (UNESCO 1984) 226–227.

52 See for example Eide (n 38) 34, 39, 47–53.

53 See Cicero, *De Officiis* (Walter Miller tr, GP Putnam's Sons 1913) Book III, vi [27] 293–295, [30]–[31] 297, vi [32] 299; Thomas Aquinas, 'Commentary on the Sentences of Peter Lombard' in AP Entrèves (ed), *Aquinas: Selected Political Writings* (JG Dawson tr, Oxford University Press 1948) Book II, 'The Obedience Owed by Christians to the Secular Power and in particular to Tyrants' di 44, q 2, a 2; Thomas Aquinas, *De regno ad regum Cypri: On Kingship, To the King of Cyprus* (Gerald B Phelan tr, IT Eschmann rev edn, Pontifical Institute of Medieval Studies 1949) Book I ch 7; Thomas Aquinas, 'Summa Theologiae' in William P Baumgarth and Richard J Regan (eds), *On Law, Morality and Politics* (Richard J Regan tr, 2nd edn, Hackett Publishing 2002) II-II q 40 'On War', a 1 'Is It Always Sinful to Wage War?', q 64 'On Homicide', a 7 'Is It Lawful for a Person to Kill Another in Self-Defense?', q 104 'On Obedience', a 5 'Are Subjects Obliged to Obey Their Superiors in All Things?' and a 6 'Are Christians Obliged to Obey Secular Authorities?', q 42 'On Rebellion', a 2 'Is Rebellion Always a Mortal Sin?'; Hugo Grotius, *The Rights of War and Peace* (Richard Tuck ed, Jean Barbeyrac tr, Liberty Fund 2005) generally; Emer de Vattel, *The Law of Nations, or Principles of the Law of Nature, Applied to the Conduct and Affairs of Nations and Sovereigns* (Béla Kapossy and Richard Whatmore eds, Liberty Fund 2008) Preliminaries, 'Idea and General Principles of the Law of Nations' [5] 68, [7]–[9] 70–71, [17] 74–75, [26]–[27] 78.

54 See *Vindiciae, Contra Tyrannos* (n 16) 68–78, 92–102, 104–124, 127, 129–137, 172; Grotius (n 53) Book I Chapter IV, VII, XVII 372–380; Vattel (n 53) Book I Chapter I [4] 83, Book I Chapter II [14]–[18], [21]–[22] 86–89, Book I Chapter III [26]–[30] 91–93, [32]–[34] 94–95, [37] 96, Book I Chapter IV [51] 103–105.

55 See Thomas Aquinas, *Treatise on Law: The Complete Text (Summa Theologiae I–II, Questions 90–108)* (Alfred J Freddoso tr, St Augustine's Press 2009) q 90 'The Essence of Law', a 2 'Is law Always Ordered toward the Common Good as Its End?'; Aquinas, 'Summa Theologiae' (n 53)

pursuit of aims that are internally consistent with generally accepted human rights norms, and it cannot be used to intentionally suppress the fundamental rights of others.[56] These crucial and distinctive aspects are further discussed below and in the following chapters.

As a human right, the right to resist is not exclusively an 'individual' or 'collective' or 'people's' right, but rather all of these. It is a right of individuals, groups, and peoples primarily against states, but given its elasticity it could also extend to a right against other actors exercising unlawful authority or abusing power. Likewise, within the human rights framework it does not fit neatly into the 'three generations of human rights' typology. Instead, it potentially plays a supporting role in the enforcement and realization of the full spectrum of human rights: civil, political, economic, social, cultural, and environmental. As an individual right it may concern both resistance to direct attacks on one's own person or violations of one's own human rights, and also individual resistance to more widespread or systematic human rights violations.

Conceptualizing the right to resist as a human right has implications not only for theories about its nature, but also for theories about its sources as a legal right.[57] The legal source theories for the right to resist established by the modern period pertained variously to 'natural law',[58] 'customary

II-II q 42 'On Rebellion', a 2 'Is Rebellion Always a Mortal Sin?' reply obj 1, reply obj 3, q 40 'On War', a 1 'Is It Always Sinful to Wage War?' reply obj 2; *Vindiciae, Contra Tyrannos* (n 16) 68–78, 92–102, 104–124, 127, 129–137, 157, 172; Vattel (n 53) Book I Chapter II [14]–[17] 86–88, [21] 89. Marcic sees an ongoing relationship between human rights and the common good, and consequently between the right to resist and the common good. See Marcic (n 10) 102–103.

56 See Eide (n 38) 54.

57 On 'human rights' as the positivized secular expression of its predecessor concept 'natural rights', see Philip Alston, 'Third Generation of Solidarity Rights: Progressive Development or Obfuscation of International Human Rights Law?' (1982) 29(3) *Netherlands International Law Review* 307, 307, 319. For a detailed account of the historical evolution from one to the other, see Costas Douzinas, *The End of Human Rights* (Hart 2000) 23–145. On the inalienability of human rights regardless of either positivization or 'whether they emanate from a "higher" natural law' see Wacks (n 6) 287. Morsink calls this the 'doctrine of inherence' established by the Universal Declaration of Human Rights. Johannes Morsink, *Inherent Human Rights: Philosophical Roots of the Universal Declaration* (University of Pennsylvania Press 2009) 17–54, 55–111.

58 See in particular the theories of Cicero and Aquinas. Cicero (n 53) Book III, iv [19], 287; Aquinas, 'Commentary on the Sentences' (n 53) Book II, 'The Obedience Owed by Christians to the Secular Power and in particular to Tyrants' di 44, q 2, a 2; Aquinas, *De regno ad regum Cypri* (n 53) Book I ch 7 'How provision might be made that the king may not fall into tyranny'; Aquinas, 'Summa Theologiae' (n 53) II-II q 40 'On War', a 1 'Is It Always Sinful to Wage War?', q 64 'On Homicide', a 7 'Is It Lawful for a Person to Kill Another in Self-Defense?', q 104 'On Obedience', a 5 'Are Subjects Obliged to Obey Their Superiors in All Things?' and a 6 'Are Christians Obliged to Obey Secular Authorities?', q 42 'On Rebellion', a

law',[59] 'Roman law' in the form of both civil law and jus gentium,[60] 'common law',[61] 'fundamental law',[62] and 'the law of nations'.[63] In contemporary theory, however, the concept of the human right to resist belongs most appropriately within the general frameworks of domestic constitutional law and international human rights law. Both of these formalize and protect the fundamental human rights of people – individually and collectively – against abuses of power by states and other actors. Indeed, the general non-recognition of the right to resist in contemporary legal scholarship contrasts with its relatively widespread codification as a fundamental right in the positive provisions of constitutional law,[64] and its reflection to some extent in international human rights law.[65] Contemporary positive law source theories are considered in greater detail in Part II.

3.3.2 A *'General Principle of Law', or a* 'Sui Generis' *Right?*

There is a difference of opinion over whether the right to resist could otherwise or also be considered a generally recognized legal principle or 'doctrine' amounting to a 'general principle of law', or is instead a legal rule emanating from another particular source or sources.[66] If general principles

2 'Is Rebellion Always a Mortal Sin?'; and the *Vindiciaen* theory in *Vindiciae, Contra Tyrannos* (n 16) 140, 149–150.

59 See in particular the Ciceronian theory in Cicero (n 53) Book III, iv [19] 287. See also the references to the Blackstonian theory in Chapter 5, Sections 5.3.1 and 5.4.1, and further discussion of theories as well as the evidence of customary law as a source in Chapters 5 and 6 generally.

60 See in particular the Bartolist theory in Saxoferrato, *On Guelfs and Ghibbellines* (n 16) Book III and Saxoferrato, *On the Tyrant* (n 16); and the *Vindiciaen* theory in *Vindiciae, Contra Tyrannos* (n 16) 149–151, 157–160, 188–190.

61 See in particular the references to Blackstone in Chapter 5, Sections 5.3.1 and 5.4.1.

62 See the source theories discussed in the context of the constitutional law provisions in Chapter 5. On the close relationship between the terms 'fundamental law', 'public law', 'constitutional law', and 'higher law', see Martin Loughlin, *Foundations of Public Law* (Oxford University Press 2010) 1–13.

63 See in particular the theories in Grotius (n 53); Vattel (n 53). See also further discussions of sources theories relating to international law in Chapters 6 and 7 generally.

64 See Chapter 5, Section 5.5.

65 See Chapters 6 and 7 generally.

66 Note the distinctions can be somewhat hazy. *Black's Law Dictionary* defines 'doctrine' as a 'principle, [especially] a legal principle, that is widely adhered to', a rule as 'an established and authoritative standard or principle ... mandating or guiding conduct or action in a given type of situation', and a 'norm' as an accepted 'model or standard ... against which society judges someone or something'. While it does not separately define 'principle', it defines 'standard' as a 'model accepted as correct by custom, consent or authority' and 'a criterion for measuring acceptability'. Garner (n 4) 216, 617, 661. See also Duncan Kennedy, A *Critique of*

must meet a strict criterion of commonality to all legal systems,[67] the right to resist probably falls short of this. However, as an established natural law concept, also found in numerous domestic constitutional codifications, it potentially fulfills the criteria of both main approaches to general principles as a distinct 'source' of law.[68] That general principles require recognition but not also practice, unlike custom,[69] may further suggest the right to resist as a candidate for this category.

For Lauterpacht the right to resist is not only an 'inherent' and 'inalienable' right,[70] it may also be a general principle of law. This conclusion can be extrapolated from his general explanation that the 'law of nature' or 'natural law' – to which his predecessors attributed the 'natural rights' that Lauterpacht styled 'inherent' rights, including the right to resist – in fact represents 'what we should describe as general principles of law arrived at by way of a generalization and synthesis of the principal systems of

Adjudication (Harvard University Press 1997) 305, cited in Henry J Steiner, Philip Alston, and Ryan Goodman (eds), *International Human Rights in Context: Law, Politics, Morals* (3rd edn, Oxford University Press 2007) 482–483; Joost Pauwelyn, *Conflict of Norms in Public International Law* (Cambridge University Press 2003) 6; Martti Koskenniemi, 'Function and Scope of the *Lex specialis* Rule and the Question of "Self-Contained Regimes", Preliminary Report' (2004) UN Doc ILC(LVI)SG/FIL/CRD 1 and Add 1, 4; Shaw (n 44) 98 fn 109, citing *Delimitation of the Maritime Boundary in the Gulf of Maine Area (Canada* v *United States of America)* (Judgment) [1984] ICJ Rep 246, 288–290. However, compare the clear distinction between 'rules' and 'standards' in Emerson H Tiller and Frank B Cross, 'What Is Legal Doctrine?' (2006) 100(1) *Northwestern University Law Review* 517.

67 Cheng further defines general principles as an auxiliary source of 'latent rules', in the form of 'general propositions' of a recognized 'legal character' applied 'in the absence of specific legal provisions or of custom' but admits that the 'exact meaning and scope' of this concept is controversial. Nevertheless, 'in practice' general principles act to either guide the application of rules 'or to decide cases where no specific rule exists'. See Bin Cheng, *General Principles of Law as Applied by International Courts and Tribunals* (2006 edn, Cambridge University Press 1953) xiii–xv, 19, 24–25.

68 See Brownlie (n 43) 16–17; Shaw (n 44) 99–100; Hugh Thirlway, *The Sources of International Law* (Oxford University Press 2014) 93–115, 95–99. Brownlie maintains that the restrictive 'domestic law analogy' interpretation is the prevalent one. However, both Brownlie and Shaw cite the more expansive position as regards both natural law and constitutional law potentially informing what constitutes the general principles, particularly with respect to human rights protection, in *South-West Africa (Ethiopia* v *South Africa; Liberia* v *South Africa)* (Second phase Judgment) [1966] ICJ Rep 6, Dissenting Opinion of Judge Tanaka 250, 294–299. On 'general principles' as 'resembling', analogous to, or derived from 'natural law principles', with application in both domestic and international legal contexts, see also Cheng (n 67) 3–5, 14, 16–17, 22.

69 On the distinction between general principles as a source and custom as a source see Cheng (n 67) 23–24.

70 Lauterpacht, 'Law of Nations, Law of Nature, Rights of Man' (n 38) 23; Lauterpacht, *International Bill of the Rights of Man* (n 9) 43; Lauterpacht (n 7) 116.

jurisprudence'.[71] He is not the only one to suggest this. Marcic also implies that the right to resist is a general principle as a 'doctrine', itself arising from the natural law 'doctrine of conditional obedience'.[72] Bassiouni draws an analogy between the right to resist and the individual and collective self-defence exception that is a general principle of law.[73] However, Hessbruegge concludes that the rare right that has status as a 'recognized general principle of law' is consequently a 'sui generis right', not a 'human right'.[74] If Lauterpacht's – admittedly under-elaborated – theory is correct, and Hessbruegge's theory is also correct, then surely the *sui generis* categorization would also apply to the right to resist.[75] This is an intriguing possibility.

3.3.3 *An 'Unenumerated', 'Implied', or 'Latent' Right, or* 'Non Liquet'?

As will be seen from the evidence reviewed in Part II, one of the particular challenges for discussing the contemporary legal concept is that many theories of the right to resist are premised not on the express legal provisions available for analysis from constitutional law, but instead concern 'unenumerated', 'implied', or 'latent' rights, particularly in international law.[76] The recognition

[71] Hersch Lauterpacht, 'The Grotian Tradition in International Law' (1946) 23 *British Yearbook of International Law* 1, 9.

[72] According to the latter doctrine, there is no requirement to obey authority exercised beyond the bounds of its competence. Marcic (n 10) 104–105, 107–108.

[73] Bassiouni therefore styles the right to resist as a 'right to political self-defense'. See M Cherif Bassiouni, 'Ideologically Motivated Offenses and the Political Offense Exception in Extradition – A Proposed Juridical Standard for an Unruly Problem' (1969) XIX *De Paul Law Review* 217, 254–255.

[74] Jan Hessbruegge, *Human Rights and Personal Self-Defense in International Law* (Oxford University Press 2017); Jan Hessbruegge, 'The Right to Life as the Jus ad Bellum of Non-International Armed Conflict' (*JustSecurity*, 27 October 2016).

[75] Hessbruegge stops short of applying this conclusion to his theory of the right to resist itself. See Hessbruegge, *Human Rights and Personal Self-Defense* (n 74) 293–244. Honoré also seems to suggest that it is *sui generis* but does not use that term. See Honoré (n 38) 42.

[76] See for example Cassese (n 16) 946; Honoré (n 38) 35, 36, 43; Falk and Weston (n 16) 154; Richard Falk, 'Azmi Bishara, the Right of Resistance, and the Palestinian Ordeal' (2002) XXXI (2) *Journal of Palestine Studies* 19, 26–27; Frédéric Mégret, 'Causes Worth Fighting For: Is There a Non-State *jus ad bellum*?' in Aristotle Constantinides and Nikos Zaikos (eds), *The Diversity of International Law: Essays in Honour of Professor Kalliopi K Koufa* (Martinus Nijhoff 2009) 186. As a right implied in the Universal Declaration of Human Rights see Cassese (n 16) 946–947; Jordan J Paust, 'Political Oppression in the Name of National Security: Authority, Participation, and the Necessity within Democratic Limits Test' (1982) 9 (1) *Yale International Law Journal* 178, 180 (fn 12), 181–183; Falk and Weston (n 16) 156–157; Paust (n 38) 560 (fn 63), 567; Jordan J Paust, 'International Law, Dignity, Democracy and the Arab Spring' (2013) 46 *Cornell International Law Journal* 1, 1, 6, 11 (fn 48); Allan Rosas, 'Article 21' in Gudmunder Alfredsson and Asbjörn Eide (eds), *The Universal*

and interpretation of such rights requires differing degrees of and approaches to dynamic interpretation, depending on the source in question. This raises important questions about the distinctions between legal 'silence' and 'ambiguity' or 'ambivalence' – and lack of competence. In ordinary construction, 'ambiguous' means 'inexact' because a choice between alternatives has not been made, or 'having an obscure or double meaning' and therefore open to more than one interpretation.[77] Likewise, 'ambivalent' means the 'coexistence of opposing feelings'.[78] Depending on the source of law in question, one may be confronted with one or even all of these possibilities. This gives rise to conclusions by some that the concept is incapable of attracting sufficient agreement to yield clarity in the law, implying that attempts to determine the validity of claims are doomed to *non liquet* results.[79] Therefore, the right to resist is *non liquet* – or at least partially so – in international law.[80]

Declaration of Human Rights: A Common Standard of Achievement (Martinus Nijhoff 1999) 432, 441–442, 449, 451; Rosas (n 38) 247–249; Kälin and Künzli (n 38) 49, 51–53. As a right implied in the Refugee Convention see generally Kälin and Künzli (n 38). As a right implied in the International Covenant on Civil and Political Rights see Paust, 'Political Oppression' (n 76) 181–183, 189–191; Paust, 'International Law, Dignity, Democracy' (n 76) 4–6, 11 (fn 48), 15 (fn 62); Falk and Weston (n 16) 156–157; Rosas, 'Article 21' (n 76) 432, 441–442, 449, 451; Rosas (n 38) 242–244, 249; Manfred Nowak, *UN Covenant on Civil and Political Rights – CCPR Commentary* (2nd edn, NP Engel 2005) 24 [34]; Bruno Simma, Hermann Mosler, Albrecht Randelzhofer, Christian Tomuschat, Rüdiger Wolfrum, Andreas Paulus, and Eleni Chaitidou (eds), *The Charter of the United Nations: A Commentary* (2nd edn, Oxford University Press 2002) vol 1, B [15] 52, C [40] 58. As a right implied in the United Nations Charter and interpretive General Assembly Resolution 2625 or 'Declaration on Principles of International Law Concerning Friendly Relations and Cooperation among States in Accordance with the Charter of the United Nations' see for example Cassese (n 16) 947; Paust, 'Political Oppression' (n 76); Paust (n 38) 550; Jordan J Paust, 'Aggression against Authority: The Crime of Oppression, Politicide and Other Crimes against Human Rights' (1986) 18 *Case Western Reserve Journal of International Law* 283, 286–290, 298; Falk and Weston (n 16) 156–157; Rosas (n 38) 247–249; Paust, 'International Law, Dignity, Democracy' (n 76) 2–4, 10 (fn 39). As a right implied in the Nuremberg Principles, see for example Falk, 'Nuremberg Defence' (n 16) 232–233, 235–237.

77 Judy Pearsall and Bill Trumble (eds), *Oxford English Reference Dictionary* (2nd edn, Oxford University Press 2002) 41.

78 Ibid.

79 For example, see Jessup (n 38) 185–186; 'The Inter-American Council of Jurists' (1951) 4(4) *International Law Quarterly* 521, 523. See Cassese's initially contradictory but later firmer position regarding the *non liquet* nature of the internal right to resist in Cassese (n 16) 949–950, 958; Antonio Cassese, *Self-Determination of Peoples: A Legal Reappraisal* (Cambridge University Press 1995) 124–126, 151–154, 197–198. See also Anyssa Bellal and Louise Doswald-Beck, 'Evaluating the Use of Force during the Arab Spring' (2012) 14 *Yearbook of International Humanitarian Law* 3, 11–14, 20–23, 32–33.

80 The usage of '*non liquet*' here in its original sense is complementary to, but also distinct from, its specific usage as a 'not proven' verdict in Roman law, or the usage of 'a' *non liquet* to

Where express provisions on the right to resist are absent in international law, opinions diverge as to whether this means that there really are gaps in the law, or whether the legal consequence of 'silence' is not a gap but rather effective permission due to non-prohibition.[81] Alternatively, it may be that these apparent gaps are already filled by the 'doctrine of a right to resist' as a 'general principle of law' as some suggest. Conversely, if the position that there are gaps is correct, should they be filled by use of a 'legal fiction', or can other provisions be extended by analogy and dynamic interpretation to recognize the right? These are further questions linking the question of the nature of the right to resist with that of its sources.

3.3.4 A '*Legal Fiction*'?

The right to resist as a legal concept would seem potentially vulnerable to certain arguments about 'legal fictions'.[82] Yet distortions of the legal fiction concept resulting from misconception of the fiction and its role are not uncommon.[83] Despite its usage by some as a pejorative, the legal fiction concept is distinct from the 'sham law' critique by those who maintain that legalization of the right to resist delivers a 'device of little significance'.[84] The latter argument holds that positive law provision for judicial determination of valid exercise would be moot under conditions where judicial review is not available, since by definition the judiciary has been rendered either powerless or compromised, and redundant in circumstances where judicial review is functional. In such instances a right to resist indicates nothing more than

describe 'a judicial finding that a particular claim can be neither upheld nor rejected, for lack of any existing applicable rule of law'. See Thirlway (n 68) 93, 111–115.

81 For example, Wright derives his assertion of a recognition in international law at least in part from the absence of a prohibition rule. See Quincy Wright, 'United States Intervention in the Lebanon' (1959) 53 *American Journal of International Law* 112, 121; Quincy Wright, 'Intervention and Cuba in 1961' (1961) 55 (27–29 April 1961) *Proceedings of the American Society of International Law at Its Annual Meeting* (1921–1969) 2, 3–4. See further discussion in Chapter 6, Section 6.2.

82 See the critiques in Bentham (n 1) 69; Jeremy Waldron, 'Jeremy Bentham's *Anarchical Fallacies*' in Waldron, *Nonsense upon Stilts* (n 1) 34–37.

83 Pierre JJ Olivier, *Legal Fictions in Practice and Legal Science* (Rotterdam University Press 1975) 81–82. Compare Olivier's Bartolist civil law concept in answer to Fuller's common law concept. See ibid 5–18, 33–36, 59–82; Lon L Fuller, *Legal Fictions* (Stanford University Press 1967).

84 Lewy (n 12) 595–596. The 'sham law' theory of constitutional provisions is discussed further in Chapter 5, Sections 5.5.3 and 5.5.4.

'a mere procedural right of appeal, regulated by law, or it will have no practical effects whatever'.[85]

However, a 'legal fiction' is instead another interpretive device applied to address gaps in the law 'in order to achieve an equitable result' which the law as it stands would otherwise not allow.[86] It involves 'an assumption of fact deliberately, lawfully and irrebuttably made, contrary to the facts proven or provable in a particular case, with the object of bringing a particular legal rule into operation or explaining a legal rule, the assumption being permitted by law or employed in legal science'.[87] To constitute a fiction, all of these core elements must be met.[88]

In general, the right to resist as a concept probably does not fit the definition of a theoretical fiction.[89] Yet some particular conceptualizations of the right to resist create the potential for use of legal fictions rather than analogies, in given cases. For example, claiming a right to resist in self-defence – in situations not involving a genuine case of self-defence as typically understood and defined, but classed as such in order to permit recognition of a right to resist claim as valid – could be making use of a fiction as to the nature of the exception, if not using an analogy instead.[90] Similarly, since many believe that international law recognizes the right to resist in assertion of external self-determination but is silent or ambiguous on its recognition in assertions of internal self-determination,[91] this could lead to a case that is really internal self-determination being treated 'as if' it were a matter of external self-determination in order to validate a claim. This could potentially constitute another use of a fiction if it does not rely on interpretative extension by analogy or independent recognition.

Alston maintains that law 'has always made good use of legal fictions ... as assumptions of a beneficial or at least harmless character which are intended

[85] Ibid. Lewy uses positivist arguments to dismiss positive legal provisions.
[86] Olivier (n 83) 85.
[87] Ibid 81 [emphasis added]. Consequently, a legal fiction is not 'analogous application of norms ... if no false factual assumption is required', or 'metaphors ... which do not require a false factual assumption', but nor does it constitute 'fraud and simulation which are not permitted by law'. Ibid 81–82.
[88] Ibid 61–79.
[89] 'Theoretical fictions' are 'used to analyse or explain the [rules of positive] law' and are therefore 'not a fiction in law, but a fiction concerning the law'. Ibid 156.
[90] In which case the fiction would be to treat a particular case that could not meet the relevant tests for self-defence 'as if it were' an instance of a right to resist in 'self-defence', whereas the analogy would treat it 'like' an instance of self-defence.
[91] See further discussion in Chapter 4, Section 4.6.1.3 and Chapter 6, Sections 6.3 and 6.4.

to promote a just outcome.'[92] Yet he urges that it matters 'whether the cause of international human rights law is furthered by the maintenance of the fiction' or 'whether [it] might actually be harmful in some ways',[93] by impeding necessary developments and changes in the law. Olivier likewise cautions against non-restrictive or unjust use of legal fictions, and in particular their unnecessary use when analogies are available.[94] These risks warrant consideration in the evaluation of right to resist theories or claims.

3.3.5 *An Enforceable 'Claim' Right*

Another major question about the nature of the right to resist upon which there is no agreement is whether it is the kind of right that can ground a legal claim, that can itself be enforced.[95] This prompts reflection on what constitutes 'enforcement' when exercising the right is, in and of itself, a form of direct enforcement of other primary rights. Yet at the same time, in certain conceptions of the right, it also activates immunities, defences, mitigations, or other protections for the rights-holders and related obligations on third parties. Bassiouni, for example, suggests that the right is enforceable by individuals in a court, by way of a claim to protection against extradition, whereby denial of extradition is the duty imposed on the third party.[96] Kälin and Künzli advance a similar theory of enforcement by way of refugee claim, involving a third-party duty of protection and denial of a request for exclusion.[97] Boyle, Lippman, Kittrie, and others have constructed theories relying on the right to resist for the purpose of defence against criminal charges, as another form of enforcement of the right itself.[98] Thus it seems that the right to resist may indeed be an enforceable 'claim' right, but not one that fully conforms to the orthodox type because it is also more than that.

92 Philip Alston, 'Introduction' in Philip Alston (ed), *Peoples' Rights* (Oxford University Press 2001) 6 (fn 11).
93 Ibid 6.
94 Olivier (n 83) 85, 156–167.
95 Compare for example Marcic (n 10); Honoré (n 38) 36, 43, 49–51; Baxi (n 38) 5ff.
96 See Bassiouni (n 73) 254–257. This theory of indirect or corroborative recognition in customary law is discussed further in Chapter 6, Section 6.6.3.
97 See generally Kälin and Künzli (n 38). This theory of indirect or corroborative recognition in treaty law is further discussed in Chapter 7, Sections 7.2.2 and 7.2.3.
98 See Francis A Boyle, *Defending Civil Resistance under International Law* (Transnational 1988); Boyle (n 38); Lippman (n 38); Matthew Lippman, 'Nuremberg and American Justice' (1991) 5 *Notre Dame Journal of Ethics, Law and Public Policy* 951; Kittrie (n 16) 243–350, in particular his 'Bill of Rights for Just Governance and Just Resistance' 342–344 and 'Typology of Political Offenses' 350 D1–F5. These theories are further discussed below and in Chapter 6, Section 6.5.

Therefore, while Baxi relies upon it for the laudable purpose of encouraging greater precision in relation to conceptualizing the right to resist,[99] the Hohfeldian definitional typology of legal rights in his theory of 'jural opposites' and 'jural correlatives'[100] may be of only limited relevance. This is not least because, as discussed below, in some conceptualizations the 'right' to resist is either derived from a prior 'duty' to resist, or else it is a hybrid 'right-duty' wherein the consequent duties correlated to the right are those imposed not only on the opposite party and on third parties respectively, but also include distinct duties imposed on the rights-holders themselves that have the effect of reinforcing the right by rendering its exercise non-optional.

On the other hand, it would seem that enforcement challenges would not in and of themselves disqualify the right to resist from being a 'right'. In some jurisdictions, the right to resist may be a 'substantial [or substantive] right' that 'potentially affects the outcome of a lawsuit and is capable of legal enforcement and protection, as distinguished from a mere technical or procedural right'.[101] Thus it would seem that in certain contexts the right to resist can be considered a 'perfect right' that is 'recognized by the law and is fully enforceable'.[102] Conversely, in other contexts it will be an 'imperfect right' that is 'recognized by the law but is not [practically] enforceable'.[103] However, the right to resist is not inherently one or the other. Moreover, the absence of judicial enforcement of the right is not necessarily determinative. As Lauterpacht points out, 'the existence of a right and the power to assert it by judicial process are not identical'.[104]

Additionally, the right to resist has positive and negative aspects, insofar as a 'positive right' is a 'right entitling a person to have another do some act for the benefit of the person entitled',[105] whereas a 'negative right' is a 'right entitling a person to have another refrain from doing an act that might harm the person entitled'.[106] These latter two aspects describe the theories of valid claims to third-party assistance or non-obstruction available to those with a right to resist.[107] All of the above would seem to reinforce the idea that the right to

99 Baxi (n 38) 6–10.

100 See Wesley Newcomb Hohfeld, *Fundamental Legal Conceptions as Applied in Judicial Reasoning and Other Legal Essays* (Yale University Press 1919) 35 ff.

101 Bryan A Garner (ed), *Black's Law Dictionary* (7th deluxe edn, West Group 1999) 1324.

102 Ibid 1323.

103 Ibid.

104 Lauterpacht (n 7) 54.

105 Garner (n 101) 1323.

106 Ibid.

107 See for example the proposal for a 'non-rigid' approach to the international regulation of intervention in Richard Falk, 'Janus Tormented: The International Law of Internal War' in

resist has potential as an enforceable 'claim right', but that is not an exhaustive characterization.

3.3.6 A 'Right' or 'Duty', or Hybrid 'Right-Duty'?

While the historical theoretical literature mostly conceived of the right to resist as derived from a duty to resist, contemporary theories conceptualize the right to resist variously as a standalone 'right', a standalone 'duty', or a hybrid 'right-duty'. Regardless of which of these most accurately describes its nature, one can find examples of formulations in contemporary positive law that fall into each of these categories, as will be shown in Part II. However, it is worth emphasizing that regimes can easily abuse formulations of an exclusive 'duty' to resist resulting in a legal obligation. For example, as Agamben warns, a duty to resist unconstitutional action may effectively render the constitution 'absolutely untouchable'.[108] Indeed, contemporary proponents of exclusive and compulsory 'duty' formulations are rarer, and the position is probably not consistent with the right to resist as a 'human right'.

The somewhat more common hybrid approach suggests that there is both a right to resist and a duty to resist.[109] While this right-duty is held by all citizens, the duty especially falls on the most powerful and influential citizens and officials as they are least vulnerable.[110] For Marcic, the general duty is one of critical examination of all laws for conformity with the highest norm, and

James N Rosenau (ed), *International Aspects of Civil Strife* (Princeton University Press 1964) 210–240, 246–248. See also Paust, 'Aggression against Authority' (n 76) 297–298, 300; Honoré (n 38) 36, 41, 43; Paust, 'International Law, Dignity, Democracy' (n 76) 2, 12–13, 15–16, 19–20. Compare the more equivocal Cassese, *Self-Determination* (n 79) 152–153, 155–158. Third-party obligation theories are discussed further in Chapter 4, Section 4.5 and in Part II, Chapters 6 and 7.

108 Agamben (n 25) 11, 17.

109 On the 'right' see Pribilla (n 10) 5ff; on the 'duty' see ibid 23–28. On the right-duty, or right which 'transforms' into a duty, see Marcic (n 10) 105–106, 108–109, 110–111, 113. On the Middle Ages origins of the 'right-duty' iteration of the concept, see Bielefeldt (n 2) 1098. For a modern iteration of a right-duty see Falk, 'Nuremberg Defense' (n 16) 208–210, 212, 237–238; Richard Falk, 'Telford Taylor and the Legacy of Nuremberg' (1998) 37 *Columbia Journal of Transnational Law* 693, 689–699; Candice Delmas, 'Disobedience, Civil and Otherwise' (2017) 11(1) *Criminal Law and Philosophy* 195; Tom Dannenbaum, 'The Criminalization of Aggression and Soldiers' Rights' (2018) 29(3) *European Journal of International Law* 859; and, more critically, Tom Dannenbaum, *The Crime of Aggression, Humanity, and the Soldier* (Cambridge University Press 2018) 20–24, 272–276, 292–299, 322–328; and, more comprehensively, Candice Delmas, A *Duty to Resist: When Civil Disobedience Should Be Uncivil* (Oxford University Press 2018).

110 Pribilla (n 10) 7, 23; Marcic (n 10) 110–111. Compare the theory of 'legitimated interposition' as a 'power and right' of officials. Kadish and Kadish (n 25) 47–67.

refusal of unlawful orders that violate human rights and human dignity, as per the doctrine of conditional obedience and principle of exceptionally conferred competence-competence on individual conscience.[111] Pribilla clarifies that, as regards the duty aspect, 'refusal to undertake active resistance [with force] cannot be made a ground for penal action'.[112] Schwarz takes the opposite view on penalties, attaching legal liability for damages in cases of failure of obligation. Significantly, however, he limits this right-duty of resistance to unlawful 'orders, regulations, decrees, edicts or laws'.[113]

Notwithstanding the above variants, contemporary theories most frequently conceptualize the right to resist as a standalone 'right'. The concern regarding duties is now generally with those arising from or correlated to the right, including both direct and third-party duties, that can also be appealed to as a matter of law. The who and what of these associated duties are discussed in more detail in Chapter 4, as 'elements' of the right.

3.3.7 *A Primary Political Right or Secondary Procedural Right, or Both?*

In contemporary terms, the right to resist is usually considered a 'remedial right' meaning a 'secondary right to have a remedy that arises when a primary right is broken'.[114] It is therefore considered also to be a 'conditional right' – that is, a 'right that depends on an uncertain event' which 'may or may not exist' depending on whether those conditions have been met.[115] Consequently, the right to resist is often classified as a 'secondary right'.[116] However, this may not be entirely straightforward.

A 'primary right' or substantive right is a 'right prescribed by the substantive law' and a 'secondary right' or procedural right is a 'right prescribed by procedural law to enforce a substantive [primary] right'.[117] Yet various theorists suggest that the right to resist itself can be enforced, either directly in a court or by third parties by way of extrajudicial assistance. The possibility is not inherently excluded, since the enforcement of a secondary right is 'variously termed secondary enforcement, remedial enforcement, or sanctional

[111] Marcic (n 10) 106, 108–109, 111.
[112] Pribilla (n 10) 23. Marcic sets the limit on the duty at not requiring the sacrifice of one's own life. Marcic (n 10) 110.
[113] Schwarz (n 10) 129–131.
[114] Garner (n 101) 1324.
[115] Ibid 1323.
[116] Honoré (n 38) 38.
[117] Garner (n 101) 1323–1324.

enforcement'.[118] This raises the question of whether the right to resist is in fact wholly procedural or also partially substantive. Furthermore, it is logical to characterize the right to resist as a 'political right', being a 'right to participate in the establishment or administration of government',[119] albeit one involving unconventional forms. Political rights are generally considered substantive and therefore primary. Thus, while perhaps predominantly secondary-procedural, the right to resist also exhibits certain characteristics of a primary-substantive right.

3.3.8 A *Superordinate Compound Right or a Subordinate Part of Another Compound Right*

As a final aspect of the nature of the right to resist, there remain differences on whether the right to resist is a 'principal right', being a 'right to which has been added a supplementary right in the same owner',[120] or a 'peripheral right', being a 'right that surrounds or springs from another right'.[121] As set out in Chapter 2, a review of the historical theories provides evidence that the right to resist has evolved as a superordinate compound right – that is, a principal or general right that can contain more specific or peripheral cognate rights within it, notwithstanding that these subordinate cognate rights may also be considered separately. However, some scholars place the right to resist itself as a subordinate cognate of other theorized superordinate compound rights, such as the 'right to peace' discussed in Chapters 4 and 7. Still others consider it a concomitant or corollary right – for example, of Marcic's 'principle of human dignity',[122] or even of Arendt's 'right to have rights'.[123] Such conceptualizations are not necessarily mutually exclusive.

3.4 FUNCTION OF THE RIGHT

In addition to the debates about its nature, there is also ongoing diversity of opinion on the question of the legal function of a right to resist.

[118] Ibid 1324.
[119] Ibid 1323.
[120] Ibid.
[121] Ibid.
[122] Marcic (n 10) 92–95, 101–105, 114. See also Paust, 'Political Oppression' (n 76) 181; Honoré (n 38) 37, 41, 43, 54; Paust, 'International Law, Dignity, Democracy' (n 76) 2–3.
[123] For example, Kesby's fifth explanatory category related to Arendt's concept of the 'right to have rights' involves 'the rightless taking up, claiming and enacting denied rights'. Though she does not identify it as such, it is the right to resist in all but name. See Alison Kesby, *The Right to Have Rights: Citizenship, Humanity and International Law* (Oxford University Press 2012).

In contemporary times it has been conceptualized as functioning as a self-help remedy for enforcement or prevention by deterrence, and as an exceptional immunity, or justification defence, or temporary permission by license. Its function has also been characterized variously as *actio popularis*, *jus ad bellum*, and *lex specialis*.

3.4.1 *Self-Help Remedy for Enforcement or Prevention by Deterrence*

In a carry-over from its earliest formulations and those of its conceptual antecedent, the function of the right to resist is still generally conceived as a form of 'self-help remedy' when judicial remedy is not available.[124] A 'remedy' is the 'means of enforcing a right or preventing or redressing a wrong'.[125] The term captures both enforcement after the fact of violation, and preventative enforcement for deterrence. 'Self-help' is defined as an 'attempt to redress a perceived wrong by one's own action rather than through the normal legal process'.[126] A 'self-help remedy' is therefore a type of 'extrajudicial remedy',[127] meaning a 'remedy not obtained from a court',[128] and is also known as 'extrajudicial enforcement'.[129] Judicial and extrajudicial remedies are not inherently and in all cases mutually exclusive, but rather can be complementary. This has been the case since the times of the ancient Athenian democracy[130] and the Roman Republic.[131] In this sense, the right to resist may be considered as a self-help counterpart to judicial review and/or international criminal proceedings, as a method of ending violations and enforcing international or constitutional law.

The right to resist is therefore seen by some theorists as falling into the smaller category of 'rights as remedies' and therefore linked to the right to an 'effective remedy', which is broader than its specific judicial sense.[132] Shelton clarifies that the term 'remedy' in fact contains 'two separate concepts, the first

[124] See for example Paust, 'Aggression against Authority' (n 76) 283–286, 297; Eide (n 38) 39; Christian Tomuschat, 'The Right of Resistance and Human Rights' in *Violations of Human Rights: Possible Rights of Recourse and Forms of Resistance* (UNESCO 1984) 20; Lippman (n 38) 353; Rachel E Schwartz, 'Chaos, Oppression, and Rebellion: The Use of Self-Help to Secure Individual Rights under International Law' (1994) 12 *Boston University Law Journal* 255; Falk, 'Azmi Bishara, the Right of Resistance' (n 76) 23–24, 31.
[125] Garner (n 4) 598.
[126] Ibid 632.
[127] Garner (n 101) 1297.
[128] Garner (n 4) 599.
[129] Garner (n 101) 1364.
[130] See further discussion in Chapter 5, Section 5.2.
[131] See further discussion in Chapter 5, Section 5.1.
[132] See for example Honoré (n 38) 38–39.

being procedural and the second substantive', and furthermore that remedies can serve four distinct purposes: compensatory justice, retributive justice, deterrence, and restorative justice.[133] Exercising the right to resist as a self-help remedy therefore potentially involves either prevention by deterrence or two complementary phases: the first consisting of removal of the violation/s and the second being restoration of the primary right/s. Conceptualized as such, the right to resist must therefore operate as a means to an end rather than an end in itself. As a human right, that end must be an internally consistent 'object and purpose'. Lawful exercise of the right also requires a necessity test to demonstrate that other effective remedies, including in particular judicial remedies, are not available.[134] Both of these latter aspects are further discussed in Chapter 4 as 'elements' of the right.

Conceptualizing the right to resist as a preventive deterrent, as some theorists do,[135] may seem intuitively risky. Yet that is precisely how it appears in many of its constitutional forms discussed in Chapter 5.

3.4.2 *Exceptional Immunity or Justification Defence, or Temporary Permission by License?*

The right to resist is traditionally also considered to function as an exception providing grounds for immunity from prosecution, in the form of an exemption from the duty of obedience and from liability for certain otherwise unlawful acts.[136] Such arguments were pioneered by Bartolus in the Middle Ages,[137] but latterly also by Mégret in the context of an evolving *jus post-bellum*.[138] Other contemporary theorists argue that a valid claim of right to resist functions to ground a justification defence or mitigation based on

[133] Dinah Shelton, *Remedies in International Human Rights Law* (2nd edn, Oxford University Press 2005) 7–16.

[134] See for example Hermann Weinkauff, *Über das Widerstandsrecht* ['On the Right of Resistance'] (Karlsruhe 1956) 18, as synoptically translated in Lewy (n 12) 583 (fn 11).

[135] See Pribilla (n 10) 5, 8–9, 30, 32, 34–35; Kaufmann (n 1) 575–576; Honoré (n 38) 39.

[136] See Baxi (n 38).

[137] See Saxoferrato, *On the Tyrant* (n 16) 9 (fn 74), 10–11 (fn 83–85, 87–92).

[138] On the need for a 'coherent' normative standard to guide the currently ambiguous 'law of amnesties', particularly as regards 'taking up arms' itself, see Frédéric Mégret, 'Should Rebels Be Amnestied?' in Carsten Stahn, Jennifer S Easterday, and Jens Iverson (eds), *Jus Post Bellum: Mapping the Normative Foundations* (Oxford University Press 2014). He proposes what he calls variously a 'non-state *jus ad bellum*' or a '*jus ad rebelium*', applying by analogy the general principles and standards under general international law on inter-state use of force, which would be combined 'dynamically' with *jus in bello* performance to provide a basis for *jus post-bellum* evaluation.

necessity or even duty,[139] or to validate a refugee claim or claim against extradition.[140]

However, because the right to resist is circumstantially limited, rather than constantly available like many other human rights, some theorists have likened its function instead to a temporary permission in the form of a 'license' rather than a real 'right'.[141] A 'license' is generally understood as a 'revocable permission to commit some act that would otherwise be unlawful'.[142] While appealing in certain ways, such theories tend not to specify who would grant or revoke this 'license', and by what process. The 'license' concept may also pose problems if it permits more discretion on the part of the grantor than may be warranted or desirable once the appropriate criteria are fulfilled. Without further development, this idea of a 'license to resist' lacks persuasiveness as an alternative, since its advantages over the right to resist as a regulated lawful exception remain unclear.

3.4.3 Actio Popularis?

Exercising the right to resist may also function as a form of enforcement by *actio popularis*, or as a way of activating this process.[143] As Abi-Saab describes, the *actio popularis* is an institution dating back to ancient Rome, where every citizen could denounce certain violations of public order and property before a judge. The *actio popularis* thus made citizens the guardians of the legality, thereby palliating the weakness of the public means available.[144] Even where not expressed as such, this idea of collective citizen action in the interest of everyone in respecting the rules protecting common values and interests[145] is

139 See Falk, 'Nuremberg Defense' (n 16) 208–213, 226, 229, 232–233, 235–238; Falk, 'Telford Taylor and the Legacy of Nuremberg' (n 109) 698–699; Boyle, *Defending Civil Resistance* (n 98); Boyle, *Protesting Power* (n 38); Lippman (n 38) 359–372; Lippman (n 98); Kittrie (n 16) 243–296, 329–350. The right to resist offers the potential of a 'justification' defence as 'warranted action', in contrast to an 'excuse' defence being 'unwarranted action for which the actor is not to blame'. See Kent Greenawalt, 'The Perplexing Borders of Justification and Excuse' (1984) 84(8) *Columbia Law Review* 1897, 1897, 1900, 1903, 1927.

140 Bassiouni (n 73); Kälin and Künzli (n 38); Kittrie (n 16) 193–242, 329–350.

141 See Cassese, *Self-Determination* (n 79) 151, 153–154, 197–198. See also the theory of 'legitimated disobedience', conceptualized as neither 'right' nor 'duty' nor 'right-duty' of the individual but rather as some form of fourth alternative – both a 'power and right', and also a 'permission' or 'license'. Kadish and Kadish (n 25) 4–8, 71–101.

142 Garner (n 4) 418.

143 Marcic (n 10) 111–112.

144 Georges Abi-Saab, 'Preface' in François Voeffray, *L'actio popularis ou la défense de l'intérêt collectif devant les jurisdictions internationales* (Graduate Institute Publications 2004) xx.

145 Ibid xx–xxii.

clearly present in certain contemporary theories of the right to resist. In particular, application of source theories relying on the Nuremberg Principles can involve the actors deliberately bringing themselves before a judge in order to make denunciations and seek corroborative rulings.[146] This effectively conceptualizes the function of the right to resist as *actio popularis*.

3.4.4 Jus ad Bellum?

Numerous contemporary theories take their cue from Grotius and Vattel,[147] conceptualizing the right to resist to function either primarily or exclusively as '*jus ad bellum*': a right to either 'use force' or 'make war' against one's own state.[148] Mégret, for example, sometimes uses the terms '*jus ad bellum* of non-State actors', '*jus insurrectionis*' or '*jus ad rebelium*' when talking about the 'right to resist' and 'right to rebel'.[149] Indeed, a growing body of complementary legal, political, and ethics theory seeks to address the absence of a parallel *jus ad bellum* regulatory framework applicable to non-state actors and in non-international armed conflicts, properly locating this in international human rights law, including by adapting traditional 'just war' principles for this purpose.[150]

[146] See Lippman (n 98) 954. On theories of the Nuremberg Principles as constituting a source of customary principles of international law including an implied right to resist, see the discussion in Chapter 6, Section 6.5.

[147] See Grotius (n 53); Vattel (n 53).

[148] Honoré cites the 'etymological root of rebellion' as 'bellum' or 'the right to make war on one's society'. Honoré (n 38) 53, though he stops short of using this terminology in his earlier work. See also Falk (n 107) 217 (fn 49), 240–242; Falk (n 76) 28. See also, for example, Cassese (n 16) 947; Paust, 'Human Right to Armed Revolution' (n 38) 548–549; Georges Abi-Saab, 'Wars of National Liberation and the Laws of War' [1972] *Annales d'Étdues Internationales* 93, 98–102; Bert VA Röling, 'The Legal Status of Rebels and Rebellion' (1976) 13(2) *Journal of Peace Research* 149, 152–154, 158–161; Robert E Gorelick, 'Wars of National Liberation: Jus Ad Bellum' (1979) 11(1) *Case Western Reserve Journal of International Law* 71; Mégret (n 76) 179, 173, 175; Noelle Higgins, *Regulating the Use of Force in Wars of National Liberation: The Need for a New Regime* (Martinus Nijhoff 2010) 89–90, 229, 231, 237, 230; Mégret (n 138) 520, 537–538, 540; Paust, 'International Law, Dignity, Democracy' (n 76) 12–13. See also Christopher J Finlay, *Terrorism and the Right to Resist* (Cambridge University Press 2015) 3, 6–7, 9 11–12, 19–154; Christopher J Finlay, 'The Perspective of the Rebel: A Gap in the Global Normative Architecture' (2017) 31(2) *Ethics and International Affairs* 213; Christopher J Finlay, 'The Deadly Serious Causes of Legitimate Rebellion: between the Wrongs of Terrorism and the Crimes of War' (2018) 12(2) *Criminal Law and Philosophy* 271. Compare Cassese, *Self-Determination* (n 79) 153–154.

[149] Mégret (n 76) 179, 173, 175; Mégret (n 138) 520, 537–538, 540.

[150] See Mégret (n 76) 179, 173, 175; Mégret (n 138) 520, 537–538, 540; Finlay, *Terrorism and the Right to Resist* (n 148); Eliav Lieblich, 'Internal Jus Ad Bellum' (2016) 67 *Hastings Law Journal* 687; Finlay, 'Perspective of the Rebel' (n 148); Finlay, 'Deadly Serious Causes of

However, in both its superordinate and discrete senses, the 'right to resist' includes measures well short of war.[151] Conceptualization of the right to resist as an exclusively *jus ad bellum* right is unsatisfactory because it comes too late, leaving a crucial gap. If there is a right to make war on your state, it must be preceded by a right to take lesser action. To jump directly from a right of exclusively peaceful and non-disruptive protest – the current standard in international human rights law, which may not include a right to civil disobedience[152] – to a right to make war, with no intermediate right in between, hardly makes sense. Presumably, therefore, there can be no *jus ad bellum* where a prior right to resist cannot be positively established. That is, one can have a right to resist but not yet a right to 'make war' against one's own state – because the appropriate necessity and proportionality thresholds have not been met – but the reverse cannot be true.[153]

Thus, the right to resist may become a *jus ad bellum* right only when it meets additional criteria. Alternatively, the right to resist is a necessary but not sufficient basis for a *jus ad bellum*, which is a form of auxiliary extension of the basic right, imposing higher thresholds. Rather than the right to resist being a species of *jus ad bellum* right, the reverse is true: a *jus ad bellum* against your own state is in fact a cognate of the right to resist, taking the form of either the 'right of rebellion' or 'right of revolution' as appropriate to the circumstance. This holds whether one conceptualizes the term *jus ad bellum* narrowly to mean the right to resort to levels of force that reach the thresholds of armed conflict, or whether one takes its broadest usage of generally employing forceful means. Either way, the right to resist is more inclusive than is *jus ad bellum*, as it takes in not only forceful means that under the most extreme circumstances may amount to armed conflict but also non-forceful means

Legitimate Rebellion' (n 148); Tom Dannenbaum, 'War Crimes and Just War Theory' in Kimberly Kessler Ferzan and Larry Alexander (eds), *The Palgrave Handbook of Applied Ethics and Criminal Law* (Palgrave Macmillan 2019). Compare Anthony Dworkin, 'Individual, Not Collective: Justifying the Resort to Force against Members of Non-State Armed Groups' (2017) 93 *International Law Studies* 477. See also for example, Cécile Fabre, 'Cosmopolitanism, Just War Theory and Legitimate Authority' (2008) 84(5) *International Affairs* 963; Cécile Fabre, 'Cosmopolitanism and Wars of Self-Defence' in Cécile Fabre and Seth Lazar (eds), *The Morality of Defensive War* (Oxford University Press 2014) 95, 100–101, 105–106; Seth Lazar, 'Authorization and the Morality of War' (2016) 94 *Australasian Journal of Philosophy* 211. See further discussion in Chapter 4, Sections 4.3 and 4.7 and Chapter 6, Sections 6.6.1, 6.6.2, 6.6.4.

[151] See in particular the discussions in Chapter 2, Sections 2.3 and 2.4 and Chapter 4, Section 4.7.

[152] See discussion in Chapter 7, Section 7.2.1.

[153] The application of the necessity condition and the proportionality limitation are further discussed in Chapter 4, Sections 4.3 and 4.7 and Chapter 6, Sections 6.3.1.4, 6.3.1.5, and 6.4.6.

amounting to civil disobedience. For these reasons, attempts to either substitute the narrower public international law concept of *jus ad bellum* for the right to resist, or squeeze the right to resist into the *jus ad bellum* concept, are ultimately inadequate and can be misleading.

3.4.5 *Lawful Exception and* Lex Specialis *Rule*

Taking into account all of the preceding, this study suggests that the human right to resist functions principally as a form of '*lex specialis*' exception to the '*lex generalis*' limitations applying to 'ordinary political rights' protected and regulated by international human rights law and also protected in constitutional law, acting mostly to lift certain ordinarily applicable restrictions on means of protest. The well-established doctrine '*lex specialis derogat legi generali*' or 'special laws repeal general laws', applies in both domestic and international law, and relates to the application and interpretation of laws in a situation whereby two different rules may govern the same factual situation. That is, the special rule can prevail even though it may contradict the general rule that would otherwise apply. This recognizes that sometimes 'special rules are better able to take account of particular circumstances'.[154]

Koskenniemi describes the *lex specialis* concept as constituting the 'two ways in which the law takes account of the relationship of a particular rule to a general rule'.[155] In one of these, 'a particular rule may be considered an application of the general rule in a given circumstance', and in the other, 'a particular rule may be conceived as an exception to the general rule. In this case, the particular derogates from the general rule'.[156] He emphasizes that 'the point of the *lex specialis* rule is to indicate which rule should be applied. In both cases, the special, as it were, steps in to replace the general'.[157]

The assertion that the right to resist is a *lex specialis* comprises three assumptions. First, international human rights law, providing standards that apply at all times and under all conditions to some extent,[158] is the source of the *lex generalis*, since it also provides standards that cannot be overridden but rather must be met by domestic constitutions. Second, within international human rights law, political rights are the *lex generalis* in question. That is, the ordinary rights of political participation and the freedoms of expression,

[154] See Koskenniemi (n 66) 4.
[155] Ibid.
[156] Ibid.
[157] Ibid.
[158] This is recognized by the International Court of Justice in *Legality of the Threat or Use of Nuclear Weapons* (Advisory Opinion) [1996] ICJ Rep 226 [25].

association, and assembly apply under general conditions. As such, they may be subject to broad limitations, in addition to the absolute peacefulness requirement.[159] These rights may also be lawfully suspended in times of emergency, provided there is state compliance with the law of derogation where applicable. Third, the right to resist is the *lex specialis*, or the law of application, only under certain conditions. It governs matters that overlap with ordinary political rights. For example, it may include assembly that is peaceful or forceful but unlawful under normal conditions when the general law of freedom of expression, assembly, and association applies. The right to resist applies only under those conditions where the resort to otherwise unlawful means can be established as a necessity. In other words, primary violations are either occurring or are at substantial risk of occurring, and there is no reasonable prospect of judicial remedy and other forms of effective remedy are demonstrably unavailable. In such situations the law of the right to resist as a limited and conditional permission overrides otherwise lawful limitations on the exercise of freedom of expression, assembly, and association. In certain cases it also overrides the peacefulness requirement in particular, where both necessity and proportionality can be demonstrated. Additionally, the law of the right to resist applies wherever there is derogation of the ordinary rights but non-compliance with the lawful derogation regime. It may also apply to some extent where there is either apparent compliance or partial compliance. That is, the right to resist qualifies the state right of derogation.[160]

The right to resist may apply not only under 'peacetime' conditions, but also under conditions of 'armed conflict' where international humanitarian law applies in addition to international human rights law and international criminal law. Importantly, the right to resist can apply in those gap conditions that fall short of the strict threshold for 'armed conflict'. Hence it is a *lex specialis* that cuts across these, potentially – although not exclusively – acting as a form of *jus ad bellum* for non-state actors regardless of whether armed conflict thresholds are reached.[161] On this basis, it acts as a form of exception to the otherwise applicable state monopoly on the lawful use of force, and as an additional exception to the otherwise applicable restriction of lawful use of

[159] See further discussion in Chapter 7, Section 7.2.1.

[160] On the right to resist as an effective limitation on state competence see Marcic (n 10) 109–110. See also Paust, 'Political Oppression' (n 76) 181–191; Paust, 'International Law, Dignity, Democracy' (n 76) 6, 11 (fn 48). See further discussion in Chapter 7, Sections 7.2.1, 7.3.2.

[161] Compare Falk, 'Adequacy of Contemporary Theories' (n 16) 255–256; Frédéric Mégret, 'Beyond "Freedom Fighters" and "Terrorists": When, If Ever, Is Non-State Violence Legitimate in International Law?' (SSRN 2009); Mégret (n 76).

force by non-state actors exclusively to situations in which the strict criteria for self-defence can be met.[162] It does not, however, act as an exception to international criminal law or the similar *jus in bello* restrictions on means.[163] In this sense, the right to resist functions in a manner similar to the right of self-defence exception for states: it does not extend to permission to engage in activities considered to constitute crimes under international law.

Conceptualizing the right to resist as a lawful exception, derived from a *lex specialis* rule related to the limitations otherwise imposed on ordinary political rights under the *lex generalis* of international human rights law, provides a contemporary expression that brings the legal concept of the right to resist up to date in the twenty-first century. This is not only generally consistent with its origins in the ancient doctrine of tyrannicide as lawful exception to the general prohibition on killing another human, but also its later evolution as a lawful exception when used against an unlawful regime or manifestly unjust laws. However, since the right to resist is much broader than tyrannicide, the exception refers to employing 'otherwise unlawful' means,[164] without specifying what these specific means are under every circumstance. This is consistent with the traditional concept and the historical theories.[165] With this in mind, it is of course advisable to conceptualize the right to resist exception carefully and with due regard to the applicable conditions and limitations, as well as possible conflicts of norms and other human rights which may compete in a given situation.

The right conceived in this way has a necessary relationship with criminal law. It implies the need for immunity provisions, or at least available defences or mitigations based on the exception.[166] This could apply to a range of criminal charges commonly available in domestic jurisdictions, such as

[162] Compare the various positions of, for example, Kopel et al, 'Is Resisting Genocide a Human Right?' (n 38); Kopel et al, 'Human Right to Self-Defense' (n 38); Mégret, 'Beyond "Freedom Fighters"' (n 161); Mégret (n 76); Jens David Ohlin, 'The Right to Exist and the Right to Resist' (SSRN 2014); Bellal and Doswald-Beck (n 79) 20–23; Hessbruegge, *Human Rights and Personal Self-Defense* (n 74) 293–344.

[163] This point is emphasized by Cassese (n 16) 947–950, 958; Falk, 'Azmi Bishara, the Right of Resistance' (n 76).

[164] Honoré (n 38) 36.

[165] See Kaufmann's definition of the elements of the 'traditional right' referenced in Chapter 2, Section 2.4.1. Kaufmann (n 1) 574–575.

[166] See Falk, 'Nuremberg Defense' (n 16); Richard Falk, 'Introduction' in Francis A Boyle, *Defending Civil Resistance under International Law* (Transnational Publishers 1988) xvii–xxii; Falk, 'Telford Taylor and the Legacy of Nuremberg' (n 109) 698–699; Lippman (n 38) 359, 361–362, 369; Lippman (n 98); Kittrie (n 16) 243–350, 342–344. It could also provide a basis for lawful discretionary non-prosecution, or nullification where available. See Kadish and Kadish (n 25) 96–99. Emphasizing the importance of mounting such defenses together with jurisdictionally specific statutory defences, see Boyle, *Protesting Power* (n 38) 7, 9–10, 22.

'sedition', 'treason', 'criminal damage', 'riot', 'civil commotion', 'mob action against the state', 'insurrection' – and conspiracy or incitement to any of these. Whether it could potentially also defend against a charge of 'terrorism' is a separate question. Most likely, the right to resist could only constitute a defence where the specific counterterrorism law is drawn or interpreted over-inclusively – to include resort to forceful or non-forceful means that would not otherwise be prohibited under international criminal law, or violate *jus cogens* norms or the core principles of international humanitarian law: necessity, proportionality, and distinction.[167] As a human right, the exception does not function as a 'right to resort to terrorism',[168] as alleged by some opponents – and even some proponents.

3.5 CONCLUSION: A POTENTIALLY ENFORCEABLE HUMAN RIGHT AND *LEX SPECIALIS* RULE OF EXCEPTION

As the unresolved debates outlined above show, there is no contemporary consensus on the nature and function of the 'right' to resist, even among its advocates. Nevertheless, the evidence demonstrates that the hypotheses regarding its nature that are consistent with the study of its positive law in Part II are viable, at least to the extent employed for the present pragmatic purposes. That is, the right to resist can indeed be coherently conceptualized as a legal right compatible with the rule of law. As such, it is a predominantly secondary right to self-help remedy for the purpose of enforcement of primary fundamental rights or deterrence of their violation. It can provide a legal basis for claims to immunity from prosecution, justification defences or mitigations, as well as for claims to protection from extradition or exclusion from refugee status. Other variations of type and function of the legal right may be possible depending on how a given theory, recognition, or provision is formulated. For example, theoretically at least it can in certain forms function as a basis for *actio popularis* or *jus ad bellum*. In general, it is conceptually possible to conclude, as this study does, that the right to resist is indeed a potentially enforceable inalienable human right, theoretically capable of interpretation as such even where unenumerated, and this is the basis for its function as a *lex specialis* rule of exception. Though it is itself a superordinate compound right

[167] See for example Cassese (n 16) 947–950, 958; Ben Saul, *Defining Terrorism in International Law* (Oxford University Press 2006) 70–71, 75, 116–120, 128. While the *jus in bello* is not a source of the right to resist, it can regulate its exercise under certain circumstances. See further discussion in Chapter 6, Section 6.6.2.

[168] See Cassese (n 16) 947–950, 958. Compare Saul (n 167); Mégret, 'Beyond "Freedom Fighters"' (n 161); Mégret (n 76); Finlay, *Terrorism and the Right to Resist* (n 148) 3–8.

as established in Chapter 2, it may equally be coherently conceptualized as a subordinate right, for example as cognate to the right to dignity or even Arendt's 'right to have rights'.

What remains to complete the picture of the human right to resist as a contemporary legal concept is to identify the content of the right in all its elements, thereby establishing a framework for the purpose of individual and comparative analysis. That is the subject matter of the following chapter.

4

Identifying the Elements and Legal Content of the Right

4.1 INTRODUCTION

Even among those who accept the possibility of the 'right' to resist as a legal right compatible with the rule of law, and who conceptualize it as a human right with a *lex specialis* exception function, there remain areas of disagreement on its content. However, systematic comparison of positions taken in contemporary theories both general and applied demonstrates better prospects for answering the 'what, when, who, why, and how' questions about what the contemporary human right 'to resist' might mean.

Building on the findings in Chapters 2 and 3, this chapter uses those questions to identify the elements that help establish the legal content of the right both generally and in any given case. Section 4.2 addresses the question of the 'right to resist what?' by reviewing the three possible primary triggers for activation of the right. Section 4.3 addresses the question of the 'right to resist when?' by considering secondary triggers or conditions for activation, including those related to 'necessity'. Section 4.4 addresses the question of 'who may resist?' by considering the personal scope dimension as to rights-holders. Section 4.5 addresses the related question of '*who* has the corresponding duty?' by considering possible duty-bearers and the consequent scope of their obligation. Section 4.6 addresses the question of the 'right to resist why?' by identifying a four-fold classification as to object and purpose: for 'higher' law and fundamental rights enforcement; for self-defence; for self-determination; or for promotion of 'positive peace' or 'human security'. Section 4.7 addresses the question of the 'right to resist how?' by considering the right's material scope of application, or permissible means, identifying three approaches and the applicability of proportionality limitations, as well as other limitations in international human rights law and international criminal law. It also briefly addresses the question of 'prudence' as a discretionary limitation element. The chapter concludes at Section 4.8 by proposing this approach as establishing a general analytical framework for identifying the legal elements and therefore content of the human right to resist, either as theorized or as found in positive law provisions or other recognitions such as those reviewed in Part II.

4.2 PRIMARY TRIGGERS OR CONDITIONS FOR ACTIVATION: THE 'RIGHT TO RESIST WHAT?'

One of the most important conceptual elements of the human right to resist is the 'triggers' that describe the threshold conditions allowing the exception or *lex specialis* to activate. This is because the right to resist remains 'in abeyance' until such conditions have been met.[1] Reference to these primary trigger conditions answers the question of 'the right to resist what?' As explained below, in current conceptualizations of the right these conditions are, variously: 'tyranny', 'oppression', or other 'violations' of human rights. The critical issue is how to identify and test for these conditions. This can pose particular challenges where legal definitions are absent, or facts disputed.

4.2.1 *Resistance to 'Tyranny'*

The ancient regime-type trigger threshold of 'tyranny' continues to be relevant, but in modified form. It was first revised in the Middle Ages and early modern period, including by application of a test developed by Bartolus for one of two types of tyranny: tyranny by 'defect of title' or tyranny by 'reason of conduct'.[2] By the mid-modern period it had evolved still further. A 'defect of title' could be internal or external – that is, the defect could signify a domestic

[1] René Marcic, 'The Persistence of Right-Law: An Inquiry into the Foundations of the Right to Resist' (1973) 59 *Archives for Philosophy of Law and Social Philosophy* 87, 108.

[2] See for example Bartolus de Saxoferrato, *On the Tyrant* (Jonathan Robinson tr, Creative Commons Attribution-Non-Commercial ShareAlike 3.0 Unreported License 2012 (rev 1.0a) 2016 (rev 1.2)) 4 (fn 31), 7–8 (fn 58, 60), 10 (fn 81), 14–17 (fn 143–146, 149, 152, 154, 156–157, 160–161, 166–167), 18 (fn 173–176, 180–181), 21–24. See also the earlier Thomas Aquinas, 'Commentary on the Sentences of Peter Lombard' in AP Entrèves (ed), *Aquinas: Selected Political Writings* (JG Dawson tr, Oxford University Press 1948) Book II, 'The Obedience Owed by Christians to the Secular Power and in Particular to Tyrants' di 44, q 2, a 2, 183; and the subsequent *Vindiciae, Contra Tyrannos: or, Concerning the Legitimate Power of a Prince over the People, and of the People over a Prince* (George Garnett ed/tr, 2003 edn, Cambridge University Press 1994) 140–141, 143–148, 172.

usurper or a foreign occupier, each lacking the consent of the population.[3] A 'reason of conduct' could also be internal or external – that is, the reason could be internal 'oppression' or external 'aggression'.[4] As will be shown in Part II, the principal continued relevance of 'tyranny' as a trigger is that it represents a legal tradition of the right based on either internal or external defect of title rendering lawful action against usurpation or occupation, or by reason of internal or external conduct rendering lawful action against oppression or aggression. Yet, even with such modifications and conceded continuing relevance, the contemporary right to resist has evolved beyond the 'tyranny' requirement as its only possible primary trigger condition.[5]

The diversification of positions on whether there can ever be a right to resist in a democratic state is the first complicating factor.[6] Those advocating the tyranny threshold often adopt what is effectively a variation of the traditional position, arguing that only those resisting in order to establish, maintain, or restore democracy have the right.[7] Within this cohort, some take a more

[3] See *Vindiciae, Contra Tyrannos* (n 2) 149–150; Locke's concepts of 'conquest' as 'foreign usurpation' and 'usurpation' as 'domestick conquest', each violating the imperative of consent, in John Locke, 'The Second Treatise of Government: An Essay Concerning the True Original, Extent and End of Civil Government' in *Two Treatises of Government* (P Laslett ed, rev edn, Cambridge University Press 1988) Chapter XVI 'Of Conquest' [175]–[196] 384–397, Chapter XVII 'Of Usurpation' [197]–[198] 397–398, Chapter XIX 'Of the Dissolution of Government' [218] 410, [239] 425.

[4] See *Vindiciae, Contra Tyrannos* (n 2) 140–141, 143–148, 155–160; Locke (n 3) Chapter XVII 'Of Usurpation' [197]–[198] 397–398, Chapter XVIII 'Of Tyranny' [199]–[210] 398–405, and the grounds of 'unjust war' in Locke (n 3) Chapter XVI 'Of Conquest' [176]–[187], [189], [191]–[192] 385–394, [196] 396.

[5] See for example Frédéric Mégret, 'Causes Worth Fighting For: Is There a Non-State *jus ad bellum*?' in Aristotle Constantinides and Nikos Zaikos (eds), *The Diversity of International Law: Essays in Honour of Professor Kalliopi K Koufa* (Martinus Nijhoff 2009) 175, 183–184; Pacifique Manirakiza, 'Towards a Right to Resist Gross Undemocratic Practices in Africa' (2019) 63(1) *Journal of African Law* 81, 84, 96–97. However, for continued emphasis on tyranny as the primary or exclusive trigger, compare John D Lewis, 'The Development of the Theory of Tyrannicide to 1660' in Oscar Jászi and John D Lewis (eds), *Against the Tyrant: The Tradition and Theory of Tyrannicide* (The Free Press 1957) 4–7, 26–28, 34, 52, 89, 95–96; Mario Turchetti, '"Despotism" and "Tyranny": Unmasking a Tenacious Confusion' (2008) 7 (2) *European Journal of Political Theory* 159, 160.

[6] Characterizing this as one of the last remaining debates on this topic in the field of political science, see Heiner Bielefeldt, 'The Right to Resist' in Wilhelm Heitmeyer and John Hagan (eds), *International Handbook of Violence Research* (Kluwer 2003) 1100–1101, 1105–1106.

[7] On the probable content of related discrete primary 'democratic rights', see Henry J Steiner, 'Political Participation as a Human Right' (1988) 1 *Harvard Human Rights Yearbook* 77; Thomas M Franck, 'The Emerging Right to Democratic Governance' (1992) 86 *American Journal of International Law* 46. On violation of such 'democratic rights' as potentially triggering a right to resist see Jordan J Paust, 'The Human Right to Participate in Armed Revolution and Related Forms of Social Violence: Testing the Limits of Permissibility' (1983) 32 *Emory Law Journal* 545, 547–548; Jordan J Paust, 'International Law, Dignity, Democracy

extreme position of democratic exceptionalism – that a right to resist exists, but not in a democratic state.[8] Others concede only a greatly reduced right to resist in a democratic state, insisting that its role is strictly that of defence of the democratic constitution.[9] However, a third group has a more expansive view of its role in reinforcing democracy as going beyond mere defence of existing law, extending to a 'legitimate and necessary' element in the process of law formation and change, to correct defects.[10] If the right to resist potentially plays a role not only in maintaining democracy but also in changing defective law to strengthen it, then the tyranny trigger is not always relevant to this.

The second complicating factor is that the rule of law can be manipulated to justify oppression, which increasingly takes place within as well as outside of legal frameworks, including human rights law.[11] Since 'tyranny' conceptually requires arbitrary rule outside or otherwise in violation of law, this is another ground on which it is insufficient as a sole primary trigger for the human right to resist in the twenty-first century.

For these reasons, the specification of 'tyranny' as a trigger for the right to resist is now probably more incidental than determinative. Hence the previously established Bartolist test, based on the Aristotelian binary concept of tyranny, is no longer exclusively used to determine the triggering of a right to resist.

and the Arab Spring' (2013) 46 *Cornell International Law Journal* 1, 7 (fn 32). Note that arguments for a unilateral right of third-party intervention premised on a right to resist with the object of establishing democracy are not consistent with the human rights concept developed in this book.

8 See for example Carl Joachim Friedrich, *The Philosophy of Law in Historical Perspective* (2nd edn, University of Chicago Press 1963) 150, 181–182. Such a position appears to influence the doctrines of the European Convention on Human Rights and American Convention on Human Rights. See the discussion in Chapter 7, Sections 7.3.2.1 and 7.3.2.2.

9 For example, see David Spitz, 'Democracy and the Problem of Civil Disobedience' (1954) 48 *American Political Science Review* 386, 391, 402–403; Arthur Kaufmann, 'Small Scale Right to Resist' (1985–1986) 21 *New England Law Review* 571, 580.

10 See for example Mortimer R Kadish and Sanford H Kadish, *Discretion to Disobey: A Study of Lawful Departures from Legal Rules* (Stanford University Press 1973, repr Quid Pro Books 2010) 146–156. Compare Pierre Rosanvallon, *Counter-Democracy: Politics in an Age of Distrust* (Arthur Goldhammer tr, Cambridge University Press 2008) 121–122, 125–149, 290–318; Candice Delmas, 'Disobedience, Civil and Otherwise' (2017) 11(1) *Criminal Law and Philosophy* 195; Daniela Bifulco and Angelo Jr Golia, 'The Right of Resistance as a State Law Basis for Transnational Regimes' Self-Contestation' (2018) 45 *Journal of Law and Society* 94; Zsolt Kapelner, 'Revolution against Non-Violent Oppression' (2019) 25(4) *Res Publica: A Journal of Moral, Legal and Political Philosophy* 445.

11 See Kaufmann (n 9) 575–576; Upendra Baxi, 'Otonomic Prowess and Existential Impotence: Reflexions on René Marcic's Sydney Papers' (conference paper for 'René Marcic: Sydney Commemorative Symposium (54)' University of Sydney, Faculty of Law, Department of Jurisprudence and International Law, Institute for Advanced Studies in Jurisprudence, Sydney, 1972) 11–14.

What has augmented or replaced the tyranny trigger is, however, less clear.[12] Contemporary legal theory deals comparatively straightforwardly with external defects and reasons as triggers – generally under the reasonably well-established rubrics of foreign 'aggression' or 'unlawful occupation' or 'colonization'.[13] However, it is considerably less specific in how it deals with internal defects and reasons as triggers – now generally referred to as 'tyranny and other forms of oppression', or simply 'oppression', as discussed below, neither of which benefits from a comparable extent of agreed definition for legal purposes.[14] In addition, the right to resist has become associated with four distinct

12 For example, Neumann's proposed grounds are essentially a rephrasing of the Bartolist test. See Franz L Neumann, 'On the Limits of Justifiable Disobedience' in Franz L Neumann, *The Democratic and Authoritarian State: Essays in Political and Legal Theory* (The Free Press 1957) 158.

13 See for example Richard Falk, 'Janus Tormented: The International Law of Internal War' in James N Rosenau (ed), *International Aspects of Civil Strife* (Princeton University Press 1964) 243–249; Richard Falk and Burns H Weston, 'The Relevance of International Law to Palestinian Rights in the West Bank and Gaza: In Legal Defense of the Intifada' (1991) 32(1) *Harvard International Law Journal* 129, 133, 142–148, 150–152, 155; Richard Falk, 'Azmi Bishara, the Right of Resistance, and the Palestinian Ordeal' (2002) XXXI(2) *Journal of Palestine Studies* 19, 22–27; Antonio Cassese, 'Human Rights and Humanitarian Law: Terrorism and Human Rights' (1982) 31 *American University Law Review* 945, 947; Georges Abi-Saab, 'Wars of National Liberation and the Laws of War' [1972] *Annales d'Étdues Internationales* 93, 100–101; Bert VA Röling, 'The Legal Status of Rebels and Rebellion' (1976) 13(2) *Journal of Peace Research* 149, 152–154; Noelle Higgins, *Regulating the Use of Force in Wars of National Liberation: The Need for a New Regime* (Martinus Nijhoff 2010) 2, 229, 231; Robert E Gorelick, 'Wars of National Liberation: Jus Ad Bellum' (1979) 11(1) *Case Western Reserve Journal of International Law* 71, 93; Frédéric Mégret, 'Beyond "Freedom Fighters" and "Terrorists": When, If Ever, Is Non-State Violence Legitimate in International Law?' (SSRN 2009); Mégret, 'Causes Worth Fighting For' (n 5) 173–175, 177. Compare the more equivocal Heather A Wilson, *International Law and the Use of Force by National Liberation Movements* (Clarendon 1988) 135–136, 186–187; Antonio Cassese, *Self-Determination of Peoples: A Legal Reappraisal* (Cambridge University Press 1995) 150–159, 197–198. See further discussion in Chapter 6, Section 6.3 and Chapter 7, Section 7.3.1.

14 Neumann (n 12) 158. Compare for example the wide variety of descriptors for this trigger in Max Pribilla, *The Right to Resist* (Catholic Social Guild 1952) 21; Cassese, 'Human Rights and Humanitarian Law' (n 13) 947, 949, 950, 958; Jordan J Paust, 'Political Oppression in the Name of National Security: Authority, Participation, and the Necessity within Democratic Limits Test' (1982) 9(1) *Yale International Law Journal* 178, 178 (fn 4); Paust, 'Human Right to Armed Revolution' (n 7) 550; Christian Tomuschat, 'The Right of Resistance and Human Rights' in *Violations of Human Rights: Possible Rights of Recourse and Forms of Resistance* (UNESCO 1984) 29–30, 33; Tony Honoré, 'The Right to Rebel' (1988) 8(1) *Oxford Journal of Legal Studies* 34, 36, 38, 45, 48, 51; Falk and Weston (n 13) 133, 136, 156–157; Richard Falk and Burns H Weston, 'The Israeli-Occupied Territories, International Law, and the Boundaries of Scholarly Discourse: A Reply to Michael Curtis' (1992) 33(1) *Harvard International Law Journal* 191, 192, 196; Walter Kälin and Jorg Künzli, 'Article 1F(b): Freedom Fighters, Terrorists and the Notion of Serious Non-Political Crime' (2000) 12 supp *International Journal of Refugee Law* 46, 49–50, 52–53; Roberto Gargarella, 'The Last Resort:

types of 'object and purpose', as set out further below, each of which has distinct triggers that relate to the denial or violation of primary fundamental human rights. Thus we now have a situation where a series of triggers are recognized, many of which do not impose a 'tyranny' threshold per se.

4.2.2 *Resistance to 'Oppression'*

The term 'oppression' often either supplements or takes the place of the 'tyranny' trigger in relation to the contemporary human right to resist.[15] The *Black's Law Dictionary* definition of 'oppression', both concise and open-textured, is in general the 'act or instance of unjustly exercising authority or power' and, more specifically for the purpose of prosecuting individuals, 'an offense consisting in the abuse of discretionary authority by a public officer who has an improper motive, as a result of which a person is injured'.[16] This would constitute considerably wider trigger conditions than those required by the 'tyranny' trigger.

Yet the absence of a more developed shared understanding of exactly what 'oppression' legally entails has generated a range of suggested interpretations of this term, none of which have gained general acceptance. For example, Paust defines 'oppression' more narrowly as 'the intentional or highly foreseeable denial of effective [political] participation ... when such is not actually necessary ... under colour of national security'.[17] He has alternatively characterized it as constituting a 'war against human rights' in the form of internal 'aggression' against the will of the people, including forcible violations of the

The Right of Resistance in Situations of Legal Alienation' (Yale Law School SELA (Seminario en Latinoamérica de Teoría Constitucional y Política) Papers, 2003) 1; Roberto Gargarella, 'The Right of Resistance in Situations of Severe Deprivation' in Thomas Pogge (ed), *Freedom from Poverty as a Human Right: Who Owes What to the Very Poor?* (Oxford University Press and UNESCO 2007) 362–364, 368 and fn 12, citing John Rawls, *A Theory of Justice* (Harvard University Press 1999) 322–323, 342; Paust, 'International Law, Dignity, Democracy' (n 7) 10 (fn 39). See also further discussion in Chapter 6, Section 6.4 and Chapter 7, Sections 7.2.1, 7.3.1.1.

15 See for example M Cherif Bassiouni, 'Final Document: Conclusions and Recommendations' in M Cherif Bassiouni (ed), *International Terrorism and Political Crimes* (Charles C Thomas 1975) xxi; Falk and Weston, 'Boundaries of Scholarly Discourse' (n 14) 192, 200. The French revolutionary Declaration on the Rights of Man and of the Citizen embedded this new formulation, starting in the modern period, according to Mitsukuni Yazaki, 'Legality and the Right of Resistance' [1957] *Osaka University Law Review* 26, 27. For further discussion see Chapter 5, Section 5.5.2.6. See also in particular the international human rights law formulations proposed by Humphrey and Cassin, discussed further in Chapter 6, Section 6.4.1.

16 Bryan A Garner, *Black's Law Dictionary* (2nd edn, West Group 2001) 504.

17 Paust, 'Political Oppression' (n 14) 178 (fn 4), 179.

right to self-determination and the human right to participate, sometimes amounting to what he calls 'politicide'.[18] Where the *Black's* definition may be too broad to provide sufficient guidance when applied to the right to resist, Paust's definition of 'political oppression' may be over-specific in certain respects, and reliant on associated concepts lacking widespread acceptance.

Other legal theorists insist that there is a distinct economic dimension to the concept of 'oppression' that should not be overlooked. This idea of 'economic oppression' suggests a possible right to resist not only 'tyranny' but also oligarchy or plutocracy or kleptocracy, which could be of particular relevance in these times of increasing concentration of global wealth. For example, Honoré suggests 'exploitation', which he defines as profit from oppression, as an additional related primary trigger.[19] Meanwhile, the Marxist variation in contemporary theory sometimes expresses this concept as a right to resist capitalism or imperialism, on the basis that these constitute 'systemic' or 'structural' forms of oppression.[20] However, it is also possible to boil these structural phenomena down to an aggregation of human rights violations, therefore not necessarily requiring discrete systemic triggers.

The advantage of the 'tyranny' concept is that the Bartolist test is available for use, modification, or updating to contemporary circumstances. No such test has yet been established for 'oppression' per se. Honoré proposes a three-prong test for 'oppression' as a trigger, providing that the violations concerned must be 'weighty, crucial and severe', amounting to 'sustained disinterest or contempt and/or discrimination'.[21] Again, while this is not entirely satisfactory it may provide a starting point for further development.

[18] Jordan J Paust, 'Aggression against Authority: The Crime of Oppression, Politicide and Other Crimes against Human Rights' (1986) 18 *Case Western Reserve Journal of International Law* 283, 283–284, 293–294, 304–305.

[19] See Honoré (n 14) 48, 51. Compare the earlier proposal for recognition of a right to resist 'economic exploitation' in Röling (n 13) 158–161; and more recently for a right to resist 'workplace oppression' in Alex Gourevitch, 'The Right to Strike: A Radical View' (2018) 112 (4) *American Political Science Review* 905. See also further discussion of the right to resist for economic self-determination later in this chapter, at Section 4.6.1.3.

[20] See for example Issa G Shivji, *The Concept of Human Rights in Africa* (CODESRIA Book Series 1989) 69–87. See also Baxi, who describes it as a right of the 'rightless' systemically excluded from the benefits of rule of law, and also from political and economic structures. Baxi (n 11) 13. In more general terms, see the proposed right to resist economic oppression in the form of a 'right to resist impoverishment' in Gwilym David Blunt, 'Is There a Human Right to Resistance?' (2017) 39(4) *Human Rights Quarterly* 860, 861, 868, 872; Gwilym David Blunt, 'Illegal Immigration as Resistance to Global Poverty' (2018) 69(1) *Raisons Politiques* 83, 87–89; Gwilym David Blunt, *Global Poverty, Injustice, and Resistance* (Cambridge University Press 2019).

[21] See Honoré (n 14) 48, 51.

Finally, 'oppression', like 'tyranny', is not a codified international crime as such. The 'crimes against humanity' threshold is available from international criminal law and undoubtedly such crimes, with their 'widespread and systematic' nature, would constitute 'oppression'.[22] The question is whether human rights violations that occur at a lower threshold, or other violations of constitutional rights, can also constitute 'oppression' or could independently trigger a right to resist and, if so, what level of seriousness would need be reached.

4.2.3 *Resistance to 'Violations'*

It remains open as to whether 'tyranny' and 'oppression' are the only possible primary trigger thresholds for the right to resist, or whether a mere 'violation' could in some instances act as a trigger provided that secondary trigger conditions and other limitation elements are met.[23] Constituting a distinct third category, such 'violation' triggers may or may not intersect with, or otherwise meet, the relevant tests for 'tyranny' or 'oppression'.

In the historical theories, such third-category triggers for the right to resist included 'unjust law'[24] or other particular violations of fundamental law.[25] However, some restricted this trigger to actions constituting a threat to life, in

[22] Compare Paust's suggestion that under certain circumstances the 'crime of oppression' can constitute a 'crime against humanity'. Paust (n 18) 294.

[23] For example as suggested by Cassese, 'Human Rights and Humanitarian Law' (n 13) 947, 950, 958. See the extended discussion of possible trigger violations that fall between the 'systemic' and the 'aberrational' in Asbjörn Eide, 'The Right to Oppose Violations of Human Rights: Basis, Conditions and Limitations' in *Violations of Human Rights: Possible Rights of Recourse and Forms of Resistance* (UNESCO 1984) 34, 39, 47–53, 60. Compare also Kadish and Kadish (n 10) 72–100.

[24] See in particular the theories of Aquinas, 'Commentary on the Sentences' (n 2) 183; Thomas Aquinas, 'Summa Theologiae' in William P Baumgarth and Richard J Regan (eds), *On Law, Morality and Politics* (Richard J Regan tr, 2nd edn, Hackett Publishing 2002) II-II q 104 'On Obedience', a 5 'Are Subjects Obliged to Obey Their Superiors in All Things?', a 6 'Are Christians Obliged to Obey Secular Authorities?' reply obj 3; Thomas Aquinas, *Treatise on Law: The Complete Text (Summa Theologiae I-II, Questions 90–108)* (Alfred J Freddoso tr, St Augustine's Press 2009) q 90 'The Essence of Law', a 2 'Is law always ordered toward the common good as its end?', q 95 'Human Law', a 2 'Does every humanly made law stem from the natural law?', q 92 'The Effects of Law', a 1 'Is it the role of law to make men good?' reply obj 4, q 96 'The Force of Human Law', a 4 'Does human law impose an obligation in conscience on a man?', reply obj 2–3, a 5 'Is everyone subject to human law?' For a contemporary variation, see Baxi (n 11) 6, 9–10.

[25] See for example the *Vindiciaen* and Lockean theories. *Vindiciae, Contra Tyrannos* (n 2) 155–156; Locke (n 3) Chapter XIV [168] 379–380.

either narrow or broad terms,[26] or to 'security'.[27] In the contemporary theories, the prospect of other 'violation' triggers yields a similar diversity of proposed answers as to just how low the threshold conditions go.

It is possible that primary trigger violations need to be of a particular character. For some, such as Bassiouni, they either are or should be limited to the violation of *jus cogens* norms,[28] or those violations otherwise constituting international crimes, therefore including but not limited to the right to resist: aggression; other denial of the right to self-determination; war crimes; genocide; crimes against humanity; apartheid and racial discrimination; slavery; torture.[29] For others, however, such as Eide, primary trigger violations can also include 'lesser' or 'ordinary' human rights violations – whether these concern civil, political, economic, social, cultural, or environmental rights.[30] On this logic, violations of other areas of 'higher' law

[26] See in particular the Hobbesian theory arising from *Leviathan* 14–15, 21, *Elements of Law* 2.1.5, 1.17.2 and *De Cive* 2.18, 3.1.4 as assessed in Deborah Baumgold, 'Pacifying Politics: Resistance, Violence and Accountability in Seventeenth-Century Contract Theory' (1993) 21 (1) *Political Theory* 6, 13–15, 24; Glenn Burgess, 'On Hobbesian Resistance Theory' (1994) XLII *Political Studies* 62; David Dyzenhaus, 'Hobbes and the Legitimacy of Law' (2001) 20 *Law and Philosophy* 461, 467–469; Peter J Steinberger, 'Hobbesian Resistance' (2002) 46 *American Journal of Political Science* 856, 857; Eleanor Curran, 'Can Rights Curb the Hobbesian Sovereign? The Full Right to Self-Preservation, Duties of Sovereignty and the Limitations of Hohfeld' (2006) 25 *Law and Philosophy* 243; Suzanne Sreedhar, *Hobbes on Resistance: Defying the Leviathan* (Cambridge University Press 2010).

[27] See in particular Emer de Vattel, *The Law of Nations, or Principles of the Law of Nature, Applied to the Conduct and Affairs of Nations and Sovereigns* (Béla Kapossy and Richard Whatmore eds, Liberty Fund 2008) Book I Chapter II [14]–[18] 86–88, [21]–[22] 88–89, Book II Chapter IV 'Of the Right to Security, and the Effects of Sovereignty and Independence of Nations' [49]–[52] 288–289, [65]–[69] 296–297.

[28] On the question of what constitutes a *jus cogens* or 'peremptory' norm of general international law, see International Law Commission, 'Draft Conclusions on Identification and Legal Consequences of Peremptory Norms of General International Law (*jus cogens*)' (2022) [2022] *Yearbook of the International Law Commission* vol II, pt. 2, including the 'non-exhaustive list' at Conclusion 23, 6.

[29] For example, though he does not use this terminology, Bassiouni's trigger theory essentially describes a right to resist crimes against humanity. See M Cherif Bassiouni, 'Ideologically Motivated Offenses and the Political Offense Exception in Extradition – A Proposed Juridical Standard for an Unruly Problem' (1969) XIX *De Paul Law Review* 217, 252–256. See also discussions of 'object and purpose' in this chapter at Section 4.6, and further discussions of the right to resist internationally criminal acts in Chapter 6, Section 6.5 and Chapter 7, Section 7.2.3.

[30] Eide (n 23) 34, 39, 47–53, 60. See also proposed thresholds of 'injustice', 'unjust action by the State', 'unlawful arrest', and 'impoverishment' in, respectively, Candice Delmas, *A Duty to Resist: When Civil Disobedience Should Be Uncivil* (Oxford University Press 2018); Jason Brennan, 'Resistance: The Fourth Option' in Jason Brennan, *When All Else Fails: The Ethics of Resistance to State Injustice* (Princeton University Press 2019); J Christopher Clark, '"Unhand Me, Gentlemen!" The Right to Resist Unlawful Arrest in South Carolina' (2017) 69 (1) *South Carolina Law Review* 247; Blunt, 'Is There a Human Right to Resistance?' (n 20).

analogous to human rights, such as international environmental law and the 'rights of nature' – including the nascent international crime of 'ecocide' – are potentially also included.[31]

In addition, it is possible that the primary trigger violations must be of a certain severity. For some, they must approximate the 'widespread and systematic' standard applying to crimes against humanity. For example, Bassiouni's theory identifies the categories of human rights violations that would trigger a right to resist as limited to those that are 'serious' and prolonged, systematic rather than sporadic, and the rights involved must be 'fundamental'.[32] For others, however, the trigger violations can include individual instances or more limited patterns of abuse, that might generally warrant only exercise of the more limited *lex generalis* primary political or procedural rights. For example, Eide maintains that while the right to resist is only rarely an individual right concerning individual violations, 'in principle' it could be triggered by 'any [human rights] violation whatsoever', whether of 'commission', 'omission', or 'exclusion', provided that violation is 'clear and incontrovertible'.[33]

Finally, a right to resist in international law or in constitutional law – or in ordinary law for that matter – logically links to trigger violations of that body of law. However, this does not necessarily mean that a right to resist will always be defensive or 'conservative', as claimed by some.[34] Provisions of ordinary law

[31] See further discussion of enforcement of 'higher' law as an 'object and purpose' in this chapter, at Section 4.6.1.1.

[32] Bassiouni (n 29) 252–256. See also Tomuschat's high threshold of 'extreme gravity' involving 'deliberate, large-scale policies of government' in Tomuschat (n 14) 24–25, 29–30, 33 or 'extraordinary illegal government action' in Cecile Fabre, 'Cosmopolitanism and Wars of Self-Defence' in Cecile Fabre and Seth Lazar (eds), *The Morality of Defensive War* (Oxford University Press 2014). Similarly, see the suggestion that the violations of human rights must be 'gross' or 'large-scale', 'severe', 'persistent', and 'systematic' in Falk and Weston (n 13) 133, 136–137, 156–157; Falk and Weston, 'Boundaries of Scholarly Discourse' (n 14) 196, 201; and in Chiara Redaelli, 'The Right to Rebel against Violations of Human Rights: A New Role for the Responsibility to Protect?' (2020) 19(1) *Palestine Yearbook of International Law* 8; or that violations must be 'massive and serious' in Manirakiza (n 5). For extended discussion of the judicial interpretation of such descriptors in assessing violations, see generally Roger-Claude Liwanga, 'The Meaning of Gross Violation of Human Rights: A Focus on International Tribunals' Decisions over the DRC Conflicts' (2015) 44(1) *Denver Journal of International Law and Policy* 67.

[33] Eide (n 23) 34, 39, 47–53, 60. Similarly, see the suggestion that such violations of human rights can include 'official disrespect' for law by authorities, 'open illegal practices', 'deliberative ignorance', or 'concealed misconduct' in Delmas (n 10); or 'intransigent non-compliance' in Blunt, 'Is There a Human Right to Resistance?' (n 20). For 'unlawful arrest' constituting a sufficient trigger, see related literature, for example Clark (n 30).

[34] See for example Honoré (n 14) 35–36, 45–52; David C Williams, 'The Constitutional Right to "Conservative" Revolution' (1997) 32 *Harvard Civil Rights-Civil Liberties Law Review* 413, 413–415, 414 fn 5, 431, 434, 438–439, 440–441, 444.

must be consistent with constitutional law, and in turn constitutional provisions need to be consistent with international standards in order to be valid. Where existing legal protections fall short of international human rights standards in particular – or where these standards are in the process of expansion – the right to resist could be foundational or 'revolutionary', as claimed by others.[35]

In sum, the primary triggers set out above generally establish necessary but not sufficient conditions to activate a human right to resist. They are not enough to ground a valid claim if that claim cannot also establish secondary triggering conditions. Only the primary and secondary trigger conditions together can sustain a claim.

4.3 SECONDARY TRIGGERS OR CONDITIONS FOR ACTIVATION: THE 'RIGHT TO RESIST WHEN?'

Only once a primary triggering condition has been established can one proceed to answer the question of 'the right to resist when?' by reference to the secondary trigger condition, which is 'necessity'.[36] That is, the right to resist finally activates when resort to that right has been rendered necessary by the absence of other equally effective remedies, judicial or otherwise.

4.3.1 *The Necessity Condition and its Variants*

Necessity is a concept that has applications in domestic law, in human rights law, and in both *jus ad bellum* and *jus in bello* applications in international law.[37] Under conditions of 'armed conflict', *jus in bello* necessity is a related

[35] See for example proposals for an exceptional right for the purpose of either enforcing or catalyzing change in international law in Richard Falk, 'The Adequacy of Contemporary Theories of International Law: Gaps in Legal Thinking' (1964) 50(2) *Virginia Law Review* 231, 248–249, 255–256, 260; Honoré (n 14) 35–36, 45–52; Frédéric Mégret, 'Civil Disobedience and International Law: Sketch for a Theoretical Argument' (2009) 46 *Canadian Yearbook of International Law* 143. See also the theories of resistance to unjust international laws in Bhupinder Singh Chimni, 'Third World Approaches to International Law: A Manifesto' (2006) 8 *International Community Law Review* 3, 19–27; Frédéric Mégret, 'International Law and Peoples' Resistance: Foreword' (2016) 1(1) *Inter Gentes* 3–4. However, there is no right to resist in order to either establish or maintain a 'tyrannical, oppressive or exploitative regime'. Honoré (n 14) 48.

[36] On the original concept of necessity in relation to the right to resist, see Aquinas, 'Summa Theologiae' (n 24) II-II q 64 'On Homicide', a 7 'Is It Lawful for a Person to Kill Another in Self-Defense?'; Aquinas, *Summa Theologiae* (n 24) q 96 'The Force of Human Law', a 6 'Is one who is subject to the law permitted to act outside the letter of the law?', reply obj 1, q 97 'Changes in Human Law', a 3 'Can custom acquire the force of law or nullify a law?' reply obj 2.

[37] See Jens David Ohlin and Larry May, *Necessity in International Law* (Oxford University Press 2016).

condition regulating conduct in the exercise of the right to resist that must also be met, but it constitutes a legal question separate from whether conditions exist to activate the right itself. Rather, the human rights law and *jus ad bellum* applications of necessity are the most relevant to consideration of the right to resist triggering conditions.

The application of a necessity condition as a secondary trigger for activation of the right to resist is rarely contradicted.[38] However, there is not full consensus on whether that should be set as high as the 'last resort' standard in the 'traditional' variant of the right,[39] at the similar 'exhaustion' standard,[40] or whether unavailability or 'no reasonable prospect' of an effective legal remedy is sufficient to meet the test.[41]

Theorists such as Kaufmann complain that the 'last resort' standard constituting an 'emergency' is too high because it activates 'too late', leading to a right that cannot be exercised because conditions by that stage render it virtually impossible to do so effectively without use of force and without exposure to disproportionate peril, which could be averted by a right that activates at a lower preventive threshold. His alternative theory proposes to act as a 'first remedy' extending to a preventive function, activating against a regime that has not yet reached the point of 'manifest unlawfulness'. This would require, in Kaufmann's view, less restrictive trigger conditions but greater consequent limitations as to means.[42] Bassiouni's more practical proposal focuses exclusively on setting the trigger lower, whereby the necessity test is met if 'a local or international remedy or legal method of redress' is not 'reasonably available'.[43]

38 However, compare Paust, 'Human Right to Armed Revolution' (n 7) 568–569, 577, 581. For Paust, necessity is not a condition of the right to revolution cognate. Rather, permissibility depends exclusively on the will of the majority, as an exercise of self-determination.

39 Compare Bassiouni (n 15) xxi; Kaufmann (n 9) 574; Tomuschat (n 14) 27, 30.

40 For example, see Pribilla (n 14) 21; Marcic (n 1) 111; Bassiouni (n 15) xxi; 'Meeting of experts on the analysis of the basis and forms of individual and collective action by which violations of human rights can be combated, Freetown, Sierra Leone, 3–7 March 1981: Final Report' in *Violations of Human Rights: Possible Rights of Recourse and Forms of Resistance* (UNESCO, 1984) 222–223. Proponents insist that the exhaustion standard must be reasonably applied: incremental escalation from legal and constitutional means, through peaceful other means before forceful means may not always be possible, for example in situations of 'imminent danger'. See Honoré (n 14) 46–47, 49, 52–53.

41 Compare Gargarella, 'Right of Resistance in Situations of Legal Alienation' (n 14) 16–19; Gargarella, 'Right of Resistance in Situations of Severe Deprivation' (n 14) 372. See also Philip C Jessup, *A Modern Law of Nations: An Introduction* (Macmillan 1948) 185–186.

42 See Kaufmann (n 9) 574–579. See the critical response to Kaufmann's model in Marcic (n 1) 87–114.

43 Bassiouni (n 29) 255, 256. See also Falk, 'Azmi Bishara, the Right of Resistance' (n 13) 29.

As a secondary trigger for this right, the necessity condition potentially operates not only as exception, but also as constraint.[44] That is, the absence of demonstrated 'necessity' can negate an otherwise well-grounded claim. It therefore constitutes a pivotal element. However, it generally proves more difficult to establish than primary trigger conditions. Therefore, this element requires particularly careful analysis by those making, defending, or otherwise assessing a claim.[45]

4.4 PERSONAL SCOPE, THE RIGHTS-HOLDERS: 'WHO MAY RESIST?'

In its ancient conceptual antecedent, and in the early concept of Middle Ages theory, the right to resist was primarily an individual right that could also be exercised collectively.[46] The debate over the personal scope of the right only emerged in earnest in the modern period, with some theories suggesting the right is never individual but always delegated to official representatives,[47] others suggesting that the right is always individual but never collective,[48] and still others maintaining that in almost all cases the right to resist – particularly with force – is a majority right that can only be exercised collectively.[49]

This diversity of opinion has inflected the contemporary conceptions. It is also demonstrated in the diversity of rights-holders in the contemporary legal provisions set out in Part II. Some describe the right to resist as broadly as possible, as a 'right of everyone' whether they are 'affected or not

44 For more on these two functional forms, see Ohlin and May (n 37) 2–6.

45 Potentially useful supplementary analytical frameworks for evaluating 'necessity' are supplied by contemporary just war theorists working in ethics and political philosophy. For example, see Lazar's theory of evidence-based necessity establishing, among other things, that evaluations of 'collectivist necessity' and 'individual necessity' will differ. See Seth Lazar, 'Necessity in Self-Defense and War' (2012) 40 *Philosophy and Public Affairs* 3.

46 See the Ciceronian, Thomasian, and Bartolist theories. Cicero, *De Officiis* (Walter Miller tr, GP Putnam's Sons 1913) Book III, iv [19], 287, vi [32] 299; Aquinas, 'Commentary on the Sentences' (n 2); Aquinas, 'Summa Theologiae' (n 24); Bartolus de Saxoferrato, *On Guelfs and Ghibbellines* (Jonathan Robinson tr, Creative Commons Attribution-Non-Commercial ShareAlike 3.0 Unreported License 2014 rev 1.1a) 5.

47 See the *Vindiciaen* theory. *Vindiciae, Contra Tyrannos* (n 2) 131–138, 157–160.

48 See certain interpretations of the Hobbesian theory in *Leviathan* 21.15, such as Ursula Goldenbaum, 'Sovereignty and Obedience' in Desmond M Clarke and Catherine Wilson (eds), *The Oxford Handbook of Philosophy in Early Modern Europe* (Oxford University Press 2011) 510–511.

49 See for example the Lockean and Vattelian theories. Locke (n 3) Chapter XVIII [209] 404–405, Chapter XIX [226] 415–416, [240] 426–427, [242]–[243] 427–428; Vattel (n 27) Book I Chapter III [32]–[34] 94–95, Book I Chapter IV [50]–[51] 105, [54] 111.

affected'.[50] Some focus on its conceptualization as a right exercisable by individuals.[51] Others specify that it is an exclusively majoritarian group right not exercisable either by minorities or by individuals.[52] Those characterizing it as an exclusively collective right sometimes identify the right as 'attribution of state sovereignty', on the understanding that under the principle of self-determination particular governments are not representatives of 'states', but rather must act as agents for a state's sovereign 'people' as a whole.[53] Those for whom the right to resist is an inherently collective *jus ad bellum* right tend to further restrict its application to 'national liberation movements'.[54]

It seems that in contemporary theory there is no single right or wrong answer to this question solely on the basis of whether the ostensible rights-holder is an individual, minority, or majority.[55] Any or all of these may apply depending on the particular circumstances or the particular legal provision in question.[56] Just as some more specific forms of the right to resist can only be exercised collectively, other forms must be exercised at individual level at least in the first instance, such as the right to disobey manifestly unlawful orders,[57] and, where legally recognized, the right to resist unlawful action by police.

50 Neumann (n 12) 158. See also Marcic (n 1) 108, 110–111, 113; Baxi (n 11) 5, 6; Honoré (n 14) 36–37.

51 See for example Kadish and Kadish (n 10).

52 For example, the position of Hermann Weinkauff as cited in Walter Schwarz, 'The Right of Resistance' (1964) 74(2) *Ethics* 126, 129. See also Paust, 'Human Right to Participate in Armed Revolution' (n 7) 553–556, 549; Paust, 'International Law, Dignity, Democracy' (n 7) 13–14.

53 See for example Quincy Wright, 'Intervention and Cuba in 1961' (1961) 55 (27–29 April 1961) *Proceedings of the American Society of International Law at Its Annual Meeting* (1921–1969) 2, 3–4. See also Paust, 'Human Right to Participate in Armed Revolution' (n 7) 546, 550–551; Paust, 'International Law, Dignity, Democracy' (n 7) 5–6.

54 Cassese is, at least initially, somewhat less restrictive and more equivocal on this point. See Cassese, 'Human Rights and Humanitarian Law' (n 13) 949–950, 958. Compare Abi-Saab (n 13) 100–101; Röling (n 13) 152–154, 158–161; Gorelick (n 13) 72–83, 93; Tomuschat (n 14) 18, 20–21, 26–27; Higgins (n 13) 7–90, 229–237.

55 Compare for example Gargarella's conception of it as a majority right in Gargarella, 'Right of Resistance in Situations of Legal Alienation' (n 14) 5, 11; and as either majority or minority right in Gargarella, 'Right of Resistance in Situations of Severe Deprivation' (n 14) 367–372. Compare also Eide (n 23) 60, 63.

56 Explanatory theories vary as well. Again, see the work of contemporary just war theorists in ethics and political philosophy working on the question of 'legitimate authority'. For example, see Fabre's theory of 'legitimacy transfer' from the state to individuals and groups who resist, where government has, through its actions, lost the claim to obedience. Cecile Fabre, 'Cosmopolitanism, Just War Theory and Legitimate Authority' (2008) 84(5) *International Affairs* 963. See also Lazar's alternative theory of 'authorization' by 'community consent'. Seth Lazar, 'Authorization and the Morality of War' (2016) 94 *Australasian Journal of Philosophy* 211.

57 See further discussion in Chapter 6, Section 6.5 and Chapter 7, Section 7.2.3.

In addition, since the individual is not only increasingly recognized as a subject of international law, but also has an increasing role in its enforcement, this poses no insurmountable barrier for a potential rights-holder.[58]

Of course, any account of the personal scope element of the human right to resist that only identifies the rights-holders is incomplete. The corresponding duty-bearers must also be identified.

4.5 PERSONAL SCOPE, THE DUTY-BEARERS: 'WHO HAS A CORRESPONDING DUTY?'

Among contemporary theorists proposing that the right to resist either arises from a duty to resist, or that it contains or correlates to a corresponding duty, there appears to be some level of agreement that the right to resist imposes both positive and negative obligations on direct parties and/or third parties. Like the rights-holders, the duty-bearers will differ depending on the theory or specific legal provision in question. Constitutional law provisions concern both right-duties of individual citizens and corresponding duties imposed on the state. International law provisions primarily concern the duties imposed on direct and third parties by human rights and certain other obligations.

Theorized direct duties on the individual include duties: (1) to take action at a time, in a manner and for an end consistent with the right's principal object and purpose – amounting to a positive obligation; (2) to observe applicable conditions and not exceed applicable limitations – amounting to a negative obligation.[59] Direct duties on the state include correlated duties: (1)

58 See Richard Falk, 'Nuremberg: Past, Present and Future' (1971) 80 *Yale Law Journal* 1501, 1516–1517; Richard Falk, 'The Nuremberg Defense in the Pentagon Papers Case' (1974) 13 *Columbia Journal of Transnational Law* 208, 208–210; Richard Falk, 'Introduction' in Francis A Boyle, *Defending Civil Resistance under International Law* (Transnational 1988); Richard Falk, 'Telford Taylor and the Legacy of Nuremberg' (1998) 37 *Columbia Journal of Transnational Law* 693, 716; Francis A Boyle, *Defending Civil Resistance under International Law* (Transnational 1988) 17; Francis A Boyle, *Protesting Power: War, Resistance, and Law* (Rowman and Littlefield 2008) 7–34; Matthew Lippman, 'The Right of Civil Resistance under International Law and the Domestic Necessity Defense' (1990) 8 *Dickinson Journal of International Law* 349, 350; Nicholas N Kittrie, *Rebels with a Cause: The Minds and Morality of Political Offenders* (Westview 2000) 243–350, in particular his 'Bill of Rights for Just Governance and Just Resistance' 342–344.

59 See for example the right-duty conceptualized as deriving from the Nuremberg Principles according to Falk, 'Nuremberg Defense' (n 58); Falk, 'Introduction' (n 58); Falk, 'Telford Taylor and the Legacy of Nuremberg' (n 58) 698–699; Boyle, *Defending Civil Resistance* (n 58); Francis A Boyle, Martin Hird, Lynn Burnaby, Ramsey Clark, David Wright, Avigdor Feldman, and Edward Dumbauld, 'Citizen Initiatives under International Law' (1988) 82 *Proceedings of the American Society of International Law* 555, 569; Boyle, *Protesting Power* (n 58); Matthew Lippman, 'Nuremberg and American Justice' (1991) 5 *Notre Dame Journal of*

to legislate in accordance with the right – amounting to a positive obligation to protect; (2) of immunization, non-prosecution and/or acceptance of defences as grounds for exoneration or mitigation in criminal cases, where there is a valid right – amounting to a negative obligation to respect;[60] (3) to concede grounds for extending refugee protection or refusing extradition, where there is a valid right – amounting to a positive obligation to protect.[61]

Third-party correlated duties are either to assist – amounting to a positive obligation to protect or to fulfill – or not obstruct – amounting to a negative obligation to respect – those with a valid right to resist.[62] Exercise of the third-party duty may therefore be active or passive, military or otherwise, but ultimately turns on the question of the extent to which such actions are either permitted or prohibited as a matter of the law on intervention, or are covered by a lawful exception.[63]

Ethics, Law and Public Policy 951. Compare Tom Dannenbaum, *The Crime of Aggression, Humanity, and the Soldier* (Cambridge University Press 2018) 'The Duty to Disobey Illegal Orders' 20–24; 'The Timing of Disobedience Protection' 272–276, 'A Limited Right to Disobey Orders to Fight in Illegal Wars' 292–299, 'The *Jus ad Bellum* and the Human Rights of Rights Defenders' 322–328; general argument in Delmas (n 30). See further discussion in Chapter 6, Section 6.5.

60 This theory goes back to Bartolus. See Saxoferrato, *On the Tyrant* (n 2) 9 (fn 74), 10–11 (fn 83–85, 87–92). See also Lippman (n 58) 359–362; Kittrie (n 58) 243–350, in particular his 'Bill of Rights for Just Governance and Just Resistance' 342–344.

61 On the duty of non-extradition, see Bassiouni (n 29) 254–257. On the duty of non-exclusion and refugee protection see Kälin and Künzli (n 14) 46–78; Kittrie (n 58) 193–242, 297–350, in particular his 'Bill of Rights for Just Governance and Just Resistance' 342–344 and 'Typology of Political Offenses' 350. On the respective related doctrines of political offence exception and protected political activity see further discussion in Chapter 6, Section 6.6.3 and Chapter 7, Section 7.2.2.

62 Compare Honoré (n 14) 36, 41, 43; Wright (n 53) 7; Quincy Wright, 'The Goa Incident' (1962) 56 *American Journal of International Law* 617, 626–628; Vladimir Ilyich Lenin, *Critical Remarks on the National Question – The Right of Nations to Self-Determination* (1914, Foreign Languages Publishing House edn 1954) 185. See also Blunt's three-fold theory of the negative obligations content as: non-interference; non-obstruction; non-collaboration. Gwilym David Blunt, 'Doing Nothing as Resistance', *Qrius* (6 April 2020).

63 This theory goes back to the *Vindiciae*, Grotius, and Vattel. See *Vindiciae, Contra Tyrannos* (n 2) Fourth Question 173–185; Hugo Grotius, *The Rights of War and Peace* (Richard Tuck ed, Jean Barbeyrac tr, Liberty Fund 2005) Book II Chapter XXV 'Of the Causes for which War Is to Be Undertaken on the Account of Others' I 1151, VI 1156, VII 1158, VIII 1159–1162; Vattel (n 27) Book I Chapter IV 'Of the Sovereign, His Obligations and His Rights' [52] 109, Book II Chapter IV 'Of the Right to Security, and the Effects of Sovereignty and Independence of Nations' [56] 289–291, Book II Chapter V 'Of the Observance of Justice between Nations' [65]–[69] 296–297, Book II Chapter XII 'Of Treaties of Alliance and other Public Treaties' [168] 344 [196]–[197] 364–365, Book III Chapter XVIII 'Of Civil War' [296] 648–649. See also further discussions in Chapter 6, Sections 6.2.2, 6.2.3, 6.3.1.6, 6.4.6, and 6.5, and Chapter 7, Sections 7.2.1.1, 7.2.2, and 7.3.1.1, in particular the discussion of Wright's theory in Chapter 6, Sections 6.2.2 and 6.2.3. See also as implied in Falk, 'Janus Tormented' (n 13);

Baxi emphasizes the critical importance of specifying the type of right for the purpose of identifying the party or parties responsible for the corresponding correlated duties of assistance and non-obstruction. He argues that if the right to resist is '*paucital* (*in personam*)', thus imposing the duty on an 'ascertainable range of persons', it is available exclusively against the state. However, if '*multital* (*in rem*)', so imposing the duty on 'a very large and indefinite class of people', this extends the duty beyond the state to potentially cover non-state sources of oppression and other violations.[64] Related is the question of whether this amounts to an *erga omnes* obligation – that is, a general, non-contract-specific obligation – between peoples rather than states.[65]

One complicating factor is that international law may impose other apparently conflicting duties, permissions, or constraints on states. For example, all states will have competing human rights duties to protect the human rights of others, including in particular their positive obligations to prevent and punish violations of the right to life, even where those arise from the exercise of a valid right to resist.[66] The application of the 'Responsibility to Protect' doctrine in its current iteration would only permit internationally authorized assistance to resistance against genocide or crimes against humanity, but not tyranny, other oppression, or other human rights violations.[67] Conversely, the permission of unilateral intervention upon invitation by the state concerned, for assistance in suppression of civil unrest in situations short of civil war, lacks an unambiguous human rights exception.[68] Absent general agreement on how to interpret such competing obligations and principles in light of the human right to resist, it may be difficult to hold duty-bearers to account.

Even where rights-holders and duty-bearers are correctly identified, and primary and secondary triggers are both present, one further element is ultimately determinative. Unless a human rights-compatible 'object and purpose' can also be shown, it will not be possible to validate a claimed human right to resist.

Falk, 'Nuremberg Defense' (n 58) 225. Compare the more equivocal Cassese, *Self-Determination* (n 13) 152–153, 155–158.

64 Baxi (n 11) 7–10.

65 This is implied in Paust, 'International Law, Dignity, Democracy' (n 7) 8; Mégret, 'International Law and Peoples' Resistance' (n 35) 3–4.

66 See further discussion in Chapter 7, Sections 7.2.1.1, 7.2.1.2, 7.3.1.1, 7.3.2.1, and 7.3.2.2.

67 On the limitation of third-party assistance to situations of 'serious, massive and systematic violations' see UNESCO, 'Meeting of Experts: Final Report' (n 40) 225. See also further discussion in Chapter 6, Sections 6.2.1, 6.2.3, 6.3, 6.3.1.6, and 6.4.6.

68 See further discussion in Chapter 6, Section 6.2.3.

4.6 OBJECT AND PURPOSE: THE 'RIGHT TO RESIST WHY?'

Identifying the 'object and purpose' ultimately helps answer the reason 'why' element of the right 'to resist'. A legal 'object' is generally understood as 'something sought to be attained or accomplished; an end, goal or purpose'.[69] The 'object of a right' is 'the thing in respect of which a right exists; the subject matter of a right'.[70] As discussed in Chapter 3 and above, the right to resist is generally considered a secondary right, meaning that it exists in order to secure a primary right or rights, and therefore only activates or 'triggers' in the context of the primary right's violation. Thus, any given concept of a right to resist must be understood in the context of its particular 'object and purpose', which is the primary right/s that it is meant to secure.

Moreover, when conceptualized as a human right, the object and purpose of the right to resist must be consistent with the overall objects and purposes of human rights law. In short, an object and purpose involving oppression or exploitation of others is excludable.[71] Therefore, the various conceptions of the human right to resist may be classified as relating to a particular human rights 'object and purpose' or legal macro-concept. The term 'object and purpose' also takes on a particular meaning in relation to treaty interpretation.[72] It is therefore especially relevant to consideration of the theories of the right to resist as an unenumerated or implied right in several such instruments.[73]

4.6.1 *A Four-Fold Typology of Object and Purpose*

Four schools of thought as to the object and purpose of the right to resist emerge from the works of the major historical and contemporary theorists

[69] Garner (n 16) 491 – the definition of 'purpose' being not significantly different: 'an objective, goal, or end'. Ibid 573.

[70] Ibid 491; as against the 'subject of a right', being '[t]he owner of a right; the person in whom a legal right is vested'. Ibid 672.

[71] Honoré (n 14) 45–49.

[72] See Richard Gardiner, *Treaty Interpretation* (Oxford University Press 2008) 189–202. This general rule of interpretation, as later established in article 31 of the Vienna Convention on the Law of Treaties, has been relied on by the International Court of Justice since the 1950s. See *Reservations to the Convention on the Prevention and Punishment of Genocide* (Advisory Opinion) [1951] ICJ Rep 15, 21–24, 26–27, 29; Vienna Convention on the Law of Treaties (adopted 22 May 1969, entered into force 27 January 1980) 1155 UNTS 331, article 31. Despite this, Klabbers insists that 'object and purpose' remains 'indeterminate' as a concept and is an 'abstract category' that is intentionally 'open-textured' and 'flexible' and 'cannot have a single fixed meaning'. See Jan Klabbers, 'Some Problems Regarding the Object and Purpose of Treaties' (1997) 8 *Finnish Yearbook of International Law* 138, 139, 141.

[73] See further discussion in Chapter 7, Sections 7.2 and 7.3.2.

surveyed. The right to resist is conceptualized, in the narrowest terms, as related to the assertion of a particular fundamental right: as an exercise of either the right of self-defence,[74] or what we now call the right to self-determination.[75] In the broadest terms, it is conceptualized as a means of enforcement of 'higher' law – whether 'natural', constitutional, or

[74] For examples of the historic theory, see Hobbes and Grotius. On Hobbes's *Leviathan* 14–15, 21, *Elements of Law* 2.1.5, 1.17.2 and *De Cive* 2.18, 3.1.4 see Baumgold (n 26) 13–15, 24; Burgess (n 26); Dyzenhaus (n 26) 267–269; Steinberger (n 26) 857; Curran (n 26); Sreedhar (n 26). See also Grotius (n 63) Book I Chapter IV, VII 360. In contemporary theory see for example Paust, 'Aggression against Authority' (n 18) 283–284, 286–290, 298; Honoré (n 14) 46–48, 53–54; Tomuschat (n 14) 22, 29–30; David B Kopel, Paul Gallant, and Joanne D Eisen, 'Is Resisting Genocide a Human Right?' (2006) 81(4) *Notre Dame Law Review* 1275; David B Kopel, Paul Gallant, and Joanne D Eisen, 'The Human Right of Self-Defense' (2008) 22 *Brigham Young University Journal of Public Law* 43; Mégret, 'Beyond "Freedom Fighters"' (n 13); Mégret, 'Causes Worth Fighting For' (n 5) 176; Frédéric Mégret, 'Not "Lambs to the Slaughter": A Program for Resistance to Genocidal Law' in René Provost and Payam Akhavan (eds), *Confronting Genocide* (Springer 2011); Paust, 'International Law, Dignity, Democracy' (n 7) 2–5, 10 (fn 39), 12–13, 17–18; Jan Arno Hessbruegge, *Human Rights and Personal Self-Defense in International Law* (Oxford University Press 2017) 293–344; Brennan (n 30). Compare Annyssa Bellal and Louise Doswald-Beck, 'Evaluating the Use of Force during the Arab Spring' (2012) 14 *Yearbook of International Humanitarian Law* 3, 20–23; Jens David Ohlin, 'The Right to Exist and the Right to Resist' (SSRN 2014).

[75] For examples of the historic theory, see Locke (n 3); Vattel (n 27) Preliminaries [15], [16], [18]–[19], [21], [22] 74–77, Book I Chapter III [37] 96, Book II Chapter I 'Of the Common Duties of a Nation towards Others or of the Offices of Humanity between Nations' [7] 265, Book II Chapter IV 'Of the Right to Security, and the Effects of Sovereignty and Independence of Nations' [54]–[57] 289–292, Book II Chapter XII 'Of Treaties of Alliance and other Public Treaties' [196]–[197] 364–365, Book III Chapter XVIII 'Of Civil War' [293] 645–647, [296] 648–649. In contemporary theory see for example Quincy Wright, 'International Law and Civil Strife' (1959) 53 *Proceedings of the American Society of International Law at Its Annual Meeting* (1921–1969) 145, 147–149, 152; and clarification comment by Wright in 'Diverse Systems of World Public Order Today – Panel I: Security Problems among Diverse Systems of World Public Order, Discussion' (1959) 53 *Proceedings of the American Society of International Law at Its Annual Meeting* (1921–1969) 166, 167; Abi-Saab (n 13) 100–101; Röling (n 13) 152–154; Cassese, 'Human Rights and Humanitarian Law' (n 13) 947; Paust, 'Human Right to Armed Revolution' (n 7) 547–548, 556–559, 567–57; Paust, 'Aggression against Authority' (n 18) 286–290; Eide (n 23) 57–63; Tomuschat (n 14) 18, 20–21, 26–27, 29–30, 33; Honoré (n 14) 35–36; Falk and Weston, 'Relevance of International Law' (n 13) 155–157; Allan Rosas, 'Article 21' in Gudmunder Alfredsson and Asbjörn Eide (eds), *The Universal Declaration of Human Rights: A Common Standard of Achievement* (Martinus Nijhoff 1999) 432, 441–442, 449, 451; Allan Rosas, 'Internal Self-Determination' in Christian Tomuschat (ed), *Modern Law of Self-Determination* (Martinus Nijhoff 1993) 227, 239–249; Falk, 'Azmi Bishara, the Right of Resistance' (n 13) 27; Fatsah Ouguergouz, *The African Charter on Human and Peoples' Rights: A Comprehensive Agenda for Human Dignity and Sustainable Democracy in Africa* (Martinus Nijhoff 2003) 203–269; Mégret, 'Beyond "Freedom Fighters"' (n 13); Mégret, 'Causes Worth Fighting For' (n 5) 176; Higgins (n 13) 2, 231; Gargarella, 'Right of Resistance in Situations of Legal Alienation' (n 14) 6; Paust, 'International Law, Dignity, Democracy' (n 7) 2–4, 12–13, 17–18.

international – and any of the fundamental rights that law protects.[76] Less often it is even, somewhat counter-intuitively and perhaps less effectively, conceptualized as a means to ultimately achieve peace by enforcing a right to human security.[77] Since all four categories ultimately constitute varying emphases within the overall objective of enforcement of fundamental human rights, enforcement can be considered as a superordinate object and purpose, to which all other more specific object and purpose variants are subordinate.

The resulting four-fold teleological or purposive typology can have a bearing on what a particular theory or conceptualization of the right to resist assumes about the right's triggers and personal scope, as well as its appropriate scope of permissible means. These represent some of the conceptual

[76] For examples of the historic theory, see Aquinas, 'Commentary on the Sentences' (n 2) Book II, 'The Obedience Owed by Christians to the Secular Power and in particular to Tyrants' di 44, q 2, a 2; Thomas Aquinas, *De regno ad regum Cypri: On Kingship, To the King of Cyprus* (Gerard B Phelan tr, IT Eschmann rev edn, Pontifical Institute of Medieval Studies 1949) Book I ch 7 'How provision might be made that the king may not fall into tyranny'; Aquinas, *Summa Theologiae* (n 24) II-II q 40 'On War', a 1 'Is It Always Sinful to Wage War?', q 64 'On Homicide', a 7 'Is It Lawful for a Person to Kill Another in Self-Defense?', q 104 'On Obedience', a 5 'Are Subjects Obliged to Obey Their Superiors in All Things?' and a 6 'Are Christians Obliged to Obey Secular Authorities?', q 42 'On Rebellion', a 2 'Is Rebellion Always a Mortal Sin?'; *Vindiciae, Contra Tyrannos* (n 2) 155–156; Grotius (n 63); Vattel (n 27) Preliminaries [15], [16], [18]–[19], [21], [22] 74–77, Book I Chapter I [4] 83, Book I Chapter II [14]–[18], [21]–[22] 86–89, Book I Chapter III [26]–[30] 91–93, [32]–[34] 94–95, [37] 96, Book I Chapter IV [51] 105. In contemporary theory see for example Marcic (n 1) 87, 100, 104, 105, 111, 113; Falk, 'Adequacy of Contemporary Theories' (n 35) 249, 255–256; Falk, 'Janus Tormented' (n 13) 209; Falk, 'Nuremberg Defense' (n 58) 209–210; Falk, 'Introduction' (n 58); Cassese, 'Human Rights and Humanitarian Law' (n 13) 947; Eide (n 23) 39, 54; Boyle, *Defending Civil Resistance* (n 58) 347–350, 353–355; Lippmann (n 58) 350, 353, 361; Rosas, 'Internal Self-Determination' (n 75) 227, 232, 249; Kälin and Künzli (n 14) 46–78; Kittrie (n 58) 243–350; Mégret, 'Causes Worth Fighting For' (n 5) 180. Baxi conceives of the rights-holder as an enforcement 'agent of otonomic law'. Baxi (n 11) 5. For Honoré, the purpose of the right is to either enforce *or to change* higher law. See Honoré (n 14) 35–36, 38–39, 44–52.

[77] For an example of the historic theory, see Vattel (n 27) Book I Chapter II [14]–[18] 86–88, [21]–[22] 88–89, Book II Chapter IV 'Of the Right to Security, and the Effects of Sovereignty and Independence of Nations' [49]–[52] 288–289, [65]–[69] 296–297. In contemporary theory see for example Ouguergouz (n 75) 334–335, 345, 353; Gloria María Gallego García, 'El amplio derecho a la resistencia en la Declaración de Luarca: Objeción de conciencia, desobediencia civil y resistencia contra la opresión y la barbarie' in Carlos Villán Durán and Carmelo Faleh Pérez (eds), *Contribuciones regionales para una declaración universal del derecho humano a la paz* (Asociación Española para el Derecho Internacional de los Derechos Humanos 2010). Undoubtedly this conceptualization is more controversial. Note that Chemillier-Gendreau acknowledges only three categories: self-defence, self-determination, and human rights enforcement. See Monique Chemillier-Gendreau, 'Resistance, Right to, International Protection' in Rüdiger Wolfrum (ed), *Max Planck Encyclopedia of Public International Law* (Oxford University Press 2012) vol III: PA-SA 954–959, respectively 955–956 [9]–[12], 956 [13]–[15], 956–957 [16]–[17]. See also Honoré (n 14) 34–54.

continuities and divergences over the centuries that continue to provide not only fuel for scholarly debate but also diversity in legal expressions of the right.

Classifying the theories accordingly is also helpful to the extent that they act as indicators of potential conflicts of norms or conflicting rights associated with the particular object and purpose, which must be taken into account in any framing or interpreting of legal provisions, or in any assessment of claim. Though not all such apparent conflicts or 'divergences' can be entirely eliminated by applying the principle of harmonization and related interpretive methods, most can be thereby resolved.[78]

4.6.1.1 For Enforcement of 'Higher' Law and Fundamental Rights

The traditional conceptualization of the right to resist as a form of 'higher law' and rights enforcement has antecedents in the ancient and Middle Ages secular and theological theories of enforcement of natural law as well as customary law,[79] in the modern concept of social contract within which the right to resist is a form of contractual enforcement,[80] and in legal provisions from all three periods intended for the enforcement of constitutional law or its equivalent.[81] That is, it was originally conceptualized as a mechanism for the purpose of constraining power, and for challenging both absolute power and the otherwise unjust exercise of power.[82] In contemporary secular terms, the object and purpose of the right to resist may concern general self-help enforcement of specific 'higher' bodies of law that fulfill a similar

78 For detailed guidance see International Law Commission, 'Conclusions of the Work of the Study Group on the Fragmentation of International Law: Difficulties Arising from the Diversification and Expansion of International Law' (2006) [2006] *Yearbook of the International Law Commission* vol II, pt 2.

79 See Cicero (n 46) Book III, iv [19] 287, vi [27] 293–295, [30]–[31] 297, vi [32] 299; Aquinas, 'Commentary on the Sentences' (n 2) Book II, 'The Obedience Owed by Christians to the Secular Power and in Particular to Tyrants' di 44, q 2, a 2; Aquinas, *De regno ad regum Cypri* (n 76) Book I ch 7 'How Provision Might Be Made That the King May Not Fall into Tyranny'; Aquinas, *Summa Theologiae* (n 24) II–II q 40 'On War', a 1 'Is It Always Sinful to Wage War?', q 64 'On Homicide', a 7 'Is it Lawful for a Person to Kill Another in Self-Defense?', q 104 'On Obedience', a 5 'Are Subjects Obliged to Obey Their Superiors in All Things?' and a 6 'Are Christians Obliged to Obey Secular Authorities?', q 42 'On Rebellion', a 2 'Is Rebellion Always a Mortal Sin?'.

80 See *Vindiciae, Contra Tyrannos* (n 2) 68–78, 92–102, 104–124, 127, 129–137, 158, 172; Grotius (n 63) Book I Chapter IV, viii–xvii 372–380; Locke (n 3) Chapter XIV [168] 379–380, Chapter XIX [211]–[212] 406–408; Vattel (n 27) Book I Chapter I [4] 83, Book I Chapter II [14]–[18], [21]–[22] 86–89, Book I Chapter III [26]–[30] 91–93, [32]–[34] 94–95, [37] 96, Book I Chapter IV [51] 105.

81 See Chapter 5, Sections 5.2, 5.3, and 5.4.

82 Pribilla (n 14) 5, 7, 16, 19–20, 27, 30.

function – for example, 'fundamental' law such as constitutional law or international law. Otherwise, it may concern the enforcement of particular fundamental rights deriving from such 'higher' laws.[83]

Specifically locating the right to resist in a human rights law enforcement framework as to object and purpose deprives of their legal purchase certain manifestly specious interpretations or claims. For example, it would discount claims to a right to resist as enforcement appropriated for a theological or ideological 'higher purpose' – that is, 'to spread doctrine' or seize control as part of a proselytizing or 'civilizing' or similar mission – that could otherwise potentially furnish justifying rationales associated with human rights-violating 'crusades' such as European colonialism or other imperialism, Nazi conquest, Soviet expansionism, or the twenty-first-century jihad of Islamic State/Daesh.[84]

Identifying triggers and rights-holders – as well as potential normative barriers and conflicting rights – for the enforcement conceptualization of the right to resist is somewhat complicated because this may depend on the specific primary right concerned in each case. As to the correlative duty of assistance, some contemporary theories in this category would apply this exclusively to cases of enforcement of the 'highest' of 'higher' law. In the sphere of international law, this would mean distinguishing between violations of *jus cogens* norms or the 'most serious crimes of concern to the international community' in international criminal law and those constituting 'tortious' human rights violations.[85] However, this suggestion is not agreed by all.

4.6.1.2 For Self-Defence

The right to resist is often instead conceptualized more narrowly, as either analogous to, or deriving from, the right of individual and/or collective self-defence.[86] With its western root in the Roman customary legal principle *vim*

[83] See for example Murray (n 25) 307; Marcic (n 1) 87, 100, 104, 105, 111, 113.

[84] It is however recognized that the human rights law framework itself, as well as individual constitutional frameworks, are not immune from manipulation as part of a 'lawfare' strategy. This is a separate problem.

[85] See for example, Hessbruegge (n 74) 312–344.

[86] See for example Kopel et al, 'Human Right of Self-Defense' (n 74); Mégret, 'Causes Worth Fighting For' (n 5) 181; Mégret, 'Not "Lambs to the Slaughter"' (n 74); Hessbruegge (n 74) 293–244. See also Honoré (n 14) 46–48, 53–54; Georg Gesk, 'Right to Resistance and Terrorism – The Example of Germany' (2012) 13 *German Law Journal* 1075, 1092. Compare Bassiouni's theory, which draws on the self-defence analogy but is conceptualized as a broader fundamental human rights enforcement right. See Bassiouni (n 29) 254–257. Compare Ohlin (n 74).

vi repellere licet,[87] the similar common law principle,[88] and the 'generally recognized principle of international law',[89] this concept of the right to resist is consistent with the established principle of the self-defence exception regarding the use of force in contemporary domestic and international law and governed by associated trigger tests. For some, the right to self-defence is itself a secondary right vindicating the primary right to life and related primary rights, including the collective 'right to existence' which is the correlative of the prohibition on genocide.[90] Its personal scope includes individual as well as internal and external collective dimensions.

As a concept related to self-defence at domestic level, it is sometimes expressed as an individual and collective right to resist state violence or 'internal aggression' in the form of unlawful use of police powers such as arrest, search and seizure, and violations of the principle of minimum force.[91] This variant is particularly prominent in the US debates on the right to resist unlawful state force, conceptualized variously as a 'householder right', a 'right to bear arms',[92] and a right against corrupt, racist, or sexual-predator law enforcers.

At international level, the variant is a right to resist in collective self-defence or the right to resist to defend others from attack. It is associated with the use-of-force regime, and primarily conceptualized as a right to resist 'external aggression'. This is typified by the complementary customary legal concept of the levée en masse.[93] While this is as much related to self-determination as to direct self-defence, it strongly links the two – particularly where the issue is not merely defeating domination by another group but actual survival of communities as constituted, sometimes known as the 'right

87 See Andrew Lintott, *Violence in Republican Rome* (Oxford University Press 1999) 11, 23.

88 See Joyce Lee Malcolm, *To Keep and Bear Arms: The Origins of an Anglo-American Right* (Harvard University Press 1994) ix–xii, 1–15.

89 See Bin Cheng, *General Principles of Law as Applied by International Courts and Tribunals* (2006 edn, Cambridge University Press 1953) 25–32. Compare Hessbruegge (n 74); Jan Arno Hessbruegge, 'The Right to Life as the Jus ad Bellum of Non-International Armed Conflict (A Reply to Lieblich)', *JustSecurity* (27 October 2016).

90 See for example Tomuschat (n 14) 22, 29–30, 33; Kopel et al, 'Is Resisting Genocide a Human Right?' (n 74); Hessbruegge (n 74) 293–344. Compare Mégret, 'Beyond "Freedom Fighters"' (n 13); Mégret, 'Causes Worth Fighting For' (n 5) 181; Ohlin (n 74).

91 On the theory of 'internal aggression' in the form of 'oppression' as a violation of UN Charter articles 1(2), 1(3), 2(4), 55(c), and 56 and related instruments triggering a right to resist in self-defence, see Paust, 'Aggression against Authority' (n 18) 283–284, 286–290, 298; Paust, 'International Law, Dignity, Democracy' (n 7) 2–5, 10 (fn 39), 12–13, 17–18. However, compare the distinctions made in Hessbruegge (n 74) 301–312 and 312–344.

92 See for example, Kopel et al, 'Human Right of Self-Defense' (n 74); Malcolm (n 88) in general; Brennan (n 30). See further discussion in Chapter 5, Section 5.4.1.

93 See Mégret, 'Causes Worth Fighting For' (n 5) 178. See further discussion in Chapter 6, Section 6.6.2.

to exist'.[94] What has become known as the 'Nuremberg obligation', or the right to resist in defence of others, is also related to this conceptualization.[95]

The international concept of the right to resist has a strong nexus with sovereignty and anti-intervention norms.[96] Conversely, however, some situate it within the human security framework, or alongside the 'responsibility to protect', as a basis for lawful multilateral intervention when undertaken with United Nations Security Council authorization. What is not necessarily clear is the extent to which, and the point at which, the concept of the right to resist converges with or diverges from these norms.[97]

Within the international human rights law framework, the right to resist in individual and collective self-defence relates primarily but not exclusively to the right to life.[98] It may also relate to the right to bodily integrity, hence the right to freedom from torture, and cruel, inhuman, and degrading treatment. It may even relate to certain economic, social, and cultural rights in extreme cases where their denial constitutes a threat to individuals and groups.[99] Given the international criminal prohibitions against such acts, there may be a correlated customary right to resist genocide,[100] and a customary right to resist

94 Compare Kopel et al, 'Is Resisting Genocide a Human Right' (n 74); Ohlin (n 74); Hessbruegge (n 74) 325–343.

95 See Falk, 'Nuremberg Defense' (n 58); Falk, 'Introduction' (n 58); Falk, 'Telford Taylor and the Legacy of Nuremberg' (n 58) 698–699, 717–718; Boyle, *Defending Civil Resistance* (n 58); Lippman (n 58) 359, 364–372; Lippman (n 59). Compare Dannenbaum (n 59); Tom Dannenbaum, 'The Criminalization of Aggression and Soldiers' Rights' (2018) 29(3) *European Journal of International Law* 859. On the term 'Nuremberg obligation' or 'Nuremberg privilege' as preferable over 'Nuremberg defence', since the latter term is also used to describe the archaic defence of 'superior orders', see Boyle, *Protesting Power* (n 58) 46–47, 62. On the Nuremberg Principles as valuable for encoding a right-duty to resist, but of questionable viability as a criminal defence, see Kittrie (n 58) 265–266, 274–276, 320–321. See further discussion in Chapter 6, Section 6.5.

96 See Quincy Wright, 'Recognition and Self-Determination' (1954) 48 (22–24 April 1954) *Proceedings of the American Society of International Law at Its Annual Meeting* (1921–1969) 23, 26–27; Wright, 'International Law and Civil Strife' (n 75) 147–152; Quincy Wright, 'United States Intervention in the Lebanon' (1959) 53 *American Journal of International Law* 112, 121–124; Quincy Wright, 'Subversive Intervention' (1960) 54 *American Journal of International Law* 521, 529–530; Wright, 'Intervention and Cuba' (n 53) 3–11; Wright, 'Goa Incident' (n 62) 617–618, 628; Falk, 'Janus Tormented' (n 13) 207, 219–220; Falk, 'Nuremberg Defense' (n 58) 225. See further discussion in Chapter 6, Sections 6.2, 6.3, and 6.3.1.6.

97 See further discussion below in Section 4.6.1.3 and in Chapter 6, Sections 6.2, 6.3, and 6.3.1.6.

98 See Hessbruegge (n 74) 293–344.

99 See for example Gargarella, 'Right of Resistance in Situations of Severe Deprivation' (n 14) 359–360, 368–370, 372.

100 See for example Tomuschat (n 14) 22, 29–30, 33; Kopel et al, 'Is Resisting Genocide a Human Right?' (n 74). See also Mégret, 'Beyond "Freedom Fighters"' (n 13); Mégret, 'Causes Worth Fighting For' (n 5) 181; Mégret, 'Not "Lambs to the Slaughter"' (n 74). Compare Hessbruegge

war crimes and crimes against humanity, analogous to or derived from the right to resist in self-defence.[101] In such cases the third-party 'assist or do not obstruct' obligation at international level becomes an aspect of the duty to prevent mass atrocities, whether as a deterrent or as a remedy.[102] All of these are indeed contemporary 'just war' or *jus ad bellum* concepts.[103]

A number of potential normative barriers and conflicting rights are associated with the right to resist for self-defence. For example, it may interfere with other state obligations, including to protect the human rights of others from harm. It has obvious implications for the exceptions permitted the state under the derogation regimes in the major human rights treaties – that is, it could conflict with state claims to necessity for a legitimate purpose. The notion of third states providing aid on behalf of a besieged community, against the will of the state involved, raises a prima facie conflict with the fundamental *jus cogens* rule of non-intervention based on the principle of state sovereignty. However, as Ouguergouz argues, these are apparent conflicts, not inherent conflicts. There is also potential for compatibility if the latter norms and rights are interpreted in light of the former,[104] or are otherwise interpreted in an integrated way.[105]

4.6.1.3 For Self-Determination

Another common contemporary conceptualization of the right to resist is that it arises from, and is for the purpose of enforcing, the collective right of political and economic 'self-determination'.[106] To an extent, clarification

(n 74) 325–343. See further discussions in Chapter 6, Sections 6.3.1.3 and 6.5 and Chapter 7, Section 7.4.1 and implications for discussions in Chapter 7, Sections 7.2, 7.3.1.1, 7.3.1.2, and 7.3.2.

[101] For example, as implied in Paust, 'Political Oppression' (n 14); Paust, 'Aggression against Authority' (n 18). See also Mégret, 'Beyond "Freedom Fighters"' (n 13); Mégret, 'Causes Worth Fighting For' (n 5) 181. Compare Kopel et al, 'Is Resisting Genocide a Human Right?' (n 74); Kopel et al, 'Human Right of Self-Defense' (n 74); Ohlin (n 74); Hessbruegge (n 74) 312–344. See further discussions in Chapter 6, Sections 6.3 and 6.5 and Chapter 7, Section 7.4.1 and implications for discussions in Chapter 7, Sections 7.2, 7.3.1.1, 7.3.1.2, and 7.3.2.

[102] See for example Mégret, 'Not "Lambs to the Slaughter"' (n 74).

[103] See also Eliav Lieblich, 'Internal Jus Ad Bellum' (2016) 67 *Hastings Law Journal* 687; Anthony Dworkin, 'Individual, Not Collective: Justifying the Resort to Force against Members of Non-State Armed Groups' (2017) 93 *International Law Studies* 477; Tom Dannenbaum, 'War Crimes and Just War Theory' in Kimberly K Ferzan and Larry Alexander (eds), *The Palgrave Handbook of Applied Ethics and Criminal Law* (Palgrave Macmillan 2019).

[104] Ouguergouz (n 75) 334–335, 345, 353.

[105] This has implications for further discussions in Chapter 6, Sections 6.2–6.5 and Chapter 7, Sections 7.2 and 7.3.

[106] See Wright, 'International Law and Civil Strife' (n 75) 147–149, 152; Wright, 'Diverse Systems of World Public Order Today' (n 75) 166, 167. See also Abi-Saab (n 13) 98–102; Röling (n 13) 152–154; Gorelick (n 13) 71–93; Eide (n 23) 57–63; Shivji (n 20) 72–87; Falk and

regarding the triggers and personal scope of this variant of the right to resist concept depends on the conceptual status of the right to self-determination itself, as the primary right. However, defining the right to self-determination in contemporary legal terms is even more complicated than defining the right to self-defence, involving a paradox that although it is recognized as a right in international treaty provisions, and has been affirmed as such also by the International Court of Justice, '[n]o one is very clear as to what it means, at least outside the colonial context'.[107] Notwithstanding this difficulty, it is generally agreed that the right to resist in the exercise of self-determination has internal and external dimensions corresponding to the bifurcated nature of the primary right.[108]

The external dimension of the right to resist for self-determination is comparatively settled and uncontested, involving the enforcement of rights to freedom from foreign invasion and occupation or colonization, and other intervention or exploitation.[109] The internal dimension of the right to resist for self-determination is less settled and more contested.[110] Firstly, it involves enforcement of the right to constitute or reconstitute a political and economic system, including the right to amend a constitution or adopt a new one.[111] Secondly, it can involve enforcement of the full spectrum of rights to political participation. Such primary rights are not limited to elections and referenda but include other citizen-initiated mechanisms to prompt policy changes and

Weston, 'Relevance of International Law' (n 13) 155–157; Falk, 'Azmi Bishara, the Right of Resistance' (n 13) 27; Ouguergouz (n 75) 261–269; Tomuschat (n 14) 18, 20–21, 26–27, 29–30, 33; Rosas, 'Internal Self-Determination' (n 75) 227, 239–249; Mégret, 'Beyond "Freedom Fighters"' (n 13); Mégret, 'Causes Worth Fighting For' (n 5) 176; Higgins (n 13) 2, 231.

107 James Crawford, 'The Right of Self-Determination in International Law: Its Development and Future' in Philip Alston (ed), *Peoples' Rights* (Oxford University Press 2001) 7, 10, 37–39. Compare Rosas, 'Internal Self-Determination' (n 75). See further discussions in Chapter 6, Sections 6.2.3 and 6.3 and Chapter 7, Sections 7.2.1, 7.3.1.1, and 7.3.1.2.

108 See the Lockean theory. Locke (n 3) Chapter XVI 'Of Conquest' [175]–[196] 384–397, Chapter XVII 'Of Usurpation' [197]–[198] 397–398, Chapter XVIII 'Of Tyranny' [199]–[210] 398–405.

109 See for example Cassese, 'Human Rights and Humanitarian Law' (n 13) 947. See further discussion in Chapter 6, Sections 6.2.3 and 6.3 and Chapter 7, Section 7.3.1.

110 See for example ibid 949, yet compare ibid 950–958; Rosas, 'Internal Self-Determination' (n 75); Cassese, *Self-Determination* (n 13) 52–55, 124–126, 126–133, 346–351; Kalana Senaratne, *Internal Self-Determination in International Law: History, Theory, and Practice* (Cambridge University Press 2021). See further discussion in Chapter 6, Sections 6.2.3, 6.3, and 6.4 and Chapter 7, Sections 7.2.1 and 7.3.1.1.

111 Soviet theory also used this conception of the right to resist in order to change specific underlying oppressive systems, to support the assertion of a right to resist capitalism and colonialism, and pledge an interventionist policy in pursuit of socialist internationalism. See for example Lenin (n 62) 64ff.

systemic reforms, free from unwarranted interference or suppression.[112] In addition, recent developments recognizing the human rights of indigenous peoples have the potential to significantly change understanding of the minority right to resist in exercise of internal self-determination, where this is unrelated to demands for statehood.[113]

Increasingly relevant but also controversial is the legally recognized but still under-developed and under-applied concept of internal and external economic self-determination. It would be particularly important to determine what a consequent right to resist in the exercise of that right might imply regarding 'neo-colonial resource exploitation', resource conflicts between indigenous and non-indigenous populations, and the right of populations to decide economic and related policy free of corporate interference.[114] Indeed, a further concept of salience in the twenty-first century may be derived from the right to self-determination and begs for further development: the right to resist plutocracy and kleptocracy.

The potential normative barriers and conflicting rights in relation to this conceptual variant are similar to those described above in relation to the right to resist in self-defence. The main additional conflict relates to the customary legal principle of 'territoriality', or state right to territorial integrity, in the case of those claiming exercise of the right on behalf of a minority 'people' rather than a majority. Such may prove more challenging but not impossible to harmonize using Ouguergouz's method, as shown in Chapter 7.

4.6.1.4 For Peace: That is, 'Positive Peace' or 'Human Security'

The fourth main contemporary object and purpose conceptualization of the right to resist is that it arises from, and is a means to enforce, the human right to 'peace'.[115] Yet the very existence of something called a 'right to peace' is itself not fully agreed.[116] Even less so is its content, never mind its relation to the right to resist. The concept is generally more contested than the right to self-determination which, by comparison, is widely recognized and accepted.

[112] Compare Paust, 'Aggression against Authority' (n 18) 302; Rosas, 'Internal Self-Determination' (n 75) 230, 232, 249. For more detail on the probable content of such rights, see Steiner (n 7); Franck (n 7); Cassese, *Self-Determination* (n 13) 52–55, 346–348.

[113] See further discussion in Chapter 6, Sections 6.3 and 6.4 and Chapter 7, Sections 7.2.1, 7.3.1.1, and 7.3.2.

[114] Compare the proposal for recognition of a right to resist 'economic exploitation' in Röling (n 13) 158–161. Suggesting that a right to resist economic, social, and cultural rights violations would only apply in 'exceptional circumstances' see Tomuschat (n 14) 25.

[115] See for example Ouguergouz (n 75) 334–335, 345, 353; Gallego García (n 77).

[116] See further discussion in Chapter 7, Section 7.4.

This makes it difficult to clarify not only the triggers and personal scope of the right to resist associated with the right to peace, but also the material scope of permissible means.[117]

While this conception of the right to resist is not without potential contradictions, neither is it necessarily illogical. Its inclusion as a right subordinate to the superordinate right to peace relates to the concept of 'positive peace', with its emphasis on creating conducive conditions by eliminating both physical and structural violence.[118] This idea is crucial to understanding how to reconcile the otherwise seemingly antithetical right to resist, given that under certain conditions it may involve the use of forceful means. That is because the elimination of structural violence is the real precondition without which peace cannot exist or last. It recognizes that, without the right to resist as both a deterrent and a safeguard, there is little hope of peace becoming 'perpetual', even if a population is temporarily pacified. According to this idea, exercising the right to resist is not axiomatically a barrier and, under certain circumstances, can act as a necessary accelerant towards peace.

Obviously, traditional state-centric notions of security cannot accommodate this conception. It belongs instead within the alternative paradigm of 'human security', in which the security of individuals and peoples is paramount and state security is secondary, or may in some instances even be contrary to this objective.[119] In such cases the latter must be sacrificed to the former. In this way, the right to resist is conceptualized as a means of protecting and fulfilling the right to peace either by its use in conflict prevention through deterrence, in prevention of conflict escalation towards atrocities, or in the restoration of peace as an outcome of the exercise of the right. This proceeds from and reflects the understanding set out in the preamble of the Universal Declaration of Human Rights, that human rights are both a prerequisite to and a consequence of peace.[120] In its preventative form, the right to resist is a deterrent against the destabilizing abuse of power by the state which often precedes conflict. In its restorative form, the right to resist is a self-help mechanism for removing a human rights-abusing regime and establishing a more peaceful equilibrium, when other methods fail.

117 See discussion of material scope below, Section 4.7.

118 In contrast to 'negative peace' meaning simply the absence of war, traditionally associated with orthodox concepts of state security and international security. See for example Gallego García (n 77).

119 See ibid. On the proposed relationship between the right to peace and human security, see also Patrick Hayden, 'Constraining War: Human Security and the Human Right to Peace' (2004) 6 *Human Rights Review* 35.

120 See further discussion in Chapter 6, Section 6.4 and Chapter 7, Section 7.4.

The right to resist in pursuit of positive peace and human security shares the common potential normative barriers and conflicting rights described above. In addition, at a most basic level, it may represent an interference with the right of others to peace. Human security considerations may also, in some instances, constitute a valid source of discretionary, prudential self-limitation on the exercise of the right, where attendant human security risks – for example, those arising from state failure – outweigh human security gains.[121] Indeed, one interpretation of the human security doctrine leads to a conclusion that the state should maintain a monopoly on the use of force in order to prevent state failure, in direct contradiction of the human right to resist. The assertion that human security 'does not entail the threat or the use of force or coercive measures' and 'does not replace State security' apparently provides corroboration.[122] On the other hand, 'empowerment' is an established 'key pillar' of human security, recognizing that individuals can 'act on their own behalf and on behalf of others, to ensure their own security' and 'stand up when their rights, and the rights of others, are violated'.[123] This embrace of individual agency would seem at least potentially consistent with the human right to resist for human security, or peace. Admittedly, however, interpretations of this doctrine remain somewhat unsettled and the relationship between the two concepts is not without tensions requiring further exploration and clarification.[124]

The right to resist conceptualized with the right to peace as its primary object and purpose is probably the least developed, least successful, and least entrenched theory of the right to date.[125] Though the idea holds a certain

[121] See discussion of prudential limitations related to material scope below, Section 4.7.

[122] UN General Assembly 'Follow-Up to Paragraph 143 on Human Security of the 2005 World Summit Outcome' UNGA Res 66/290 (25 October 2012) [3].

[123] Ibid; Commission on Human Security, *Human Security Now: Protecting and Empowering People* (Commission on Human Security 2003) 11–12. On 'Narrow–Broad approaches' to the doctrine, and the embrace of individual agency in providing for one's own security, see, respectively, Shahrbanou Tadjbakhsh, 'In Defense of the Broad View of Human Security' in Mary Martin and Taylor Owen (eds), *Routledge Handbook of Human Security* (Routledge 2014); Des Gasper, 'Human Security: From Definitions to Investigating a Discourse' in Mary Martin and Taylor Owen (eds), *Routledge Handbook of Human Security* (Routledge 2014).

[124] Compare, for example, apparently opposing views in Rhoda E Howard-Hassman, 'Human Security: Undermining Human Rights?' (2012) 34(1) *Human Rights Quarterly* 88; the narrower view of what constitutes empowerment in Sadako Ogato and Johan Cels, 'Human Security? Protecting and Empowering the People' (2003) 9(3) *Global Governance* 273.

[125] Indeed, most approaches to the right to peace and to human security tend to substitute the responsibility to protect for the right to resist. See for example Natalie Oman, 'Hannah Arendt's "Right to Have Rights": A Philosophical Context for Human Security' (2010) 9(3) *Journal of Human Rights* 279; Robert J Hanlon and Kenneth Christie, *Freedom from Fear,*

appeal and has been formally advanced,[126] ultimately one struggles to find a persuasive argument in its favour over the other three categories.

4.7 MATERIAL SCOPE OF APPLICATION: THE 'RIGHT TO RESIST HOW?'

The final element of the legal content of the human right to resist concept concerns the material scope of its application. This pertains to the types of otherwise unlawful conduct to which the right applies as a rule of exception. In other words, in general terms, it concerns permissible means arising from the right, once the primary and secondary trigger conditions have been met and where the object and purpose is compatible with human rights.

4.7.1 *Three Competing Approaches to Permissible Means*

It is worth emphasizing that, as demonstrated by the evidence from the historical theory, the term 'resistance' is not about use of force per se, but rather about defiance – of the law, for example. Hence resistance may involve use of force, or it may not. Therefore, the 'right to resist' should not be understood reductively as the 'right to use force'.

In the contemporary period debate has emerged as to permissible means covered under the right to resist. Three approaches may be identified. Many maintain the historical inclusive means approach, described as 'traditional'.[127] Others, however, take a narrower approach. Some would limit what is 'resistance' to forceful means,[128] occasionally on the possibly inaccurate premise that all peaceful means are already covered by ordinary political rights.[129]

Freedom from Want: An Introduction to Human Security (University of Toronto Press 2016) 133–158.

[126] This was the underlying premise of the case made by those promoting the inclusion of the right to resist in the draft UN Declaration on the Right to Peace. See further discussion in Chapter 7, Section 7.4.

[127] Kaufmann (n 9) 574–575. See also for example Pribilla (n 14) 7, 9–10, 21–22; Marcic (n 1) 110–111; Baxi (n 11) 5–6, 8; Eide (n 23) 40, 53–54; Tomuschat (n 14) 25–27; UNESCO, 'Meeting of Experts: Final Report' (n 40) 222–223, 226; Falk, 'Azmi Bishara, the Right of Resistance' (n 13) 26–28. Gargarella later modified his position to an inclusive one. Compare Gargarella, 'Right of Resistance in Situations of Legal Alienation' (n 14) 1–3; Gargarella, 'Right of Resistance in Situations of Severe Deprivation' (n 14) 366–367, 370. See also Mégret, 'Causes Worth Fighting For' (n 5); Mégret, 'Civil Disobedience and International Law' (n 35); Mégret, 'Not "Lambs to the Slaughter"' (n 74). Compare Delmas (n 30).

[128] For example Cassese, 'Human Rights and Humanitarian Law' (n 13) 946–950.

[129] See further discussion of treaty-based limitations on the use of peaceful means under provisions for ordinary political rights in Chapter 7, Sections 7.2.1.2, 7.2.1.3, 7.3.1.1, and 7.3.2.

Still others would limit what is 'lawful resistance' to the use of peaceful means also known in contemporary terms as 'civil disobedience' or 'civil resistance' but historically specified as a 'right of disobedience'.[130] Arguably, a concept that is at least potentially inclusive of the full spectrum of illegal action from peaceful to forceful means is justified, among other reasons because this better corresponds to how it works in the real world where escalation is usually incremental and often reactive. Moreover, unnecessary exclusive focus on forceful or non-forceful means can lead to conceptual distortions.

This study suggests that the *lex generalis* of ordinary political human rights provides a useful inverse indicator as to content of this element. That is, the 'right to resist' covers the use of non-forceful and forceful means that would not be permitted, and would be considered legitimately unlawful, under ordinary conditions in which the *lex generalis* pertains – provided other elements and conditions are met, and applicable *lex specialis* limitations discussed below are observed.

4.7.2 *Proportionality Limitations*

More promising than absolute restrictions on means is the generally accepted traditional 'proportionality' limitation on the right to resist.[131] Proportionality is another concept that has domestic and human rights law applications, as well as both *jus ad bellum* and *jus in bello* applications in international law.[132] As with the principle of necessity as a secondary trigger condition, the *jus ad bellum* and human rights law applications of proportionality are the most relevant to consideration of the right to resist in the first instance. While *jus in bello* proportionality may also become relevant to regulating the exercise of the right to resist,[133] this is again a secondary legal question.

[130] For example Schwarz (n 52) 129–131, 133; Boyle et al, 'Citizen Initiatives under International Law' (n 59) 569; Lippman (n 58) 350, 354, 361. Compare Bedau's more contingent characterization: not all civil disobedience involves a 'right to disobey' that is ultimately 'lawful' in the sense of higher law. See Hugo Adam Bedau, 'On Civil Disobedience' (1961) 58 (21) *Journal of Philosophy* 653, 653–656, 660 (fn 12), 663.

[131] See the original application of this concept to the right to resist in Aquinas, *Summa Theologiae* (n 24) II-II q 64 'On Homicide', a 7 'Is It Lawful for a Person to Kill Another in Self-Defense?' This is because 'breaches of [the state] duty [of protection of its citizens] can be of various degrees of gravity which in turn can justify recourse to different remedies'. See also the extended discussion of proportionality considerations as applied to the various categories of potential rights-holders in Eide (n 23) 54–56, 57–63; UNESCO, 'Meeting of Experts: Final Report' (n 40) 222–223; Honoré (n 14) 53.

[132] See Michael Newton and Larry May, *Proportionality in International Law* (Oxford University Press 2014) 2–3, 13, 19, 33, 60.

[133] See further discussion in Chapter 6, Sections 6.3.1.5, 6.4.6, 6.5, and 6.6.2.

Weinkauff succinctly sets the proportionality limitation as permitting 'only those means which promise success with a minimum infringement of ordinary legality'.[134] He extends this so far as to include tyrannicide in appropriate situations of extremity, which 'will not have the legal character of murder but rather that of the lawful execution of a criminal'.[135] However, as further discussed below, assessment of the contemporary legality of tyrannicide is not straightforward.[136]

When considering the possibility of resistance with force, Pribilla imposes a proportionality limitation such that '[o]nly so much force should be exerted as is required to gain the desired end', together with an additional public interest limitation also familiar from the traditional theory, stipulating that such resistance cannot be undertaken for 'private advantage' or 'to satisfy personal revenge or envy' but rather exclusively 'for the general good'.[137] However, as a rider or companion limitation attached to proportionality, the 'public interest' concept may not be sufficiently precise compared with the other human rights object and purpose categories outlined above.

Bassiouni's approach probably better captures proportionality as applied to the contemporary human right to resist. It specifies those means limited to, and not extending beyond, what are required for remedy consisting in ending the violations, that follow the principle of minimum force, and do not themselves include violations of fundamental rights,[138] or international crimes.[139]

4.7.3 *Applicable Limitations in International Human Rights Law and International Criminal Law*

The right to resist is sometimes misrepresented as an absolute right, to be exercised 'by any means necessary' without limitations – of proportionality or

[134] Guenter Lewy, 'Resistance to Tyranny: Treason, Right or Duty?' (1960) 13(3) *Western Political Quarterly* 581, 583 (fn 12). This is his synoptic translation of Hermann Weinkauff, 'Die Militäropposition gegen Hitler und das Widerstandsrecht' ['The Military Opposition against Hitler and the Right of Resistance'] in *Die Vollmacht des Gewissens* ['The Power of Conscience'] 149.

[135] Ibid. See also Schwarz (n 52) 128.

[136] It is conceded more rarely than the right to resist, according to Jászi and Lewis (n 5) 'Preface' vi. Yet compare Kaufmann (n 9) 574–576.

[137] Pribilla (n 14) 22. For Honoré, the use of force is only justified if the relevant breach is 'so serious and sustained' that it 'dissolves legal bonds'. Honoré (n 14) 53–54.

[138] Bassiouni (n 29) 256–257.

[139] Ibid 241–243. Gargarella prefers imposing the 'least harm' as a limitation supplementary to proportionality. See Gargarella, 'Right of Resistance in Situations of Severe Deprivation' (n 14) 371–372. Proportionality debates in the contemporary just war literature from ethics and political philosophy supply other tests for permissibility/impermissibility, possibly applicable in modified form, such as the 'ours=theirs assessment' in Adil Ahmad Haque, 'Proportionality' in *Law and Morality at War* (Oxford University Press 2017) 190.

otherwise. It is difficult to take that position if the right to resist is conceptualized as a 'human right'. Therefore, most contemporary theorists recognize that a human right to resist must be situated within certain applicable limitations and conditions imposed by international human rights law and international criminal law.[140] That is, there cannot be a human right that makes an exception for torture or genocide in the name of resistance, for example. This would fall afoul of *jus cogens* prohibitions, to which there are no exceptions, and would therefore be impossible to prove lawful in public international law. Nevertheless, the distortion does serve to highlight that, within reasonable limitations, the right to resist is in fact about taking certain actions that would otherwise be considered unlawful, and thus by definition will involve going beyond the much stricter limitations imposed under the *lex generalis* of ordinary political rights under international human rights law.

That the right to resist authorizes necessary and proportionate means within certain limitations, but not any and all means, is illustrated by the complex contemporary status of tyrannicide.[141] In today's terms, to effectively argue for a right of assassination sounds perilously close to a right of extrajudicial execution that would generally be incompatible with a human rights framework. Indeed, the entire body of international criminal law exists as an alternative to the self-help doctrine of tyrannicide, to bring such individuals to justice by trial in a court of law – where possible. Under this law, removing the 'tyrant' from power and prosecuting them is the objective, whereas extrajudicial killing is itself made potentially subject to prosecution. That is not to say that in the course of lawful resistance it would be unlawful to aim to remove a tyrant from power using necessary and proportionate means and

[140] See for example Bassiouni (n 15) xii–xiv, xvi–xviii, xxi; Eide (n 23) 34–35, 39, 54–55; UNESCO, 'Meeting of Experts: Final Report' (n 40) 222–223, 226; Bielefeldt (n 6) 1104; Paust, 'International Law, Dignity, Democracy' (n 7) 13–14. See further discussion in Chapter 6, Sections 6.3.1.5, 6.4.6, and 6.5 and Chapter 7, Sections 7.2.1.1, 7.2.2, 7.2.3, 7.3.1.1, and 7.3.2. Detailed consideration of these limitations is beyond the scope of this study but amply covered by other specialist scholars, such as Andrew Clapham, *Human Rights Obligations of Non-State Actors* (Oxford University Press 2006) 271–298; Jo Hyeran, *Compliant Rebels: Rebel Groups and International Law in World Politics* (Cambridge University Press 2015); Tilman Rodenhäuser, *Organizing Rebellion: Non-State Armed Groups under International Humanitarian Law, Human Rights Law, and International Criminal Law* (Oxford University Press 2018). See also Lieblich (n 103); Dannenbaum (n 103).

[141] See Shannon Brincat, 'The Legal Philosophy of Internationally Assisted Tyrannicide' (2009) 34 *Australian Journal of Legal Philosophy* 151; Jean D'Aspremont, 'Le tyrannicide en droit international' in Christian Tomuschat, Evelyne Lagrange, and Stefan Oeter (eds), *The Right to Life* (Brill 2010) 288–289, 308–312. On tyrannicide as 'generally impermissible' outside exceptional circumstances meeting necessity and proportionality tests, and where it also does not constitute 'aggression' or 'terrorism', see Paust, 'Aggression against Authority' (n 18) 298–299.

otherwise adhering to the general prohibitions in international human rights law and international criminal law.[142] Indeed, there are foreseeable circumstances in which there is no realistic possibility of capture and trial, in which case tyrannicide could conceivably be assessed as justifiable or even lawful.[143] Without consideration of specific context, however, it is difficult and inadvisable to make categorical statements about the contemporary lawfulness or unlawfulness of actions amounting to tyrannicide. The important conclusion is that tyrannicide would no longer be considered lawful unless it was the result of actions otherwise compliant with international criminal law and international human rights law. Similarly, the right to resist exercised in other guises would also be held to these general standards, as applicable in the particular circumstances.

Cassese is emphatic that there must be no confusion on the important conceptual point of limitations. A valid right to resist can act as a human rights exception to the state monopoly on lawful use of force, and can be additional to the self-defence exception. However, it is not an exception to the prohibitions on genocide, crimes against humanity, and war crimes – or the use of certain specific means most commonly agreed as 'terrorist' – in international law.[144]

4.7.4 *'Expedience' or 'Prudence' as Discretionary Limitations*

Lastly, the Thomasian doctrine of double-effect,[145] reiterated in one form or another in the historical theories, is sometimes also included in contemporary theories of the right to resist as a form of discretionary limitation on means. This can take the form of an 'expedience' limitation restricting the right's exercise to situations in which there is a 'reasonable prospect of success', and a 'prudence' requirement so that 'nothing be undertaken which will increase

[142] Compare tyrannicide's characterization as not unlawful but also not 'lawful' or protected in Brincat (n 141); D'Aspremont (n 141).

[143] There is no consensus on this. Compare for example Brincat (n 141); D'Aspremont (n 141); Ohlin and May (n 37) on the duty of custody 235–258; implications of overall discussion in Christopher J Finlay, *Terrorism and the Right to Resist: A Theory of Just Revolutionary War* (Cambridge University Press 2015) 15–16, 219–285.

[144] See for example Cassese, 'Human Rights and Humanitarian Law' (n 13) 947–950, 958, in which he particularly emphasizes the applicability of the principle of distinction and absolute prohibition of 'indiscriminate' attacks on civilians, and inhuman and degrading treatment. See also Bassiouni (n 15) xii–xiv, xvi–xviii, xxi; Honoré (n 14) 54; Falk, 'Azmi Bishara, the Right of Resistance' (n 13) 26–28. With the exception of aggression, international criminal prohibitions apply to non-state as well as state actors. On the more controversial issue of what might be commonly agreed as 'terrorist' means, and their relation to the right to resist, see discussion in Chapter 6, Section 6.6.4. Compare the non-legal theory of Finlay (n 143) 3–8, 15–16.

[145] See Aquinas, *Summa Theologiae* (n 24) II-II q 64 'On Homicide', a 7 'Is It Lawful for a Person to Kill Another in Self-Defense?'

rather than diminish' wrongs.[146] This amounts to a plea for discretion, involving a moral or strategic choice to refrain from exercising a valid right if this cannot be done without inducing greater harm. Strictly speaking, however, these discretionary limitations do not work to disqualify an otherwise valid right to resist in the same way that the proportionality, human rights, and international criminal law limitations can.

4.8 CONCLUSION: AN ANALYTICAL FRAMEWORK TO IDENTIFY AND COMPARE ELEMENTS AND CONTENT

Taking all of the preceding into account, it would seem that the contemporary legal concept of the right to resist retains many traditional features, though in modified or updated form. At its most basic, it is a right – under certain conditions, for certain generally lawful purposes, and within certain constraints – to commit otherwise unlawful acts or use otherwise unlawful means. It is therefore a form of limited and conditional right to disobey the law. When conceptualized as a human right, this modifies that basic definition to suggest a right to resist human rights violations where no other effective remedy is available, in pursuit of objectives that are consistent with human rights – subject to certain human rights limitations on scope of action already imposed on non-state actors, in particular by international criminal law – using means beyond those permitted under the *lex generalis*. Within this general framework, and provided all the elements are met, the right can embrace a full spectrum of objectives from overthrow and replacement of a given political-constitutional, economic, and/or social order, to more modest objectives such as specific grievance redress. It can employ a broad spectrum of appropriate means from the peaceful to the forceful. It can be exercised on one's own behalf or on behalf of a group including a minority, or by a representative group, mass movement, or majority on behalf of a people as a whole.

Of course, looking at the theoretical legal concept of the right to resist or *lex ferenda* in isolation from its *lex lata* place in positive law can lead to distortions. Indeed, for centuries, the right to resist – or its *exceptio tyrannoctonos* antecedent – has not been just a theory or a purely moral doctrine without legal expression. For example, despite relatively little evidence of theory in ancient Athens, there is comparatively good evidence of the positive law. From the Middle Ages onward, there is evidence of theory and law in the form of both doctrine and express provisions. Adding the contemporaneous law illuminates the theory. This positive law of the right to resist will therefore be examined in Part II, providing evidence of how it compares with the

[146] See for example Pribilla (n 14) 21; Marcic (n 1) 112.

term usage and working definition proposed in Chapter 2, the general features as to nature and legal function identified in Chapter 3, and the content elements identified in the present chapter.

The Alstonian method, outlined in Chapter 1 and used here, yields a proposed analytical framework that may be equally applied to identify the content elements of individual theories as well as legal provisions and other recognitions, and also can be used for comparative analysis. It involves the identification of the:

- source of the right;
- primary and secondary trigger conditions;
- rights-holders;
- duty-bearers;
- object and purpose; and
- permissible means including applicable limitations.

This analytical framework likewise provides the basis for generating potentially appropriate general tests, as well as jurisdictionally specific tests, for assessing claims to a right to resist in its multiple contemporary modalities.

Examination of this type of evidence best answers the question of the right's status in law. Assessing the positive legal provisions and other recognitions both past and present will also help partially answer the question of sources – at least with respect to customary and constitutional law, treaty law, customary international law, and the possibility that the right to resist may constitute a general principle of law. It will shed further light on the question of enforceability of the right in any given instance. The positive law analysis can also help explore the question of the right's relationship to the rule of law – particularly whether it is integral or complementary and compatible but separate. Consideration of this material is essential for scholars in the twenty-first century, since sufficient positive sources are available for both individual and comparative analysis. Therefore, the following chapters in Part II will draw on the empirical *lex lata* evidence to chart the horizons of the right in contemporary law and map the contours of its landscape.

Is it ultimately correct to conclude, as Chemillier-Gendreau does in her encyclopedic entry on this subject, that 'the demand for a right of resistance has not received any sufficient formal response in either domestic or international law'?[147] Part II uses the Alstonian analytical framework established here and used in Part I to further examine this question of whether and to what extent the theories examined in Part I find adequate expression in law.

[147] Chemillier-Gendreau (n 77) 958 [24].

PART II

The Law

5

Domestic Provision in Constitutional Law

5.1 INTRODUCTION

The human right to resist hails from a legal tradition more than a thousand years old. It can now be found in nearly one in five constitutions, and in all main regions of the world.[1] Constitutional law is a crucial source of this right – historically, quantitatively, and as potentially enforceable domestic 'higher' law. Indeed, as the evidence in this chapter will show, it is no exaggeration to describe the right to resist as 'profoundly constitutional'.[2]

Even so, contemporary scholarship frequently ignores the constitutional or functionally equivalent provisions, and the few existing comparative studies are limited in various ways. The historical studies are period- and

[1] See Tom Ginsburg, Daniel Lansberg-Rodriguez, and Mila Versteeg, 'When to Overthrow Your Government: The Right to Resist in the World Constitutions' (2013) 60 *UCLA Law Review* 1184, 1217–1218.

[2] Shannonbrooke Murphy, 'Unique in International Human Rights Law: Article 20(2) and the Right to Resist in the African Charter on Human and Peoples' Rights' (2011) 11(2) *African Human Rights Law Journal* 465, 467. Similarly, see Roberto Gargarella, 'The Last Resort: The Right of Resistance in Situations of Legal Alienation' (2003) (Yale Law School SELA (Seminario en Latinoamérica de Teoría Constitucional y Política) Papers) 2, 4–6, 16; Roberto Gargarella, 'The Right of Resistance in Situations of Severe Deprivation' in Thomas Pogge (ed), *Freedom from Poverty as a Human Right: Who Owes What to the Very Poor?* (Oxford University Press and UNESCO 2007) 360–361, 365 (fn 10); Ginsburg et al (n 1) 1188. However, compare the more modest characterization of the constitutional right in Tony Honoré, 'The Right to Rebel' (1988) 8(1) *Oxford Journal of Legal Studies* 34, 49; David C Williams, 'The Constitutional Right to "Conservative" Revolution' (1997) 32 *Harvard Civil Rights-Civil Liberties Law Review* 413, 414.

region-specific.[3] Recent studies of the modern and contemporary law take a socio-legal approach, concentrating on establishing prevalence, or proposing predictors to explain the adoption of these ostensibly counterintuitive provisions.[4] Comparative analysis as to legal content, meaning, and value remains rudimentary. Yet, as the longest-standing source of the positive law, it has the potential to shed light on issues relevant to contemporary codification, interpretation, and application of this right – not only domestically but also at international level.

Because 'constitutional' law dates back to ancient times,[5] but formal written constitutions are largely a modern phenomenon,[6] some evidence of the ancient and Middle Ages antecedent or 'proto-right to resist' necessarily concerns unwritten constitutions or customary laws that bear on 'fundamental' matters but are 'constitutional' only in function rather than form.[7] A comprehensive comparison of all historical constitutional and 'quasi-constitutional' provisions, building on existing scholarship, would prove useful in the development of a more complete history of the evolution of this legal right,

[3] See for example comparative studies on the ancient or Middle Ages antecedents such as David A Teegarden, *Death to Tyrants! Ancient Greek Democracy and the Struggle against Tyranny* (Princeton University Press 2014); Fritz Kern, *Kingship and Law in the Middle Ages: The Divine Right of Kings and the Right of Resistance in the Early Middle Ages* (S Chrimes tr, Basil Blackwell 1939) 1–146.

[4] The leading study is Ginsburg et al (n 1), discussed in further detail in Section 5.5.

[5] Not only does constitutional law date back to ancient times, so does comparative constitutional study. See Rosalind Dixon and Tom Ginsburg, 'Introduction' in Rosalind Dixon and Tom Ginsburg (eds), *Research Handbook on Comparative Constitutional Law* (Edward Elgar 2011) 1; Michel Rosenfeld and András Sajó, 'Introduction' in Michel Rosenfeld and András Sajó (eds), *The Oxford Handbook of Comparative Constitutional Law* (Oxford University Press 2012) 3. See also Peter John Rhodes, A *Commentary on the Aristotelian Athenaion Politeia* (Clarendon Press 1981) 1–63; Andrew Lintott, *The Constitution of the Roman Republic* (Oxford University Press 1999) 1–8, 27–39; Adriaan Lanni and Adrian Vermeule, 'Constitutional Design in the Ancient World' (2012) 64 *Stanford Law Review* 907; Kern (n 3) 1–146; Martin Loughlin, *Foundations of Public Law* (Oxford University Press 2010) 1–13. Compare Dieter Grimm, 'Types of Constitutions' in Rosenfeld and Sajó (n 5) 100–105.

[6] See Vicki C Jackson and Mark Tushnet, 'Preface' in Vicki C Jackson and Mark Tushnet (eds), *Comparative Constitutional Law* (Foundation Press 1999) v; compare Dixon and Ginsburg (n 5) 2. As to the major legal features that distinguish modern 'constitutional' from other law, see the 'functional' and 'formal' characteristics suggested in Grimm (n 5) 103–115.

[7] Comparative constitutional studies take a variety of approaches to inclusion and exclusion criteria. Compare Jon Elster, 'Forces and Mechanisms in the Constitution-Making Process' (1995) 45 *Duke Law Journal* 364, 365–366; Zachary Elkins, Tom Ginsburg, and James Melton, *The Endurance of National Constitutions* (Cambridge University Press 2009) 36–40, 49; Dixon and Ginsburg (n 5) 4–5; David S Law and Mila Versteeg, 'The Evolution and Ideology of Global Constitutionalism' (2011) 99(5) *California Law Review* 1163, 1187–1188; Benedikt Goderis and Mila Versteeg, 'The Transnational Origins of Constitutions: Evidence from a Global Data Set on Constitutional Rights' (2013) (Tilburg University CentER Discussion Paper 2013-010) 19.

as would a more exhaustive study to establish prevalence in customary law and other ordinary domestic law provisions.[8] This chapter cannot fill such a large gap in the scholarship. Instead, it considers a sample of the more historically significant domestic constitutional or functionally equivalent provisions,[9] and all of the current provisions in overview. By applying the Part I findings and Chapter 4 analytical framework identifying legal features for comparative content analysis, it establishes a map of basic continuities and divergences over time. Section 5.2 examines the post-Solonian 'proto-right' in the Decree of Demophantos and Law of Eukrates of ancient Athens. Section 5.3 assesses the Magna Carta's 'proto-right' in the context of the broader Middle Ages pan-European phenomenon of similar provisions in customary fundamental law, coronation oaths as constitutional 'contracts', and early independence declarations. Section 5.4 considers the right to resist in modern foundational declarations and constitutional provisions including the American Declaration of Independence and United States Constitution, French Declaration of the Rights of Man and Citizen and French Constitution, and subsequent Latin American independence constitutions. Section 5.5 takes a more comprehensive approach, comparing the approximately forty current constitutional provisions on the right to resist identified by Ginsburg and colleagues, drawing on English translations of written constitutions from 1789 to present developed by Hein Online World Constitutions Illustrated and Oxford Constitutions of the World, coded by the Comparative Constitutions Project. It then briefly discusses their legal meaning and legal value.

5.2 PROVISION IN 'ANCIENT CONSTITUTIONS' OR EQUIVALENT LAW

A narrow 'proto-right to resist' was first codified in ancient 'constitutional' law as lawful tyrannicide, functionally an exception to the prohibition on homicide.

[8] For example, though it is potentially relevant to all civil law countries, establishing the customary Roman law basis of the 'proto-right' is highly complex due to the lack of primary evidence and because the Bartolist interpretation may be more legal fiction than fact. See Bartolus de Saxoferrato, *On Guelfs and Ghibbellines* (Jonathan Robinson tr, Creative Commons Attribution-Non-Commercial ShareAlike 3.0 Unreported License 2014 rev 1.1a) Book III 4–6; Bartolo de Saxoferrato, *On the Tyrant* (Jonathan Robinson tr, Creative Commons Attribution-Non-Commercial ShareAlike 3.0 Unreported License 2012 (rev 1.0a) 2016 (rev 1.2)); Hans Julius Wolff, *Roman Law: An Historical Introduction* (University of Oklahoma Press 1951) 189–190. Definitive treatment of this subject would be welcome, building on the evidence of lawful self-help measures directed against usurpation or other abuse of public authority gathered in the broader research works of Wilfried Nippel, *Public Order in Ancient Rome* (Cambridge University Press 1995); Andrew Lintott, *Violence in Republican Rome* (Oxford University Press 1999).

[9] In certain instances, acceptance as such is not universal but rather sufficiently widespread to warrant examination.

The Athenian tyrannicide laws were not unique in their time,[10] but they are among the earliest and comparatively good – inscription or stele – evidence available.[11] Their content is therefore worth considering in detail as a baseline against which to compare what followed as the right evolved in later periods.[12]

5.2.1 *Lawful Tyrannicide in Customary Law and the 'Solonian Constitution' of Athens (594 BCE)*

The ancient Athenian law of tyrannicide was one component of the broader tyranny law covering the substantive outlawing of tyranny, penalties, and procedures.[13] This was a law of the *polis* or public law,[14] the primary purpose of which was to deter or punish and remedy the unlawful usurpation of political power contrary to the *politeia* or constitution,[15] and later specifically

[10] See Teegarden (n 3) 57–84, 115–214, who documents similar laws in the city-states of Eretria, Eresos, Erythrai, and Ilion, influenced by the Athenian laws. See also Ilias Arnaotoglou, *Ancient Greek Laws: A Sourcebook* (Routledge 1998) 76.

[11] See Arnaotoglou (n 10) xv. See also in particular the photograph of the inscription of the Law of Eukrates reproduced in Teegarden (n 3) 107 figure 3.1.

[12] Of course, comparing and contrasting these with the legal provisions of later periods demands attention to specialists' cautions. Regarding assumptions about ancient Greek 'rights' concepts that were closer to 'quasi-rights' based on immunities, and on the legal value of the oath, see Josiah Ober, 'Law and Political Theory' in Michael Gagarin and David Cohen (eds), *Cambridge Companion to Ancient Greek Law* (Cambridge University Press 2005); David Carter, 'Could a Greek Oath Guarantee a Claim Right? Oaths, Contracts and the Structure of Obligation in Classical Athens' in Alan H Sommerstein and Judith Fletcher (eds), *Horkos: The Oath in Greek Society* (Bristol Phoenix Press 2007); Peter J Rhodes, 'Oaths in Political Life' in Sommerstein and Fletcher, *Horkos* (n 12). On the distinctive features of Athenian law including vagueness and flexibility, amateurism, and overlapping procedures, see SC Todd, *The Shape of Athenian Law* (Clarendon Press 1993) 3–70. On the prevalence of lawful self-help enforcement as linked to the participatory nature of the radical Athenian democracy in decision-making and prosecution-adjudication, and as intrinsic to, rather than representing a rupture from, the emerging concept of the rule of law, see David Cohen, 'Crime, Punishment and the Rule of Law in Classical Athens' in Gagarin and Cohen, *Cambridge Companion to Ancient Greek Law* (n 12). On the evolving concept and law of citizenship, and in particular the radical democratic concept of active participatory citizenship, see Cynthia Patterson, 'Athenian Citizenship Law' in Gagarin and Cohen, *Cambridge Companion to Ancient Greek Law* (n 12). All of these provide important context for noting the origins and similarities but also emphasizing and understanding the differences between the ancient and later legal provisions, particularly the contemporary provisions for the right to resist.

[13] See for example Douglas M MacDowell, *The Law in Classical Athens* (Cornell University Press 1978) 175–191.

[14] Arnaotoglou (n 10) xiv–xv.

[15] See McGlew's theory of tyrannicide as a circular remedy of regime change, for the violation of regime change. James F McGlew, 'Fighting Tyranny in Fifth Century Athens: Democratic Citizenship and the Oath of Demophantus' (2012) 55(2) *Bulletin of the Institute of Classical Studies* 91, 92.

contrary to the democratic *politeia*. Thus, tyrannicide was conceptualized as a self-help means of enforcing the fundamental law of the people, and the particular constitutional form.[16] Given its link to the substantive offence of tyranny, which was considered 'an attempt to deprive people of their political/constitutional rights',[17] the implicit secondary purpose of the law was rights-enforcement to halt such violations.

It was not a general individual right per se, but rather an individual citizen's public duty from which immunity rights derived. As it authorized homicide outside situations of self-defence under certain conditions, it was clearly intended as a law of exception.[18] The tyrannicide law was however distinct from the *lex talionis* or law of retaliation, for example, as it was not permitted for the purpose of private retribution or private good, but rather exclusively to uphold the *politeia* and the political and other rights of the *polis* or public good.[19]

The Athenian tyrannicide law predates documentary evidence in the form of surviving inscription. Therefore, while its existence and general content are not in dispute, its original source and consistency over its two main phases of legal development remain contested.[20] Evidence of its codification in the 'archaic law' – covering the pre-Draconian customary law, the seventh-century BCE Draconian code and sixth-century BCE Solonian code and 'constitution' – is partial at best.[21] In comparison, the 'classical law' of the late fifth and fourth

16 See for example MacDowell (n 13) 113–114.

17 See Martin Ostwald, 'The Athenian Legislation against Tyranny and Subversion' (1955) 86 *American Philological Association* 103, 104–105.

18 Hence Ostwald's theory that it originated as, and formed part of, Draco's 621 BCE homicide law. Ibid 107–108 (fn 26).

19 See Cohen (n 12).

20 In particular, there remain disagreements and gaps in knowledge as to whether the earliest tyrannicide law was Solonian, Draconian, or customary in origin, and whether the application of the customary law was continuous or periodically discontinued or updated. Compare James F McGlew, *Tyranny and Political Culture in Ancient Greece* (Cornell University Press 1993) 87–88, 92–93, 114–115, 119; Ostwald (n 17) 107–108 (fn 26); and Michael Gagarin, 'The Thesmothetai and the Earliest Athenian Tyranny Law' (1981) 111 *Transactions of the American Philological Association* 71, 74, 77; Rhodes (n 5) 79–88, 110–112, 130–134, 154–159, 220–223; Aristotle, *The Athenian Constitution* (Peter J Rhodes tr, Penguin Books Ltd 2002) 42, 120.

21 For literary evidence of the archaic tyranny law, in which provision for lawful tyrannicide is merely implied rather than explicit, see the 'Aristotelian' account of the customary and possibly also Solonian law at 16.10 *Athenion Politeia*. Aristotle, 'Constitution of Athens' in Jonathan Barnes (ed), *The Complete Works of Aristotle* (FG Kenyon tr, Princeton University Press 1984) vol 2, 2351. Compare the later Rhodes translation: 'This is an ordinance and tradition of the Athenians: if men rise with the aim of tyranny, or if any one joins in setting up a tyranny, he and his issue shall be without rights.' Aristotle, *Athenian Constitution* (n 20) 58–59. See also the account of Plutarch 'Solon and Publicola' in *Lives* (Bernadotte Perrin tr, Harvard University Press 1914) vol I, Book I, XIX 455–457, Book III, II-III 569, 571–573.

century BCE associated with the radical democratic period is better-documented and therefore less controversial.[22] The first such evidence of codification of an explicit tyrannicide law is the Decree and Oath of Demophantos.[23]

5.2.2 *The Decree of Demophantos (410 BCE) and the Law of Eukrates (336 BCE)*

The Decree of Demophantos provides that '[w]hoever abolishes the democracy in Athens, or serves in any public office, while democracy is abolished, he shall be enemy of the Athenians and he shall be slain with impunity . . . [and] the person who has killed him, or conspired to, shall be free of defilement'.[24] It thus establishes the primary trigger as commission of the offence of constitutional change and the consequent exceptional right of tyrannicide by way of immunity. In fact, the term 'tyrannicide' may be a slight misnomer, since it was equally intended for use against oligarchic usurpation, and not exclusively 'tyranny' as then generally understood.[25] The related oath sworn by all Athenian citizens formalizes tyrannicide as a duty, for the purpose of constitutional defence: 'I will kill by word and deed and vote and my own hand, if it is in my power, anyone who overthrows the democracy in Athens, who holds any public office while democracy is abolished, who attempts to become a

[22] For the literary and inscription evidence of the classical tyranny law, see the texts of the Decree and Oath of Demophantos cited in *Andocides i (On the Mysteries)* 96–98, and the Law of Eucrates cited in *Supplementum Epigraphicum Graecum* vols 1–42, republished in Arnaotoglou (n 10) 74–76. See also the alternative translations used by Teegarden. Teegarden (n 3) 31, 87.

[23] There are also competing theories as to whether and to what extent the tyranny law prior to codification by Demophantos alternated between harsher and more lenient forms of penalty, including the extent to which tyrannicide was permissible. Compare Ostwald (n 17) 103–117; Gagarin (n 20); Rhodes (n 5) 79–88, 110–112, 130–134, 154–159, 220–223; Aristotle, *Athenian Constitution* (n 20) 124, 128; McGlew (n 20) 111–121. Disagreement centres in part on the legal meaning of the penalty of *atimia*, which involves the loss of rights and protection of the law, long characterized as a more lenient approach. However, *atimia* could lead to confiscation, exile, or death as a consequence of the impunity that would apply to such actions against the *atimos*. See Todd (n 12) 116–118, 142–143, 182–183, 365; Adele C Scafuro, 'Atimia' in *Encyclopedia of Ancient History Online* (John Wiley 2012); Rhodes (n 5) 158–159, 220–223; Aristotle, *Athenian Constitution* (n 20) 177–178, 184. *Atimia* is thus a potentially broader and more flexible penalty that could yield the same result as the impeachment, ostracism, and tyrannicide laws. In this way, perhaps it is the law of *atimia* applying to tyrants that more closely resembles the later and even contemporary right to resist, in its implicit authorization of a broader range of otherwise unlawful actions.

[24] See Arnaotoglou (n 10) 74–75; Teegarden (n 3) 31.

[25] See Julia L Shear, 'The Oath of Demophantos and the Politics of Athenian Identity' in Sommerstein and Fletcher, *Horkos* (n 12) 148, 150.

tyrant or helps to establish one.'[26] Successful tyrannicides could expect compensation: 'because he has killed an enemy of the Athenians ... I will sell all the property of the killed [tyrant or oligarch] and give half of it to his killer, without depriving him of anything'. Moreover, the oath promises public honours in the event of failed tyrannicide: 'I will treat him and his children in the same way as Harmodios and Aristogeiton and their descendants.'[27] The similar Law of Eukrates passed approximately seventy-five years later: 'if anyone revolts in order to install a tyrannical regime or helps to this aim or abolishes democracy or deprives the Athenian people of their constitution, whoever kills this person shall not need purification'.[28]

The ancient Athenian law of tyrannicide was both customary and quasi-constitutional and only later expressed in written form. Like its successor, the constitutional right to resist, its primary purpose was constitutional enforcement, acting as both deterrent and remedy. It functioned as an exception to a general legal prohibition, extending an immunity or license. It also appears from the evidence that, like its successors, this extrajudicial remedy coexisted with judicial remedies over the centuries, rather than becoming redundant and obsolete following the adoption of more sophisticated legal mechanisms.[29] In another similarity, the extent to which the tyrannicide law was used or effective remains unknown – although in its case it is also possibly unknowable as no litigation evidence survives, or firm evidence of its exercise.[30] Specialist conclusions on this matter differ,[31] and the account of the operation of the tyrannicide law remains incomplete.[32]

The ancient Athenian law also provides certain contrasts with its successors. For example, the right of tyrannicide derived from a duty on all citizens but

[26] See Arnaotoglou (n 10) 74–75; Teegarden (n 3) 31.

[27] See Arnaotoglou (n 10) 74–75; Teegarden (n 3) 31. For further analysis of the Decree and Oath of Demophantos, see Teegarden (n 3) 15–53.

[28] See Arnaotoglou (n 10) 75–76; Teegarden (n 3) 87. For further analysis of the Law of Eukrates, see Teegarden (n 3) 85–112.

[29] See MacDowell (n 13) 64, 73–75, 169–170, 170–172, 183–186, 254–259; Todd (n 12) 112–118, 139–143, 154–156, 158–160, 302–303, 305–306, 372; Aristotle, *Athenian Constitution* (n 20) 179, 183–184. There is similar evidence of coexistence and complex interplay between the judicial and the lawful but extrajudicial self-help measures in the Roman Republic. See Nippel (n 8) 35–46; Lintott (n 8) 4–34, 66.

[30] However, according to Ostwald there is also no evidence of use of the Solonian law providing for trial for the offence of tyranny. See Ostwald (n 17) 111.

[31] For example, Teegarden makes ambitious claims for the law's effectiveness. See Teegarden (n 3) 6–7, 215. Yet compare McGlew (n 15) 97–98; Shear (n 25) 152, 155, 158–159; Anthony E Raubitschek, 'The Origin of Ostracism' (1951) 55 *American Journal of Archaeology* 221, 225–226.

[32] See Teegarden's partial reconstruction and claims for the law in use. Teegarden (n 3) 6–11, 215–219.

not all people, and it therefore stops short of a general right, much less a human right. Its trigger was exclusively related to change in constitutional form, without regard to reasons of conduct or need for a secondary trigger involving exhaustion of other means of remedy, and without the constraint of proportionality. In is also quite unclear whether any acts short of tyrannicide were covered by the Athenian law. Many scholars assume that no other forms of resistance were exceptionally authorized.[33] However, McGlew points to an apparent range of authorized actions covered under the Oath of Demophantos – to 'kill' by 'word', 'deed', 'vote', or 'own hand' – arguing that the actual scope of the law matches the scope of resistance, and not merely tyrannicide.[34] Teegarden draws a similar conclusion of implicit authorization for resistance, on the basis that tyrannicide was only one in a series of necessary enforcement acts.[35]

In the intervening centuries, the constitutional right to resist has evolved from this cruder antecedent, though some of the core features remain and a few contemporary provisions still resemble the rigid Athenian archetype in certain respects.[36] Beyond setting the baseline for comparison with what followed, the lasting legacy of the ancient 'proto-right to resist' is its close relationship with constitutionalism. That feature persists to this day, as the evidence in the following sections demonstrates.

5.3 MIDDLE AGES 'CONSTITUTIONS' OR PUBLIC LAW EQUIVALENTS, INCLUDING CUSTOMARY LAW

A right to resist – with a broader scope of means and potentially lower trigger threshold than that of the 'proto-right' – was first positivized in the 'constitutional' law of the Middle Ages. As with the positive law of the ancient period, specialists do not always agree on its origins, or on the explanation for its development and diffusion. However, certain features of the right are reasonably well-established. Kern identifies two secular forms of the right operating across Europe in the Middle Ages – customary and feudal contractual. These differ from each other, and also from the ecclesiastical form, in 'origins and in

[33] This may be partly due to the specialist scholarship's near exclusive focus on the tyrannicide provisions. For a fuller account, compare David Daube, *Civil Disobedience in Antiquity* (Edinburgh University Press 1972) 2–3.

[34] McGlew (n 15) 92.

[35] Teegarden (n 3) 216–217.

[36] See for example the current Ghanaian provisions examined in Lydia A Nkansah, 'The Right of Resistance and the Defence of Ghana's Fourth Republican Constitution' (2014) 6 *Kwame Nkrumah University of Science and Technology Law Journal* 129, factored into the analysis of contemporary provisions in Section 5.5 below.

methods'.[37] The customary form he describes is associated with pre-feudal 'constitutional' law, providing both an individual right of self-help against customary rights violations by the monarch and a collective right of forcible deposition.[38] Generally, there was no formal condemnation, no associated legal procedure, and no death sentence – though death could result if force was required. Rather, the people withdrew their obedience, transferring it to a new ruler.[39] The later feudal contractual form operating from the ninth through fifteenth centuries was similar but more formalized as a 'constitutional' right, often recognized by coronation oath.[40]

5.3.1 *Clause 61 of the Magna Carta (1215)*

The quasi-constitutional English Magna Carta is one of the earliest sources of written legal provision for the right to resist – in all but name – in the positive law of the Middle Ages.[41] Clause 61 of the first Magna Carta includes an unusually elaborate and mostly procedural variant of a self-help form of fundamental rights enforcement.[42] It was meant as a preventive deterrent but also as a remedy for violations of charter rights.

By virtue of clause 61 the king undertakes that 'the barons are to choose any twenty-five barons of the realm they wish, who with all their might must observe, maintain and cause to be observed the peace and liberties . . . granted to them and confirmed by this our present charter'.[43] Its potential substantive scope therefore would have extended beyond the enforcement of its well-

37 See Kern (n 3) 96.

38 See ibid 83–87, 89–90, 92, 121.

39 This last step was legally formalized. See ibid 86–87, 92.

40 See ibid 91, 121–131.

41 Ibid 128–129. Silving identifies it as the precedent for the later concept of a constitutional 'right to resist oppression', discussed in Section 5.4. See Helen Silving, 'The Origins of the Magnae Cartae' (1965) 3 *Harvard Journal on Legislation* 117, 121–122, 124, 127. Not all are agreed, however. Compare JC Holt, *Magna Carta* (3rd edn, George Garnett and John Hudson eds, Cambridge University Press 2015) 288; Barna Horvath, 'Rights of Man: Due Process of Law and Excès de Pouvoir' (1955) 4(4) *American Journal of Comparative Law* 539, 548.

42 Vincent calls it the 'sanctions clause'. Nicholas Vincent, *Magna Carta: The Foundation of Freedom 1215–2015* (Third Millennium Publishing 2015) 71, 72, 73, 75, 82. Holt, Garnett, and Hudson call it the 'security clause'. George Garnett and John Hudson, 'Introduction' in Holt, *Magna Carta* (n 41) 6–7. Kern maintains it established 'rules for constitutional resistance', amounting to the 'constitutional organization of self-help'. Kern (n 3) 129–131.

43 See Magna Carta (1215) clause 61, translated and reprinted in Holt (n 41) Appendix 6, 395. Silving describes the twenty-five barons as an 'enforcement committee'. See Silving (n 41) 121–122, 124, 127. Others have described it as a 'court' empowered to authorize the activation of the lawful right to resist under clause 61. See Holt (n 41) 288.

known civil and political rights forerunners to certain functional equivalents to economic and social rights also recognized in its provisions, including but not limited to those relating to forest law.[44] The provision is a safeguard against unlawful rule, to guarantee the customary fundamental rights of subjects, which are 'to be enjoyed fully and undisturbed in perpetuity'.[45] Its primary trigger is violation of the charter rights or terms: 'if we or our justiciar or our bailiffs or any other of our ministers offend against anyone in any way, or transgress any of the articles of peace or security',[46] the self-help enforcement procedure is followed. It establishes an initial requirement of grievance notification by way of petition: 'the offence is indicated to four barons of the aforesaid twenty-five barons, those four barons shall come to us or to our justiciar, if we are out of the kingdom, and bring the transgression to our notice and ask that we have the transgression addressed without delay'.[47] Failing rectification of the grievance, the secondary trigger of exhaustion of other means is reached upon expiry of a time-limited grace period: 'if we, or our justiciar should we be out of the kingdom, do not redress the transgression within forty days from the time when it was brought to the notice of us or our justiciar … the aforesaid four barons shall refer the case to the rest of the twenty-five barons'.[48] This necessity condition effectively restricts exercise of the right where there is reasonable prospect of another remedy.

The consequent right to resist is limited, yet the scope of means is inclusive of forceful and non-forceful otherwise unlawful means.[49] That is: 'those twenty-five barons with the commune of all the land shall distrain and distress us in every way they can, namely by seizing castles, lands and possessions, and in such other ways they can, saving our person and those of our queen and of our children'.[50] So this is explicitly not a right of tyrannicide, but instead a right to resist without taking the life of the monarch and family – and only 'until, in their judgment, [the trigger grievance] has been redressed', whereupon the enforcement right ceases and the obedience duty resumes.[51] Other limitations or safeguards against misuse of the right include a requirement of

44 See Holt (n 41) 286–288; Geraldine Van Bueren, 'Socio-economic Rights and a Bill of Rights – An Overlooked British Tradition' [2013] *Public Law* 821, 824–825.

45 See Magna Carta (1215) clause 61 (n 43).

46 Ibid.

47 See ibid.

48 See ibid.

49 On its authorization of forceful means, see Vincent (n 42) 75.

50 See Magna Carta (1215) clause 61 (n 43).

51 Ibid. Kern emphasizes this was not a right of deposition, or tyrannicide, nor was it a revolutionary right, but a right limited to the correction of injustice, which protected the king from deposition and the people from misrule. See Kern (n 3) 128–129.

majority agreement by the barons on the activating grievance, and the clause 63 stipulation of 'good faith' exercise.[52]

The personal scope of the right is not limited to the barons who control its exercise, as all rights are relevant including those held by persons other than barons, and as the immunity from punishment for use of these enforcement means extends beyond the barons.[53] The immunity provision reads: 'anyone in the land who wishes may take an oath to obey the orders of the said twenty-five barons in the execution of all the aforesaid matters ... and we publicly and freely permit anyone who wishes to take the oath, and we will never forbid anyone to take it',[54] provided the other conditions are met. It is not only a right but also a duty: the barons agree to 'faithfully observe' and 'do all they can do to secure' these procedures, and others shall be 'compelled and ordered' to support the barons in following these procedures.[55] Finally, revocation or diminution of these 'concessions and liberties' is 'null and void'.[56]

There was little time for application of clause 61 as it was deleted from subsequent amended versions of the Magna Carta.[57] No later 'constitutional' formulation made similar provision.[58] However, if the prevailing scholarly view that the Magna Carta generally formalized pre-existing rights rather than creating new rights is accurate,[59] then clause 61 is merely a procedural

52 See Magna Carta (1215) clause 61 (n 43) 395, 397; clause 63, 397.

53 However, Vincent estimates that the Magna Carta rights extended to only 10–20 per cent of the population. See Vincent (n 42) 15, 72.

54 See Magna Carta (1215) clause 61 (n 43).

55 Ibid 395, 397.

56 See ibid 397.

57 There is only a single instance of enforcement of clause 61 – where distraint was applied in the case of Nicholas de Stuteville. See Holt (n 41) 291–292, 303–304. The clause was removed from the 1216 version, and thus the 1215 version 'endured for less than twelve weeks'. Most remaining provisions were also repealed by 1966, starting in 1828. See Vincent (n 42) 13–15, 82; Garnett and Hudson (n 42) 7, 33. Kern concludes that clause 61 was 'ineffective'. Kern (n 3) 133.

58 The English Bill of Rights (1689), still in effect as a document of the uncodified British 'constitution', institutionalized a limited and elite 'right to bear arms' cognate to the 'right to rebel', but does not acknowledge the 'right to resist' per se. According to Malcolm, the 'right of ordinary citizens to possess weapons' or 'right to bear arms' is not in fact a 'true, ancient, and indubitable right' as sometimes claimed and is 'no longer a right' in that jurisdiction. See Joyce Lee Malcolm, *To Keep and Bear Arms: The Origins of an Anglo-American Right* (Harvard University Press 1994) ix, 9–11, 113–134, 165, 172, 170–177. However compare 'The Right to Disobey the Law' in Geoffrey Marshall, *Constitutional Theory* (Clarendon Press 1971) 210.

59 Or at least it formalized contemporaneous perception of what these rights were. This is not straightforward. See Vincent (n 42) 15, 17, 24, 26–27, 29–35, 70; Holt (n 41) 73–75, 81, 83–87, 102, 254–259. Compare the alternative attribution to an earlier codification of 1099 that reads: 'If it happens that the King acts in any way contrary to his undertakings, he denies God, for he has repudiated his oath, and neither his vassals nor his people ought to

specification relating to a pre-existing customary right. Ostensibly, then, the right itself would have been unaffected by the dropping of the clause in subsequent versions of the Magna Carta. This is also suggested by Blackstone's modern theory of an inalienable 'fifth auxiliary' natural or common law right to resist oppression persisting from custom,[60] that would become influential on the framing of constitutional rights to resist starting in the modern period. Either way, it provides an important example of a right to resist fundamental rights violations, consistent with an increasingly widespread custom in coronation oaths across Europe in the Middle Ages.[61]

5.3.2 *Other Quasi-constitutional Sources Including Coronation Oaths and Intervention Appeals*

The Magna Carta may have been the most elaborate, but it was not the only provision of a quasi-constitutional right to resist in this period. Kern cites evidence of 'special measures' providing for a right and duty to resist unlawful acts of the king in Germanic customary law predating the Magna Carta, as later recorded in the Sachsenspiegel (1220 or 1235), the first German law code recording customary and feudal law.[62] Indeed, he maintains that the Capitulary of Quierzy (857), in which the king 'bound himself to definite obligations, and conceded his subjects the right to refuse him obedience if he failed to fulfill his commitments', contains the earliest recorded feudal contractual provision for the right to resist, which 'thereby became a contractual penalty, and precisely for that reason acquired something of a preventive character'.[63] Similarly, there is a '*ius resistendi*' immunity provision in clause

endure it'. Charles d'Eszlary, 'Magna Carta and the Assises of Jerusalem' (1958) 2(3) *American Journal of Legal History* 189, 193–194, 206–208, 213–214. Garnett and Hudson suggest that the main innovation in clause 61 was the application of the custom of 'distraint' to the king. Garnett and Hudson (n 42) 5, 6–7, 287–288.

60 William Blackstone, *Commentaries on the Laws of England*, vol. 1 (1765, repr University of Chicago Press 1979) 139 [5]. See more detailed explanation below in n 80.

61 On the spread of similar provisions see Kern (n 3) 83–97, 115, 117–127; Péter László, '*Ius Resistendi* in Hungary: Resistance as a Right' in Péter László and Miklós Lojkó (eds), *Hungary's Long Nineteenth Century* (Brill 2012); Holt (n 41) 88, 91–93.

62 It states that 'a man must resist his king and judge, if he does wrong, and must hinder him in every way ... he does not thereby break his fealty'. Kern maintains that similar traditions derived from Nordic customary law. See Kern (n 3) 83–85. See also the right of resistance in the customary coronation oath of the Polish kings, later codified in the first Pacta Coventa or Acta Henriciana (1574). Daniel H Cole, 'From Renaissance Poland to Poland's Renaissance' (1999) 97(6) *Michigan Law Review* 2062, 2069. On successor laws, see Felicia Roşu, 'Free from Obedience: Constitutional Expressions of the Right of Resistance in Early Modern Transylvania and Poland-Lithuania' (2017) 47(1) *European History Quarterly* 6.

63 See Kern (n 3) 122, 127.

31 of the Hungarian Bulla Aurea or Golden Bull (1222).[64] Like the Magna Carta, this rights-enforcement clause conditionally authorized limited resistance not including deposition, tyrannicide, or regime change.[65] The 'discontinuity' of this provision's application from 1222 to 1917 was not uncommon for similar provisions of the period.[66] Other examples of customary coronation oaths with similar provisions, discontinuous history and comparative longevity include the Brabantian 'charter of liberties', the Joyeuse Entrée (1356),[67] nullified in 1794 but later reanimated in the Constitution of Belgium (1831).[68] These examples demonstrate that such laws, though perhaps comparatively crude in form, were not uncommon. Indeed, such customary law was also not limited to Europe. For example, contemporaneous to this period, in what later became known as North America post-colonization, the Kayanerenkó:wa or 'Great Law of Peace' of the Haudenosaunee Confederacy included provision for an analogous right that may also reflect codification of an earlier customary law.[69]

Thus, provision for the Middle Ages quasi-constitutional right to resist carried over certain core features from its ancient predecessor. It started as customary law, later codified. Its object and purpose 'was the enforcement of

64 It reads: '[s]hould we, or any of our successors, at any time seek to violate this disposition of ours, both the bishops and other lords and nobles of the regnum collectively and singly, present and future can, by this authority, be free in perpetuity to resist and oppose us and our other successors without the imputation of high treason'. From the translation cited in László (n 61) 116. Note that Rady's use of the same translation differs in several places. See Martyn Rady, 'Hungary and the Golden Bull of 1222' (2014) 24(2) *Banatica* 87, 92. On its impact into the twentieth century, see Horvath (n 41) 548 (fn 7).

65 See Rady (n 64) 89–90.

66 Clause 31 was periodically removed from and reinstated into subsequent versions of the Golden Bull sworn between 1231 and 1490, then 'permanently' reinstated and formally incorporated into the Tripartium law code in 1517. It remained in effect until 1687 when declared 'permanently' invalid by the Hungarian Diet. Thereafter it was expressly excluded through formal statements in the Golden Bulls of 1711, 1741, 1790, 1792, 1836, 1867, and 1917, to prevent reversion to it as customary law. See László (n 61) 113–133, 117–119, 121–123, 125–127; Rady (n 64) 104–116.

67 It is cited as an example analogous to the right to resist as it 'required a new duke to acknowledge the rights and privileges of Brabanters and to protect the customs of the Duchy; if the latter broke his undertakings, a clause ordained that his subjects might disobey him until he mended his ways'. See *Vindiciae, Contra Tyrannos: or, Concerning the Legitimate Power of a Prince over the People, and of the People over a Prince* (George Garnett ed/tr, 2003 edn, Cambridge University Press 1994) 137–140, 137 fn 475. Compare Brecht Deseure, 'From Pragmatic Conservatism to Formal Continuity: Nineteenth Century Views on the Old Regime Origins of the Belgian Constitution' (2016) 32 *Giornale di Storia Costituzionale* 257.

68 See the critical account of claims to this effect in Deseure (n 67).

69 See Kayansenh Paul Williams, *Kayanerenkó:wa – The Great Law of Peace* (University of Manitoba Press 2018) 368–375.

fundamental law and rights. Its function was that of both deterrent and remedy, as a rule of exception conferring immunity, and extending license. Its form was that of a right-duty, and directly enforceable claim. The evidence of its use and effectiveness is similarly limited. However, the pan-European form also exhibited some significant differences not only from the ancient proto-right discussed above, but also from the subsequent modern and contemporary constitutional rights to resist discussed below. First, it was an elite right of subjects rather than a general right of all citizens – much less a 'human right'. The primary trigger could include reason of conduct contrary to law, distinct from and at a lower threshold than the ancient trigger for tyrannicide. The secondary trigger of necessity due to exhaustion of other means, absent from the ancient right, started to appear. The permissible means were usually left open, but in some instances limited to exclude tyrannicide. Distinct from the later modern underlying concepts of social contract and popular sovereignty, the Middle Ages right derived from the belief that law is sovereign, that obligation to the monarch is therefore conditional on his or her obedience to law, and that law must be consistent with custom meaning that legal innovation is beyond monarchic power.[70]

In another category from this period are the enforcement claims equivalent to the right to resist foreign invasion and occupation, as expressed in intervention appeals such as the Remonstrance of the Irish Chiefs (1317)[71] and the Scottish Declaration of Arbroath (1320).[72] For its legal basis the former relied

[70] See Kern (n 3) 82–83, 89.

[71] The Remonstrance of the Irish Chiefs is an appeal for intervention combining defect of title with reason of conduct arguments against the English king and his predecessors, in a claim to be 'defending as we can the rights of our law and liberty against cruel tyrants and usurpers'. Further, 'we do nothing unlawful … and we neither can nor should be held guilty of perjury or disloyalty on this account, since neither we nor our fathers have ever done homage or taken any other oath of fealty to him or his fathers'. Citing the 'stress of necessity', therefore 'we will fight against them in defence of our right' until 'they shall desist from unjustly injuring us … [through] tyrannous oppression'. See Domhnall Ó Néill, 'Remonstrance of the Irish Chiefs to Pope John XXII' (1317) (Edmund Curtis tr) in Edmund Curtis and RB McDowell (eds), *Irish Historical Documents 1172–1922* (Barnes and Noble 1943 repr 1968) vol 1, 38, 44, 45, as listed in the CELT (Corpus of Electronic Texts) database T310000-001 (University College Cork 2007–2010).

[72] The Declaration of Arbroath in favour of King Robert the Bruce is another appeal for intervention cited as an example in Emer de Vattel, *The Law of Nations, or Principles of the Law of Nature, Applied to the Conduct and Affairs of Nations and Sovereigns* (Béla Kapossy and Richard Whatmore eds, Liberty Fund 2008) Book I Chapter IV [51] 106–107 (fn). It describes allegiance to a chosen king as conditional by law, to be withdrawn in the event of an attempt to 'make us or our kingdom subject to the King of England or the English', at which point the barons and earls would lawfully 'drive him out as our enemy and a subverter of his own right and ours, and make some other man who was well able to defend us our King;

in part upon the customary Brehon law by which Gaelic chieftains or kings were selected and their authority regulated, including by deposition for violations,[73] supplemented by appeals to just war doctrine.[74] This category of claim basis, also quasi-contractual and public law-equivalent, with an international law dimension relating to external self-determination, would become more important and influential on the law of the right to resist from the modern period.

5.4 MODERN REVOLUTIONARY REPUBLICAN AND ANTI-COLONIAL FOUNDATIONAL DECLARATIONS AND CONSTITUTIONS

The modern provisions for the right to resist first appeared bi-continentally in Europe and the Americas in quasi-constitutional declaratory instruments and in written constitutions, starting with the sixteenth-century Declaration of Independence of the Republic of the Seven United Provinces of the Netherlands, the Plakkat van Verlatinghe or Dutch 'Act of Abjuration' (1581),[75] and continuing with the more influential eighteenth-century American Declaration of Independence and United States Constitution and French Declaration of the Rights of Man and of the Citizen and French

for, as long as a hundred of us remain alive, never will we on any conditions be subjected to the lordship of the English'. See Declaration of Arbroath (1320) (National Archives of Scotland, state papers (SP13/7) Alan Borthwick tr, 2005).

73 See Bart Jaski, *Early Irish Kingship and Succession* (Four Courts Press 2000) 48–49, 57, 72–77, 277–278.

74 See James Muldoon, 'The Remonstrance of the Irish Princes and the Canon Law Tradition of the Just War' (1978) 22 *American Journal of Legal History* 309.

75 This sets out the primary trigger conditions, amounting to reason of conduct: when the monarch, who should act in the interests of his subjects, instead 'oppresses them, seeking opportunities to infringe their ancient customs and privileges, exacting from them slavish compliance, then he is no longer a prince, but a tyrant'. It further stipulates secondary trigger conditions, amounting to necessity by reason of exhaustion of other means: when this is 'the only method left for subjects whose humble petitions and remonstrances could never soften their prince or dissuade him from his tyrannical proceedings'. Then the subjects 'may not only disallow his authority, but legally proceed to the choice of another prince for their defense', as the permissible means. Finally, it sets out the source of the right as both natural and contractual: because 'this is what the law of nature dictates for the defense of liberty' therefore 'most of the Provinces receive their prince upon certain conditions, which he swears to maintain' but if violated 'he is no longer sovereign'. See Plakkat van Verlatinghe (1581) (University of Groningen tr, Department of Alfa-Informatica 1994–2012) [1]. For the influences on the Act of Abjuration including the *Vindiciae Contra Tyrannos*, its posited link to the Joyeuse Entrée, and its influence on the later Grotian and Althusian theories of the right to resist, see John Witte Jr, 'Natural Rights, Popular Sovereignty, and Covenant Politics: Johannes Althusius and the Dutch Revolt and Republic' (2009–2010) 87 *University of Detroit Mercy Law Review* 565, 565–576.

Constitution, and the series of nineteenth-century Latin American independence constitutions discussed below. Jägerskiöld calls these republican constitutions 'the culmination of the doctrine of the right of resistance' and its 'recognition in constitutional theory and in law'.[76] This period also introduced the formalization of the newer cognate concept of a right of revolution.

5.4.1 *The American Declaration of Independence (1776) and United States Constitution as Amended by its Bill of Rights (1791)*

Probably the most famous example of a right of resistance and right of revolution variant is found in the second paragraph of the preamble to the American Declaration of Independence (American Declaration).[77] An equally famous but more controversial variant on, or subordinate cognate of, the right to resist or to rebel is the provision for the 'right to bear arms' in the Bill of Rights second amendment to the United States Constitution. Indeed, similar provisions are included in many of the state constitutions.[78] Influences on the main drafters Jefferson and Madison included prominent

[76] Stig Jägerskiöld, 'Tyrannicide and the Right of Resistance, 1792–1809 – A Study on JJ Anckarström' (1964) 8 *Scandinavian Studies in Law* 67, 79. This case study examines theories of a Swedish constitutional right to resist in an indirect provision at article 14 of the constitutions of 1720 and 1772. See ibid 80–81, 83–87, 95–96.

[77] Concurring that both the American Declaration and French Declaration are examples including formulations of a right to resist, see Ginsburg et al (n 1) 1188 (fn 6–8), 1203 (fn 79, 81), 1206 (fn 98).

[78] Two dozen state constitutions provide for the right of revolution, many of which are triggered by majority will rather than oppression. See the Maryland Constitution (1776) Declaration of Rights section IV; Virginia Constitution (1776) Bill of Rights section 3; Pennsylvania Constitution (1776) Declaration of the Rights of the Inhabitants of the Commonwealth, or State of Pennsylvania, article V; Massachusetts Constitution (1780) Declaration of Rights article VII; New Hampshire Constitution (1784) Bill of Rights article X; Pennsylvania Constitution (1790) article IX section 2; Delaware Constitution (1792) preamble; Kentucky Constitution (1792) article XII section 2; Tennessee Constitution (1796) article XI section 1; Kentucky Constitution (1799) article XII section 2; Ohio Constitution (1802) article VIII section 1; Indiana Constitution (1816) article I section 2; Mississippi Constitution (1817) article I section 2; Connecticut Constitution (1818) article I section 2; Alabama Constitution (1819) article I section 2; Maine Constitution (1819) article I section 2; Missouri Constitution (1820) article XIII section 2; Michigan Constitution (1835) article I section 2; Arkansas Constitution (1836) article II section 2; Texas Constitution (1836) Declaration of Rights section 2; Florida Constitution (1838) article I section 2; Pennsylvania Constitution (1838) article VIII section 2; Kentucky Constitution (1850) article XII section 2; Oklahoma Constitution (1907) article II section 1. See Christian G Fritz, 'Recovering the Lost Worlds of America's Written Constitutions' (2004) 68 *Albany Law Review* 261, 274–277, 280 (fn 55–59, 66–73, 80). See also Ginsburg et al (n 1) 1204–1205 (fn 85–86, 88). In addition, forty-four state constitutions expressly protect the more specific cognate 'right to bear arms' according to Malcolm (n 58).

theorists who recognized the right to resist as a natural right.[79] Blackstone's suggestion of a 'fifth auxiliary right' in customary English common law deriving from the natural right of resistance is particularly relevant.[80] However, neither the Declaration's clauses nor the United States Constitution's second amendment amounts to an express constitutional 'right to resist' named as such. The right is logically implied, but not agreed among specialists. The extent of its legal recognition is, at best, questionable given the available United States Supreme Court interpretations.[81] Yet paradoxically the United States jurisdictions yield the densest available case law or *obiter dicta* on the subject. The status of the constitutional right to resist in relation to the United States provisions is therefore complex compared to the other express, or otherwise generally undisputed, quasi-constitutional and constitutional provisions discussed elsewhere in this chapter.

79 See the theories of John Locke, 'The Second Treatise of Government: An Essay Concerning the True Original, Extent and End of Civil Government' in *Two Treatises of Government* (Peter Laslett ed, rev edn, Cambridge University Press 1988) Chapter XVI 'of Conquest' [175]–[196] 384–397, Chapter XVII 'Of Usurpation' [197]–[198] 397–398, Chapter XVIII 'Of Tyranny' [199]–[200] 398–405, Chapter XIX 'Of the Dissolution of Government' [211]–[243] 406–428; Vattel (n 72) Book I Chapter IV 'Of the Sovereign, His Obligations and His Rights' [51]–[54] 103–112, Book II Chapter I 'Of the Common Duties of a Nation towards others or of the Offices of Humanity between Nations' [7] 265, Chapter IV 'Of the Right to Security, and the Effects of Sovereignty and Independence of Nations' [49]–[52] 288–289, [54]–[57] 289–292, Chapter V 'Of the Observance of Justice between Nations' [65]–[70] 296–297, Chapter XII 'Of Treaties of Alliance and other Public Treaties' [168] 344 [196]–[197] 364–365, Book III Chapter XVIII 'Of Civil War' [288]–[289] 641–642, [290]–[293], [295] 642–647; Blackstone (n 60, see also n 80 below).

80 The 'fifth auxiliary right of the subject' being 'that of having arms for their defence, suitable to their condition and degree, and such as are allowed by law', which is 'a public allowance, under due restrictions, of the natural right of resistance and self-preservation, when the sanctions of society and laws are found insufficient to restrain the violence of oppression'. Blackstone (n 60) 139 [5]. For Blackstone's fuller analysis of the position of the right to resist in the English common law system, including the distinct and separate position of the right to revolution, see *Commentaries on the Laws of England* Book I 'Of the Rights of Persons', Chapter I 'Of the Absolute Rights of Individuals'; Chapter II 'Of the Parliament'; Chapter III 'Of the King, and His Title'; Chapter VI 'Of the King's Duties'; and especially Chapter VII 'Of the King's Prerogative', all of which should be taken together with certain relevant explanations in Section II of the Introduction 'Of the Nature of Laws in General'. Ibid 119–121, 125–140, 142–145, 147–149, 151, 153–157, 159, 164–165, 172–179, 183–186, 188–190, 202–211, 226–227, 230–239, 243–244, 249–250, 253–254. Citing Blackstone's assessment but not including the second amendment provision on the right to bear arms in their list of constitutional right to resist provisions – without explanation – see Ginsburg et al (n 1) 1204–1205.

81 On its limited constitutional recognition as a consequence of a series of United States Supreme Court decisions, see Jordan J Paust, 'The Human Right to Participate in Armed Revolution and Related Forms of Social Violence: Testing the Limits of Permissibility' (1983) 32 *Emory Law Journal* 545, 545–546, 550–560, 567–569.

The American Declaration states, with reference to the 'laws of nature' and 'certain unalienable rights', that 'to secure these rights, governments are instituted among men, deriving their just powers from the consent of the governed'.[82] Therefore, it recognizes a right of revolution 'whenever any form of government becomes destructive to these ends, it is the right of the people to alter or to abolish it, and to institute new government . . . on such principles and organizing its powers in such form, as to them shall seem most likely to effect their safety and happiness'.[83] One secondary trigger, therefore, is the will of the majority. This activates a 'right . . . [and] duty' of resistance, 'to throw off such government' where the primary trigger is 'a long train of abuses and usurpations' amounting to 'the establishment of an absolute tyranny'.[84] Another secondary trigger is the necessity condition, due to exhaustion of other remedies: '[i]n every stage of these oppressions we have petitioned for redress in the most humble terms: our repeated petitions have been answered only by repeated injury'.[85] The scope of means is inclusive and unspecified and the sole limitation is prudence, which 'will dictate that governments long established should not be changed for light and transient causes'.[86]

Despite the clear articulation of legal elements in the American Declaration,[87] the right to resist and right to revolution were never incorporated as such into the United States Constitution, and the Declaration's legal effect is still controversial among constitutional scholars.[88] Early commentary

[82] See American Declaration of Independence (4 July 1776) preamble, paragraph 2.

[83] Ibid [emphasis added].

[84] Ibid. The list of grievances, rights abuses, and usurpations set out in the 'indictment' section cumulatively form the basis of the primary 'tyranny' trigger, and the 'self-defence' ground essential to establishing the position in international law. The 'denunciation' section sets out the conclusion that the conditions have been met.

[85] Ibid. The 'indictment' and 'denunciation' sections indicate that the secondary 'necessity' condition has been met.

[86] Ibid preamble, para 2. On the strength of the discretionary prudential limitation, see Kevin Portteus, 'The Right of Revolution in the American Founding' (RealClear Public Affairs, 18 May 2021).

[87] Also asserting elements of a *jus ad bellum* basis for the exercise of the right to resist – unconstitutional rule beyond established jurisdiction and violation of fundamental rights; threat and use of force constituting aggression; necessity due to exhaustion of legal means of remedy – see the earlier 'Declaration by the Representatives of the United Colonies of North-America, Now Met in Congress in Philadelphia, Setting Forth the Causes and Necessity of Their Taking Up Arms' (1775).

[88] For a concise account of the three main arguments in the scholarly debate – that the American Declaration either is part, is not part, or is relevant to interpretation of the United States Constitution – see Lee J Strang, 'Originalism's Subject Matter: Why the Declaration of Independence Is Not Part of the Constitution' (2016) 89 *Southern California Law Review* 637, 637–640.

on the United States Constitution seems to affirm the right of revolution as being a natural and therefore inalienable right rather than a consequence of its recognition in the Declaration, or specifically constitutional.[89] A similar view is advanced by certain contemporary scholars.[90] The constitutional viability of such arguments would likely rest on the non-diminution provision in the ninth amendment, that '[t]he enumeration in the Constitution, of certain rights, shall not be construed to deny or disparage others retained by the people'.[91] Others, however, dismiss assertions of constitutional recognition of a right to resist or right of revolution, and theorize a doctrine of denial by relying on a series of United States Supreme Court cases which seem to prioritize the right of the state to defend itself.[92] Nevertheless, Paust proposes a doctrinal theory of limited Supreme Court recognition of a majoritarian right of revolution, by reading across more than two dozen decisions including those cited as definitive by denialists, most of which concern litigation of constitutionally acceptable limits on ordinary rights, principally those protected by the first amendment.[93] In other words, this is an implied right at best, and even if memorably articulated by the American Declaration, that is apparently not its constitutional 'source'. In contrast, the cognate right of revolution was independently and expressly incorporated into many state constitutions, with somewhat less doubtful status.[94]

Equally contentious as to whether it guarantees a right to resist, right to rebel, or right to revolution – or none of the above – is the second amendment to the United States Constitution, which reads: '[a] well regulated Militia, being necessary to the security of a free State, the right of the people to keep

89 See St George Tucker, *Blackstone's Commentaries with Notes of Reference to the Constitution and Laws* (William Young Birch and Abraham Small 1803) 74–75; William Rawle, *A View of the Constitution of the United States of America* (2nd edn, PH Nicklin 1829) 94–95; Joseph Story, *Commentaries on the Constitution of the United States* (Hilliard, Gray and Co 1833) 305–306 [337] and 374–375 [395]. Compare however the identification of the right of revolution as a 'fundamental right' and 'general principle' of the United States Constitution, in Thomas Cooley, *General Principles of Constitutional Law* (Little, Brown 1880) 25–26.

90 For example, see Williams (n 2) 416–417, 419–420, 422, 432, 441 and fn 11.

91 Constitution of the United States of America (1787, as amended 1791) ninth amendment.

92 See the list of cases relied on in Raymond E Hayes, 'Revolution as a Constitutional Right' (1938) 13 *Temple Law Quarterly* 18, 22, 26; Horvath (n 41) 556–557 (fn 35, 37); Williams (n 2) 425.

93 See the list of cases relied on in Paust (n 81) 545–568 (fn 22, 24, 28–29, 33, 38–41, 43–60, 62).

94 For an account of the constitutional right of revolution arising from the sovereignty of the people as a central constitutional idea extensively expressed in the state constitutions, distinctive to the American constitutional tradition, see Fritz (n 78) 272–278, 280, 282–284, 291–293.

and bear Arms, shall not be infringed'.[95] This provision was adapted from a narrower formulation in the English Bill of Rights (1689).[96] Early commentary on the second amendment seems to generally corroborate the Blackstonian interpretation of its relation to a natural right to resist also embedded in customary and common law.[97] This interpretation is not agreed by all,[98] but it was endorsed by the United States Supreme Court in its first ruling on the core content of the second amendment in *District of Columbia* v *Heller*.[99] While this decision does not fully and finally resolve the question of whether and to what extent the second amendment represents a constitutional right to resist, the Court's acceptance of Blackstone's fifth auxiliary right as the interpretive basis of the second amendment would seem to leave the possibility open for future clarification.[100] Recent comparative constitutional studies treat the second amendment 'right to bear arms' as *sui generis*, excluding it from lists of constitutional 'right to resist' provisions,[101] rather than seeing the former as a specific and consequential cognate form of the

[95] Constitution of the United States of America (n 91) second amendment. On this right as 'capable of an amazing range of interpretations' but only correctly understood by reference to its predecessor English right, that is, as a logical corollary of the right of individual and collective self-defence, and right to resist in defence of primary natural and constitutional rights as per Blackstone's interpretation, see Malcolm (n 58) 121–122, 128–130, 135–136, 138–164.

[96] Malcolm (n 58) 119. The sixth of thirteen rights 'endangered' by the king, it reads: 'That the Subjects which are Protestants may have Arms for their Defence suitable to their Conditions and as allowed by Law.' Since this was restricted to citizens of a particular religion, rank, and income – essentially only a full right of the wealthy – it was broadened rather than adopted verbatim in the second amendment. Ibid 117–118, 120–123, 136.

[97] See Story (n 89) 746–747 [1889]–[1890]; Cooley (n 89) 270–272. However compare Tucker (n 89) 'Editor's Appendix Note D: View of the Constitution of the United States' 300; Rawle (n 89) 125–126, 142, associating the second amendment principally with a right of self-defence not necessarily related to the right to resist.

[98] See for example Williams (n 2) 413, 416–417 and fn 45. For an account of the general contours of the debate, identifying a reluctance to fully engage with the second amendment by non-conservative legal scholars, see Sanford Levinson, 'The Embarrassing Second Amendment' (1989) 99 *Yale Law Journal* 637.

[99] See *District of Columbia* v *Heller*, 554 US 570 (2008) Part II; Joyce Lee Malcolm, 'The Supreme Court and the Uses of History: District of Columbia v Heller' (2009) 56 *UCLA Law Review* 1377; David B Kopel, 'The Right to Arms in the Living Constitution' (2010) *Cardozo Law Review* de novo 99, 100.

[100] Of potential relevance to the right to resist are the Court's holdings that: the decision does not exhaust the provision's full scope; it does protect an individual right, not an exclusively collective right; the right is a natural or common law or otherwise pre-existing right that cannot be alienated or otherwise extinguished by virtue of the Constitution; the Blackstonian elaboration is accepted; the right is not unlimited; the operative clause is controlling and the prefatory clause is clarifying but not limiting. See *DC* v *Heller* (n 99) Part IIA 1a–3e; Part III.

[101] In this regard Ginsburg and colleagues follow Law and Versteeg (n 7) 1202; David S Law and Mila Versteeg, 'The Declining Influence of the United States Constitution' (2012) 87 *New York University Law Review* 762, 775. See Ginsburg et al (n 1) 1204–1205.

latter and treating the two rights as distinct but related.[102] Additionally, popular belief in the concept of a second amendment constitutional guarantee of the right to resist endures regardless of scholarly or judicial opinion.[103]

Settling the question of the contemporary meaning of this provision is beyond the scope of the present study,[104] as is the question of whether there is an implied right to resist to be found otherwise in the United States Constitution.[105] Indeed, to the extent that one accepts an implied right, other provisions may offset this interpretation, such as the disqualification of convicted rebellion participants from holding public office, by virtue of section 3 of the fourteenth amendment.[106] It suffices that, as the contemporary comparative studies demonstrate, while the second amendment 'right to bear arms' formulation is nearly unique among national constitutions,[107] the American Declaration and similar state constitution formulations influenced subsequent constitutional provisions in other jurisdictions, as discussed below, and continue to provide a point of reference for the modern legal concept.

5.4.2 *The French Declarations of the Rights of Man and of the Citizen (1789 and 1793) and the French Constitution (1791 and 1958)*

The first codification of a 'right to resist oppression' is at article 2 of the 1789 French Declaration of the Rights of Man and Citizen (French

[102] See for example, Malcolm (n 58) 122, 128–130, 162–164, 167, 172.

[103] For a scholarly historical analysis of the salience of the second amendment right as both right of resistance and right of self-defence for marginalized citizens whom the state is unwilling or unable to protect from racist violence, see Robert J Cottrol and Raymond T Diamond, 'The Second Amendment: Toward an Afro-Americanist Reconsideration' (1991) 80 *Georgetown Law Journal* 309.

[104] Also beyond its scope is the currently controversial legal right to resist unlawful arrest or search and seizure, recognition, and regulation of which varies state-by-state. The related substantial case law and growing secondary literature is worthy of separate study as a subset of the right as encoded at domestic level.

[105] Hence it does not consider Paust's theory in detail, or others relying on constitutional rights such as the first or ninth amendments, or consideration of the case law cited in Francis A Boyle, *Defending Civil Resistance under International Law* (Transnational 1988); Francis A Boyle, *Protesting Power: War, Resistance, and Law* (Rowman and Littlefield 2008); Matthew Lippman, 'The Right of Civil Resistance under International Law and the Domestic Necessity Defense' (1990) 8 *Dickinson Journal of International Law* 349; Matthew Lippman, 'Nuremberg and American Justice' (1991) 5 *Notre Dame Journal of Ethics, Law and Public Policy* 951; Nicholas N Kittrie, *Rebels with a Cause: The Minds and Morality of Political Offenders* (Westview 2000).

[106] Albeit that such 'disability' is removable by a two-thirds majority vote.

[107] See further discussion in Sections 5.5.1 and 5.5.2.

Declaration), which includes it as a 'natural and imprescriptible' right.[108] Its successor 1793 Declaration, which never took legal effect, is even more emphatic. Article 11 states that '[a]ny act done against man outside of the cases and without the forms that the law determines is arbitrary and tyrannical; the one against whom it may be intended to be executed by violence has the right to repel it by force'. Article 27 proposes to '[l]et any person who may usurp the sovereignty [of the people] be instantly put to death by free men'. Article 33 claims that '[r]esistance to oppression is the consequence of the other rights of man'. Article 34 elaborates that '[t]here is oppression against the social body when a single one of its members is oppressed: there is oppression against each member when the social body is oppressed'. Article 35 further establishes that '[w]hen the government violates the rights of the people, insurrection is for the people and for each portion of the people the most sacred of rights and the most indispensible of duties'.[109] While only the 1789 version, as incorporated into the 1791 Constitution, had and has constitutional effect in France,[110] both versions had influence on the framing of the constitutional right to resist in other jurisdictions in successive generations.[111]

As Alpaugh has observed, '[n]o codified precedent existed for such a broad right of resistance',[112] and its provenance is still not definitively

[108] Article 2 reads in full: 'The aim of all political association is the preservation of the natural and imprescriptible rights of man. These rights are liberty, property, security, and resistance to oppression.' On the provision's drafting history see Micah Alpaugh, 'The Right of Resistance to Oppression: Protest and Authority in the French Revolutionary World' (2016) 39(3) *French Historical Studies* 567, 568–569. For the positivist attack on its formulation as 'imprescriptible' see Jeremy Bentham, 'Anarchical Fallacies; Being an Examination of the Declaration of Rights Issued during the French Revolution' reprinted in Jeremy Waldron (ed), *Nonsense upon Stilts: Bentham, Burke and Marx on the Rights of Man* (Methuen 1987) 49, 52–59, 68–69.

[109] See Declaration of the Rights of Man and of the Citizen (1793) articles 11, 27, 33–35 in Frank Maloy Anderson (ed), *The Constitutions and Other Select Documents Illustrative of the History of France 1789–1901* (HW Wilson 1904).

[110] Ultimately the 1793 Constitution was never officially enacted. Instead, the Thermidorean Constitutional Convention of 1795 delivered the more conservative abbreviated 'Constitution of the Year III', which eliminated the right to resist oppression. The 'Constitution of the Year VIII' eliminated the Declaration of Rights altogether following Napoleon's Brumaire coup. See Alpaugh (n 108) 590–592.

[111] See Georg Jellinek, *Declaration of the Rights of Man and of Citizens: A Contribution to Modern Constitutional History* (Henry Holt 1901) 2–3; Mitsukuni Yazaki, 'Legality and the Right of Resistance' [1957] *Osaka University Law Review* 26, 27. On the French Declaration's general influence on subsequent constitutional drafting in other jurisdictions, see Rosenfeld and Sajó (n 5) 4. On the French revolutionaries' active promotion of the constitutional right to resist as a model for emulation, see Alpaugh (n 108) 585–586.

[112] Ibid 582.

determined.[113] It was formally proposed in a draft Declaration presented by the Marquis de Lafayette, but records are otherwise unsatisfactory.[114] The Constitutional Committee of forty did not make a final record of proceedings, and the provision passed the National Assembly without explanation or debate.[115] It is generally agreed however that this was not a French concept, but rather borrowed from Anglo-Americans.[116] Yet, as shown above, none of these was as broad or expressed in such explicit terms: this is the substance of the French revolutionary innovation to the antecedent formulations of the right. In 1791 a series of 'catéchismes' appeared to explain its meaning.[117] They described it as an individual and collective right to 'reclaim' denied rights and to 'arm oneself against manifest violence or illegal and tyrannical oppression'.[118] The trigger was unlawful or unconstitutional action by the state, and the right was distinguished from unlawful 'rebellion' or 'revolt' as these contradict the general will.[119] However, the Assembly did not provide formal clarifications regarding what means the right authorized, in response to two citizen petitions presented on this issue in 1792.[120] When a Girondin-led constitutional committee set out to revise the 1791 Constitution and the 1789 Rights of Man, evidence of the debates shows that the Jacobins in general and Robespierre in particular objected to proposed changes to the right to resist provision.[121] The stronger wording and clearer conceptualization of the right to resist oppression in the provisions of the 1793 Declaration are also attributable to Robespierre, and would have provided an even broader formulation of the right of resistance.[122]

The French National Assembly ultimately 'decreed that the Constitution should be preceded by the Declaration. The intention, apparently, was to endow the latter with an authority superior even to that of the Constitution', consequently giving the constitutional right to resist the form of a permanent

[113] No texts in the Project for American and French Research on the Treasury of the French Language (ARTFL) database include the two terms 'resistance' and 'oppression' in the same sentence before 1789, according to ibid 574.

[114] Ibid 576–577.

[115] Ibid 579–580.

[116] See Jellinek (n 111) 8–16, 18–20, 24–25, 27–82; Alpaugh (n 108) 567, 569–570, 576; Rosenfeld and Sajó (n 5) 3–4.

[117] Such as *Catéchisme de la constitution francoise* and *Catéchisme de la Déclaration des droits de l'homme*. Alpaugh (n 108) 583–584.

[118] Ibid 583.

[119] Ibid.

[120] Ibid 584.

[121] Alpaugh cites the *Archives parlemantaires* (63:113–115) in ibid 586–587 fn 95–97.

[122] Ibid 587–588.

guarantee of fundamental rights.[123] Lauterpacht explains that '[w]hile subsequent French constitutional enactments did not refer *expressis verbis* to the right of resistance, it is arguable that they recognised it inasmuch as they confirmed the principles of the Declaration of 1789'.[124] Indeed, the French Declaration continues to have constitutional value by virtue of preambular reference in the Constitution of the Fifth French Republic (1958). Conseil Constitutionnel Decision 71-44 DC affirmed the binding nature of the provisions of the Declaration, and that its principles can act as a 'constitutional block' on proposed legislation in the same way as other provisions of the constitution.[125] However, despite this apparent legal entrenchment, some scholars still claim that the French Declaration right to resist is 'not a right'.[126]

5.4.3 *The Latin American Independence Constitutions (1814–1886)*

The American and French Declarations – as well as the Constitution of the United States of America and various of its state constitutions – influenced the formulation of right to resist provisions in several post-colonial Latin American constitutions adopted in the nineteenth century.[127] These included article 14 of the Constitution of Apatzingán or Constitutional Decree for the Liberty of Mexican America (1814), one of the earliest republican independence constitutions adopted during the Mexican War of Independence but which

[123] Hersch Lauterpacht, *International Law and Human Rights* (Stevens and Sons 1950) 91–2.

[124] He was writing then of the Constitution of the Fourth French Republic (1946). Ibid 326 fn 4.

[125] *Conseil Constitutionnel Decision* 71–44 *DC* (1971) [2] *Journal officiel* 18 July 1971, 7114.

[126] For example, Monique Chemillier-Gendreau, 'Resistance, Right to, International Protection' in Rüdiger Wolfrum (ed), *Max Planck Encyclopedia of Public International Law* (Oxford University Press 2012) 954 [1]. On the institutionalization, neutralization, and obsolescence of article 2 as a consequence of the *recours pour excès* de pouvoir regime, see Horvath (n 41) 561, 566–568.

[127] On their general influence see Hersch Lauterpacht, 'Law of Nations, Law of Nature, Rights of Man' (1943) 29 *Transactions of the Grotius Society* 1, 9; Russell H Fitzgibbon, 'The Process of Constitution-Making in Latin America' (1960) 3 *Comparative Studies in Society and History* 1, 1, 2, 6; Gargarella, 'Right of Resistance in Situations of Legal Alienation' (n 2) 5–6; Gargarella, 'Right of Resistance in Situations of Severe Deprivation' (n 2) 361; Rosenfeld and Sajó (n 5) 4; Roberto Gargarella, *Latin American Constitutionalism 1810–2010* (Oxford University Press 2013) 2, 6–11. On the alternative attribution of primary influence to the 'liberal 1812 Spanish Constitution of Cadiz' see Dixon and Ginsburg (n 5) 2; MC Mirow, *Latin American Constitutions: The Constitution of Cádiz and Its Legacy in Spanish America* (Cambridge University Press 2015) 4–7. However, the latter was a monarchic and colonial constitution that did not include a functional equivalent to the right to resist. It is therefore not the primary influence on the provisions under discussion.

never entered into force;[128] article 1 of the now defunct revolutionary republican Constitution of the United Provinces of Rio de la Plata (Argentina, Uruguay, Bolivia) (1828);[129] article 134 of the first Constitution of Uruguay (1830), still in force under a new article number;[130] and articles 8 and 9 of the Constitution of El Salvador (1886),[131] that country's most durable to date but succeeded by several subsequent constitutions. The Mexican and United Provinces provisions, with minor modifications, follow the right of revolution wording of the American Declaration.[132] The Uruguayan and El Salvadorean provisions are right to resist variants, but do not use the specific 'right to resist oppression' wording of the French Declaration.[133]

Unlike the American and French Declarations, these Latin American constitutions and their right to resist provisions have generally been superseded. Subsequent constitutions of Mexico, El Salvador, and Argentina continued to provide for the right to resist,[134] but of these original provisions the only one still in effect is that of the 1830 Constitution of

[128] Article 14 of the Constitution of Apatzingán (Mexico) (1814) recognizes the 'undeniable popular right [to] establish … alter, modify, or completely abolish the government, whenever necessary for the people's happiness.' See Ginsburg et al (n 1) Appendix I, 1253. For reference to an earlier provision in the Banda Oriental [del Uruguay] Constitution (1813) see Gargarella, 'Right of Resistance in Situations of Legal Alienation' (n 2) 5–6.

[129] According to article 1 of the Constitution of the United Provinces of Rio de la Plata (Argentina, Uruguay, Bolivia) (1828): since 'it is a responsibility of the state to secure [natural, essential and inviolable] rights … should the state fail to do so the people have a right to alter the government and take any actions necessary for restoring their security, prosperity and happiness'. See Ginsburg et al (n 1) Appendix I, 1258.

[130] Article 134 of the Constitution of Uruguay (1830) – now article 10 of the Constitution of Uruguay (1966, reinstated 1985, revised 2004) – provides that: 'No inhabitant of the state will be forced to do what the law does not require, nor prevented from doing what is not prohibited.' See Ginsburg et al (n 1) Appendix I, 1259.

[131] Article 8 of the Constitution of El Salvador (1886) provides that 'Salvador recognizes rights and obligations anterior and superior to the positive laws, derived from the principles of liberty, equality, and fraternity'. Article 9 provides that 'Every inhabitant … holds the incontestable right to preserve and defend his life, liberty, and property … in conformity with law'. See Ginsburg et al (n 1) Appendix I, 1247.

[132] As such they fall within Gargarella's category of republican and majoritarian models. See Roberto Gargarella, 'Towards a Typology of Latin American Constitutionalism 1810–60' (2004) 39 *Latin American Research Review* 141, 142–151; Gargarella, *Latin American Constitutionalism* (n 127) 4–11.

[133] They bear instead the hallmarks of Gargarella's category of liberal and individualist models. See Gargarella, 'Towards a Typology of Latin American Constitutionalism' (n 132) 142–151; Gargarella, *Latin American Constitutionalism* (n 127) 4–7, 14–17.

[134] See the Constitution of Mexico (1917) [revised 2015] article 136; Constitution of El Salvador (1945) article 36; Constitution of El Salvador (1950) articles 5 and 175; Constitution of Argentina (1956) [(1853, reinstated 1983, revised 1994)] article 36; Constitution of El Salvador (1996) [(1983, revised 2014)] articles 87 and 88. See Ginsburg et al (n 1) Appendix I, 1242, 1247–1248, 1253.

Uruguay.[135] Nevertheless, these four nineteenth-century provisions initiated what became a regional tradition of constitutional codification of the right to resist that has continued into the twentieth and twenty-first centuries,[136] spreading to other countries in widely varied formulations.[137] Indeed, much like the French, Latin American legal scholars and members of delegations to international organizations actively promoted recognition and positivization of this right at international level, advocating inclusion of express provisions in constitutions as well as international declarations.[138]

[135] Constitution of Uruguay (1830) article 134 is now Constitution of Uruguay (1966, reinstated 1985, revised 2004) article 10.

[136] Right to resist provisions appear in all Gargarella's identified constitutional periods, but they are concentrated in the two most recent 'social' constitutions and 'new' constitutions periods, with only five of twenty-seven – according to the list in Ginsburg et al – appearing in prior periods. See Ginsburg et al (n 1) Appendix I, 1242, 1244–1248, 1250–1254, 1258–1259. On Gargarella's five-fold periodization theory, see Gargarella, *Latin American Constitutionalism* (n 127) ix. Those from the independence constitutions period (1810–1850) and 'foundational' constitutions period (1850–1890) are discussed above. In addition are those from the 'post-colonial crisis' constitutions period (1890–1930): Constitution of Mexico (1917) article 136 – though note that Mirow identifies this as the first 'social' constitution in Mirow (n 127) 258, 271; the 'social' constitutions period (1930–1950s/60s): Constitution of Cuba (1940) article 40; Constitution of El Salvador (1945) article 36; Constitution of Guatemala (1945) article 50; Constitution of El Salvador (1950) articles 5 and 175; Constitution of Argentina (1956) article 36; Constitution of Honduras (1957) article 4; Constitution of Venezuela (1961) article 250; Constitution of the Dominican Republic (1963) article 81; Constitution of Guatemala (1965) article 7; Constitution of the Dominican Republic (1966) articles 8(5), 46 and 99; and the 'new' constitutions period (1980s–present): Constitution of Honduras (1982) article 3; Constitution of Guatemala (1982) preamble; Constitution of Guatemala (1985) articles 5 and 45; Constitution of Paraguay (1992) article 138(1); Constitution of Peru (1993) article 46; Constitution of El Salvador (1996) articles 87 and 88; Constitution of Ecuador (1998) article 4(6); Constitution of Venezuela (1999) articles 333 and 350; Constitution of Ecuador (2008) articles 98 and 416(8). Note that Gargarella's scheme appears to leave three right to resist provisions without a periodization 'home'. These are: Constitution of Cuba (1972) articles 3 and 12; Constitution of Ecuador (1978) article 4; Constitution of Peru (1979) article 82. Of the historical total of twenty-seven Latin American right to resist provisions identified by Ginsburg and colleagues, just under half (eleven, or 40 per cent) were introduced during the 'second phase' identified by Mirow (1978–2008), which concentrates on constitutional rights and mechanisms for their enforcement. Of the fifteen constitutions he attributes to this period, nearly three-quarters (eleven, or 73 per cent) include right to resist provisions. See Mirow (n 127) 247–248.

[137] The right to resist was not included in Cuba's original anti-colonial constitution (1869) or its first post-colonial constitution (1901), but the third Constitution of Cuba (1940) introduced a right to resist at article 40. See Ginsburg et al (n 1) Appendix I, 1244. For its invocation in the most famous use of a constitutional right to resist as a legal defence in a criminal trial see Fidel Castro, *History Will Absolve Me* (Pedro Álvarez Tabío and Andrew Paul Booth tr) (Editorial de Ciencias Sociales 1975), referring to it variously as the 'right to resist oppression and injustice', the 'right to rebel' against usurpation, and 'right of insurrection against tyranny'.

[138] See Ramón Infiesta's lecture course on 'The Right to Resist Oppression in Comparative Constitutional Law' referred to in George A Finch, 'Inter-American Academy of Comparative

Thus the modern constitutional provisions for the right to resist retained certain common features with their predecessors, but also introduced further distinctions. The right was still considered to function as both deterrent and remedy for violations of fundamental rights, to operate as an exception provided trigger conditions were met, and to grant immunity for otherwise unlawful conduct. The scope of exceptional means continued to include both forceful and non-forceful means. The secondary trigger of necessity was still relevant. As previously, related rights claims were not necessarily meant to be litigated but rather directly enforced through action. However, the modern right was also reconceptualized as one of 'all citizens' individually, or of 'the people' acting as a unit or a majority. In introducing the specific 'right to resist oppression' it formalized this as a primary trigger. The principal object and purpose was still the enforcement of existing rights but not always the existing constitutional order. The newly introduced right of revolution also had a much lower secondary trigger threshold, potentially requiring only the will of the majority, as a matter of discretion. In short, the constitutional right to resist as understood today became more recognizable in the modern period.

5.5 CONTEMPORARY CONSTITUTIONAL PROVISIONS

Several studies by leading comparative constitutional scholars using empirical methods make findings pertinent to the contemporary constitutional right to resist.[139] In general, compilation of comprehensive comparative constitutional datasets and subsets is relatively recent,[140] and notoriously difficult due to a number of factors.[141] So far, establishment of legal prevalence of the

and International Law' (1957) 51(1) *American Journal of International Law* 97, later published in *Cursos Monográficos* (1959) (Academia Interamericana de Derecho Comparado e Internacional 1959) vol VII; Robert D Hayton, 'Untitled Review' (1961) 55(1) *American Journal of International Law* 187, 189. See also further discussion in Chapter 6, Section 6.4 and Chapter 7, Section 7.4.

139 See in particular, Law and Versteeg (n 7); Law and Versteeg (n 101); Goderis and Versteeg, (n 7); Ginsburg et al (n 1).

140 See Elkins et al (n 7) 6; Zachary Elkins, Tom Ginsburg, and James Melton, 'The Comparative Constitutions Project: A Cross-National Historical Dataset of Written Constitutions' (CCP Survey Instrument, 11 May 2010) under 2.3 Basic Principles at v63, 13–14; Benedikt Goderis and Mila Versteeg, 'The Transnational Origins of Constitutions: An Empirical Analysis' (2011) (SSRN 1865724, 2011); later revised as Goderis and Versteeg, 'Transnational Origins' (n 7) 19–21, 40–41; and Benedikt Goderis and Mila Versteeg, 'Diffusion of Constitutional Rights' (2014) 39 *International Review of Law and Economics* 1; Law and Versteeg (n 7) 1191, 1194, 1200–1202, 1223; Law and Versteeg (n 101) 771–776, 856–858.

141 See Jackson and Tushnet (n 6) v–ix; Dixon and Ginsburg (n 5) 4–5, 13; Rosenfeld and Sajó (n 5) 12–13; Law and Versteeg (n 7) 1167–1168, 1187–1188, 1246–1249.

constitutional right to resist is the main contribution of this scholarship. Explanatory analysis as to its legal meaning and legal value remains rudimentary. More detailed comparative doctrinal work is also pending. However, using the results of the prevalence studies it is possible to establish and compare basic legal features and content of the provisions.

5.5.1 *Legal Prevalence of the Constitutional Right to Resist*

Domestic constitutions are by far the most quantitatively significant source of contemporary law on the right to resist. For example, recent studies estimate that between 16 and 20 per cent of nearly 200 contemporary constitutions contain some variation on provision for a right to resist.[142] In contrast, only three sources of an implied right to resist are identifiable in customary international law,[143] along with two express right to resist provisions in regional treaty law and two sources of implied right in universal treaty law – in an overall dataset of more than 500 international treaties.[144] This represents a tiny fraction compared to the approximately one in five prevalence in constitutional law.

Most contemporary provisions were originally adopted in the twentieth century, and many were retained or reaffirmed in subsequent constitutional amendment processes in the current century – some as recently as 2020.[145] Indeed, Goderis and Versteeg and Law and Versteeg find that inclusion of constitutional right to resist provisions is on the increase, having doubled from 8 to 16 per cent in the six decades between 1946 and 2006.[146] This contrasts with the narrower 'right to bear arms', which is not only the least common

[142] Compare the estimate of 16 per cent of all contemporary constitutions as of 2006 in Law and Versteeg (n 7) 1202; Law and Versteeg (n 101) 775; Goderis and Versteeg (n 7) 40, with the more recent estimate of 20 per cent in Ginsburg et al (n 1) 1217–1218.

[143] See further discussion in Chapter 6, Sections 6.3, 6.4, and 6.5.

[144] See the United Nations Treaty Collection online database; Treaty Section-Office of Legal Affairs, *Treaty Handbook* (United Nations rev 2012) iv. This includes 'over three hundred human rights instruments, including one hundred global and regional multilateral human rights [treaties] currently in force' cited in Law and Versteeg (n 101) 834 (fn 186). See further discussion in Chapter 7, Sections 7.2.1, 7.2.2, and 7.3.1.

[145] According to the Comparative Constitutions Project updated and searchable online Constitute database.

[146] Law and Versteeg (n 7) 1202; Law and Versteeg (n 101) 775; Goderis and Versteeg (n 7) 40.

right but is also declining.[147] This evidence suggests continuing salience, rather than obsolescence of the right to resist as a legal idea.

That said, the extent of provision for the right to resist compared to other types of constitutional rights should not be overstated. For example, Law and Versteeg's 'constitutional rights index' identifies elements that meet a 70 per cent prevalence threshold for inclusion in a 'generic model'.[148] They find that the right to resist is not sufficiently common to be considered a 'generic' right.[149] This may have negative implications for any argument that the right to resist constitutes a 'general principle of law' for the purposes of international legal recognition, if based exclusively or primarily on domestic legislative prevalence.[150] Nevertheless, right to resist provisions are still more common than constitutional prohibitions on genocide and crimes against humanity[151] – both of which ostensibly represent more widely accepted legal concepts.

Ginsburg and colleagues have published the leading comparative study specific to the constitutional right to resist,[152] building a data subset based on the original comprehensive dataset by Elkins and colleagues.[153] It compares over 900 new and interim or amended constitutions covering over 200 countries from 1781 to 2011, but deliberately excludes unwritten constitutions, pre-1781 documents, 'quasi-constitutions', and state constitutions from federal systems.[154] As such, the Ginsburg data subset identifies sixty-one

[147] It comes last in their index of constitutional rights, in sixtieth place, now represented in only 2 per cent of constitutions. See Law and Versteeg (n 7) 1202; Law and Versteeg (n 101) 775–776; Goderis and Versteeg (n 7) 40.

[148] See Law and Versteeg (n 7) 1187–1202; Law and Versteeg (n 101) 773–776, 856–858.

[149] This conclusion is based on the lower estimated prevalence rate of 16 per cent, which ranks it fifty-fifth in their index of sixty. Law and Versteeg (n 7) 1202; Law and Versteeg (n 101) 775.

[150] Alternatively, any suggestion that the right to resist is a 'general principle of law' would need to demonstrate that 20 per cent constitutes sufficient domestic prevalence, if using the more recent data in Ginsburg et al (n 1) 1217–1218.

[151] This comes in at fifty-seventh place in the index. Law and Versteeg (n 7) 1202; Law and Versteeg (n 101) 775.

[152] Ginsburg et al (n 1).

[153] They also draw on the earlier datasets of Goderis and Versteeg and Law and Versteeg. See Ginsburg et al (n 1) 1217 (fn 155–156).

[154] See the earlier Tom Ginsburg, Daniel Lansberg-Rodriguez and Mila Versteeg, 'When to Overthrow Your Government: The Right to Resist in the World's Constitutions' (SSRN 2012) 31 (fn 151–152). These exclusion criteria necessarily mean that, despite the claim that the data subset represents 'all' historical constitutional right to resist provisions, it is not in fact fully historically comprehensive.

relevant current and former constitutions overall, covering forty-one countries and a defunct federation, including thirty-nine constitutions with right to resist provisions listed as 'current' at time of publication.[155] Though it may not be absolutely accurate in every regard,[156] it is still the most authoritative dataset available.[157]

5.5.1.1 Regional Distribution of Right to Resist Provisions

Regional distribution of the constitutional right to resist provisions is particularly relevant to the current and future status of the right in international law, as discussed in the two subsequent chapters. First, it helps establish whether this legal concept is geographically concentrated or confined to certain regions and not others, which would significantly constrain the viability of initiatives for wider codification at international level. Second, it helps determine whether adoption or non-adoption of constitutional right to resist provisions corresponds with recognition or non-recognition in international law at the regional level, which has implications for standard-setting and supplementary recognition. For these reasons, the regional units used for the following analysis generally correspond to the regional human rights treaties, the principal source of justiciable human rights at international law level: Africa, the Americas, Europe, and Asia.[158]

[155] See Ginsburg et al (n 1) Appendix I, 'Full Text of All (Historical) Constitutional Right-to-Resist Provisions' 1242–1259.

[156] As constitutions are amended and new constitutions adopted, figures current at any given time will fluctuate. For example, the Constitution of Thailand (2017) no longer contains a provision. In addition, not all constitutions containing such provisions are included. For one example, the Constitution of Turkey (1982 revised 2011, 2017) is not listed despite its article 137 provision for a limited right-duty to resist unlawful orders. See also the shortcomings in their compilation of African constitutions (see below n 159). On the other hand, several defunct constitutions are erroneously listed as 'current'. For one example, the United Provinces of the Rio de la Plata was dissolved in 1831 and succeeded by the states of Argentina, Uruguay, Bolivia, and Brazil. See Ginsburg et al (n 1) 1255, 1257–1259.

[157] A discrepancy between the Ginsburg et al data subset classification terminology and the comparative search term function in the Constitute database renders the former generally the more useful for the purposes of this study, as the latter generates a significant prevalence under-estimation. However, all updates to the constitutions and provisions are sourced from the Constitute database, indicated by square brackets. All subsequent references are to the constitutions in force at time of writing unless otherwise indicated.

[158] The more detailed United Nations geoscheme classification was therefore not the most appropriate for the purpose of the present analysis. Note however the continuing absence of a pan-Asian regional human rights treaty.

In absolute terms, Africa has the greatest number of constitutions with provisions (13),[159] followed by the Americas (12),[160] Europe (11),[161] and

[159] The Ginsburg et al data subset lists these as: Constitution of Algeria (1976) [(1989, reinstated 1996, revised 2008 and 2020)] articles 27 and 33 [note the correct articles were 30 and 39, although article 30 is now article 32, and article 39 was eliminated as of the 2020 amendments]; Constitution of Benin (1990) article 66; Constitution of Burkina Faso (1991) [revised 2012] article 167; Constitution of Cape Verde (1996) [(1980, revised 1992)] article 18; Constitution of Chad (1996) [revised 2005, 2018] preamble; Constitution of the Democratic Republic of the Congo (2005) [revised 2011] article 64; Constitution of Ghana (1992) [revised 1996] article 3(4)–(7); Constitution of Guinea (2010) article 21; Constitution of Mali (1992) article 121; Constitution of Mozambique (1990) [(2004, revised 2007)] article 80; Constitution of Rwanda (2003) [revised 2015] article 48 [now article 49]; Constitution of Togo (1992) [revised 2007] articles 45 and 150; Constitution of Uganda (1995) [revised 2005] article 3(4)–(6). See Ginsburg et al (n 1) 1242, 1243, 1244, 1249, 1251, 1252, 1253, 1255, 1256, 1258. In addition, Christof Heyns and Waruguru Kaguongo, 'Constitutional Human Rights Law in Africa' (2006) 22 *South African Journal of Human Rights* 673, 678 (fn 20) identifies the still-current Constitution of Cameroon (1972 [revised 2008]) preamble [7]; Constitution of Benin (1990) article 19; Constitution of Congo (Brazzaville) (2002) article 10; Constitution of the Democratic Republic of the Congo (2005 [revised 2011]) article 28; Constitution of Gambia (1996, revised 2004) article 6(2)–(3); Constitution of Niger [revised 2010] article 15; Constitution of Togo (1992 [revised 2007]) article 21. See also the Interim Constitution of Southern Sudan (2005) article 4(2); Transitional Constitution of the Republic of South Sudan (2011) article 4(3) identified in Murphy (n 2) 470 (fn 19–20). According to the Constitute database, the latter provision appears in the Constitution of South Sudan (2011, revised 2013) as article 4(3).

[160] The Ginsburg et al data subset lists these as: Constitution of Argentina (1956) [(1853, reinstated 1983, revised 1994)] article 36; Constitution of Cuba (1972) [(1976, revised 2002 and 2019)] articles 3 and 12 [now articles 4 and 16]; Constitution of the Dominican Republic (1966) [(2015)] articles 8(5), 46 and 99 [now articles 6, 40(15) and 73]; Constitution of Ecuador (2008) [revised 2015] articles 98 and 416(8); Constitution of El Salvador (1996) [(1983, revised 2014)] articles 87 and 88; Constitution of Guatemala (1985) [revised 1993] articles 5 and 45; Constitution of Honduras (1982) [revised 2013] article 3; Constitution of Mexico (1917) [revised 2015] article 136; Constitution of Paraguay (1992) [revised 2011] article 138(1); Constitution of Peru (1993) [revised 2009] article 46; Constitution of Uruguay (1830) [(1966, reinstated 1985, revised 2004)] article 134 [now article 10]; Constitution of Venezuela (1999) [revised 2009] articles 333 and 350. See Ginsburg et al (n 1) 1242, 1245, 1246, 1248, 1251, 1252, 1253, 1254, 1259.

[161] The Ginsburg et al data subset lists these as: Constitution of Armenia (2005) [(1995, revised 2005)] article 18; Constitution of Azerbaijan (1995) [revised 2009] article 54(2) [see also article 26(1)]; Constitution of the Czech Republic (1993) [revised 2013] article 23 [of the Charter of Fundamental Rights and Basic Freedoms]; Constitution of Estonia (1992) [revised 2015] article 54(2) [now article 54]; Constitution of France (1791, reinstated 1958) [revised 2008] article 2 [of the Declaration of the Rights of Man and of the Citizen (1789)]; Constitution of Germany (1968) [(1949, revised 2014)] article 20(4); Constitution of Greece (1975) [revised 2008] article 120(4); Constitution of Hungary (2011) [revised 2013] article C (2)–C(3); Constitution of Lithuania (1992) [revised 2006] article 3; Constitution of Portugal (1989) [(1976, revised 2005)] articles 7(3) and 21; Constitution of Slovakia (1992) [revised 2014] article 32. See Ginsburg et al (n 1) 1242, 1246, 1248, 1249, 1252, 1255.

Asia (3).[162] This demonstrates a roughly even three-way split among regions not including Asia. As for regional prevalence, the right is most predominant in the Americas,[163] followed by Africa,[164] Europe,[165] and Asia.[166] At a prevalence of more than one-third of constitutions in the Americas, and nearly one-quarter of constitutions in both Africa and Europe, the right to resist could be considered significant in three out of four regions.

In comparison, the right's status in public international law at regional level is considerably shakier. It is recognized in the African system – as well as in the Arab system, which would include countries in both the African and Asian geographic regions – but not in the American or European systems, despite similarly significant levels of constitutional recognition in these regions.[167]

An additional type of regional clustering of contemporary constitutional provisions is also evident, correlated to regional experiences of specific manifestations of oppression.[168] The European constitutional provisions include a Western European cluster of post-fascist right to resist codifications,[169] and an Eastern European cluster of post-Soviet codifications.[170] The remaining codifications represent the largest, pan-regional post-colonial cluster spanning

[162] The Ginsburg et al data subset lists these as: Constitution of Maldives (2008) articles 64 and 245; Constitution of Thailand (2007) section 69 [note this provision does not appear in the subsequent Constitution of Thailand (2014) or (2017) and therefore is not current]; Constitution of Timor Leste (2002) section 28(1)–(2). See Ginsburg et al (n 1) 1252, 1255, 1256.

[163] That is, twelve of thirty-five, or approximately 34 per cent of Organization of American States countries, by the Ginsburg et al data subset.

[164] That is, thirteen of fifty-five, or approximately 23 per cent of African Union countries, by the Ginsburg et al data subset.

[165] That is, eleven of forty-seven, or approximately 23 per cent of Council of Europe countries, by the Ginsburg et al data subset.

[166] That is, three of forty-four countries in what is the forty-eight-country Asian region according to the UN, which includes countries of the Middle East, minus the three countries that are members of the Council of Europe and thus included in that group, above: Armenia, Azerbaijan, and Turkey; and minus one further country, Algeria, that is a member of the African Union and thus included in that group, above. That makes approximately 6 per cent by the Ginsburg et al data subset.

[167] The disjuncture at regional level and between regions is discussed further in Chapter 7, Section 7.3.

[168] These clusters correspond to three of seven constitutional 'waves' since 1780 identified in Elster (n 7) 368–373, who does not include the post-colonial constitutional waves in Africa, Asia, or Latin America.

[169] Constitution of Germany article 20(4); Constitution of Greece article 120(4); Constitution of Portugal articles 7(3) and 21. The Constitution of France containing a provision at article 2 of the Declaration of the Rights of Man and of the Citizen was restored in 1958, but strictly speaking it belongs to the original revolutionary republican cluster discussed in Section 5.4.

[170] Constitution of Armenia article 18; Constitution of Azerbaijan articles 26(1) and 54(2); Constitution of the Czech Republic article 23 of the Charter of Fundamental Rights and Basic Freedoms; Constitution of Estonia article 54; Constitution of Hungary article C(2)–C(3); Constitution of Lithuania article 3; Constitution of Slovakia article 32.

Africa, Asia, and Latin America.[171] It is also noticeable that right to resist provisions were not adopted uniformly across affected states. Moreover, the formulations can differ considerably within each cluster, and in no case does the language of the provisions correspond to existing international human rights law expressions of the right.[172] Since the scope of the present research is limited to comparative content analysis, it must leave open the questions of why the constitutional right to resist has been adopted by some countries and not others, why it is significantly less common in Asia despite the fact that the concept also has distinct eastern origins, and why adoptions have followed some revolutionary periods and not others. Such variations do however warrant future research into explanations, building on existing research hypotheses and comparative evidence.[173]

5.5.2 *Legal Features and Content: Comparative Analysis of the Ginsburg Data Subset*

Reviewing the Ginsburg data subset, it quickly becomes apparent that no two constitutional provisions for the right to resist are identical. While it is possible to identify certain similarities in legal features, each varies considerably as to form. Nor does any constitutional provision appear to draw from the two regional human rights treaties that include an express right.[174] What Law and Versteeg characterize as 'minor textual differences'[175] arguably instead represent a diversity in legal content worthy of closer consideration. However,

[171] According to the Ginsburg et al subset, the relevant African codifications are: Constitution of Algeria articles 27 and 33 [articles 30 and 39, now only article 32]; Constitution of Benin article 66; Constitution of Burkina Faso article 167; Constitution of Cape Verde article 18; Constitution of Chad preamble; Constitution of the Democratic Republic of the Congo article 64; Constitution of Ghana article 3(4)–(7); Constitution of Guinea article 21; Constitution of Mali article 121; Constitution of Mozambique article 80; Constitution of Rwanda article 49; Constitution of Togo articles 45 and 150; Constitution of Uganda article 3 (4)–(6). The relevant Asian codifications are: Constitution of Maldives articles 64 and 245; Constitution of Timor Leste section 28(1)–(2). The relevant Latin American codifications are: Constitution of Argentina article 36; Constitution of Cuba articles 3 and 12 [now articles 4 and 16]; Constitution of the Dominican Republic articles 8(5), 46 and 99 [now articles 6, 40(15) and 73]; Constitution of Ecuador articles 98 and 416(8); Constitution of El Salvador articles 87 and 88; Constitution of Guatemala articles 5 and 45; Constitution of Honduras article 3; Constitution of Paraguay article 138(1); Constitution of Peru article 46; Constitution of Venezuela articles 333 and 350. Certain right to resist provisions originating in earlier revolutionary republican constitutions were amended or affirmed in the twenty-first century. See Constitution of Mexico article 136; Constitution of Uruguay article 134 [now article 10].

[172] This is generally consistent with other findings in Law and Versteeg (n 101) 833–850. See further discussion in Chapter 6, Sections 6.3, 6.4, and 6.5 and Chapter 7, Sections 7.3.1 and 7.4.

[173] For example, see Goderis and Versteeg (n 7) 1–11, 15–16; Ginsburg et al (n 1) 1228–1233.

[174] See further discussion in Chapter 7, Section 7.3.1.

[175] Law and Versteeg (n 101) 771; Law and Versteeg (n 7) 1191.

the Ginsburg study focuses on other questions and does not run an analysis of the provisions against the content elements they identify as potentially relevant for classification.[176]

The Ginsburg data subset therefore provides the basis for a legal features and content comparison, using the conceptual elements identified in Chapter 4. What follows is a qualitative analysis of all provisions identified as 'current' by Ginsburg and colleagues as to certain features describing their legal nature, legal function, and legal content. The intent is to identify similarities and differences between the provisions in the thirty-nine constitutions, establish general contours, and thereby test the relevance of the Part I findings. To the extent quantitative approximations are suggested, this is for illustrative purposes only. For the same reason, the analysis exclusively considers the texts of the provisions. It does not include their judicial interpretation in the limited case law available, which could help elaborate on legal meaning. While such evidence could be relevant, its systematic assessment is beyond the scope of this immediate project. Note also that in certain instances, or with regard to certain features, the provisions can be vague or open-textured enough to permit several viable interpretations, impeding strict 'accuracy' in categorization.

5.5.2.1 Foundational Organizing Principle, Fundamental Right, Method of Enforcement

Placement of constitutional provisions is the first indicator of the conceptualization of their nature and function. One-third of the constitutions identified by Ginsburg and colleagues place the right to resist provisions with the foundational organizing principles.[177] Nearly half list them among the 'fundamental' or 'human' rights,[178] with over a quarter of these additionally listed

[176] See Ginsburg et al (n 1) 1221, 1226–1228.

[177] That is, fourteen out of thirty-nine or approximately 33 per cent. See Constitution of Algeria article 27 [article 30, now article 32]; Constitution of Benin article 66; Constitution of Cuba articles 3 and 12 [now articles 4 and 16]; Constitution of Chad preamble; Constitution of the Dominican Republic articles 6, 40(15) and 73; Constitution of Ecuador articles 98 and 416 (8); Constitution of El Salvador articles 87 and 88; Constitution of Germany article 20(4); Constitution of Honduras article 3; Constitution of Hungary article C(2)–C(3); Constitution of Lithuania article 3; Constitution of Portugal articles 7(3); Constitution of Paraguay article 138(1); Constitution of Peru article 46.

[178] That is, seventeen out of thirty-nine, or approximately 43 per cent. See Constitution of Algeria article 33 [article 39, now suspended]; Constitution of Argentina article 36; Constitution of Armenia article 18; Constitution of Azerbaijan article 26(1); Constitution of Cape Verde article 18; Constitution of the Czech Republic article 23; Constitution of the Dominican Republic articles 6, 40(15) and 73; Constitution of Estonia article 54; Constitution of France

specifically as 'political rights'.[179] One in five lists them among the constitutional enforcement provisions,[180] with only a small number identifying them exclusively under a listing of citizen duties.[181] All of these placements are corroborative of the conceptual findings described in Part I.

As with all constitutional provisions, the right to resist in each context must be read in conjunction with other provisions that may either clarify or limit its scope and application. For example, some coexist with general clauses affirming non-diminution of rights otherwise recognized, or extensive provisions for prior judicial remedy. Some coexist with general disclaimer clauses potentially limiting interpretation and application, or express obedience requirements, treason, or sedition provisions, or extensive provisions for rights suspension under a state of emergency.[182] While detailed analysis of all thirty-nine constitutions in this regard is beyond the scope of this overview of the

article 2 of the Declaration of the Rights of Man and of the Citizen; Constitution of Guatemala articles 5 and 45; Constitution of Guinea article 21; Constitution of Maldives articles 64 and 245; Constitution of Mozambique article 80; Constitution of Portugal articles 7 (3) and 21; Constitution of Slovakia article 32; Constitution of Timor Leste section 28(1)–(2); Constitution of Uruguay article 10.

179 That is, five out of seventeen, or approximately 29 per cent. See Constitution of Azerbaijan article 54(2); Constitution of the Czech Republic article 23; Constitution of the Dominican Republic article 40(15); Constitution of Mozambique article 80; Constitution of Slovakia article 32. Goderis and Versteeg (n 7) 40 includes the 'right to resist when rights are violated' under the cluster of constitutionally codified 'political, democratic and accountability rights', together with but distinct from a 'right to a remedy when rights are violated' – but separates it from a 'right to bear arms', classified as an entirely separate 'life, liberty, physical integrity and privacy' right.

180 That is, eight out of thirty-nine, or approximately 20 per cent. See Constitution of Burkina Faso article 167; Constitution of the Dominican Republic article 73; Constitution of Ghana article 3(4)–(7); Constitution of Greece article 120(4); Constitution of Mali article 121; Constitution of Mexico article 136; Constitution of Uganda article 3(4)–(6); Constitution of Venezuela articles 333 and 350. Law and Versteeg (n 101) 771 treat it as a substantive rather than enforcement right.

181 That is, three out of thirty-nine, or approximately 7 per cent. See Constitution of the Democratic Republic of the Congo article 64; Constitution of Rwanda article 49; Constitution of Togo articles 45 and 150. These are not the only constitutions that conceptualize a 'duty to resist', but rather the only ones that separate it off as such, for emphasis.

182 See, for example Constitution of Ecuador judicial remedy provisions at Title II chapters 1, 8; Title III chapters 1, 3 sections 1–7; Title IX chapter 2; non-diminution provisions at Title II, chapter 1 articles 10–11; Title IX chapter 1; state of emergency provisions at Title IV chapter 3 section 4. Indeed, the 1968 amendment introducing emergency provisions into the German Constitution (1949) accompanied the amendment introducing a right to resist provision, itself subject to non-diminution as per article 79. See Dieter Grimm, 'The Basic Law at 60 – Identity and Change' (2010) 11(1) *German Law Journal* 33, 34; Georg Gesk, 'Right to Resistance and Terrorism – The Example of Germany' (2012) 13 *German Law Journal* 1075, 1077–1078.

general features of their right to resist provisions, complementary or competing clauses must be taken into account when interpreting provisions in any particular constitution.

5.5.2.2 Express Rights Predominate, Implied Rights Also Feature

By far the majority of the constitutions identified by Ginsburg and colleagues contain express provision for the right to resist.[183] This particularly contrasts with general international law, in which the right to resist is merely implied.[184] That said, a significant number contain implied provisions,[185] and it is not uncommon for constitutions to provide for both express and implied rights.[186]

5.5.2.3 'Right to Resist' Most Common Cognate Term Used

The most common term used to describe the constitutional right is the 'right to resist' or its variants, the 'right to resistance' or 'right of

[183] That is, thirty-two out of thirty-nine, or approximately 82 per cent. See Constitution of Argentina article 36; Constitution of Armenia article 18; Constitution of Azerbaijan article 54 (2); Constitution of Benin article 66; Constitution of Burkina Faso article 167; Constitution of Cape Verde article 18; Constitution of Chad preamble; Constitution of Cuba article 3 [now article 4]; Constitution of Czech Republic article 23; Constitution of Ecuador articles 98 and 416(8); El Salvador article 87; Constitution of Estonia article 54(2); Constitution of France, Declaration article 2; Constitution of Germany article 20(4); Constitution of Ghana article 3 (4); Constitution of Greece article 120(4); Constitution of Guinea article 21; Constitution of Honduras article 3; Constitution of Hungary article C(2); Constitution of Lithuania article 3; Constitution of Maldives article 64; Constitution of Mali article 121; Mozambique article 80; Constitution of Paraguay article 138(1); Constitution of Peru article 46; Constitution of Portugal articles 7(3) and 21; Constitution of Rwanda article 48; Constitution of Slovakia article 32; Constitution of Thailand section 69 [now suspended]; Constitution of Timor Leste article 28(1)–(2); Constitution of Togo article 150; Constitution of Uganda article 3(4).

[184] See Chapter 6, Sections 6.3, 6.4, and 6.5 and Chapter 7, Section 7.2.

[185] That is, fifteen out of thirty-nine, or approximately 38 per cent. See Constitution of Algeria articles 27 and 33 [articles 30 and 39, now only article 32]; Constitution of the Democratic Republic of the Congo article 64; Constitution of Cuba article 12(g) [now article 16]; Constitution of Dominican Republic articles 6, 40(15) and 73; Constitution of El Salvador article 88; Constitution of Ghana articles 3(5)–(7); Constitution of Guatemala article 5 and article 45; Constitution of Honduras article 3; Constitution of Maldives article 245; Constitution of Mexico article 136; Constitution of Paraguay article 138(1); Constitution of Peru article 46; Constitution of Togo article 45; Constitution of Uruguay article 10; Constitution of Venezuela articles 333 and 350.

[186] That is, eight out of thirty-nine, or approximately 20 per cent. See Constitution of Cuba articles 3 and 12(g) [now articles 4 and 16]; Constitution of El Salvador articles 87 and 88; Constitution of Ghana article 3(4)–(7); Constitution of Honduras article 3; Constitution of Maldives articles 64 and 245; Constitution of Paraguay article 138(1); Constitution of Peru article 46; Constitution of Togo articles 45 and 150.

resistance'. Just under half of the constitutions in the Ginsburg and colleagues subset include this descriptor of the right.[187] The next most common cognate used to describe the right is the 'right to disobey' or 'right of disobedience'. One-quarter of the constitutions identified use this cognate.[188] Only one constitution expressly uses the 'right to oppose'.[189] None employ the cognate terms 'right of rebellion' or 'right of revolution'.[190] Several opt for more obscure cognate descriptors, as either express or implied rights.[191] There is also only a single express reference to a constitutional 'right of self-defence' among the subset.[192]

[187] That is, at least nineteen of thirty-nine, or approximately 48 per cent use the exact term or variants. See Constitution of Argentina article 36; Constitution of Azerbaijan article 54(2); Constitution of Cape Verde article 18; Constitution of Chad preamble; Constitution of Cuba article 3 [now article 4]; Constitution of Czech Republic article 23; Constitution of Ecuador article 98; Constitution of France, Declaration article 2; Constitution of Germany article 20 (4); Constitution of Ghana article 3(4); Constitution of Greece article 120(4); Constitution of Guinea article 21; Constitution of Hungary article C(2); Constitution of Paraguay article 138 (1); Constitution of Portugal article 21; Constitution of Slovakia article 32; Constitution of Thailand section 69 [now suspended]; Constitution of Timor Leste article 28(1); Constitution of Uganda article 3(4). In addition, the right to resist is implied in a further three constitutions: Constitution of Algeria articles 27 and 33 [articles 30 and 39, now only article 32]; Constitution of Mexico article 136; Constitution of Venezuela articles 333 and 350. See also further reference to more obscure alternative cognates (n 191 below). Using the Constitute database's alternative translations, usage of the exact term or variants could be somewhat greater than identified by Ginsburg et al.

[188] That is, ten of thirty-nine, or approximately 25 per cent, although several of these use slightly different terminology. See Constitution of Benin article 66; Constitution of Burkina Faso article 167; Constitution of Cape Verde article 18; Constitution of Chad preamble; Constitution of Maldives articles 64 and 245; Constitution of Mali article 121; Constitution of Mozambique article 80; Constitution of Rwanda article 48; Constitution of Timor Leste article 28(1); Constitution of Togo article 150. In addition, the right of disobedience is implied in a further five constitutions: Constitution of Dominican Republic articles 6, 40(15) and 73; Constitution of Guatemala article 5; Constitution of Honduras article 3; Constitution of Paraguay article 138(1); Constitution of Uruguay article 10.

[189] See Constitution of Lithuania article 3. A further two imply the right to 'oppose'. See Constitution of the Democratic Republic of the Congo article 64; Constitution of Guatemala article 45.

[190] Ginsburg et al (n 1) 1189 (fn 11) expressly follows Honoré in considering these terms synonymous with the 'right to resist'. This is questionable for the reasons set out in Chapter 2, and is not reflected in the provision texts included in the subset. Compare the consistent usage of the 'right to resist when rights are violated', deliberately separated from the narrower 'right to bear arms' in Law and Versteeg (n 7) 1194, 1202; Law and Versteeg (n 101) 775, 857.

[191] See Constitution of Armenia article 18; Constitution of Cuba article 12(g) [now article 16]; Constitution of El Salvador article 87 and 88; Constitution of Estonia article 54; Constitution of Honduras article 3; Constitution of Peru article 46; Constitution of Portugal articles 7(3) and 21; Constitution of Togo article 45.

[192] See Constitution of Timor Leste article 28(2).

5.5.2.4 Primarily a 'Right' of 'All Citizens'

Among the identified constitutions, express or implied rights provisions are by far the most common, appearing in all but two of the constitutions. Either hybrid 'right-duty' provisions, or provision for both 'right' and 'duty' within the same constitution, feature in nearly a quarter of the subset.[193] Only two constitutions refer exclusively to a 'duty' or 'obligation'.[194] Arguably, however, these duties also imply derived rights.

In almost all of these provisions, the right-holders are identified as 'all citizens' or the equivalent.[195] In some, the right-holders are the citizens only when acting as a majority – 'the people'.[196] In a few cases, the right-holders are 'peoples' more generally, extending recognition beyond the citizens of the state.[197] In a very few cases additional rights are conferred on public servants

[193] That is, nine of thirty-nine, or approximately 23 per cent. See Constitution of Benin article 66; Constitution of Chad preamble; Constitution of El Salvador articles 87 and 88; Constitution of Ghana article 3(4); Constitution of Greece article 120(4); Constitution of Hungary article C (2); Constitution of Maldives articles 64 and 245; Constitution of Togo articles 45 and 150; Constitution of Uganda article 3(4).

[194] See Constitution of the Democratic Republic of the Congo article 64; Constitution of Venezuela articles 333 and 350.

[195] That is, in thirty-six of thirty-nine constitutions, or approximately 92 per cent. See Constitution of Algeria article 33 [article 39, now suspended]; Constitution of Argentina article 36; Constitution of Armenia article 18; Constitution of Azerbaijan article 54(2); Constitution of Benin article 66; Constitution of Burkina Faso article 167; Constitution of Cape Verde article 18; Constitution of Chad preamble; Constitution of Cuba article 3 [now article 4]; Constitution of Czech Republic article 23; Constitution of the Democratic Republic of the Congo article 64; Constitution of Dominican Republic articles 6, 40(15) and 73; Constitution of Ecuador article 98; Constitution of Estonia article 54(2); Constitution of France, Declaration article 2; Constitution of Germany article 20(4); Constitution of Ghana article 3 (4)–(7); Constitution of Greece article 120(4); Constitution of Guatemala article 5; Constitution of Guinea article 21; Constitution of Honduras article 3; Constitution of Hungary article C(2); Lithuania article 3; Constitution of Maldives article 64; Constitution of Mozambique article 80; Constitution of Paraguay article 138(1); Constitution of Peru article 46; Constitution of Portugal article 21; Constitution of Rwanda article 48; Constitution of Slovakia article 32; Constitution of Thailand section 69 [now suspended]; Constitution of Timor Leste article 28(1)–(2); Constitution of Togo articles 45 and 150; Constitution of Uganda article 3(4); Constitution of Uruguay article 10; Constitution of Venezuela article 333.

[196] See Constitution of El Salvador article 87; Constitution of Guatemala article 45; Constitution of Honduras article 3; Constitution of Mali article 121; Constitution of Mexico article 136; Constitution of Venezuela article 350.

[197] See Constitution of Portugal article 7(3). See also Constitution of Algeria article 27 [article 30, now article 32]; Constitution of Cuba article 12(g) [now article 16]; Constitution of Ecuador article 416(8).

or representatives.[198] Likewise, in the even fewer cases where duty-bearers are specified, with only rare exceptions these are 'all citizens'.[199] Of course in all cases, by virtue of constitutional codification and guarantee, the duty on the state to respect, protect, and fulfill the right is implied.

5.5.2.5 Enforcement as Predominant Object and Purpose

Nearly all constitutional provisions for the right to resist are premised on its conceptualization as a form of 'higher' law or rights enforcement. Most intend constitutional enforcement.[200] About one-third of the constitutions include provisions that intend human rights enforcement, whether constitutional or international.[201] A small number of provisions also intend the enforcement of

[198] See Constitution of Benin article 66; Constitution of Maldives article 245; Constitution of Togo article 150.

[199] See Constitution of Benin article 66; Constitution of Chad preamble; Constitution of Cuba article 12(g) [now article 16]; Constitution of the Democratic Republic of the Congo article 64; Constitution of El Salvador article 88; Constitution of Ghana article 3(4)–(7); Constitution of Greece article 120(4); Constitution of Hungary article C(2); Constitution of Maldives article 245; Constitution of Togo articles 45 and 150.

[200] That is, thirty-four out of thirty-nine, or approximately 87 per cent. See Constitution of Argentina article 36; Constitution of Azerbaijan article 54(2); Constitution of Benin article 66; Constitution of Burkina Faso article 167; Constitution of Cape Verde article 18; Constitution of Chad preamble; Constitution of Cuba article 3 [now article 4]; Constitution of Czech Republic article 23; Constitution of the Democratic Republic of the Congo article 64; Constitution of Dominican Republic articles 6, 40(15) and 73; Constitution of Ecuador article 98; Constitution of El Salvador articles 87 and 88; Constitution of Estonia article 54(2); Constitution of France, Declaration article 2; Constitution of Germany article 20(4); Constitution of Ghana article 3(4); Constitution of Greece article 120(4); Constitution of Guatemala article 45; Constitution of Guinea article 21; Constitution of Honduras article 3; Constitution of Hungary article C(2); Constitution of Lithuania article 3; Constitution of Mali article 121; Constitution of Mexico article 136; Constitution of Mozambique article 80; Constitution of Paraguay article 138(1); Constitution of Peru article 46; Constitution of Portugal articles 7(3) and 21; Constitution of Slovakia article 32; Constitution of Thailand section 69 [now suspended]; Constitution of Timor Leste article 28(1); Constitution of Togo articles 45 and 150; Constitution of Uganda article 3(4); Constitution of Venezuela articles 333 and 350. This purpose is most often express, but in a few instances is implied. While Ginsburg et al (n 1) 1192 maintains that the right to resist is designed to achieve 'the wholesale restructuring of an entire regime', this is generally contradicted by the provisions themselves.

[201] That is, thirteen of thirty-nine, or approximately 33 per cent. See Constitution of Algeria article 33 [article 39, now suspended]; Constitution of Armenia article 18; Constitution of Cape Verde article 18; Constitution of Czech Republic article 23; Constitution of France, Declaration article 2; Constitution of Guatemala article 45; Constitution of Guinea article 21; Constitution of Mozambique article 80; Constitution of Portugal articles 7(3) and 21; Constitution of Rwanda article 48; Constitution of Slovakia article 32; Constitution of Timor Leste article 28(1)–(2); Constitution of Venezuela article 350.

the public international law prohibition on aggression,[202] but none has the sole intent of enforcing international law.

A small but significant cluster conceptualizes the right to resist as a form of effective remedy when judicial and other forms have failed.[203] While none of the provisions is expressly constructed as a deterrent, this purpose is arguably at least implied by those constitutions making provision for a right or duty to disobey unconstitutional or otherwise unlawful orders.

Notwithstanding the predominance of the enforcement conception, the four-fold typology of object and purpose set out in Chapter 4 is faintly reflected in the constitutional provisions identified, in that some provisions appear to draw on more than one legal macro-concept. For example, the very fact of the right to resist's expression as a constitutional right implies its conceptualization as part of a right to self-determination. However, only a comparatively small number of these constitutional provisions specifically conceptualize the right to resist as 'self-determination',[204] or as a collective form of 'self-defence'.[205] This again contrasts with international law, where treaty law provision and customary law recognition of the right derive primarily from these two concepts. Similarly, none of the constitutional provisions is expressly conceptualized as instrumental to realizing the 'right to peace'. This contrasts with the most recent initiative to codify the right to resist as such in international law.[206]

5.5.2.6 Primary and Secondary Triggers

The specific term 'right to resist tyranny' is not used at all and reaching that threshold is not a requirement in the identified constitutions. However, in general the primary triggers do otherwise roughly correspond with the

[202] This may be either express or implied. See Constitution of Algeria article 27 [article 30, now article 32]; Constitution of Cape Verde article 18; Constitution of Cuba article 12(g) [now article 16]; Constitution of Ecuador article 416(8); Constitution of Lithuania article 3.

[203] That is, seven of thirty-nine, or approximately 17 per cent. See Constitution of Cape Verde article 18; Constitution of Cuba article 3 [now article 4]; Constitution of Czech Republic article 23; Constitution of Estonia article 54(2); Constitution of Germany article 20(4); Constitution of Portugal article 21; Constitution of Slovakia article 32.

[204] This may be either express or implied. See Constitution of Algeria article 27 [article 30, now article 32]; Constitution of Cuba articles 3 and 12(a) and (g) [now articles 4 and 16]; Constitution of Ecuador article 416(8); Constitution of Guinea article 21; Constitution of Lithuania article 3.

[205] This may be either express or implied. See Constitution of Cape Verde article 18; Constitution of Cuba article 12(g) [now article 16]; Constitution of Lithuania article 3; Constitution of Portugal article 21; Constitution of Timor Leste article 28(2).

[206] See further discussion in Chapter 7, Section 7.4.

associated Bartolist thresholds of 'defect of title' or 'reason of conduct'.[207] Virtually all the constitutional provisions identified are triggered by some form or forms of unconstitutional exercise of power.

Clearly related to defect of title is the 'usurpation' of power, with or without the use of force, appearing as a trigger in more than half of the identified constitutions.[208] Similar but not identical is the trigger specifying change of the constitutional order itself, again with or without force, present in more than half of the identified constitutions.[209] Only a few provisions specify a right to resist 'coup d'état'.[210]

As for reasons of conduct, constitutional violations provide the primary trigger in more than half of the identified constitutions,[211] and human rights

[207] See discussion in Chapter 4, Section 4.2.

[208] That is, twenty-three of thirty-nine, or approximately 58 per cent. For provisions specifying forcible usurpation, see Constitution of Argentina article 36; Constitution of Azerbaijan article 54(2); Constitution of Benin article 66; Constitution of Burkina Faso article 167; Constitution of Chad preamble; Constitution of Democratic Republic of Congo article 64; Constitution of Estonia article 54(2); Constitution of Greece article 120(4); Constitution of Hungary article C (2); Constitution of Lithuania article 3; Constitution of Togo articles 45 and 150. For provisions where usurpation by force is either not specified or can include 'other unlawful means', see Constitution of Cuba article 3 [now article 4]; Constitution of Dominican Republic articles 40(15), 73; Constitution of El Salvador articles 87 and 88; Constitution of Germany article 20(4); Constitution of Ghana article 3(4); Constitution of Honduras article 3; Constitution of Mali article 121; Constitution of Mexico article 136; Constitution of Paraguay article 138(1); Constitution of Peru article 46; Constitution of Thailand section 69 [now suspended]; Constitution of Uganda article 3(4).

[209] That is, twenty-five of thirty-nine, or approximately 64 per cent. For provisions specifying forcible change, see Constitution of Argentina article 36; Constitution of Azerbaijan article 54 (2); Constitution of Benin article 66; Constitution of Burkina Faso article 167; Constitution of Chad preamble; Constitution of Democratic Republic of the Congo article 64; Constitution of Estonia article 54(2); Constitution of Greece article 120(4); Constitution of Lithuania article 3; Constitution of Paraguay article 138(1); Constitution of Slovakia article 32; Constitution of Togo articles 45 and 150. For provisions where forcible change is either not specified or may include 'other unlawful means', see Constitution of Cuba article 3 [now article 4]; Constitution of Czech Republic article 23; Constitution of El Salvador articles 87 and 88; Constitution of Germany article 20(4); Constitution of Ghana article 3(4); Constitution of Honduras article 3; Constitution of Hungary article C(2); Constitution of Mali article 121; Constitution of Mexico article 136; Constitution of Peru article 46; Constitution of Thailand section 69 [now suspended]; Constitution of Uganda article 3(4); Constitution of Venezuela article 333.

[210] See Constitution of Benin article 66; Constitution of Burkina Faso article 167; Constitution of Mali article 121; Constitution of Togo article 150.

[211] That is, twenty-three of thirty-nine, or approximately 58 per cent, most of which are express but some are implied. See Constitution of Algeria article 33 [article 39, now suspended]; Constitution of Armenia article 18; Constitution of Burkina Faso article 167; Constitution of Cape Verde article 18; Constitution of Chad preamble; Constitution of Czech Republic article 23; Constitution of Dominican Republic articles 6 and 40(15); Constitution of

violations in one-third.[212] The specific term 'right to resist oppression' is used, but only in a few instances.[213]

In a very few cases, certain other violations of public international law that bridge contemporary concepts of defect of title and reason of conduct can also trigger a constitutional right to resist. These triggers are 'aggression'[214] and imposition of a colonial, neo-colonial, or racist regime.[215]

Fewer than one in five of the identified constitutions also specifies a secondary trigger for the right to resist, requiring that no other effective remedy be available.[216] More than four out of five provisions do not specify this – or any other secondary trigger condition. Where the provisions in question effectively contain a necessity requirement, no provision actually uses that term. Nor is the term 'last resort' used, or 'exhaustion'. This suggests that, even where specified, the secondary trigger threshold of these provisions may be lower.[217]

Democratic Republic of the Congo article 64; Constitution of Ecuador article 98; Constitution of El Salvador article 87; Constitution of France, Declaration article 2; Constitution of Ghana article 3(4); Constitution of Guatemala article 45; Constitution of Guinea article 21; Constitution of Mexico article 136; Constitution of Mozambique article 80; Constitution of Portugal articles 7(3) and 21; Constitution of Rwanda article 48; Constitution of Slovakia article 32; Constitution of Timor Leste article 28(1); Constitution of Uganda article 3(4); Constitution of Uruguay article 10; Constitution of Venezuela article 350.

212 That is, thirteen of thirty-nine, or approximately 33 per cent, most of which are expressed as such but some of which are implied. See Constitution of Algeria article 33 [article 39, now suspended]; Constitution of Armenia article 18; Constitution of Cape Verde article 18; Constitution of Czech Republic article 23; Constitution of France, Declaration article 2; Constitution of Guatemala article 45; Constitution of Guinea article 21; Constitution of Mozambique article 80; Constitution of Portugal articles 7(3) and 21; Constitution of Rwanda article 48; Constitution of Slovakia article 32; Constitution of Timor Leste article 28(1); Constitution of Venezuela article 350.

213 For use of the exact term see Constitution of France, Declaration article 2; Constitution of Guinea article 21. For use of variants see Constitution of Ecuador article 416(8); Constitution of Portugal article 7(3).

214 See Constitution of Benin article 66; Constitution of Cape Verde article 18; Constitution of Cuba article 12(g) [now article 16]; Constitution of Portugal article 21.

215 See Constitution of Algeria article 27 [article 30, now article 32]; Constitution of Cuba article 12(g) [now article 16]; Constitution of Ecuador article 416(8).

216 That is, seven of thirty-nine, or only approximately 17 per cent. See Constitution of Cape Verde article 18; Constitution of Cuba article 3 [now article 4]; Constitution of Czech Republic article 23; Constitution of Estonia article 54(2); Constitution of Germany article 20 (4); Constitution of Portugal article 21; Constitution of Slovakia article 32.

217 See Constitution of Cape Verde article 18; Constitution of Cuba article 3 [now article 4]; Constitution of Czech Republic article 23; Constitution of Estonia article 54(2); Constitution of Germany article 20(4); Constitution of Portugal article 21; Constitution of Slovakia article 32.

5.5.2.7 Scope of Permissible Means

It is significant that most of the identified constitutions either expressly provide for inclusive means, or do not specify the permissible means,[218] and therefore do not automatically prohibit the use of force. However, they also generally indicate that whatever means are employed must be used for a specific and limited purpose. That purpose in well over half of the identified constitutions is restoration of the constitutional order.[219] More than one in four specify another human rights purpose such as restoration of constitutional or other human rights.[220]

[218] That is, thirty of thirty-nine, or approximately 76 per cent. See Constitution of Algeria articles 27 and 33 [articles 30 and 39, now article 32 only]; Constitution of Argentina article 36; Constitution of Armenia article 18; Constitution of Azerbaijan article 54(2); Constitution of Benin article 66; Constitution of Cape Verde article 18; Constitution of Chad preamble; Constitution of Cuba articles 3 and 12(g) [now articles 4 and 16]; Constitution of Czech Republic article 23; Constitution of the Democratic Republic of the Congo article 64; Constitution of Ecuador articles 98 and 416(8); Constitution of El Salvador articles 87 and 88; Constitution of Estonia article 54(2); Constitution of France, Declaration article 2; Constitution of Germany article 20(4); Constitution of Ghana article 3(4); Constitution of Greece article 120(4); Constitution of Guatemala article 45; Constitution of Guinea article 21; Constitution of Honduras article 3; Constitution of Lithuania article 3; Constitution of Mexico article 136; Constitution of Paraguay article 138(1); Constitution of Peru article 46; Constitution of Portugal articles 7(3) and 21; Constitution of Slovakia article 32; Constitution of Timor Leste article 28(1)–(2); Constitution of Togo articles 45 and 150; Constitution of Uganda article 3(4); Constitution of Venezuela articles 333 and 350. Those that simply provide for an express or implied right of 'disobedience' also do not specify peaceful means. For example, see Constitution of Benin article 66; Constitution of Dominican Republic articles 6, 40(15), and 73; Constitution of Guatemala article 5; Constitution of Maldives articles 64 and 245; Constitution of Mozambique article 80; Constitution of Rwanda article 48; Constitution of Uruguay article 10.

[219] That is, twenty-five of thirty-nine, or approximately 64 per cent. See Constitution of Argentina article 36; Constitution of Azerbaijan article 54(2); Constitution of Benin article 66; Constitution of Burkina Faso article 167; Constitution of Chad preamble; Constitution of Cuba article 3 [now article 4]; Constitution of Czech Republic article 23; Constitution of the Democratic Republic of the Congo article 64; Constitution of El Salvador articles 87 and 88; Constitution of Estonia article 54(2); Constitution of Germany article 20(4); Constitution of Ghana article 3(4); Constitution of Greece article 120(4); Constitution of Honduras article 3; Constitution of Hungary article C(2); Constitution of Lithuania article 3; Constitution of Mali article 121; Constitution of Mexico article 136; Constitution of Paraguay article 138(1); Constitution of Peru article 46; Constitution of Slovakia article 32; Constitution of Thailand section 69 [now suspended]; Constitution of Togo articles 45 and 150; Constitution of Uganda article 3(4); Constitution of Venezuela article 333.

[220] That is, eleven of thirty-nine, or approximately 28 per cent. See Constitution of Algeria article 33 [article 39, now suspended]; Constitution of Armenia article 18; Constitution of Cape Verde article 18; Constitution of Czech Republic article 23; Constitution of Ecuador articles 98 and 416(8); Constitution of Guatemala article 45; Constitution of Portugal articles 7(3) and

A small group of provisions specifies peaceful means only.[221] Likewise, only two constitutions specify that forceful means are permissible,[222] and only two that this may include international military assistance.[223] Thus there is a similar incidence of express authorization of exclusively peaceful means and express authorization of forceful means.

The term 'proportionality' is not used in any of the identified constitutional provisions. Two provisions ambiguously specify that the permissible means are 'lawful only'.[224] As indicated above, other limitations as to means must be read from the context of each provision.

By making constitutional provision for a right, immunity from prosecution is implied. However, only two provisions actually specify that the actions undertaken are legally protected from prosecution.[225]

5.5.3 *Legal Meaning: A Two-Fold Typology*

The detailed content analysis above demonstrates that the 'right to resist' in contemporary constitutional law cannot be reduced to a single overarching legal meaning, but a basic two-fold typology can be identified, which has some consistency with what Bartolus identified centuries ago as a two-fold typology of 'defects of title' and 'reasons of conduct' providing legal bases for the right.[226] One version of the concept intends to protect people from abuse by their own state. The other intends to protect the state from interference by

21; Constitution of Rwanda article 48; Constitution of Slovakia article 32; Constitution of Timor Leste article 28(1)–(2); Constitution of Venezuela article 350.

221 See Constitution of Burkina Faso article 167; Constitution of Hungary article C(2)–(3); Constitution of Mali article 121; Constitution of Thailand section 69 [now suspended]. See n 218 above regarding the further group of right of 'disobedience' provisions possibly implying peaceful means, but not actually specifying this. For example, there are conceivably circumstances in which 'disobedience' or 'defiance' of unlawful orders could necessitate force.

222 See Constitution of Cape Verde article 18; Constitution of Cuba articles 3 and 12(g) [now articles 4 and 16]. Yet compare the assumption that the right to resist definitionally involves forceful means, and the conflated definition of the right to resist with the right to rebel, as 'the right of an individual or group to resort to violence' in Ginsburg et al (n 1) 1189 (fn 11), 1192. This is not indicated by the provisions themselves. Indeed, compare the acknowledgement elsewhere that the provisions relate to a spectrum of means from disobedience to force in ibid 1227–1228.

223 See Constitution of Benin article 66; Constitution of Cuba article 12(g) [now article 16].

224 See Constitution of Armenia article 18; Constitution of Hungary article C(2).

225 See Constitution of Ghana article 3(5)–(7); Constitution of Uganda article 3(5)–(6). Arguably these are not the only provisions that effectively confer immunity. See as one example the Constitution of Paraguay article 138(1), excusing citizens from compliance with the law if validly exercising the 'right to resist oppression', and similar provisions.

226 See further discussions in Chapter 4, Section 4.2.

unauthorized people. In other words, it amounts to either 'defence against the state' or 'defence of the state'. Neither meaning is overwhelmingly predominant in the contemporary constitutional law. The split is nearly even, with just over half of the constitutions in the subset intending to provide people protection from their state,[227] and just over half intending to provide the state protection from either a proportion of its people or from outsiders.[228] Some right to resist provisions do both, and thus seem to allow that there are times when the state should be defended and such action should be lawful, and times when the state should be resisted, and such action should also be lawful. Indeed, this latter unified but qualified meaning may come closer to what the right to resist means as a 'human right'.

The contemporary constitutional subset evidence does not entirely corroborate other two-fold typology theories that the right to resist is either 'conservative' or 'revolutionary' in form.[229] However, it does largely sustain the Ginsburg and colleagues two-fold classification of provisions as either 'democratic' or 'undemocratic' in intent,[230] and Law and Versteeg's finding that

[227] That is twenty-four of thirty-nine, or approximately 61 per cent. See Constitution of Algeria article 33 [article 39, now suspended]; Constitution of Armenia article 18; Constitution of Burkina Faso article 167; Constitution of Cape Verde article 18; Constitution of Chad preamble; Constitution of Czech Republic article 23; Constitution of the Democratic Republic of the Congo article 64; Constitution of Dominican Republic articles 6 and 40(15); Constitution of Ecuador articles 98 and 416(8); Constitution of El Salvador article 87; Constitution of France, Declaration article 2; Constitution of Ghana article 3(4); Constitution of Guatemala articles 5 and 45; Constitution of Guinea article 21; Constitution of Hungary article C(2); Constitution of Maldives articles 64 and 245; Constitution of Mexico article 136; Constitution of Mozambique article 80; Constitution of Paraguay article 138(1); Constitution of Portugal articles 7(3) and 21; Constitution of Rwanda article 48; Constitution of Slovakia article 32; Constitution of Timor Leste article 28(1); Constitution of Venezuela article 350.

[228] That is twenty-five of thirty-nine, or approximately 64 per cent. See Constitution of Argentina article 36; Constitution of Azerbaijan article 54(2); Constitution of Benin article 66; Constitution of Burkina Faso article 167; Constitution of Chad preamble; Constitution of Cuba article 3 [now article 4]; Constitution of Czech Republic article 23; Constitution of Democratic Republic of the Congo article 64; Constitution of Dominican Republic articles 40(15), 73; Constitution of El Salvador articles 87 and 88; Constitution of Estonia article 54 (2); Constitution of Germany article 20(4); Constitution of Ghana article 3(4); Constitution of Greece article 120(4); Constitution of Honduras article 3; Constitution of Hungary article C (2); Constitution of Lithuania article 3; Constitution of Mali article 121; Constitution of Mexico article 136; Constitution of Paraguay article 138(1); Constitution of Peru article 46; Constitution of Thailand section 69 [now suspended]; Constitution of Togo articles 45 and 150; Constitution of Uganda article 3(4); Constitution of Venezuela article 333.

[229] See for example Williams (n 2); Honoré (n 2) 45–52. That said, the evidence does not refute the assertion that the right to resist is sometimes but not always 'conservative' or 'revolutionary' in its intent.

[230] Ginsburg et al (n 1) 1207–1217, 1232–1233, 1237.

such provisions are adopted by both 'undemocratic' and democratic states.[231] All of these efforts demonstrate that we cannot presume a legal meaning from the mere presence of a constitutional right to resist provision – which in and of itself tells us relatively little about either the intent of the provision or the nature of the state in question.[232]

The above findings on legal meaning also serve to underline that some of these provisions do not uphold the central premise of contemporary constitutionalism itself – the idea that people have a right to consent to governance and also to withdraw that consent. The most restrictively framed provisions in the subset actually appear to reflect a contrary assumption. That is, the only possible form of 'unconstitutional government' or constitutional subversion is that involving unconstitutional seizure of power. Such provisions cannot contemplate the possibility that there may be some instances where this could be in the public interest, for example if that constitution is too easily either used or subverted against the common good. This leaves open the possibility for a government to maintain power by virtue of constitutional mechanisms and procedures and yet still govern in ways that violate important aspects of that constitution – for example, constitutionally recognized fundamental rights.[233] Such provisions do not really function as an accountability mechanism limiting the abuse of power. Indeed, they function more like an extreme manifestation of the principle of entrenchment.[234] Viewed in this way, arguably the key distinction between these provisions therefore arises from their overall legal meaning.

This also suggests that recognition of the right to resist in domestic constitutions is not sufficient. People in some states with a constitutional right need

[231] Law and Versteeg (n 7) 1223, 1225–1226, 1229.

[232] On the German provision for example, see the varying perspectives in Edgar Bodenheimer, 'Significant Developments in German Legal Philosophy Since 1945' (1954) 3 *American Journal of Comparative Law* 379, 381–383, 385–387; Gerhard Brinkmann, 'Militant Democracy and Radicals in the West German Civil Service' (1983) 46 *Modern Law Review* 584, 593–594; Donald P Kommers, *The Federal Constitutional Court* (American Institute for Contemporary German Studies and Johns Hopkins University 1994) 5, 30; Hans Mommsen, *Germans against Hitler: The Stauffenberg Plot and Resistance under the Third Reich* (Angus McGeoch tr, IB Tauris 2008) 19–20; Claudia E Haupt, 'The Scope of Democratic Public Discourse: Defending Democracy, Tolerating Intolerance, and the Problem of Neo-Nazi Demonstrations in Germany' (2008) 20 *Florida Journal of International Law* 169, 177–178, 208–209; Donald P Kommers and Russell A Miller, *The Constitutional Jurisprudence of the Federal Republic of Germany* (3rd edn, Duke University Press 2012) 51–52, 285–301; Heiner Bielefeldt, 'The Right to Resist' in Wilhelm Heitmeyer and John Hagan (eds), *International Handbook of Violence Research* (Kluwer 2003) 1100; Gesk (n 182) 1077–1078.

[233] See for example the concerns raised in Nkansah (n 36) 129, 132, 145–146, 148–149, 157–158.

[234] For a concise description of this principle, see Dixon and Ginsburg (n 5) 357.

supplementary protection from abuse of power in situations when the constitutional order may well be left intact – at the hands of their own constitutional rulers, as is frequently the case. In this context the need for positive recognition of a human right to resist, enforceable at international level, becomes more obvious. Where an international standard for the right to resist is considered binding, either by way of treaty or otherwise through custom, those constitutional provisions that permit systematic violations of constitutional and other human rights would need to be revisited or interpreted in a compatible manner.

State refusal to recognize or uphold a constitutional right to resist is one thing. Citizen failure to exercise the right where recognized and warranted is another matter. Yet either of these can contribute to its under-utilization or a lack of adjudication. This leads to the more complicated question of the legal value of these provisions.

5.5.4 *Legal Value and the Question of 'Sham Law' Provisions*

One indicator of legal value is the extent of enforcement. Initially, it appears that the right to resist would fall into the category of 'under-enforced' constitutional norms due to generally low levels of litigation and therefore limited case law. However, this does not necessarily mean that the right has no legal value.[235] Under-enforcement, particularly by way of adjudication, may not always be an indicator of a 'sham' provision.[236] There may be other explanations.

Contrary to what might be expected according to the obsolescence/replacement theories, the lack of case law does not appear to result from a general correlation between the right to resist and limited judicial review competence. In Latin America, for example, there is considerable correlation between the countries that have recently introduced better judicial mechanisms for enforcement of constitutional rights and those that have introduced a

[235] See Lawrence Gene Sager, 'Fair Measure: The Legal Status of Underenforced Constitutional Norms' (1978) 91(6) *Harvard Law Review* 1212, 1213, 1220–1221, 1264.

[236] On the term 'sham constitutions' as describing those that 'promise much', 'deliver little', and 'underperform', and on the startlingly low compliance rates with certain other unquestionably well-established constitutional rights such as freedom from torture, see David S Law and Mila Versteeg, 'Sham Constitutions' (2013) 101 *California Law Review* 863, 863, 880, 883, 897–899, 912–913; Goderis and Versteeg (n 7) 10. While the right to resist is not specifically examined, the data shows no correlation between such provisions and 'sham' constitutions, nor does it identify this right among those 'least honoured'. Rather, it demonstrates that these provisions are found in constitutions of both highest- and lowest-compliance countries, with slightly higher concentration in the former.

constitutional right to resist. According to Mirow, since the 1980s individuals can take constitutional actions in twelve countries,[237] two-thirds of which also include a constitutional right to resist.[238] Of the six countries that created new specialized constitutional courts and tribunals,[239] half also include a constitutional right to resist.[240] Of the five countries that created specialized constitutional chambers within their supreme courts,[241] all of them also include a constitutional right to resist.

Conversely, where there is correlation with judicial review provisions, it could instead be an indicator of systemic functionality showing that, as part of the normal democratic process, judicial review has proved a sufficient safeguard and resort to a right to resist as an enforcement mechanism has not been required. Alternatively, in certain cases the right to resist may simply be numbered among the 'dormant clauses' and 'latent rights' in constitutions involving 'language long ignored or misinterpreted', sometimes later 'awakened' by 'more effective or more active constitutional tribunals', and thereby 'rediscovered, reactivated and brought to life' to provide a remedy.[242]

Since right to resist provisions arguably should also be measured by their preventive value, one positive indicator of this would be non-use and non-enforcement. General disuse of the right to resist is not necessarily a measure of its disutility. Indeed, the existence of judicial determinations, at domestic level, may not be the most relevant measure of value for a right such as this, which is in some cases triggered only when the legal system fails. Thus, for example, the German Constitutional Court maintains that if a judicial remedy is available, that in itself is evidence of the non-necessity and irrelevance of the constitutional right to resist.[243] On the other hand, judicial corruption would supply

[237] Argentina, Bolivia, Colombia, Costa Rica, Dominican Republic, El Salvador, Guatemala, Honduras, Nicaragua, Panama, Paraguay, Venzuela. See Mirow (n 127) 251.

[238] Argentina, Costa Rica, Dominican Republic, El Salvador, Guatemala, Honduras, Paraguay, Venezuela.

[239] Ecuador, Guatemala, Chile, Peru, Colombia, Bolivia. See Mirow (n 127) 251.

[240] Ecuador, Guatemala, Peru. For an examination of the operation of the right to resist in the Constitution of Ecuador 2008 and its adjudication in three cases, see Alberto Noguera Fernandez, 'Derecho a la Resistencia y Justiciabilidad de los Derechos Sociales en Ecuador' (2016) 1 *Revista de Derecho Social Latinoamerica* 89.

[241] El Salvador, Costa Rica, Honduras, Paraguay, Venezuela. See Mirow (n 127) 251.

[242] See ibid 261–262. In general, and in most jurisdictions, constitutional adjudication is relatively recent and this is one of the reasons it lacks density. Grimm (n 5) 112–113.

[243] *Re Ratification of the Treaty of Lisbon* 2 BvE 2/08 (30 June 2009) [2010] 3 CMLR 13, 316–317, Part III [114aa] 325 [162], affirming *Communist Party (KPD) Case* 5 BVerfGE 85 (1956) 377; *Manfred Brunner and Others* v *The European Union Treaty* 2 BvR 2134/92 and 2159/92 (12 October 1993) [1994] 1 CMLR 57, 83 [31]. See also Gerhard Wegen and Christopher Kuner, 'Germany: Federal Constitutional Court Decision Concerning the Maastricht Treaty – Introductory Note' (1994) 33 ILM 388, 416 [4]–[5].

another valid reason why such provisions would likely remain un-litigated just when they are needed most. There is also the risk that litigation could render the constitutional right to resist illusory. For example, the Ghanaian Supreme Court has ruled that right to resist provisions cannot be relied on as a defence where their source is a prior constitution since overthrown by coup if the subsequent constitution came to an accommodation with the usurpers.[244] On the other hand, the potential for useful judicial clarification cannot be discounted, as these courts have demonstrated.[245]

The apparent judicial under-use of the constitutional right to resist provisions begs the further question of how we measure legal value, and the extent to which we accept certain forms of extrajudicial enforcement and extrajudicial remedy as complementary to judicial forms, or instead insist that the latter are exclusive.[246] Arguably, constitutional law is more than just a dialogue between courts and the state.[247] Thus there may be other indicators of legal salience of a right to resist provision among the subjects of such laws, despite judicial torpor. Alternatively, without further specific examination, we cannot rule out the possibility that in certain cases the right to resist really is an example of Waldron's disenfranchisement 'by the very document that is supposed to give [people] their power'.[248] 'Under-enforcement' of these provisions is therefore a more complicated question than can be addressed adequately in the context of this limited survey. It deserves more research attention.

[244] For example, in *Ekwam* v *Pianim (no 2) and Others* (1996–97) SCGLR 120 [1999] 2 LRC 242, [2] 245, 257, 273–279, 281. However, compare the dissents of Wiredu JSC and Adjabeng JSC, concluding that the defendant's actions were protected under both constitutions. Ibid [2] 245–246, 256–257, 260, 262–263.

[245] See for example the clarifications of the nature, primary and secondary triggers for, and object and purpose of, the German constitutional right to resist in *Communist Party Case* (n 243) 376, 377; *Re Ratification of the Treaty of Lisbon* (n 243) 325 [161aa]–[162]. See also the clarification of the personal scope of the Ghanaian right in *New Patriotic Party* v *Attorney General* (1997) [1999] 2 LRC 283, Dissent of Kpegah JSC 285–286, 312, 321, 322.

[246] According to Law and Versteeg (n 236) 864, in general 'neither the existence of judicial review nor the ratification of human rights treaties is statistically associated with increased respect for constitutional rights'.

[247] See Mark Tushnet, *Taking the Constitution away from the Courts* (Princeton University Press 1999); Larry D Kramer, *The People Themselves: Popular Constitutionalism and Judicial Review* (Oxford University Press 2004).

[248] Jeremy Waldron, 'Constitutionalism: A Skeptical View' in Thomas Christiano and John Christman (eds), *Contemporary Debates in Political Philosophy* (Wiley-Blackwell 2009) 267. Yet compare Bifulco and Golia's work 'reorienting the paradox' of the right to resist in state constitutions. Daniela Bifulco and Angelo Jr Golia, 'The Right of Resistance as a State Law Basis for Transnational Regimes' Self-Contestation' (2018) 45 *Journal of Law and Society* 94.

5.6 CONCLUSION

The constitutional and quasi-constitutional evidence considered above demonstrates the longevity, widespread nature, and diversity in legal provision for the right to resist and its conceptual antecedents. As a form of rights enforcement, the right to resist started out as a 'well-established' customary right in the Middle Ages, evolved into an inalienable constitutionalized 'right of man' in the modern period, and finally emerged as a fundamental and universal human right protected to a certain extent in constitutional law – and also in international law – today.

The positive law evidence provided by the constitutional provisions corroborates several main premises of this study. The first and most obvious of these is that this right is at least theoretically capable of positivization and enforcement. Yet a pronounced feature of the constitutional right to resist provisions is that their potential as judicially enforceable claim rights remains untapped. However, given their at least partially 'extrajudicial' nature, extent of adjudication is probably not the only relevant measure of their value. Lack of use could just as easily be an indicator of effectiveness as a deterrent and constraint on abuse of power, or of a functioning system of judicial review. Any contention that they amount to 'sham law' therefore remains to be proven. Pending further research on this and related questions, firm conclusions on their legal value will continue to elude us.

Secondly, analysis of the sample provisions from all periods from ancient times to the present confirms their compatibility with rule of law. The right to resist has long existed as complementary to other forms of lawful remedy, including provision for judicial enforcement. It has also been considered supplementary or alternative to judicial or political machinery that has failed. Under such circumstances, the right to resist acts as an auxiliary to limits on power by way of petition, assembly and election, judicial review or parliamentary and legislative resolution. Its constitutional enforcement functions are intended as preventive, defensive, and restorative. Yet it has also had constitutionally acknowledged foundational functions. Among its remedial functions is to constitutionally shield individuals from ordinary criminal liability and penalty including for treason, but also to create a practical deterrent and penalty for violators of the higher law. While perennial debates persist over trigger points, the evidence seems to corroborate the ongoing salience of the Aristotelian-Bartolist 'defect of title' or 'reason of conduct' primary triggers – though it also shows that as early as the Middle Ages such triggers became decoupled from the 'tyranny' threshold, with diversification of what these two categories constituted.

The third premise corroborated by content analysis of the contemporary provisions in the Ginsburg data subset is that the right to resist is now predominantly considered a human right that belongs with the cluster of political rights – belief, opinion, expression, association, participation, and peaceful assembly and protest – as a law of exception or *lex specialis*. Furthermore, as a constitutional right of 'all citizens' individually and collectively, this does not limit its valid exercise to elites or to citizens only when acting as a majority of 'the people'.

This evidence has also reinforced several other conclusions of Part I. First, it confirms that the 'right to resist' is the predominant form of legal terminology employed, and also that its 'cognate terms' are not wholly interchangeable. Whatever their potential relevance in relation to international law, the 'right to rebel' and 'right to revolution' are cognates not generally used in constitutional law.[249] Second, it confirms that the right to resist is about the exceptional right to use otherwise unlawful means that may be either peaceful or forceful, and not exclusively about the right to use force. Third, it corroborates the contention that right to resist provisions generally reflect a four-fold typology of legal macro-conception as to object and purpose, but that enforcement of 'higher law' – in this case constitutional law – and fundamental rights is the superordinate among them.[250]

Finally, the relative profusion of constitutional provisions has not eliminated the identified problem that excessively vague or under-regulated provisions are vulnerable to abuse in the absence of general standard-setting in international human rights law. Therefore, an international standard on the human right to resist could assist in interpretation or implementation of these domestic rights, preventing their abuse or conflict with international human rights law or international law generally.[251] Conversely, international standards under customary or conventional law could be relied upon in those countries where the right to resist is not protected or otherwise provided for in constitutional law. This could have a positive human rights impact on how

[249] This fact has not prevented domestic courts from adjudicating on the lawfulness or otherwise of particular revolutions, or necessarily limited judges to findings of unlawfulness. See Richard S Kay and Joel I Colón-Ríos, *Adjudicating Revolution: Courts and Constitutional Change* (Edward Elgar 2022) 1–21.

[250] The constitutional provisions represent three categories. On the fourth, see further discussion in Chapter 7, Section 7.4.

[251] For example, Peru now requires bill of rights interpretation in light of international human rights treaties. Argentina raised international human rights treaties to a constitutional level. Costa Rica and El Salvador also treat international human rights treaties as a form of higher law. Other courts have applied or otherwise used international human rights law to interpret or supplement national law. See Mirow (n 127) 259–260.

we interpret domestic treason, sedition, and incitement laws. Indeed, by clarifying human rights-compliant interpretation of an implied or explicit duty to resist in defence of a constitution, it could also reduce the risk of activating a trigger for exercise of the right in response to false information, whether deliberate or in error.

Given all the above, what are the implications of the apparent absence of clear provision in the general or 'universal' system, or the variation in regional positions on the right? This is the subject matter explored in the following two chapters on the international law of the right to resist.

6

Recognition in General or Customary International Law

6.1 INTRODUCTION

The long-established and widespread domestic tradition of the constitutional right to resist contrasts with its more precarious place in public international law. Whereas an estimated one in five current constitutions contains a right to resist provision in some form,[1] only two express provisions exist in international law. These are contained in regional human rights treaties.[2] There is no express codification in the universal treaties and all other international legal recognition is instead implied and therefore potentially open to dispute. While indeed the right's status is arguably more firmly established in general or customary international law than in treaty law,[3] disagreement persists about the extent of its recognition. For those seeking greater legal certainty, much remains to be resolved.

[1] See Chapter 5, Section 5.5.

[2] See Chapter 7, Sections 7.2 and 7.3.

[3] The term 'general or customary' is used primarily to provide contrast with conventional or treaty law sources, denoting its applicability to all states. The precise content of 'general international law' remains disputed. Acknowledging the possibility of 'conventional law' in the form of widely ratified 'general multilateral treaties' – or their individual provisions – either reflecting or evolving into custom over time, and thereby into 'general' or 'universal' international law, see Grigori Tunkin, 'Is General International Law Customary Law Only?' (1993) 4 *European Journal of International Law* 534. Treating general international law as its own distinct category used to fill legal gaps left by treaty, custom, and general principles, see Christian Tomuschat, 'General International Law: A New Source of International Law?' in Riccardo Pisillo Mazzeschi and Pasquale De Sena (eds), *Global Justice, Human Rights and the Modernization of International Law* (Springer 2018).

Clarifying its international legal status would be beneficial because international law has a distinctive role to play in recognizing and, under certain circumstances, giving effect to the right to resist as a human right. Ideally, it establishes a common framework for international validation of specific instances of the right's exercise, prior to application of any legal regime regulating particular means employed in the course of that resistance. This should include legal principles, rules, and standards[4] governing the corresponding international obligation on third parties – whether states or international organizations – to 'assist or not obstruct' those validly exercising the right.[5] Operating in conjunction with the general prohibition on intervention in strictly domestic matters, international recognition of the human right to resist could help regulate the duty of external assistance in qualifying exceptional cases, yielding a clearer legal basis for United Nations (UN) authorization. The purpose of this chapter – and indeed, this work as a whole – is to contribute to that clarification process.

Before proceeding to apply Chapter 4's analytical framework to the primary material sources of the right to resist in general or customary international law,[6] Section 6.2 of this chapter considers factors relevant to interpreting these sources with a view to clarifying the extent of recognition in the absence of express provision. Section 6.3 reviews the treatment of this right in the 'Declaration on Principles of International Law Concerning Friendly Relations and Co-operation among States in accordance with the Charter of the United Nations' (Declaration on Principles of International Law or UN General Assembly Resolution 2625), considered expressive of customary international law. In light of the proposition that the Universal Declaration

4 International legal principles are those 'binding legal statement[s]' describing 'obligations of conduct or obligations to achieve an objective', distinguished from international legal rules in that they are 'described in abstract rather than concrete terms ready for direct application', but 'may [also] be the basis for concrete obligations'. International standards are generally 'technical rules' leaving 'a wide margin of appreciation' for interpretation and application but in another usage can also constitute principles. Rüdiger Wolfrum, 'General International Law: Rules, Principles and Standards' in *Max Planck Encyclopedia of Public International Law* (Oxford Public International Law online database 2010) B1[6], B1[17], C1[65], D[108]–[109].

5 This is the corresponding duty as defined by Tony Honoré, 'The Right to Rebel' (1988) 8(1) *Oxford Journal of Legal Studies* 34, 36, 41, 43.

6 On the numerous 'material sources' of laws of general application from customary international law and general principles of international law, as referred to throughout this chapter, see Ian Brownlie, *Principles of Public International Law* (7th edn, Oxford University Press 2008) 3–19. On the non-exclusivity of the source of rules, and the common difficulty of distinguishing between codification or progressive development of customary public international law through conventional means, see David J Bederman, *Custom as a Source of Law* (Cambridge University Press 2010) 137, 155–157.

of Human Rights effectively expresses customary international human rights law in the twenty-first century,[7] or is at least interpretive of the term 'human rights' in the provisions of the UN Charter, Section 6.4 evaluates the contention that this instrument recognizes the right to resist. Section 6.5 revisits the theory that the customary Nuremberg Principles contain an implied right-duty to resist. Section 6.6 then briefly surveys other regulatory sources, or sources of complementary rights, sometimes mischaracterized as establishing recognition of the right to resist but instead best considered corroborative of customary recognition. The conclusion at Section 6.7 assesses the implications of this evidence for the controversies as to the legal status and value of the right to resist in international law, in particular the presumption that the right is *non liquet* and/or otherwise unenforceable.

6.2 CLARIFYING RECOGNITION IN THE ABSENCE OF EXPRESS PROVISION

The obvious main feature of the right to resist in international law is the general absence of express provision. Hence, discussion of international legal recognition of the right to resist generally encompasses the possibilities that it is: (1) implicitly recognized as a long-established customary right;[8] (2) permitted by virtue of non-prohibition;[9] (3) conversely, subject to state discretion by virtue of international law's 'silence';[10] (4) *non liquet* in whole or in part due to a gap or gaps in the law;[11] (5) generally beyond the jurisdiction of international law's protection by virtue of the principles of sovereignty and non-intervention;[12] (6) conversely, beyond international law's restriction or

[7] See William A Schabas, *The Customary International Law of Human Rights* (Oxford University Press 2021).

[8] See for example Quincy Wright, 'Intervention and Cuba in 1961' (1961) 55 (27–29 April 1961) *Proceedings of the American Society of International Law at Its Annual Meeting (1921–1969)* 2, 3–4; Quincy Wright, 'The Goa Incident' (1962) 56 *American Journal of International Law* 617, 628.

[9] See for example Quincy Wright, 'United States Intervention in the Lebanon' (1959) 53 *American Journal of International Law* 112, 121–124; Wright, 'Intervention and Cuba' (n 8) 3–4.

[10] This would ostensibly include the discretion to criminalize, prosecute, and punish resistance. See Ben Saul, *Defining Terrorism in International Law* (Oxford University Press 2006) 81–86.

[11] See for example Antonio Cassese, 'Human Rights and Humanitarian Law: Terrorism and Human Rights' (1982) 31 *American University Law Review* 945, 949–950, 958; Antonio Cassese, *Self-Determination of Peoples: A Legal Reappraisal* (Cambridge University Press 1995) 151–153, 197–198, 160–162.

[12] See for example Philip C Jessup, *A Modern Law of Nations: An Introduction* (Macmillan 1948) 185–186.

regulation by virtue of its status as an inalienable right;[13] (7) exclusively determined ad hoc and post hoc by the customary principle of effectiveness;[14] (8) recognized or partially recognized by virtue of contemporary customary international law;[15] (9) partially recognized with the possibility of further extension by analogy and/or progressive interpretation.[16] The remainder of this and the following sections (Sections 6.3–6.6) consider these alternative status theories in the context of the material source theories. While difficult to establish implicit recognition or permission by virtue of non-prohibition, it should nevertheless be possible to determine whether there is customary recognition and its extent, whether there are gaps in this recognition, whether recognition can be reasonably extended to fill the apparent gaps, or whether international jurisdiction over the question is instead precluded.

6.2.1 *Identification and Interpretation of Customary International Law and General Principles of International Law*

All three of the main material sources considered in Sections 6.3–6.5 derive from UN General Assembly resolutions, included here on the basis that they are widely considered to articulate customary international legal rules, principles, and/or standards. As the International Law Commission has affirmed, such resolutions cannot create a customary international legal rule, but may instead provide evidence of its existence and content or contribute to its later development, and also evidence of its acceptance as law (*opinio juris*) and/or of state practice provided state endorsement is 'sufficiently widespread and

[13] See Hersch Lauterpacht, 'The Law of Nations, the Law of Nature and the Rights of Man' (1943) 29 *Transactions of the Grotius Society* 1, 23; Hersch Lauterpacht, *An International Bill of the Rights of Man* (Columbia University Press 1945) 43; Hersch Lauterpacht, *International Law and Human Rights* (Stevens and Sons 1950) 116.

[14] See for example Hans Kelsen, *General Theory of Law and State* (Harvard University Press 1949) 116–119. For a critique of the 'moral neutrality' of Kelsen's evaluation of what makes a revolution lawful, see Ali Khan, 'A Legal Theory of Revolutions' (1987) 5 *Boston University International Law Journal* 1, 12–18.

[15] See for example Jordan J Paust, 'The Human Right to Participate in Armed Revolution and Related Forms of Social Violence: Testing the Limits of Permissibility' (1983) 32 *Emory Law Journal* 545, 548, 560–562. Compare the position that its contemporary customary recognition is only partial and otherwise *non liquet* in, for example, Heather A Wilson, *International Law and the Use of Force by National Liberation Movements* (Clarendon 1988) 135–136, 186–187; Cassese, *Self-Determination* (n 11) 151–154, 197–198; Anyssa Bellal and Louise Doswald-Beck, 'Evaluating the Use of Force during the Arab Spring' (2012) 14 *Yearbook of International Humanitarian Law* 3, 11–14, 20–23, 32–33.

[16] See Honoré (n 5) 42–45.

representative, as well as consistent'.[17] This would be the case where such resolutions are adopted by consensus, and repeatedly referred to thereafter as constituting relevant rules, principles, or standards, as with the three main material sources under consideration here. Furthermore, treaty rules or principles – for example those arising from the UN Charter – may also reflect customary international law if they codify an existing rule or principle, lead to crystallization of a rule or principle, or give rise to general practice generating a new rule or principle.[18] Since two of these material sources are intended to supply detail on the content of concepts referred to in UN Charter provisions, they are also included here on the understanding that the UN Charter simultaneously constitutes both treaty law and general or customary international law.

With respect to general principles of international law, the International Law Commission affirms that these may either derive from national legal systems or may be formed within the international legal system itself, or transposed thereto,[19] as with the principles articulated in the three main material sources considered in this chapter. Functionally they not only help 'interpret and complement' other international legal rules, but can also provide a basis for primary rights and duties or secondary or procedural rules.[20] While their identification may be tricky, express labelling as 'general principles' or 'principles' in a UN General Assembly resolution adopted by consensus – as with two of the material sources considered here – would seem to provide good evidence of their status as such.[21]

The International Law Commission provides further guidance on how to interpret the rules, principles, and standards identified from these sources. First, there is no general hierarchy between customary international law,

[17] International Law Commission, 'Identification of Customary International Law' (2018) annexed to UN Doc A/RES/73/203 (11 January 2019) 3–4, Conclusions 6[2], 8[1], 10[2], 12 [1]–[3].

[18] Ibid 3–4, Conclusion 1[1], 6[2], 10[2].

[19] See International Law Commission, 'General Principles of Law: Consolidated Text of Draft Conclusions 1 to 11 Provisionally Adopted by the Drafting Committee' UN Doc A/CN.4/L.971 (21 July 2022) Draft Conclusions 2–8.

[20] Ibid Draft Conclusion 10. See also International Law Commission, 'Third Report on General Principles of Law by Marcelo Vásquez-Bermúdez, Special Rapporteur' UN Doc A/CN.4/753 (18 April 2022). Note this work is ongoing at the time of writing.

[21] On additional methods for identifying general or customary international law by way of decisions of international courts and tribunals, or from the 'teachings of the most highly qualified publicists', see International Law Commission, 'First Report on Subsidiary Means for the Determination of Rules of International Law by Charles Chernor Jalloh, Special Rapporteur' UN Doc A/CN.4/760 (13 February 2023); International Law Commission, 'Subsidiary Means for the Determination of Rules of International Law: Titles and Texts of Draft Conclusions 1 to 3 Provisionally Adopted by the Drafting Committee' UN Doc A/CN.4/L.985 (2 June 2023). Note this work is ongoing at the time of writing.

general principles of international law, and treaty law.[22] Second, the same or a similar rule 'may exist in parallel' in all three sources, and any conflict between them must be resolved by applying relevant interpretive techniques for systemic integration,[23] including by way of the principle of harmonization,[24] or by using customary international law or general principles of law to supplement where existing treaty rules are absent or unclear.[25] Third, however, there is a hierarchy between UN Charter provisions and other sources, and also between *jus cogens* (peremptory) norms and other norms, whatever their source.[26] That is, where customary or other international legal rules conflict with a *jus cogens* norm of general international law, such rules either cease to exist or are modified thereby, or must be interpreted in a manner consistent with the *jus cogens* norm.[27]

Furthermore, where 'serious breaches' of *jus cogens* norms occur, no situation thereby created can be recognized as lawful.[28] States have a duty not to assist in the maintenance of such situations, and furthermore to use lawful means to bring those breaches to an end.[29] The norms considered peremptory include the prohibitions on aggression, genocide, crimes against humanity and war crimes, apartheid, slavery, and torture, as well as the right to

[22] International Law Commission, 'Conclusions of the Work of the Study Group on the Fragmentation of International Law: Difficulties Arising from the Diversification and Expansion of International Law' (2006) [2006] *Yearbook of the International Law Commission* vol II, pt 2 [1]–[42]; International Law Commission, 'General Principles of Law: Consolidated Text of Draft Conclusions 1 to 11 Provisionally Adopted by the Drafting Committee' (n 19) Draft Conclusion 11.

[23] International Law Commission, 'Conclusions of the Work of the Study Group on the Fragmentation of International Law' (n 22) [17]–[23].

[24] Ibid [4], [42].

[25] Ibid [20]. See also discussion in Chapter 7, Section 7.1, and proposed applications in Sections 7.2, 7.3, and 7.4.

[26] Ibid [31]–[36], [40]–[41].

[27] International Law Commission, 'Draft Conclusions on Identification and Legal Consequences of Peremptory Norms of General International Law (*jus cogens*)' (2022) [2022] *Yearbook of the International Law Commission* vol II, pt 2 Conclusions 14, 20.

[28] International Law Commission, 'Responsibility of States for Internationally Wrongful Acts' (2001) annexed to UNGA Res 56/83 (12 December 2001) article 41[2]; International Law Commission, 'Draft Conclusions on Identification and Legal Consequences of Peremptory Norms of General International Law' (n 27) Conclusion 19[2].

[29] International Law Commission, 'Responsibility of States for Internationally Wrongful Acts' (n 28) article 41[1]–[2]; International Law Commission, 'Draft Conclusions on Identification and Legal Consequences of Peremptory Norms of General International Law' (n 27) Conclusion 19[1]. Indeed, states aiding or assisting the commission of a wrongful act thereby also incur responsibility. International Law Commission, 'Responsibility of States for Internationally Wrongful Acts' (n 28) articles 16–17.

self-determination.[30] Therefore, to the extent that breaches of those norms generate right to resist claims, the International Law Commission guidance would imply that such a duty may entail 'assisting or not obstructing' those with a consequent right to resist, to the extent the law allows. These identification and interpretive rules are therefore especially relevant to gauging the theories of the right to resist in general or customary international law examined in Sections 6.3–6.5, and the competing origin theories considered in the remainder of this section.

6.2.2 *Theories of Recognition in Customary International Law Predating the United Nations Charter*

Conceptions of the right to resist in international law have been strongly associated with just war theory from the seventeenth century onwards.[31] However, scholars take opposing views on the legal recognition of the just war principles – including the right to resist – both before and during the League of Nations period.[32] Consequently, while some suggest that the right to resist was not recognized and indeed was not a topic of international law prior to the UN Charter with its associated human rights obligations,[33] others

30 See the 'non-exhaustive list' of such norms at Conclusion 23(a)–(h), International Law Commission, 'Draft Conclusions on Identification and Legal Consequences of Peremptory Norms of General International Law' (n 27).

31 In particular, see the theories of Grotius and Vattel in Hugo Grotius, *The Rights of War and Peace* (Richard Tuck ed, Jean Barbeyrac tr, Liberty Fund 2005) Book I Chapter IV 'Of a War Made by Subjects against Their Sovereigns' 336–383, Book II Chapter I-I 392, III 397, V 399, 401, Chapter XXV 'Of the Causes for Which War Is to Be Undertaken on the Account of Others' I 1151, VI 1156, VII 1158, VIII 1159–1162, Chapter XXVI 'Lawful Reasons Why Subjects of a Ruler May Go to War' III–IV 1167, 1171, 1173, 1176, 1177; Emer de Vattel, *The Law of Nations, or Principles of the Law of Nature, Applied to the Conduct and Affairs of Nations and Sovereigns* (Béla Kapossy and Richard Whatmore eds, Liberty Fund 2008) Book I Chapter IV 'Of the Sovereign, His Obligations and His Rights' [51]–[54] 103–112, Book II Chapter I 'Of the Common Duties of a Nation towards others or of the Offices of Humanity between Nations' [7] 265, Chapter IV 'Of the Right to Security, and the Effects of Sovereignty and Independence of Nations' [49]–[52] 288–289, [54]–[57] 289–292, Chapter V 'Of the Observance of Justice between Nations' [65]–[70] 296–297, Chapter XII 'Of Treaties of Alliance and other Public Treaties' [168] 344, [196]–[197] 364–365, Book III Chapter XVIII 'Of Civil War' [288]–[289] 641–642, [290]–[293], [295] 642–647.

32 See for example Hans Kelsen, 'Quincy Wright's A Study of War and the Bellum Justum Theory' (1943) 53 *Ethics* 208. Compare Daniele Archibugi, Mariano Croce, and Andrea Salvatore, 'Law of Nations or Perpetual Peace? Two Early International Theories on the Use of Force' in Marc Weller (ed), *The Oxford Handbook on the Use of Force in International Law* (Oxford University Press 2015) 56–78, 'The Right to Resist' 72–74.

33 Monique Chemillier-Gendreau, 'Resistance, Right to, International Protection' in Rüdiger Wolfrum (ed), *Max Planck Encyclopedia of Public International Law* (Oxford University Press 2012) 954 [2]–[3].

maintain that the right to resist already had an established place in customary international law. For example, Wright maintains that the right to resist and the right of revolution became recognized as customary law during the nineteenth century, expressed in the principle of neutrality and non-intervention in internal matters such as revolution.[34] This view persisted among certain scholars during the League of Nations period.[35] Indeed, Kelsen maintains that article 10 of the League of Nations Covenant itself made a distinction equivalent to an implied recognition of the right to revolution.[36]

If the contention of pre-UN customary recognition is correct, this bolsters the argument for its continuity in the absence of express prohibition. However, it is not altogether clear from other contemporaneous sources that this was indeed settled customary international law at that time.[37] That said, ultimately theories of implied recognition as a general principle and/or as customary international law during the UN period do not depend on customary recognition in previous periods.

6.2.3 *Theories of Implied Recognition in General or Customary International Law, or as a General Principle: The Two Elements in Article 1(2) and (3) of the United Nations Charter*

In her entry for the right of resistance in the Max Planck Encyclopedia of Public International Law, Chemillier-Gendreau concludes that the right 'is protected' in general international law by way of the UN Charter and Universal Declaration on Human Rights, extending thus not only to whole

34 See Quincy Wright, 'Recognition and Self-Determination' (1954) 48 (22–24 April 1954) *Proceedings of the American Society of International Law at its Annual Meeting* (1921–1969) 23, 26–27; Quincy Wright, 'International Law and Civil Strife' (1959) 53 *Proceedings of the American Society of International Law at Its Annual Meeting* (1921–1969) 145, 149–150.

35 See account in Albert Lévitt, 'Minority Report of Committee on Codification: A Proposed Code of International Criminal Law' (1939) 33 (27–29 April 1939) *Proceedings of the American Society of International Law at Its Annual Meeting* (1921–1969) 212, 212 article 2(7).

36 See Hans Kelsen, *Peace through Law* (University of North Carolina Press 1944) 52–53. This analysis follows on from the logic of Kelsen, 'Bellum Justum Theory' (n 32). Compare Quincy Wright, 'The Bombardment of Damascus' (1926) 20 *American Journal of International Law* 263, 275–277.

37 See Inter-American variations including the Convention on the Rights and Duties of States in the Event of Civil Strife (1928) 22 *American Journal of International Law* 159 Documents Supplement (July 1928) and the Tobar Doctrine (1907–1920s) 'repudiating' the right to revolution by limiting recognition to only those governments formed by constitutional means, as cited in Richard Falk, 'Janus Tormented: The International Law of Internal War' in James N Rosenau (ed), *International Aspects of Civil Strife* (Princeton University Press 1964) 215 fn 48, 231 fn 74, 232.

'peoples' but also to 'individuals or groups'.[38] She describes the UN Charter as recognizing the right to resist in self-defence,[39] in the exercise of self-determination,[40] and for human rights enforcement.[41] She characterizes the UN Charter right to resist as providing a human rights 'exception' not only to the general prohibition on the use of force, but also to the principle of territorial integrity.[42] She further identifies an implied right in the Universal Declaration's preambular reference to rebellion as a last resort, which she describes as 'an explicit reference to a right to resist'.[43] She maintains this constitutes additional acknowledgment of an exception for the purpose of human rights enforcement, equivalent to a distinction between 'authorized and prohibited force'.[44] Such claims for an international right to resist are not universally accepted. The remainder of this chapter will consider whether and to what extent they stand up.

Chemillier-Gendreau's assessment relates to chapter 1 of the Charter,[45] on the 'purposes and principles' of the United Nations. This states at article 1(2) and (3) that among its 'purposes' are: '[t]o develop friendly relations among nations based on respect for the principle of equal rights and self-determination of peoples';[46] and 'promoting and encouraging respect for human rights'.[47] These are among the 'certain elements' of article 1 that are also considered 'binding under customary international law'.[48] Nowhere does the Charter itself give any detail as to what is meant by the international legal terms 'self-determination' or 'human rights' – much less specify a right to resist on these grounds. Yet understanding what exactly constitutes the self-determination and human rights 'purposes' of the Charter is necessary to the

38 Chemillier-Gendreau (n 33) 955 [5]–[8], [16]. See also Gerald Sumida, 'The Right to Revolution: Implications for International Law and Order' in Myres S McDougal and W Michael Reisman (eds), *International Law in Contemporary Perspective: The Public Order of the World Community – Cases and Materials* (Foundation Press 1981) 168.

39 Chemillier-Gendreau (n 33) 955–956 [9]–[12].

40 Ibid 956 [13]–[15].

41 Ibid 956–957 [16]–[17].

42 Ibid 956 [9], [14].

43 Ibid 955 [5]–[7], [16]. See also Sumida (n 38) 167–169, 168.

44 Chemillier-Gendreau (n 33) 955 [6], 956 [16].

45 Ibid 956 [13].

46 Charter of the United Nations (adopted 26 June 1945, entered into force 24 October 1945) (as amended) 892 UNTS 119 (UN Charter) article 1(2).

47 Ibid article 1(3).

48 Bruno Simma, Hermann Mosler, Albrecht Randelzhofer, Christian Tomuschat, Rüdiger Wolfrum, Andreas Paulus, and Eleni Chaitidou (eds), *The Charter of the United Nations: A Commentary* (2nd edn, Oxford University Press 2002) 40 A[4]. On the UN Charter as a whole as an example of 'general multilateral treaties' reflecting or evolving into custom and thereby into general or 'universal' international law, see Tunkin (n 3) 538.

interpretation of its article 2(4) prohibition, under which Member States 'shall refrain in their international relations from the threat or use of force' not only 'against the territorial integrity or political independence of any State', but also 'in any other manner inconsistent with the Purposes of the United Nations'.[49] One possibility is that the internal dimension of these two purposes creates room for extension by analogy, to accommodate a parallel Charter prohibition on the internal use of force against a state's own population in a manner inconsistent with the self-determination and human rights purposes of the UN.[50] Another is that this complementary prohibition otherwise exists in contemporary customary international law.[51]

Prior to formal clarification of the article 1 terms 'self-determination' and 'human rights' within the meaning of the Charter – discussed in the following two sections – some scholars understood that the UN could neither regulate nor guarantee the right to resist, put beyond international law's jurisdiction as a consequence of the Charter's article 2(7) anti-intervention clause.[52] This holds that no Charter provision 'shall authorize the United Nations to intervene in matters which are essentially within the domestic jurisdiction of any State'.[53] Others however considered that article 1 of the Charter establishes respect for human rights and self-determination as matters of international concern, and therefore not 'essentially' domestic.[54] They constructed the customary law related to intervention in civil wars, including the customary rules on provision of armed assistance to either side, in light of the Charter provisions.[55] Wright, for example, built on his contention that the right to resist and right of revolution are customarily recognized in international law as a matter of sovereignty and self-determination of 'peoples' of which states are merely guardians,[56] and that there is therefore no international rule against it, concluding furthermore that externally suppressing revolution is contrary to

[49] UN Charter (n 46) article 2(4) [emphasis added].

[50] See for example the concepts of 'self-defence against colonization' and 'colonization as permanent aggression', and the theory of a separate rule of exception, as set out in Robert E Gorelick, 'Wars of National Liberation: Jus Ad Bellum' (1979) 11(1) *Case Western Reserve Journal of International Law* 71, 72–77, 77–81, 81–83.

[51] This possibility remains open since, according to the International Court of Justice, the UN Charter 'by no means covers the whole area of the regulation of the use of force in international relations'. See *Military and Paramilitary Activities in and against Nicaragua (Nicaragua* v *USA)* (Merits) [1986] ICJ Rep 14 [176].

[52] See for example Jessup (n 12) 52–55, 184–186.

[53] UN Charter (n 46) article 2(7).

[54] See for example Wright, 'Recognition and Self-Determination' (n 34), 27–30; Wright, 'Intervention and Cuba' (n 8) 3; Wright, 'Goa Incident' (n 8) 620.

[55] See Wright, 'United States Intervention in the Lebanon' (n 9) 119–123.

[56] See Wright, 'International Law and Civil Strife' (n 34) 147–148, 152.

Charter principles.[57] However, he also concluded that the consequent obligation on the UN and its Member States to 'not obstruct' did not, at that time, extend to a further obligation to 'assist'.[58] Nevertheless, given the article 2(7) caveat that the principle of non-intervention in domestic matters 'shall not prejudice the application of enforcement measures under Chapter VII',[59] Wright identified three grounds on which the UN may at its discretion lawfully override the prohibition on intervention, as the matter ceases to be domestic if: (1) warranted to prevent a threat to international peace and security;[60] (2) justified by violations of self-determination;[61] (3) justified by human rights violations.[62] These grounds, consistent with UN purposes, have implications for those claiming an international right to resist and seeking external assistance on the basis of a right protected pursuant to the Charter.

Today the Charter's self-determination and human rights purposes are further elaborated by way of several UN Declarations and other instruments.[63] These are broadly understood as imposing certain constraints on state sovereign authority. Now it is the continuing absence of clear agreed rules for UN-authorized intervention that complicates the task of establishing the extent of recognition of the human right to resist and the associated third-party duties consistent with the UN Charter.[64] Indeed, this question necessarily intersects with several as yet unresolved wider debates on intervention norms under general and customary international law, in particular the scope of the lawful

57 See ibid 147–152; Wright, 'United States Intervention in the Lebanon' (n 9) 121–123; Quincy Wright, 'Subversive Intervention' (1960) 54 *American Journal of International Law* 521, 529–530; Wright, 'Intervention and Cuba' (n 8) 3–11; Wright, 'Goa Incident' (n 8) 618, 628.

58 See Wright, 'Intervention and Cuba' (n 8) 3–11; Wright, 'Subversive Intervention' (n 57) 529; Wright, 'Goa Incident' (n 8) 626–628. See also Falk (n 37) 198.

59 UN Charter (n 46) article 2(7).

60 Wright, 'Intervention and Cuba' (n 8) 6; report of discussion in Quincy Wright, 'Diverse Systems of World Public Order Today – Panel I: Security Problems among Diverse Systems of World Public Order, Discussion' (1959) 53 *Proceedings of the American Society of International Law at Its Annual Meeting* (1921–1969) 166, 166, 167.

61 Wright, 'International Law and Civil Strife' (n 34) 149, 151–152.

62 Ibid.

63 See Sections 6.3 and 6.4.

64 Of course, non-UN-authorized unilateral or multilateral intervention, including 'humanitarian intervention', remains generally unlawful in contemporary customary international law. See Brownlie (n 6) preface, 742–745; Christine Gray, *International Law and the Use of Force* (4th edn, Oxford University Press 2018) 38–58, 60, 64–68. See also Christine Gray, 'The Use of Force and the International Legal Order' in Malcolm D Evans (ed), *International Law* (Oxford University Press 2010) 615, 621–623, emphasizing the findings in *Corfu Channel (UK v Albania)* (Merits) [1949] ICJ Rep 4 [34] and *Nicaragua v USA* (n 51) [134]–[135], [202], [268]. For background see Simon Chesterman, *Just War or Just Peace? International Law and Humanitarian Intervention* (Oxford University Press 2001).

exceptions.[65] While it is not possible to resolve these broader debates within the limitations of this study, their interrelationship with the status of the human right to resist and correlated international-level duty to 'assist or not obstruct' suggests that they cannot be resolved without taking full account of this as one potential criterion.

The first of these debates is whether, and if so under what conditions, unilateral or multilateral external intervention by invitation in support of a particular government is internationally lawful when for the purpose of suppressing resistance.[66] It is well-established that intervention by state invitation can be a lawful exception to the general prohibition on intervention, provided that certain requisite criteria are met regarding the legitimacy of the issuing authority and the legal validity of its consent.[67] Increasingly, however, scholars argue for additional regulation to mitigate the risk of abuse of the invitation doctrine – either by the requesting state or by the requested state – including restrictions to prevent third-party complicity in the denial of the right to internal self-determination and other human rights violations.[68] It is conceivable that the existence of a valid human right to resist could impose one such limitation on the state right of invitation, also activating the third-party duty of non-obstruction.

65 In general, the intervention rules are reasonably clear, agreed, and affirmed. On the rules themselves, see *Nicaragua* v *USA* (n 51) [191], [202]–[209], [228], [241], [246]; *Armed Activities on the Territory of the Congo (DRC* v *Uganda)* (Judgment) [2005] ICJ Rep 168 [162]. See also Rosalyn Higgins, 'International Law and Civil Conflict' in Evan Luard (ed), *The International Regulation of Civil Wars* (New York University Press 1972) 169–172, 177, 184, 185 (fn 21–22); Gray, *International Law and the Use of Force* (n 64) 25, 38–119. For detailed treatment of relevant debates arising from their application in practice, see Eliav Lieblich, *International Law and Civil Wars: Intervention and Consent* (Routledge 2013); Olivier Corten, *La rebellion et le droit international: le principe de neutralité en tension* (Adi-Poche, Académie de Droit International de la Haye 2015).

66 This is likewise a longstanding and recurring debate. Compare for example the opposite conclusions of Wright, 'Goa Incident' (n 8) 618 and Malcolm N Shaw, *International Law* (6th edn, Cambridge University Press 2008) 1149, 1151–1154, and more recently Lieblich (n 65); Corten (n 65).

67 *Nicaragua* v *USA* (n 51) [205]–[209], [246].

68 See for example Karine Bannelier and Theodore Christakis, 'Under the UN Security Council's Watchful Eyes: Military Intervention by Invitation in the Malian Conflict' (2013) 26 (4) *Leiden Journal of International Law* 855; Lieblich (n 65) 10–37, 209–258; Farideh Shaygan, 'Intervention by Invitation as a Tool of New Colonialism' in James Crawford, Abdul Koroma, Said Mahmoudi, and Alain Pellet (eds), *The International Legal Order: Current Needs and Possible Responses* (Brill Nijhoff 2017); Cóman Kenny and Seán Butler, 'The Legality of Intervention by Invitation in Situations of R2P Violations' (2018) 51 *New York University Journal of International Law and Politics* 135; Quoc Tan Trung Nguyen, 'Rethinking the Legality of Intervention by Invitation: Toward Neutrality' (2019) 24(2) *Journal of Conflict and Security Law* 201.

The second debate, conversely, is whether, and if so under what conditions, intervention in opposition to a particular state regime can ever be internationally lawful when for the purpose of supporting resistance.[69] It is equally well-established that intervention by invitation is not a right generally shared by opposition or rebel groups when it concerns appeals made directly to third-party states.[70] That said, intervention appeals made to the UN may be allowable – as for example under the highly limited conditions of the still unsettled doctrine of the 'responsibility to protect'.[71] Indeed, recognition of the human right to resist as a basis for lawful UN-authorized assistance may help mitigate at least two of the criticisms that doctrine has attracted: that it treats affected populations as passive 'beneficiaries' rather than active agents defending their own human rights; and that its activation thresholds are too high and narrow, therefore coming too late for prevention of atrocities.[72] Some consequent proposals suggest either that the responsibility to protect could be used as a precedent or as a basis for recognizing an analogous complementary right to

[69] See the account in Corten (n 65), especially 243–327 and his conclusions at 326–327, 356.

[70] *Nicaragua* v *USA* (n 51) [246].

[71] Under the 'responsibility to protect' concept, if states are 'unwilling or unable' to protect their own populations from grave harm or 'atrocity crimes', responsibility for this may devolve to the 'international community' acting under authority of the UN Security Council. See Gareth Evans and Mohammed Sahnoun, *The Responsibility to Protect* (International Commission on Intervention and State Sovereignty 2001) (ICISS Report) xi, 32–37; UN General Assembly, 'Follow-Up to the Outcome of the Millennium Summit: A More Secure World – Report of the High Level Panel on Threats, Challenges and Change' UNGA Res A/59/565 (2 December 2004) 8–99 (High Level Panel Report) [201]–[203], setting out basic principles of the doctrine, later affirmed by the UN General Assembly in its '2005 World Summit Outcome' UNGA Res A/RES/60/1 (24 October 2005) [138]–[139], and reaffirmed by the UN Security Council in its 'Resolution 1674 on the Protection of Civilians in Armed Conflict' SC Res S/RES/1674 (28 April 2006) [4]. Note however that as it has yet to receive the imprimatur of formal adoption by a UN General Assembly 'law-making' resolution, it is still considered an 'emerging' norm. See Shaw (n 66) 1155–1158; Ingo Winkelmann, 'Responsibility to Protect' in *Max Planck Encyclopedia of Public International Law* (Oxford Public International Law online database 2010) A[1]–[2], D[13]–[15], E1[16]–[17], E3[22], F[23]; UN Office on the Prevention of Genocide and on the Responsibility to Protect, 'Framework of Analysis for Atrocity Crimes: A Tool for Prevention' (United Nations 2014) 2–3.

[72] See these and other concerns raised in Alex J Bellamy, 'The Responsibility to Protect – Five Years On' (2010) 24(2) *Ethics and International Affairs* 143; Aidan Hehir, 'The Responsibility to Protect: Sound and Fury Signifying Nothing?' (2010) 24(2) *International Relations* 218; Jennifer D Halbert, 'A Responsibility to Protect or Preclude? Examining the Beneficiaries of the Responsibility to Protect' in André Nollkaemper and Julia Hoffman (eds), *Responsibility to Protect: From Principle to Practice* (Amsterdam University Press 2011); Jann K Kleffner, 'The Scope of Crimes Triggering the Responsibility to Protect' in André Nollkaemper and Julia Hoffman (eds), *Responsibility to Protect: From Principle to Practice* (Amsterdam University Press 2011); Lawrence Woocher, 'Responsibility to Prevent: Toward a Strategy' in W Andy Knight and Frazer Egerton (eds), *The Routledge Handbook of the Responsibility to Protect* (Taylor and Francis 2012).

resist exception,[73] or that the responsibility to protect should itself be enhanced by way of a recognition that resembles support for a duty to resist held by various components of an affected population.[74]

In addition, it remains an open question whether the previously established anti-intervention principle of international neutrality with respect to internal conflicts that have escalated into civil wars must evolve to accommodate, or instead already accommodates contraindications posed by requirements of Charter *erga omnes* obligations (of all towards all) with respect to self-determination and human rights. In his comprehensive study of the interaction between these principles and claims to a right of rebellion in international law, Corten concludes that whether general or customary international law yields a right to rebellion or a ban on rebellion cannot yet be determined, in part because state practice shows that the principle of neutrality is subject to challenge or reconfiguration according to the particularities of each case – sometimes favouring the rebels, and sometimes favouring the state authorities.[75]

In another variation on theories locating a Charter-based right to resist in general or customary international law, both Lauterpacht and Bassiouni have suggested another conception of this right as a 'general principle'.[76] As shown by the evidence in the previous chapter, domestic constitutional codifications of the right may not be sufficiently dense to warrant its characterization as a

[73] See for example Chiara Redaelli, 'The Right to Rebel against Violations of Human Rights: A New Role for the Responsibility to Protect?' (2020) 19(1) *Palestine Yearbook of International Law* 8. Similarly, see the proposition in Tom Dannenbaum, 'War Crimes and Just War Theory' in Kimberly K Ferzan and Larry Alexander (eds), *The Palgrave Handbook of Applied Ethics and Criminal Law* (Palgrave Macmillan 2019) 789.

[74] See the 'individual responsibility to protect', intended as a 'complement to the state- and institution-centric paradigm', proposed by Edward Luck and Dana Luck, 'The Individual Responsibility to Protect' in Sheri P Rosenberg, Tibi Galis, and Alex Zucker (eds), *Reconstructing Atrocity Prevention* (Cambridge University Press 2015).

[75] See Corten (n 65) 326–327, 356. Corten identifies, in effect, a continuing ambivalence resulting from pressures on the traditional principle by a progressive prohibition on rebellion against constitutional government on the one hand, and an increasing acceptance of rebellion against legal but authoritarian regimes on the other. See in general ibid 243–327.

[76] See Hersch Lauterpacht, 'The Grotian Tradition in International Law' (1946) 23 *British Yearbook of International Law* 1, 9. See also Lauterpacht, 'Law of Nations, Law of Nature, Rights of Man' (n 13) 23; Lauterpacht, *International Bill of the Rights of Man* (n 13) 43; Lauterpacht, *International Law and Human Rights* (n 13) 116; M Cherif Bassiouni, 'Ideologically Motivated Offenses and the Political Offense Exception in Extradition – A Proposed Juridical Standard for an Unruly Problem' (1969) XIX *De Paul Law Review* 217, 254–255. See also Sumida (n 38) 168; Paust (n 15) 560–562, 566; Jordan J Paust, 'International Law, Dignity, Democracy and the Arab Spring' (2013) 46 *Cornell International Law Journal* 1, 12.

'general principle of law' if this depends on universal domestic recognition.[77] However, as UN General Assembly Resolution 2625 interpreting certain clauses of the UN Charter including articles 1 and 2 is designated a 'Declaration on Principles of International Law', this would indicate that validity as such may be otherwise established.[78] Likewise, the Universal Declaration on Human Rights is understood to provide an authoritative statement of the general human rights principles or standards referred to in the UN Charter.[79] Therefore, to the extent that these two declaratory instruments recognize the right to resist, the theory that it is a general principle of international law, consistent with the purposes of the UN, becomes harder to dismiss. These sources will be considered in turn.

6.3 LIMITED IMPLIED RECOGNITION: UN GENERAL ASSEMBLY RESOLUTION 2625

One of the few comparatively 'known knowns' about the right to resist in contemporary international law concerns resistance to foreign aggression, occupation, colonization, apartheid, and other racist regimes. When such resistance has escalated to the point of 'armed conflict', these are sometimes emotively termed 'wars of national liberation'.[80] It is generally agreed that

77 Domestic or 'municipal' law is one of five categories of 'general principles' as sources of international law, as per article 38(1)(c) of the Statute of the International Court of Justice. The principles set out in articles 1 and 2 of the UN Charter, as 'generalized and further elaborated upon' in UN General Assembly Resolution 2625 and 'invoked frequently before the ICJ' as 'giving rise to concrete legal obligations', are an example of another category. See Wolfrum (n 4) B2(b)[28]–[29]; B2(b)(ii)[34]–[36]; B2(b)(v)[41]; B2(b)(v)[43]–[47], [55]. On 'natural law' as a source of 'general principles', in turn a basis for human rights concepts, see also *South-West Africa (Ethiopia* v *South Africa; Liberia* v *South Africa)* (Second Phase Judgment) [1966] ICJ Rep 6, Dissenting Opinion of Judge Tanaka 250, 294–299.

78 On the need to distinguish between 'general principles of international law' and the broader category of 'general principles of law' as a distinct source of international law to which it belongs as per article 38(1)(c) of the Statute of the International Court of Justice, see Wolfrum (n 4) B1[6]–[7], [17], [20], B2, B4(a)[58]–[59], E[125]. Yet compare Brownlie, maintaining that the category 'general principles of international law' is not rigid, is overlapping, and is in fact the broader category including 'rules of customary law [and] general principles of law as in Article 38(1)(c)' and 'are primarily abstractions from a mass of rules and have been so long and so generally accepted as to be no longer directly connected with state practice'. Brownlie (n 6) 19.

79 See discussion in Section 6.4.

80 Glazier's definition is an 'armed conflict' against 'a colonial or occupying power, or racist regime' waged by a people 'seeking independence', which 'enjoy[s] a presumption of legality' but, in his view, a limited twenty-first-century relevance. David W Glazier, 'Wars of National Liberation' in *Max Planck Encyclopedia of Public International Law* (Oxford Public International Law online database 2009) A[1]–[3], E[17]–[19]. Brownlie affirms that by virtue of state practice and that of the UN, 'national liberation movements' may acquire a 'special type' of international legal personality conferring rights and duties additional to those otherwise

where there is 'forcible deprivation' of the right to self-determination, involving the domination of one 'people' by another, resistance in defence of that right is considered lawful,[81] or at least not unlawful.[82] The source of this limited implied recognition is the UN Charter,[83] as interpreted by the UN General Assembly 'Declaration on Principles of International Law Concerning Friendly Relations and Co-operation among States in

attributed to 'belligerent and insurgent communities', and that this concept is rooted in UN General Assembly Resolution 2625. See Brownlie (n 6) 62–63. Compare Simma et al (n 48) 57 C[35]–[36], 61 D[54], 125–129 C[40]–[48] D[49]–[50]. See also further discussion in Section 6.6.2 below on usage in relation to international humanitarian law.

81 See for example Georges Abi-Saab, 'Wars of National Liberation and the Laws of War' [1972] *Annales d'Études Internationales* 93, 100–101; M Cherif Bassiouni, 'Final Document: Conclusions and Recommendations' in M Cherif Bassiouni (ed), *International Terrorism and Political Crimes* (Charles C Thomas 1975) xii; Christian Tomuschat, 'The Right of Resistance and Human Rights' in *Violations of Human Rights: Possible Rights of Recourse and Forms of Resistance* (UNESCO 1984) 18, 20–21, 26–27, 29–30, 33; Richard Falk and Burns H Weston, 'The Relevance of International Law to Palestinian Rights in the West Bank and Gaza: In Legal Defense of the Intifada' (1991) 32(1) *Harvard International Law Journal* 129, 132; Richard Falk and Burns H Weston, 'The Israeli-Occupied Territories, International Law, and the Boundaries of Scholarly Discourse: A Reply to Michael Curtis' (1992) 33(1) *Harvard International Law Journal* 191, 192; Richard Falk, 'Azmi Bishara, the Right of Resistance, and the Palestinian Ordeal' (2002) XXXI(2) *Journal of Palestine Studies* 19; Noelle Higgins, *Regulating the Use of Force in Wars of National Liberation: The Need for a New Regime* (Martinus Nijhoff 2010) 2, 7–90, 229–237. See also Brownlie (n 6) 582, 739–741; Simma et al (n 48) 62–63 F[60]–[61], 128 D[49]; Glazier (n 80) A[1]–[3]; compare Gray, 'The Use of Force and the International Legal Order' (n 64) 623–624; Gray, *International Law and the Use of Force* (n 64) 68–74. Others maintain that only resistance without force is recognized as 'lawful'. See for example Daniel Thürer and Thomas Burri, 'Self-Determination' in *Max Planck Encyclopedia of Public International Law* (Oxford Public International Law online database 2008) C1(a)[15](ii).

82 See for example Wilson (n 15) 135–136, 186–187; Cassese, *Self-Determination* (n 11) 151–154, 197–198; Walter Kälin and Jörg Künzli, 'Article 1F(b): Freedom Fighters, Terrorists and the Notion of Serious Non-Political Crime' (2000) 12 supp *International Journal of Refugee Law* 46, 56–59; Saul (n 10) 75.

83 On the UN Charter as 'a legal text, stating legal purposes and principles, specifying norms, organizing sanctions' and imposing international legal obligations see Jean-Pierre Cot, 'United Nations Charter' in *Max Planck Encyclopedia of Public International Law* (Oxford Public International Law online database 2011) B[15]. On the special status of the UN Charter among multilateral treaties, given its 'normative superiority' as per article 103 and the essentially universal nature of UN membership, see Simma et al (n 48) 15–16 A[1]–[2]; Philip Kunig, 'United Nations Charter, Interpretation of' in *Max Planck Encyclopedia of Public International Law* (Oxford Public International Law online database 2006) A[1], B[5]; Cot (n 83) C[24], D[38]–[39], F2[69]–[70], [73]–[78]. That the principles enumerated in article 2 give rise to direct rights and obligations which are to be interpreted in light of the purposes set out at article 1 as well as the Preamble, see Cot (n 83) C[22], [29]. That certain of these principles are reflective of customary international law, and others also reflect *jus cogens* norms see ibid C [31]–[32], F.2 [76]–[77]; Kunig (n 83) C1[9], C2(a)[12], C3[18]; *Nicaragua* v *USA* (n 51) [99], [408].

Accordance with the Charter of the United Nations' set out in Resolution 2625.[84] This declaration, like all UN General Assembly resolutions, is not legally binding in itself. However, since it was adopted by consensus without a vote it is usually considered as also expressing customary international law, and described as 'at a minimum, an [authoritative] aid to interpretation' of certain binding obligations under the UN Charter.[85]

The UN Charter right to resist is found in this Declaration's fifth principle, self-determination, according to which: 'In their actions against, and resistance to ... forcible action [by states depriving them of the right to self-determination and] in pursuit of the exercise of their right to self-determination ... peoples are entitled to seek and receive support in accordance with the purposes and principles of the Charter.'[86] The fifth principle creates an additional implied right to resist where a state is not 'conducting [itself] in compliance with the principle of equal rights and self-determination ... and thus [not] possessed of a government representing the whole people belonging to the territory without distinction as to race, creed or colour'.[87]

The third principle, non-intervention, establishes an important limitation on consequent international assistance. It specifies that '*no State shall* organize, assist, foment, finance, incite or tolerate subversive, terrorist or armed activities directed towards the violent overthrow of the regime of another State, or interfere in civil strife in another State'.[88] However, as qualified by the first principle, the prohibition of the threat or use of force, this '*shall [not] be construed as affecting [t]he powers of the Security Council under the*

84 UNGA Res 2625 (XXV) (24 October 1970).

85 Honoré (n 5) 44. On UNGA Res 2625 as evidence of *opinio juris* and subsequent 'practice' in application of the Charter, providing 'a basis for the progressive development of the law and the speedy consolidation of customary rules', with 'direct legal effect as an authoritative interpretation and application of the principles of the Charter', see Brownlie (n 6) 12–13, 15; Kunig (n 83) C2(a)[12]–[14], C[7], C1[9], D[19]; Cot (n 83) C[26], E[55]–[56], [60]; Simma et al (n 48) 27–30 C[26]–[32], 57 C[37]. On its consequent status as 'customary law' and a 'potential source of codification' of pre-existing customary international law principles, see Tunkin (n 3) 538; Helen Keller, 'Friendly Relations Declaration (1970)' in *Max Planck Encyclopedia of Public International Law* (Oxford Public International Law online database 2009) A[1], A[3], B[5], C1(c)[12], E1[30], E3[33]–[35], E4[36]–[39], F[40]–[41]; Gray, *International Law and the Use of Force* (n 64) 69–70, 77, 82; Gray, 'The Use of Force and the International Legal Order' (n 64) 616; *Nicaragua* v *USA* (n 51) [187]–[195], [202]–[205], [264], [408].

86 'The principle of equal rights and self-determination of peoples' or fifth principle, UNGA Res 2625 (n 84) non-numbered fifth paragraph [emphasis added].

87 Fifth principle, UNGA Res 2625 (n 84) non-numbered seventh paragraph.

88 'The principle concerning the duty not to intervene in matters within the domestic jurisdiction of any State' or third principle, UNGA Res 2625 (n 84) non-numbered second paragraph [emphasis added].

Charter . . . [or] enlarging or diminishing in any way the scope of the provisions of the Charter concerning cases in which the use of force is lawful'.[89]I

The subsequent UN General Assembly Resolution 3314 'Definition of Aggression' – also adopted by consensus – affirms this exception and thus limited right in customary international law.[90] Its article 6 clarifies that nothing in the definition 'shall be construed as in any way enlarging or diminishing the scope of the Charter . . . provisions concerning cases in which the use of force is lawful' and article 7 asserts that in particular it does not 'in any way prejudice the right to self-determination . . . as derived from the Charter, of peoples forcibly deprived of that right . . . particularly peoples under colonial and racist regimes or other forms of alien domination: nor the right of these peoples to struggle to that end and to seek and receive support' specifically 'in accordance with the principles of the Charter and in conformity with the above-mentioned Declaration' in UN General Assembly Resolution 2625.[91]

While undeniably convoluted,[92] the Declaration implicitly affirms a right to resist that includes a right to rebel – that is, to use force against one's own state or against a state that otherwise claims jurisdiction – as a rule of exception to the general rule of prohibition on the use of force applicable to all subjects of international law, exclusively for the purpose of enforcing the right to self-determination under certain conditions.[93] It is on this basis that, in addressing the question 'may racial groups and peoples resort to force when self-determination is forcibly denied?', Cassese answers with a concise formula that describes nature, function, source, rights-holders, triggers, means, and

[89] 'The principle that States shall refrain in their international relations from the threat or use of force against the territorial integrity or political independence of any State or in any other manner inconsistent with the purposes of the United Nations' or first principle, UNGA Res 2625 (n 84) non-numbered tenth and thirteenth paragraphs [emphasis added].

[90] On Resolution 3314 as another example of the General Assembly providing an elaboration or clarification of UN Charter principles and rules, and legally binding on that basis, see Kunig (n 83) C2(a)[13]. Note that the earlier 'Declaration on the Granting of Independence to Colonial Countries and Peoples' does not actually contain a recognition similar to the UNGA Res 2625 right to resist. See UNGA Res 1514 (XV) (14 December 1960). Some scholars nevertheless maintain the right to resist is also implied therein. See for example Honoré (n 5) 42 fn 17.

[91] 'Definition of Aggression' UNGA Res 3314 (XXIX) (14 December 1974) articles 6, 7.

[92] The Declaration's purpose is to clarify seven principles as 'basic rules' of international law but its vague wording is sometimes considered 'not conducive to clarification'. The lack of consensus among drafters meant that exceptions to these rules were not clearly enumerated, save for the qualification clause under the fifth principle, referred to above. See Keller (n 85) A [2]–[3], B[4]–[6], C1(b)[9], C1(c)[10], D1(b)[16], F[42].

[93] See Honoré (n 5) 43–44. Paust maintains that the right to rebel has been 'a recognized principle of international law' since at least 1975, citing the conclusions of thirty-eight experts as reported in Bassiouni (n 81) xii, xxi. See Paust (n 15) 560, 566.

object and purpose: that 'gradually a customary rule has evolved providing for an exception to the broad scope of that customary rule banning force' enumerated in article 2(4) of the UN Charter, providing that 'if peoples subjected to colonial domination or foreign occupation, as well as racial groups not represented in government, are forcibly denied the right to self-determination, such peoples or racial groups are legally entitled to resort to armed force to realize their right to self-determination'.[94] Others maintain the exception is not additional to, or separate from, but rather an analogous extension of, the narrow UN Charter article 51 self-defence exception to the article 2(4) prohibition of the use of force,[95] in the event of 'armed attack' by a state against a state.[96]

Notwithstanding the above, and partly because the question has not yet been directly adjudicated by international courts and tribunals, some still maintain that general international law remains ambiguous as neither permissive nor prohibitive and therefore *non liquet* on the right to resist.[97] Indeed, the lack of an unmistakably clear articulation of the right's recognition could cause problems for decision-makers and adjudicators in the regulation of its exercise, as well as for those engaged in or contemplating such actions, who need assistance. Yet if broken down into its constituent elements, arguably this source of the right provides basic guidance to decision-making by the UN Security Council, or advisory opinion or litigation in the International Court of Justice. As customary international law, it could also prove relevant in either international or domestic *jus post-bellum* (post-conflict justice) processes.

94 Antonio Cassese, *International Law* (2nd edn, Oxford University Press 2005) section 18.9, 374, citing UNGA Res 2625 and article 7 of UNGA Res 3314. Although Cassese finds supporting evidence in article 1(4) of Additional Protocol I to the 1949 Geneva Conventions, he does not cite it as a 'source' per se. Ibid 374 fn 30, cross-referencing Cassese, *Self-Determination* (n 11) 150–158, 197–198. Similarly, see Chemillier-Gendreau (n 33) 956 [13].

95 On the application of an analogous self-defence rule to right to resist claimants, see Simma et al (n 48) 52 B[15], 61 D[54]–[55], 128 D[49]. This possibility remains open because, as Gray points out, there is no agreement as to whether the narrow right of self-defence as described in article 51 is exhaustive, or whether there is a broader customary right. See Gray, 'The Use of Force and the International Legal Order' (n 64) 615–647, 625.

96 On the application of article 51 to states in instances relating to third-party-backed rebellion, in particular the 'armed attack' standard, necessity, and attribution requirements, compare Brownlie (n 6) 732–733; Gray, 'The Use of Force and the International Legal Order' (n 64) 627, 630; Jens David Ohlin and Larry May, *Necessity in International Law* (Oxford University Press 2016) 62–63. See also *Nicaragua* v *USA* (n 51) [109]–[110], [160], [191], [195], [210]–[211], [230], [246], [249]; *Legal Consequences of the Construction of a Wall in the Occupied Palestinian Territory* (Advisory Opinion) [2004] ICJ Rep 136 [138]–[141]; *DRC* v *Uganda* (n 65) [146]–[147], however note that the question of whether the rebels or insurgents had a right to resist was not the question before the Court in these cases.

97 See for example Bellal and Doswald-Beck (n 15) 11–14, 21–23, 32–33; Corten (n 65) 356.

6.3.1 *Elements of the Right and Ancillary Assessments Necessary to Validate a Claim*

Using the analytical framework established in Chapter 4, it is possible to identify the elements of the right to resist as recognized under UN General Assembly Resolution 2625 and thus the ancillary assessments necessary to validate a claim made on this legal basis. These relate to the rights-holders and duty-bearers, primary and secondary triggers, permissible means, and object and purpose. While such analysis demonstrates that its recognition of the right is indeed quite limited, it is not so impossibly vague as to be beyond determination.

6.3.1.1 The Object and Purpose

The decisive element of the right as recognized in this particular source of general or customary international law is its valid object and purpose, exclusively restricted to enforcing the UN Charter-protected collective right of self-determination, or a connected right of collective self-defence. This is probably not a source that recognizes a right to resist with the broader object and purpose of more general human rights or other international law enforcement – or change. Valid objects would need to be demonstrated within the context of a particular claim by reference to generally accepted authoritative international legal definitions, to the extent that these are available, bearing in mind that such definitions may be evolving, in flux, or otherwise not fully agreed.[98] In addition, meeting the valid object test would likely exclude those who would exercise their right to self-determination by denying this same right to others. This potentially complicates assessment in practice, where real-world cases can involve competing claims. Recognition of the right to self-

[98] For example, the articulation of the right to self-determination in the Declaration on Principles of International Law is considered 'the most authoritative and comprehensive so far', with a recognized 'legal character' as a right with associated duties 'directly binding' as 'part of the law of the Charter', although without a fully agreed conceptual definition and content. See UNGA Res 2625 (n 84) fifth principle, non-numbered first, fourth, and seventh paragraphs, and third principle, non-numbered first and fourth paragraphs; Simma et al (n 48) 48–49 A[1], A[3], 50–51 B[8], [12], 52 B[15], 54 B[24]; Thürer and Burri (n 81) B2[11], C[12]. However, this is not the only declaratory source. See the further elaboration of the right's elements in the UN Declaration on the Rights of Indigenous Peoples UNGA Res 61/295 (13 September 2007).

While this may not yet have ripened into settled customary international law, it is legally significant as evidence of the evolution of *opinio juris* and a source of authority on the content of the right as applied. See Sylvanus Gbendazhi Barnabas, 'The Legal Status of the United Nations Declaration on the Rights of Indigenous Peoples (2007) in Contemporary International Human Rights Law' (2017) 6 *International Human Rights Law Review* 242.

determination as a *jus cogens* norm immune to derogation provides further reinforcement for those asserting a valid claim.[99]

6.3.1.2 The Rights-Holders

Apart from the formally recognized colonization cases, establishing which 'units of self-determination' distinguish valid rights-holders is generally considered one of the most controversial aspects.[100] According to Paust, the international right of resistance, rebellion, or revolution is never a minority right but rather an exclusively majoritarian right of a 'people as a whole' – albeit one held by 'all peoples',[101] whether they constitute a majority or a minority in a given context.[102] He emphasizes that it is necessarily distinct from a claimed 'right of secession' by a minority that does not legally constitute a 'people'.[103] Indeed, it would seem that for the purposes of a claim under the UN Charter according to UN General Assembly Resolution 2625, a valid rights-holder must constitute a majority or minority 'people'.[104] Unfortunately, a longstanding conundrum associated with the international law of self-determination is its lack of an agreed legal definition of a 'people'.[105] For this reason, a separate judicial finding that a given group is a 'people' with a right to self-determination would act as a useful preliminary identification of a potential rights-holder.[106]

99 See International Law Commission, 'Draft Conclusions on Identification and Legal Consequences of Peremptory Norms of General International Law' (n 27) Conclusion 23(h).

100 Honoré (n 5) 44–45. Yet potential rights-holders are not restricted to decolonization cases. '[W]hole populations' of states constitute the most relevant group in the twenty-first century, according to Simma et al (n 48) 53 B[17]–[18], 60 C[48].

101 See Paust (n 15) 553, 567.

102 See Gudmunder Alfredsson, 'Peoples' in *Max Planck Encyclopedia of Public International Law* (Oxford Public International Law online database 2007) A[4]–[5], [7], C[13], D[18]–[20].

103 Paust (n 15) 553–555. Indeed a 'right of secession' describes a more specific remedy than a right to resist, but similar insofar as it is not available where human rights are respected by the government in question. See Simma et al (n 48) 57 C[34].

104 See ibid 58 C[40].

105 See ibid 55 C[27]; Alfredsson (n 102) A[2]; Thürer and Burri (n 81) C1(b)[18]. However see the 'objective and subjective elements' proposed in *Accordance with International Law of the Unilateral Declaration of Independence in Respect of* Kosovo (Advisory Opinion) [2010] ICJ Rep 403, Separate Opinion of Judge Cançado Trindade 523, 613–614 [228]–[229]; the definitions advanced by the African Commission and African Court of Human and Peoples Rights further discussed in Chapter 7, Section 7.3.1.1. The lack of an agreed definition has not prevented formal findings in particular cases that a discrete group constitutes a legal 'people'. Thürer and Burri (n 81) C1(b)[18]–[19].

106 See for example *Legal Consequences for States of the Continued Presence of South Africa in Namibia notwithstanding Security Council Resolution 276 (1970)* (Advisory Opinion) [1971]

Simma and colleagues identify three types of potential 'external' rights-holders: whole populations of a state subject to 'foreign domination' which could include invasion and occupation; 'colonized peoples' subject to foreign rule and exploitation; and ethnic minority 'peoples' within a multi-ethnic state politically, economically, and culturally dominated by another group.[107] Similarly, they identify two types of potential 'internal' rights-holders as 'peoples': whole populations of a state that have a right to decide their form of government; and ethnic minorities that have a right to 'self-government or other protective provisions within [that] state'.[108] Arguably, indigenous peoples could be either external or internal rights-holders, depending on their particular circumstances, which can differ widely.[109]

Honoré correctly distinguishes the right of self-determination, for those units meeting the criteria, from their right to resist or rebel in order to secure its enforcement. While the former is a right 'irrespective' of trigger conditions, the latter is not.[110] The activation of a people's potential right to resist in any particular case depends on whether the primary and secondary trigger conditions are met.

6.3.1.3 The Primary Triggers

Establishing primary trigger conditions for the right to resist pertaining to a given claim by a potentially valid rights-holder, in pursuit of the legally valid object of self-determination pursuant to the UN Charter, requires not only a primary violation of the human right to self-determination, but also reference to international legal standards or tests for the particular form of violation, where

ICJ Rep 16 [52]–[53]; *Western Sahara* (Advisory Opinion) [1975] ICJ Rep 12 [70]; *East Timor (Portugal v Australia)* (Judgment) [1995] ICJ Rep 90 [31], [37]; *Legal Consequences of the Construction of a Wall in the Occupied Palestinian Territory* (n 96) [118], [149]–[159]; *Legal Consequences of the Separation of the Chagos Archipelago from Mauritius in 1965* (Advisory Opinion) [2019] ICJ Rep 95 [146]–[147], [152], [160], [172], [174], [177]–[178]. Compare *Kosovo Advisory Opinion* (n 105) [51], [56], [79], [82]–[84], [122], where the Court deliberately does not address the question of whether there is a positive 'right' arising. Alternatively or in addition, specific UN Resolutions may be relied upon, as in Falk (n 81) 22–27.

107 See Simma et al (n 48) 55–56 C[28]–[31].

108 See ibid 56 C[32].

109 For affirmative general recognition of indigenous peoples as 'peoples' with self-determination rights in international law, including the right to an effective remedy for violations of that right, see the many detailed provisions in the UN Declaration on the Rights of Indigenous Peoples (n 98). Regardless of the overall legal status of that Declaration itself, such rights are unquestionably binding on states where incorporated into domestic law. Barnabas (n 98) 252–253.

110 Honoré (n 5) 45.

available. For example, conditions must in the first instance amount to 'aggression';[111] 'unlawful occupation';[112] 'unlawful intervention';[113] 'colonization';[114]

[111] See first principle, UNGA Res 2625 (n 84) non-numbered second paragraph, where 'aggression' is prohibited and described as a 'crime against the peace' but not otherwise defined, hence the need for supplement by UNGA Res 3314 (n 91), emphasizing in particular articles 6 and 7 which modify the definition at article 3 including article 3(g). There is a significant specialist literature on aggression in customary international law that would further assist in identifying associated trigger conditions. In general, see Yoram Dinstein, 'Aggression' in *Max Planck Encyclopedia of Public International Law* (Oxford Public International Law online database September 2015) B[9]–[12], C1[13]–[14], C2[15]–[22], C3[23]–[31],C4 [32]–[33]; Yoram Dinstein, *War, Aggression and Self-Defence* (6th edn, Cambridge University Press 2017). See also the concise account in Tom Dannenbaum, *The Crime of Aggression, Humanity, and the Soldier* (Cambridge University Press 2018) 19–21.

[112] See first principle, UNGA Res 2625 (n 84) non-numbered tenth paragraph, which specifies 'military occupation resulting from the use of force in contravention of the provisions of the Charter' and prohibiting as unlawful any other 'territorial acquisition resulting from the threat or use of force'. For a more detailed analysis of this trigger see the general points made in Falk and Weston, 'Relevance of International Law' (n 81) 132, 142–148, 150–152, 155. There is a significant specialist literature on unlawful occupation in customary international law that may further assist in identifying associated trigger conditions. In general, see Eyal Benvenisti, 'Occupation, Belligerent' in *Max Planck Encyclopedia of Public International Law* (Oxford Public International Law online database May 2009) A1[1], 3[4]–[10], B1[12]–2[13]–[15] C1 [20]–[21], D[32]; Eyal Benvenisti, *The International Law of Occupation* (2nd edn, Oxford University Press 2012); Eliav Lieblich and Eyal Benvenisti, *Occupation in International Law* (Oxford University Press 2022); Marco Longobardo, *The Use of Armed Force in Occupied Territory* (Cambridge University Press 2018) 4–61, 82–87. Also relevant will be any forthcoming Advisory Opinion of the International Court of Justice addressing the lawfulness of occupation policies and practices, and legal consequences of unlawful occupation, in response to the UN General Assembly request entitled 'Israeli Practices Affecting the Human Rights of the Palestinian People in the Occupied Palestinian Territory, including East Jerusalem' UNGA Res 77/247 (30 December 2022) [18].

[113] See first principle, UNGA Res 2625 (n 84) non-numbered first and seventh to ninth paragraphs; ibid third principle, non-numbered first to fourth paragraphs. Gray emphasizes that the International Court of Justice has affirmed that, in general, unilaterally assisting or supporting or tolerating rebels amounts to unlawful intervention, and actively arming or training them and providing other direct or indirect military support amounts to both unlawful intervention and an unlawful use of force by the assisting state. See Gray, *International Law and the Use of Force* (n 64) 25, 72, 76–84, 108–118. There is a significant specialist literature on unlawful intervention in customary international law that would further assist in identifying associated trigger conditions. In general, see Philip Kunig, 'Intervention, Prohibition of' in *Max Planck Encyclopedia of Public International Law* (Oxford Public International Law online database April 2008) A1[1]–[6], A2[7]–[9], [11]–[13, B[20], D1[29], D2[30]–[31], D3 [32]–[33], D4[34]–[36], D5[39], E[48]–[49]; Lieblich (n 65) 1–37, 122–258. See also Corten (n 65).

[114] See fifth principle, UNGA Res 2625 (n 84) non-numbered second paragraph, which at (b) specifies the duty on all states to 'bring a speedy end to colonialism, having due regard to the freely expressed will of the peoples concerned'. See also UNGA Res 1514 (n 90) [1]–[2], [4]–[5], and the *Chagos Advisory Opinion* (n 106) [150]–[153] affirming the role of that resolution

'apartheid' or other 'racist regime'.[115] Note the 'racist regime' trigger would not only imply a right to resist apartheid-equivalent regimes,[116] but also arguably

as material evidence of the customary right of colonized peoples to self-determination; the list of 'non-self-governing territories' formally entitled to self-determination and subject to decolonization on this basis, as per the criteria established under 'Principles Which Should Guide Members in Determining Whether or Not an Obligation Exists to Transmit the Information Called for under Article 73 e of the Charter of the United Nations' UNGA Res 1541 (XV) (1960) (15 December 1960); and the annual reports of the UN Special Committee on Decolonization tasked with review of implementation. However, unlisted colonized peoples also have the right of external self-determination if their status as such lacks 'the free and informed approval of the people concerned'. Alfredsson (n 102) B[11]. While an estimated 700 million people have decolonized since 1945, reducing the number of colonies from fifty-one to sixteen, with less than 1 per cent of the world's population remaining colonized, this 'impressive achievement' remains incomplete, according to Rahmatullah Khan, 'Decolonization' in *Max Planck Encyclopedia of Public International Law* (Oxford Public International Law online database 2011) A[1]–[2]. There is a significant specialist literature on colonization in customary international law that would further assist in identifying associated trigger conditions in contemporary contexts. See for example Jörn Axel Kämmerer, 'Colonialism' in *Max Planck Encyclopedia of Public International Law* (Oxford Public International Law online database January 2018) A[1]–[5], C[8]–[10], D[11]–[23]; Jaime Trinidad, *Self-Determination in Disputed Colonial Territories* (Cambridge University Press 2018); Thomas Burri and Jamie Trinidad (eds), *The International Court of Justice and Decolonisation: New Directions from the* Chagos *Advisory Opinion* (Cambridge University Press 2021). Regarding indigenous peoples subject to colonization, see the specific self-determination rights and obligations set out in the UN Declaration on the Rights of Indigenous Peoples (n 98), and the associated specialist literature: for example, Jessie Hohmann and Marc Weller (eds), *The UN Declaration on the Rights of Indigenous Peoples: A Commentary* (Oxford University Press 2018) especially chapters 3, 5–6, 8–10, 14–15, 17.

115 See fifth principle, UNGA Res 2625 (n 84) non-numbered second and seventh paragraphs, characterizing 'subjection of peoples to alien subjugation, domination and exploitation' as 'contrary to the Charter', and withdrawing 'territorial integrity' and 'political unity' protections from governments not 'representing the whole people belonging to the territory without distinction as to race, creed or colour' and thus not 'conducting themselves in compliance with the principle of equal rights and self-determination' – in other words, from racist regimes.

116 See preamble, articles I and II of the International Convention on the Suppression and Punishment of the Crime of Apartheid (adopted 30 December 1973, entered into force 18 July 1976) 1015 UNTS 243; Convention on the Elimination of All Forms of Racial Discrimination (entered into force 4 January 1969) 660 UNTS 195 article 3; UN Committee on the Elimination of Racial Discrimination, 'General Comment 19 – Article 3: The Prevention, Prohibition and Eradication of Racial Segregation and Apartheid' (1995) UN Doc A/50/18, 140 [1]–[2]. On the international legal meaning of the term 'apartheid' as any regime of 'systematic and institutionalized racial domination' that is 'configured deliberately for [that] purpose', the status of the Apartheid Convention as codification of peremptory general international law despite non-universal ratification, and thus its definition's ongoing relevance and application beyond the South African case, see for example John Dugard, 'Introductory Note to the Convention on the Suppression and Punishment of the Crime of Apartheid' (United Nations Audiovisual Library of International Law 2008) 2; John Reynolds, 'Third World Approaches to International Law and the Ghosts of Apartheid' in Keane and McDermott, *The Challenge of Human Rights* (n 1) 209–214; Richard Falk and Virginia

genocide,[117] as defined by their respective United Nations treaties. Assessment is considerably simplified where these standards are clear and agreed. The converse is true to the extent that they remain contested. Formal findings by UN adjudicative bodies or expert reports commissioned by other UN bodies, or resolutions of the UN Security Council or UN General Assembly to this effect may help corroborate the existence of primary triggering conditions in particular cases.[118]

Establishing the above 'external' self-determination trigger conditions for the right to resist can be complicated enough. Establishing what qualifies as 'internal' self-determination triggers is even more so.[119] This ambiguity regarding a right to resist to enforce the internal dimension of the right to

Tilley, 'Israeli Practices towards the Palestinian People and the Question of Apartheid' (United Nations Economic and Social Commission for Western Asia 2017) 10, 11–22; Julia Gebhard, 'Apartheid' in *Max Planck Encyclopedia of Public International Law* (Oxford Public International Law online database January 2018) B3[13], C[14]–[24], D[25]–[27], E[28]–[29].

117 See articles II and III of the Convention on the Prevention and Punishment of the Crime of Genocide (concluded 9 December 1948, entered into force 12 January 1951) 78 UNTS 277. On the customary status of the Convention's principles and definition despite its non-universal ratification, see *Reservations to the Convention on the Prevention and Punishment of Genocide* (Advisory Opinion) [1951] ICJ Rep 15; *Application of the Convention on the Prevention and Punishment of the Crime of Genocide (Bosnia and Herzegovina* v *Serbia and Montenegro)* (Judgment) [2007] ICJ Rep 43 [161]; William A Schabas, *Genocide in International Law* (2nd edn, Cambridge University Press 2009) 3–6, 8, 10–12, 15. Forthcoming International Court of Justice decisions on the merits in the *Application of the Convention on the Prevention and Punishment of the Crime of Genocide (Gambia* v *Myanmar)*; *Dispute Relating to Allegations of Genocide (Ukraine* v *Russian Federation)*; and *Application of the Convention on the Prevention and Punishment of the Crime of Genocide in the Gaza Strip (South Africa* v *Israel)* cases may also provide relevant guidance.

118 See the rare example of a specific characterization of actions as constituting 'aggression', with specific invocation of UNGA Res 2625 – although not by the UN Security Council – in UN General Assembly, 'Aggression against Ukraine' UNGA Res ES-11/1 (18 March 2022).

119 Indeed, much about the right to internal self-determination itself, including its specific content, remains unresolved. For a detailed discussion see Kalana Senaratne, *Internal Self-Determination in International Law: History, Theory, and Practice* (Cambridge University Press 2021) 1–11, 237–253. Compare Cassese, *Self-Determination* (n 11) 52–55, 126–133, 346–348; Allan Rosas, 'Internal Self-Determination' in Christian Tomuschat (ed), *Modern Law of Self-Determination* (Martinus Nijhoff 1993) 227, 230, 232, 249; Simon Chesterman, Ian Johnstone, and David M Malone (eds), *Law and Practice of the United Nations: Documents and Commentary* (Oxford University Press 2016) 435–476. Paust however argues that internal self-determination content may be logically inferred from the UN Charter, UNGA Res 2625 and article 21 of the Universal Declaration of Human Rights – discussed in Section 6.4 – together establishing this dimension of the right under customary international law. See Jordan J Paust, 'Political Oppression in the Name of National Security: Authority, Participation, and the Necessity within Democratic Limits Test' (1982) 9(1) *Yale International Law Journal* 178, 181–188.

self-determination largely correlates to the still unresolved status of a 'right to democratic governance'.[120] Some maintain the Declaration indicates a general right to revolution, by inference.[121] Others counsel caution, however, citing a lack of clarity in the document rendering the internal dimension of the right *non liquet*, or argue its restriction to racist regimes only as per the explicit provision in the text.[122] While such doubts about breadth of scope are not unreasonable, the logical consequence of the restrictive interpretation is uncertainty regarding a customary right to resist other crimes against humanity, as well as other human rights violations that do not constitute internationally criminal acts, even where these could amount to the traditional trigger conditions of 'tyranny' or 'oppression' which are not directly referenced in the Declaration's text.

Yet there may be more interpretive room than the restrictive position concedes.[123] For example, as Simma and colleagues note, dynamic interpretation is the standard method regarding the UN Charter,[124] with an emphasis not only on the importance of ordinary meaning, but also context and object and purpose.[125] The ordinary meaning of 'self-determination' is widely understood to include both external and internal dimensions.[126] Of relevance to

[120] See Senaratne (n 119) 1, 3–4, 9, 51–72. Compare Thürer and Burri (n 81) C2(b)(i)[33]–[37]; Chesterman et al (n 119) 456, 458–470, 472; and consequences for intervention rules set out in Gray, *International Law and the Use of Force* (n 64) 64–68.

[121] See for example Paust (n 119) 181–188. Yet compare Kälin and Künzli (n 82) 58.

[122] See for example Tomuschat (n 81) 28; Cassese, *International Law* (n 94) 18.9, 374. However, compare the counter-argument in Rosas (n 119) 238, 247–249. Compare also Asbjörn Eide, 'The Right to Oppose Violations of Human Rights: Basis, Conditions and Limitations' in *Violations of Human Rights: Possible Rights of Recourse and Forms of Resistance* (UNESCO 1984) 34, 39, 47–53, 57–63.

[123] Firstly, UNGA Res 2625 is 'not exhaustive'. See Gray, 'The Use of Force and the International Legal Order' (n 64) 616. Moreover, it deliberately widened the interpretive scope of the right to self-determination within the meaning of the UN Charter from that previously established in UNGA Res 1514, exclusive to situations of colonization. See fifth principle, UNGA Res 2625 (n 84) non-numbered fourth and seventh paragraphs; Keller (n 85) D5(a)[24], D5(b)[25].

[124] See Simma et al (n 48) 16–17 A[3]–[4], 18–19 B[8]–[9]–C[10], 23–30 C[19]–[23], [26]–[32], 32 C[38]–D[39]. See also Kunig (n 83) C1[9], C2(a)[12]–[13], D[19]; Cot (n 83) B[16], [19], E[50]–[51], [53]–[54], [61].

[125] That is, the 'teleological' or 'functional method' of interpretation is 'predominant', the Charter's object and purpose is of 'special significance', and the Charter as a whole is treated as providing relevant context, as are the associated interpretive declarations. See Simma et al (n 48) 15 A[1], 18–19 B[8]–[9], C[10], 25 C[22], 30–32 C[34]–[37].

[126] See Rosas (n 119); Cassese, *Self-Determination* (n 11) generally. See therefore the extended discussion of parameters of a possible limited right to resist violations of internal self-determination, grounded in established human rights standards for the 'distribution, structure and functions of authority' under the UN Charter and related instruments in Eide (n 122) 41–42, 44, 59–63.

context, and object and purpose, is the disclaimer in the second paragraph of the Declaration's General Part, that the principles must be interpreted without prejudice to existing Charter rights and duties of Member States or the rights of peoples. This would include the duty at articles 1(3) and 55(c) of the Charter to 'promote … universal respect for and observance of human rights', as understood within the meaning of the Charter.[127] Alternatively, therefore, others suggest that 'massive and systematic human rights violations … in particular exclusion from or non-representation in public life' may generate an 'acquired right' to resist by virtue of this trigger, by converting a non-enforceable right to 'internal' self-determination into an enforceable right to 'external' self-determination.[128]

Ultimately, however, the primary triggering condition is necessary but not sufficient. Activating the exception also requires meeting the secondary trigger condition.

6.3.1.4 The Secondary Trigger

The secondary trigger establishing necessity is 'forcible deprivation' of the right to self-determination. However, exactly what constitutes 'forcible deprivation' requires further analysis and interpretation of specific acts in the context of a given claim. It definitely includes the 'use of force' in its formal sense, associated with or resulting in violation of the right to self-determination in one or more of its dimensions, thereby amounting to an unlawful use of force. But whereas the use of force is inherent to some of the primary triggers outlined above, it may not be present in all cases of forcible deprivation.[129] For example, deprivation of the right to internal or external economic self-

[127] See Simma et al (n 48) 63 F[61]; UN Charter (n 46) articles 1(3), 55(c); preamble, UNGA Res 2625 (n 84) non-numbered third paragraph; first principle, UNGA Res 2625 (n 84) non-numbered first, seventh, and thirteenth paragraphs; fifth principle, UNGA Res 2625 (n 84) non-numbered third paragraph; general part, UNGA Res 2625 (n 84) [2].

[128] Alfredsson (n 102) C[14], D[20]. Compare Simma et al (n 48) 58 C[38]–[40], 61 D[56], 63 F [61]. They suggest that the problem involves establishing the 'quantity and quality of discrimination', as 'severe' violations of human rights provide 'offsets' to the traditional negative presumption against rebellion, so that 'where the oppression amounts to a crime against humanity', this may also act as a trigger for the exception in internal self-determination cases.

[129] For the purposes of the Declaration, the prohibited 'threat or use of force against the territorial integrity or political independence of any State or in any other manner inconsistent with the purposes of the United Nations' is conceived broadly as 'any forcible action which deprives peoples … of their right to self-determination … and independence'. See first principle, UNGA Res 2625 (n 84) non-numbered first to tenth paragraphs; third principle, UNGA Res 2625 (n 84) non-numbered third paragraph.

determination may be 'forcible' in the sense of 'coercion', but may not always involve the 'use of force' per se.[130] This remains to be clarified in light of particular circumstances.

It is also not established whether 'forcible deprivation' acts independently as the sole secondary trigger, or whether a separate necessity test needs to be met in addition, pertaining to the use of forceful means of resistance, forming a two-part secondary trigger.[131] For example, it is possible that customary *jus ad bellum* necessity or 'last resort' standards would need to be met additionally and independently of the 'forcible deprivation' condition.[132] Assessment of necessity is complicated by the fact that the *jus ad bellum* variant of necessity as exceptional justification, the human rights variant of necessity as constraint, and the criminal law variant of exceptional justification or excuse as generally understood and applied, while distinct from one another,[133] all have potential overlapping relevance for such right to resist claims. But none of them is tailor-made to fit exactly.[134]

Even less certain is whether other forms of unlawful state use of force – for example, where such actions would fail the appropriate human rights tests regarding acceptable conditions for the internal use of force and proper application of the minimum force principle – can trigger a UN General Assembly Resolution 2625 right to resist in self-defence, if these are unrelated

[130] On the content of 'economic self-determination' as partially expressed in the international legal principle of 'permanent sovereignty over natural resources', affirmed as customary, see 'Declaration on Permanent Sovereignty Over Natural Resources' UNGA Res 1803 (XVII) (14 December 1962); *DRC* v *Uganda* (n 65); Nico J Schrijver, 'Natural Resources, Permanent Sovereignty Over' in *Max Planck Encyclopedia of Public International Law* (Oxford Public International Law online database 2008) A[1]–[2], C2[7], C3[9]–[10], E[23]–F[25].

[131] The trigger for lawful use of force in cases other than decolonization is 'one of the most disputed' questions in the law of self-determination, according to Simma et al (n 48) 57 C [35]–[36].

[132] On *jus ad bellum* necessity as 'a criterion that must be satisfied before the recourse to force can be justified' that 'works slightly differently depending on whether it is asserted as an independent excuse' and 'invoked as an exception to general rules of conduct', or is instead 'one component of a self-defense analysis' where it 'functions as a constraint on the application of a general justification'; and on the closely associated traditional doctrine of 'last resort', requiring serious prior consideration of 'reasonable' non-forceful alternatives amounting to 'equally efficacious means', given the time constraints imposed by the further 'immediacy' or 'imminence' condition, see Ohlin and May (n 96) 6, 28–37; Michael Newton and Larry May, *Proportionality in International Law* (Oxford University Press 2014) 142–143, 147.

[133] See Ohlin and May (n 96) 2–7, 53–54.

[134] The growing 'revisionist' just war literature addressing necessity may be helpful in some cases. See for example Seth Lazar, 'Necessity in Self-Defense and War' (2012) 40(1) *Philosophy and Public Affairs* 3; Cécile Fabre, 'Cosmopolitanism and Wars of Self-Defence' in Cécile Fabre and Seth Lazar (eds), *The Morality of Defensive War* (Oxford University Press 2014). See also the discussion of necessity in Chapter 4, Section 4.3.1.

to forcible deprivation of the right of external self-determination.[135] Some suggest that such scenarios would be covered under the UN Charter's article 51 self-defence exception by extension or analogy,[136] but this remains controversial.[137] Indeed, disagreement persists as to whether all or only some right to resist claims under UN General Assembly Resolution 2625 are actually a species of self-defence to which the equivalent necessity and other criteria apply.[138] It is possible that some claims under the Declaration may instead constitute another legal category of lawful exception to which either traditional last-resort necessity, or indeed another type of necessity criteria applies.[139]

6.3.1.5 The Permissible Means

Where all other elements are in place including the secondary trigger necessity condition, the consequent permissible means are unspecified by the Declaration. Presumably, therefore, such means are inclusive. Hence, this source of the right to resist does, at least potentially in qualifying cases, constitute a lawful exception to the ordinarily assumed state monopoly on the lawful use of force.

[135] See the extensive discussion in Jan Arno Hessbruegge, *Human Rights and Personal Self-Defense in International Law* (Oxford University Press 2017).

[136] See for example, Frédéric Mégret, 'Causes Worth Fighting For: Is There a Non-State *jus ad bellum*?' in Aristotle Constantinides and Nikos Zaikos (eds), *The Diversity of International Law: Essays in Honour of Professor Kalliopi K Koufa* (Martinus Nijhoff 2009) 180 (fn 30); Saul (n 10) 87. For an argument that forcible deprivation of the right to internal self-determination constitutes 'internal aggression' and thus a violation of UN Charter article 2(4), as well as articles 1(2), 1(3), 55(c) and 56, see Jordan J Paust, 'Aggression against Authority: The Crime of Oppression, Politicide and Other Crimes against Human Rights' (1986) 18 *Case Western Reserve Journal of International Law* 283, 286–290, 298; Paust (n 76) 4–5, 10–12.

[137] Compare for example Keller (n 85) D1(b)[15]; Saul (n 10) 80, 87.

[138] On the four customary criteria applying to *jus ad bellum* self-defence claims – an unlawful 'armed attack'; its 'immediacy or imminence'; the 'necessity' of a forceful response to stop it, given the prior evaluation of 'reasonable' and 'equally efficacious' alternatives; and the general 'proportionality' of the proposed use to the nature of the threat – see Ohlin and May (n 96) 55–63.

[139] For example, the 'customary principle of necessity' in international law requires that the otherwise unlawful action is 'the only way ... to safeguard' an 'essential interest' under 'grave and imminent peril' so long as it 'does not seriously impair an essential interest ... of the international community as a whole', and barring fault or contribution to the situation giving rise to necessity. See International Law Commission, 'Responsibility of States for Internationally Wrongful Acts' (n 28) article 25; Ohlin and May (n 96) 40–45. On its application 'as a general defense to violations of public international law' see Ohlin and May (n 96) 45–53; *Gabčikovo-Nagymaros Project (Hungary* v *Slovakia)* (Judgment) [1997] ICJ Rep 7 as affirmed in *Legal Consequences of the Construction of a Wall in the Occupied Palestinian Territory* (n 96) [140]–[141].

The full spectrum of means relevant to the right to resist can include both forceful and non-forceful but 'otherwise unlawful' actions. Establishing permissible means in any given claim requires the meeting of the appropriate test for proportionality, which acts as a limitation on choices.[140] Assessment of this is complicated by the fact that international law in general and international human rights law in particular do not always rely on the same standards for 'proportionality'.[141] Where resistance with force is contemplated, customary *jus ad bellum* proportionality standards apply,[142] in addition to any other applicable international legal regulations.

Of course, the right to resist does not constitute an exception to internationally criminalized means such as aggression, genocide, war crimes, or crimes against humanity, or to other specific means violating *jus cogens* norms such as the prohibitions on torture and slavery.[143] Means generally will be regulated to varying extents by international human rights law, international criminal law, and, where applicable, the *jus in bello* or international humanitarian law of armed conflict, in particular as regards prohibited weapons and targets and particularly with respect to the principle of distinction.[144] Specifically, use of armed force in exercise of the right to resist based on a UN General Assembly Resolution 2625 claim, once it reaches the relevant 'armed conflict'

[140] On 'proportionality' as a term that 'recurs across an array of disciplines and usages' with 'very different meanings with often profound and context specific implications', but with a common basic meaning 'that a response or action must be commensurate with the anticipated goal to be achieved', see Newton and May (n 132) 2–3, 13, 15.

[141] See ibid 57–59. However, findings of state proportionality or disproportionality in the human rights sense may have an effect on the determination of triggering conditions for the right to resist.

[142] On proportionality as a potentially strict limitation that not only requires general calibration to the overall cause but also a specific design 'to eliminate the threat presented'; on disproportionality potentially ruling out an otherwise 'just cause'; on the interactive effects of proportionality requirements from the other 'branches'; and on necessity as a trump condition see Newton and May (n 132) 17, 19, 57–59, 60, 61, 66–68, 78–84, 142–143, 145, 147. The growing 'revisionist' just war literature addressing proportionality may also be helpful in some cases. See for example arguments in Seth Lazar, 'Authorization and the Morality of War' (2016) 94(2) *Australasian Journal of Philosophy* 211, 213–215, 222. See also the discussion of proportionality in Chapter 4, Section 4.7.2.

[143] See discussion in Chapter 4, Section 4.7. See also Jochen A Frowein, 'Ius Cogens' in *Max Planck Encyclopedia of Public International Law* (Oxford Public International Law online database 2013) C[6]–[8]; and the formally proposed '[n]on-exhaustive list' of *jus cogens* norms in International Law Commission, 'Draft Conclusions on Identification and Legal Consequences of Peremptory Norms of General International Law' (n 27) Conclusion 23.

[144] See for example Andrew Clapham, *Human Rights Obligations of Non-State Actors* (Oxford University Press 2006); Tilman Rodenhäuser, *Organizing Rebellion: Non-State Armed Groups under International Humanitarian Law, Human Rights Law, and International Criminal Law* (Oxford University Press 2018).

thresholds, would be regulated by the relevant Geneva Conventions and Additional Protocols.[145] As demonstrated by the specialist scholarship in this area, *jus in bello* regulation of the exercise of the right to resist raises complex intersecting questions. Detailed consideration is both beyond the scope of this study and amply provided elsewhere.[146]

6.3.1.6 The Duty-Bearers

One advantage of UN General Assembly Resolution 2625 is that it provides a reasonably clear source of the third-party duty to not obstruct, and the subsidiary right to assistance and duty to assist – within the limits of the law – those with a valid claim, according to Honoré.[147] In such cases, the duty-bearers are the UN Security Council and UN Member States acting in accordance with the UN Charter.

With regard to the non-obstruction obligation, in this context the UN Charter article 2(4) prohibition on the use of force 'in any manner inconsistent with the [article 1] Purposes of the United Nations' reads as equivalent to a ban on providing requested assistance to a state for the purpose of suppressing resistance or rebellion where this amounts to a forcible deprivation of the right to self-determination – or potentially also where a right to resist exists on other human rights grounds such as those recognized by the Universal Declaration of Human Rights.[148] This is the basis upon which one could conclude that – even with an otherwise valid invitation – it is unlawful to aid a government to suppress rebellion in any context where a valid right to resist can be established, in keeping with a minimal duty of neutrality respecting the principles of non-intervention and self-determination.

Equally, however, the duty bearers must not engage in assistive actions amounting to 'aggression' or any other unlawful 'use of force' or 'intervention' as understood in international law.[149] As Wright maintains, article 2(4)

[145] See further discussion in Sections 6.6.2 and 6.6.2.1. For treatment of forceful resistance to unlawful occupation as a specific example, see Longobardo (n 112) 134–164.

[146] See for example Clapham (n 144). See also Christopher J Finlay, *Terrorism and the Right to Resist: A Theory of Just Revolutionary War* (Cambridge University Press 2015) 87–124, 155–246; Jo Hyeran, *Compliant Rebels: Rebel Groups and International Law in World Politics* (Cambridge University Press 2015); Rodenhäuser (n 144).

[147] Honoré (n 5) 44.

[148] See Section 6.4.

[149] See first principle, UNGA Res 2625 (n 84) non-numbered paragraphs 1–10; third principle, UNGA Res 2625 (n 84) non-numbered paragraphs 1–4; *Nicaragua* v *USA* (n 51) [195], [202]–[209], [228], [241]; *DRC* v *Uganda* (n 65) [165], [297]–[299]. See also Gray, 'The Use of Force and the International Legal Order' (n 64) 618, 623, 626; Gray, *International Law and the Use of Force* (n 64) 79, 83, 114.

'cannot be construed to permit a state in its own discretion to use force in order to effect purposes of the United Nations. The determination of the means to effect these purposes belongs, according to the Charter, not to the Members individually but to the organs of the United Nations'.[150] Therefore, he concludes, explicit UN authorization is required before external force may be lawfully used to assist valid rights-holders.[151] Indeed, it is likely that a third-party duty on individual Member States which stops at 'do not obstruct', and does not extend to 'assist' without such authorization, may also apply to non-UN General Assembly Resolution 2625 claims.

As for the consequent duty on the UN Security Council, Simma and colleagues suggest that permissions and obligations are comparatively clear on this point: in external self-determination cases, support for the 'aggressor' state is 'unlawful' and assistance to the 'victim' people 'lawful'; in internal self-determination cases, assistance to the requesting state is lawful and to the rebels unlawful, unless the requesting state is engaged in forcible deprivation or 'oppression' triggering a valid right to resist, in which case the reverse is true – assistance to the requesting state is unlawful and assistance to the rebels may be permissible.[152]

Notwithstanding this, the fact that UN Security Council practice under Chapters VI and VII of the UN Charter is bound by general international law and the UN Charter itself but not by precedent means that such practice may be ad hoc.[153] Thus, the Security Council's primarily political decisions do not generally clearly articulate or consistently reflect the relevant legal obligations as described by Simma and colleagues as such, even where these involve

[150] See Wright, 'Goa Incident' (n 8) 628. See also Gray, 'The Use of Force and the International Legal Order' (n 64) 615–616, 620, 645; Gray, *International Law and the Use of Force* (n 64) 37–60.

[151] Requirements on claimants may be analogous to those generally applying to collective self-defence: acts must qualify as 'forcible deprivation' of the right to self-determination; a formal declaration as such by a victim 'people'; a formal request to the UN for assistance; necessary and proportionate action only pending Security Council-authorized measures to restore peace and security; reporting to the Council. For collective self-defence requirements see *Nicaragua v USA* (n 51) [102]–[105], [110], [127]. See also Gray, 'The Use of Force and the International Legal Order' (n 64) 615–647, in particular 633.

[152] See Simma et al (n 48) 62–63 F[60]–[61]. See also third principle, UNGA Res 2625 (n 84) non-numbered second paragraph. See also Gray, 'The Use of Force and the International Legal Order' (n 64) 615–616, 620, 645; Gray, *International Law and the Use of Force* (n 64) 59–64, 82; compare Shaw (n 66) 1148–1149 fn 157; Keller (n 85) D3(a) [19]. See the proposals for common criteria, objective tests, and approval procedures in Falk, 'Janus Tormented' (n 37) 203–204, 208–244.

[153] On this ad hoc approach made possible by the uncertainties in the law, and on the non-neutrality of UN interventions in practice, which default to the status quo to the detriment of rebels as a longstanding pattern, see Higgins (n 65) 178, 180–181.

'threat to the peace' determinations under article 39 authorizing consequent measures under articles 41 and 42.[154] It is likely to remain so in the absence of either endorsement of express legal rules governing the duty of assistance/non-obstruction in cases of a valid right to resist, or improved consistency in state practice and *opinio juris* in specific cases, or both.

If UN General Assembly Resolution 2625 provides some guidance as to a limited implied recognition of the right to resist under the UN Charter, the other piece of that puzzle depends on its status under the Universal Declaration of Human Rights. While less firmly established, it may reflect recognition of a broader right.

6.4 BROADER IMPLIED RECOGNITION: THE UNIVERSAL DECLARATION OF HUMAN RIGHTS

The Universal Declaration of Human Rights has become more widely accepted as now representing customary international law through state practice and *opinio juris* and binding as such.[155] In another view, the Declaration is not binding in itself but rather, much like UN General Assembly Resolution 2625, a formal aid to interpretation of legal obligations under the UN

[154] As noted, the Security Council rarely makes determinations on 'aggression' and the legality of self-defence claims, or attributes responsibility for unlawful intervention. Its more common determinations of a 'threat to peace' can arise out of an internal conflict, and are based on broad constructions. See Gray, 'The Use of Force and the International Legal Order' (n 64) 633–634; Michael Wood, 'United Nations, Security Council' in *Max Planck Encyclopedia of Public International Law* (Oxford Public International Law online database 2007) D3[26]–[30]; Gray, *International Law and the Use of Force* (n 64) 17–26. For a rare and controversial example of a Chapter VII authorization of the use of force to protect civilians and civilian-populated areas under rebel control and to prevent or halt crimes against humanity committed by the state during the Libyan uprising, citing a 'threat to peace', see UNSC Res 1973 (2011) (17 March 2011) preamble, non-numbered fourth, fifth, seventh, and ninth paragraphs, and [4].

[155] See Theodor Meron, *Human Rights and Humanitarian Norms as Customary Law* (Clarendon 1989) 82–88 citing Louis Sohn, 'The Human Rights Law of the Charter' (1977) 12 *Texas International Law Journal* 129; Louis Sohn, '"Generally Accepted" International Rules' (1986) 61 *Washington Law Review* 1073, 1077–1078. See also *Legal Consequences for States of the Continued Presence of South Africa in Namibia* (n 106) Separate Opinion of Judge Ammoun 76; Hurst Hannum, 'The Status of the Universal Declaration of Human Rights in National and International Law' (1995–1996) 25 *Georgia Journal of International and Comparative Law* 287, 289–290, 319–325, 352–354, though Hannum admits that perhaps not all provisions of the Universal Declaration qualify, ibid 340; Johannes van Aggelen, 'The Preamble of the United Nations Declaration of Human Rights' (2000) 28 *Denver Journal of International Law and Policy* 129, 131–132, 143; Schabas (n 7) 18–19, 103–105, 342. Among right to resist advocates taking this position, see for example Paust (n 119) 180 fn 12; Paust (n 15) 560 fn 63.

Charter.[156] Regardless of which is correct, this Declaration sets universally applicable human rights standards that are now relied upon to evaluate state behaviour by the UN Human Rights Council under its Universal Periodic Review procedure.[157] Moreover, the Universal Declaration has been identified as a source of 'fundamental principles' and thus a normative standard potentially applicable in the International Court of Justice.[158] Therefore, whether the Universal Declaration recognizes the right to resist is potentially of considerable significance.

6.4.1 *An Express Right to Resist Proposed but Not Included*

No express right to resist appears in the Universal Declaration. Instead, the preambular text reads, in its third paragraph: 'Whereas it is essential, if man is not to be compelled to have recourse, as a last resort, to rebellion against tyranny and oppression, that human rights should be protected by the rule of law'.[159]

[156] On 'the fundamental principles of human rights' as 'part of customary or general international law', for which the UN Charter provides the 'baseline', and therefore 'responsibility exists under the Charter for any substantial infringement of the provisions' on human rights despite the 'absence of a precise definition' within the Charter itself; and on the Universal Declaration as 'an authoritative guide ... to the interpretation of the provisions of the Charter' providing a 'core of reasonable certainty' with 'indirect legal effect', see Brownlie (n 6) 555–556, 559, 562–563. See also *South West Africa Cases*, Dissenting Opinion of Judge Tanaka (n 77) 250, 293; Simma et al (n 48) 18 A [7]; Kunig (n 83) C.2(a) [13]; William A Schabas, 'Introductory Essay: The Drafting and Significance of the Universal Declaration of Human Rights' in William A Schabas, *The Universal Declaration of Human Rights: Travaux Préparatoires* (Cambridge University Press 2013) vol I, lxxi–cxxv, cxiii–cxvi, cxix–cxxi.

[157] Schabas compares the scope and compliance rate of this 'voluntary' and 'non-binding' process favourably against the human rights treaty monitoring and implementation mechanisms. See Schabas, 'Introductory Essay' (n 156) lxxi–cxxv, lxxi, cxvii–cxix, cxxii–cxxiii. See also Schabas (n 7) 104–105, 343–344.

[158] See *United States Diplomatic and Consular Staff in Tehran (USA* v *Iran)* (Judgment) [1980] ICJ Rep 3 [91]. Indeed Meron finds it 'surprising' that the Universal Declaration is not more often characterized as reflecting general principles of law, but acknowledges that '[a]s in other fields of international law, the distinction between international customary law ... and general principles of law ... eventually become[s] blurred'. See Meron (n 155) 88–89. Compare the contemporaneous criticism in Hersch Lauterpacht, 'Universal Declaration of Human Rights' (1948) 25 *British Yearbook of International Law* 354. Theories of the Universal Declaration as grounded in natural rights preceding positive law are not relevant to the present discussion. For an example, see Johannes Morsink, 'The Philosophy of the Universal Declaration' (1984) 6(3) *Human Rights Quarterly* 309, 333–334.

[159] Universal Declaration of Human Rights (1948) UNGA Res 217A (III) (10 December 1948) preamble, non-numbered third paragraph [emphasis added].

Compared against the formulations in two earlier proposals, this reference seems especially oblique.[160]

In contrast, the initial Secretariat Draft Declaration prepared by Humphrey provides for a substantive right at article 29 that reads: 'Everyone has the right, either individually or with others, to resist oppression and tyranny.'[161] In the revised Drafting Committee Draft Declaration prepared by Cassin, article 25 reads: 'When a government seriously or systematically tramples the fundamental human rights and freedoms, individuals and peoples have the right to resist oppression and tyranny, without prejudice to their right of appeal to the United Nations.'[162]

[160] Vague formulations, especially in the preamble, and the rejection of controversial issues are two of five 'facilitating factors' identified that explain the successful negotiation of the text, along with the drafters' strategy of using terms and concepts that could be defined in different ways. See Åshild Samnøy, 'The Origins of the Universal Declaration of Human Rights' in Gudmundur Alfredsson and Asbjörn Eide (eds), *The Universal Declaration of Human Rights: A Common Standard of Achievement* (Martinus Nijhoff 1999) 14–20.

[161] 'Draft Outline of International Bill of Rights (prepared by the Division of Human Rights)' UN Doc E/CN.4/AC.1/3 (4 June 1947). See Schabas, *Universal Declaration of Human Rights* (n 156) vol I, 285. See also related debates as collected in the Schabas volumes: 'Drafting Committee on an International Bill of Human Rights International Bill of Rights Documented Outline' UN Doc E.CN.4/AC.1/3/Add.1 (11 June 1947) Schabas, *Universal Declaration of Human Rights* (n 156) vol I, 566–567; 'Summary Record of the Fourth Meeting [of the Drafting Committee of the Commission on Human Rights] Held at Lake Success, New York, on Wednesday, 12 June 1947, at 10.30 a.m.' UN Doc E/CN.4/AC.1/SR.4 (11 June 1947) Schabas (ibid) 744. See also Johannes Morsink, *The Universal Declaration of Human Rights: Origins, Drafting and Intent* (University of Pennsylvania Press 1999) 'The Right to Rebellion' 307–312, 309.

[162] 'Suggestions Submitted by the Representative of France for Articles 7–32 of the International Declaration of Rights' UN Doc E/CN.4/AC.1/W.2 (16 June 1947). See Schabas, *Universal Declaration of Human Rights* (n 156) vol I, 793. See also related debates as collected in the Schabas volumes: 'Summary Record of the Eighth Meeting [of the Drafting Committee of the Commission on Human Rights] Held at Lake Success, New York, on Tuesday, 17 June 1947, at 2:30 p.m.' UN Doc E/CN.4/AC.1/SR.8 (17 June 1947) ibid 810; 'Suggestions Submitted by the Representative of France for Articles 7–32 of the International Declaration of Rights' UN Doc E/CN.4/AC.1/W.2/Rev.1 (18 June 1947) ibid 815; 'Revised Suggestions Submitted by the Representative of France for Articles of the International Declaration of Rights' UN Doc E/CN.4/AC.1/W.2.Rev.2 (20 June 1947) ibid 841; 'Summary Record of the Eighteenth Meeting [of the Drafting Committee of the Commission on Human Rights] Held at Lake Success, New York, on Wednesday, 25 June 1947 at 10:30 a.m.' UN Doc E/CN.4/AC.1/SR.18 (25 June 1947) ibid 905. The draft text of article 25 also appears unamended as article 26 in 'Report of the Drafting Committee to the Commission on Human Rights' Annex D 'Suggestions Submitted by the Representative of France for Articles of the International Declaration of Human Rights' UN Doc E/CN.4/21 (1 July 1947) ibid vol II, 924. See further 'Report of the Drafting Committee to the Commission on Human Rights' Annex F 'Suggestions of the Drafting Committee for Articles of an International Declaration on Human Rights' UN Doc E/CN.4/21 (1 July 1947) ibid 936; 'Summary Record of the Seventh Meeting [of the Working Group on the Declaration of Human Rights] Held at the Palais des

Both the Humphrey draft and the Cassin draft clearly identify a human 'right to resist'. Applying the analytical framework from Chapter 4, both specify individuals as rights-holders but diverge as to whether only whole 'peoples' or also unspecified 'groups' share this right. The Humphrey draft sets a choice of two simple single-trigger conditions: either 'tyranny' or more broadly 'oppression', without appearing to require a secondary trigger of any kind provided these conditions are met. Similarly, the Cassin draft does not require a secondary trigger condition but sets a more specific single trigger of 'serious or systematic' violation of Declaration rights by a 'government'. While the Humphrey draft does not specify the duty-bearers, the Cassin draft suggests a duty on the United Nations where a direct appeal is made, implying a further right of assistance or non-obstruction. Because neither draft formulation directly identifies the valid object and purpose or any other limitations, such would need to be inferred from other draft provisions. Equally, since neither draft specifies permissible means, both imply the full inclusive range from peaceful to forceful, provided that the trigger condition is met.

Ultimately, neither the Humphrey nor the Cassin formulations survived the drafting debates.[163] However they remain a useful contrast to the obscure

Nations, Geneva, at 3 p.m. on Tuesday 9 December, 1947' UN Doc E/CN.4/AC.2/SR.7 (9 December 1947) ibid 1213; 'Summary Record of the Fortieth Meeting [of the Commission on Human Rights] Held at the Palais des Nations, Geneva on Tuesday, 16 December 1947, at 9 a.m.' UN Doc E/CN.4/SR.40 (16 December 1947) ibid 1294; 'Summary Record of the Forty-First Meeting [of the Commission on Human Rights] Held at the Palais des Nations, Geneva, on Tuesday 16 December 1947, at 3 p.m.' UN Doc E/CN.4/SR.41 (16 December 1947) ibid 1309; 'Draft International Declaration on Human Rights (Numbering of Articles corresponds to numbering in Chapter III of the Report of the Working Group on a Declaration (Document E/CN.4/57))' UN Doc E/CN.4/77/Annex A (16 December 1947) ibid 1332; 'Report to the Economic and Social Council on the Second Session of the Commission [on Human Rights] Held at Geneva, from 2 to 17 December 1947' UN Doc E/600 (17 December 1947) ibid 1347; 'Report to the Economic and Social Council on the Second Session of the Commission [on Human Rights] Held at Geneva, from 2 to 17 December 1947' UN Doc E/600 (17 December 1947) ibid 1351; 'Comments from Governments on the Draft International Declaration on Human Rights, Draft International Covenant on Human Rights and the Question of Implementation' UN Doc E/CN.4/82/Add.2 (22 April 1948) ibid 1431; 'Collation of the Comments of Governments on the Draft International Declaration on Human Rights, Draft International Covenant on Human Rights and the Question of implementation (Note by the Secretary-General)' UN Doc E/CN.4/85 (1 May 1948) Part II 'Draft International Declaration on Human Rights' B. 'Comments on the Articles of the Draft International Declaration on Human Rights' ibid 1474. See also Morsink (n 161) 'The Right to Rebellion' 309.

163 The proposal for inclusion of the right to resist as a substantive right was ultimately withdrawn, rather than voted down. See the relevant travaux documents concerning the preliminary discussions, the original Cuban proposal to include the right to resist as a substantive right, the alternative preambular proposal and counter-proposals, and the final joint Cuban–Chilean–French proposal adopted by a vote of 25 to 1 with 11 abstentions, as collected in Schabas,

reference in the third preambular paragraph as adopted. This appears to acknowledge not a 'right' per se, but rather a 'recourse' implying a self-help remedy – possibly presumed recognized elsewhere in law, or perhaps instead understood as a 'natural' or inherent moral right regardless of codification or other legal status. This 'recourse' involves 'rebellion' which potentially therefore includes the use of forceful means in response to the primary trigger conditions of 'tyranny' and 'oppression', but only provided that the high threshold secondary trigger of 'last resort' has been met. In keeping with the text elsewhere in the preamble, the rights-holders – if any – would be 'all members of the human family' or all 'human beings',[164] and the duty-bearers 'every individual and every organ of society' as the component parts of all 'the

Universal Declaration of Human Rights (n 156): 'Seventh Meeting [of the General Assembly] Monday, 14 January 1946 at 3 p.m.' UN Doc A/PV.7 (14 January 1946) ibid vol I, 11; 'Draft Declaration on Human Rights and Letter of Transmittal, Cuban Legation, Great Britain' UN Doc E/HR/1 (12 February 1946) ibid 16–18, 17; 'Analysis of Various Draft International Bills of Rights (Item 8 on the Agenda) (Memorandum by the Division of Human Rights)' UN Doc E/CN.4/W.16 (23 January 1947) 5, ibid 150; 'Observations of Governments on the Draft International Declaration on Human Rights, the Draft International Covenant on Human Rights, and Methods of Application – Communication Received from the French Government' UN Doc E/CN.4/82/Add.8 (6 May 1948) ibid vol II, 1502; 'Cuba: Amendments to Articles 23 to 27 of the Draft Declaration (E/800)' UN Doc A/C.3/261 (12 October 1948) ibid vol III, 2205; 'Argentina: Draft Resolution Concerning the Article Relative to the "Right to Resist Acts of Oppression or Tyranny" (A/C.3/307/Rev.2)' UN Doc A/C.3/377 (29 November 1948) ibid 2859; 'Chile: Alternative Text for the Additional Article Submitted by Cuba (A/C.3/307/rev 2)' UN Doc A/C.3/378 (29 November 1948) ibid 2860; 'Summary Record of the Hundred and Sixty-Fourth Meeting [of the Third Committee] Held at the Palais de Chaillot, Paris, on Monday, 29 November 1948, at 3:15 p.m.' UN Doc A/C.3/SR.164 (29 November 1948) ibid 2872–2877; 'Cuba, Chile, France: Joint Amendment to the Preamble (A/C.3/314/Rev.1)' UN Doc A/C.3/382/Rev.1 (30 November 1948) ibid 2888; 'Summary Record of the Hundred and Sixty-Fifth Meeting [of the Third Committee] Held at the Palais de Chaillot, Paris, on Tuesday, 30 November 1948, at 10 a.m.' UN Doc A/C.3/SR.165 (30 November 1948) ibid 2891–2892, 2895–2896, 2901; 'Summary Record of the Hundred and Sixty-Sixth Meeting [of the Third Committee] Held at the Palais de Chaillot, Paris, on Tuesday, 30 November 1948, at 3 p.m.' UN Doc A/C.3/SR.166 (30 November 1948) ibid 2906–2907; 'Summary Record of the Hundred and Sixty-Seventh Meeting [of the Third Committee] Held at the Palais de Chaillot, Paris, on Tuesday, 30 November 1948, at 3 p.m.' UN Doc A/C.3/SR.167 (30 November 1948) ibid 2921. See also the concise synthesized account in Morsink (n 161) 'The Right to Rebellion' 302, 307–312. Note that, contrary to Morsink and the evidence from the travaux documents collected by Schabas that the proposals on the right to resist emanated from the Latin American and French delegations, Cassese proceeds from the premise that the proposal to formally recognize this right – which he generally calls a 'right to rebel' – came instead from the socialist bloc. See Antonio Cassese, *Human Rights in a Changing World* (Polity Press 1990) 34, 36, 41–42.

[164] Universal Declaration of Human Rights (n 159) preamble, non-numbered first and second paragraphs.

peoples of the United Nations' and its 'Member States'.[165] Its object and purpose could only be the vindication of 'inherent [human] dignity' and the 'equal and inalienable rights' elaborated in the remainder of the document, under the broad categories of 'freedom of speech and belief and freedom from fear and want'.[166]

If relying exclusively on the *travaux préparatoires* to help interpret the meaning of the third preambular paragraph, it would be hard to escape the conclusion that the Universal Declaration actively avoids formal recognition of the right to resist.[167] However, the *travaux* are not considered necessarily definitive of its meaning.[168] Hence there emerge four theories of constructive ambiguity in the Universal Declaration's relation to the right to resist, described below, which would permit other interpretations. If any or all of these theories are correct, this potentially closes a crucial gap otherwise left open by the possibility that UN General Assembly Resolution 2625 does not extend recognition of the right to resist for enforcement of internal self-determination in the face of 'tyranny' or 'oppression' by one's own government, or the enforcement of human rights in the face of other types of violations.

6.4.2 *Theory of an Unenumerated Natural or Inherent Human Right to Resist Tyranny, Oppression, and Other Human Rights Abuses, Implicitly Recognized in the Third Preambular Paragraph*

Scholars have produced a number of variations on the third preambular paragraph recognition theories,[169] though usually without providing much

[165] Ibid preamble, non-numbered fifth, sixth and seventh paragraphs.

[166] Ibid preamble, non-numbered first and second paragraphs.

[167] The right to resist, to rebel, or to revolution is characterized as present but 'submerged' or 'demoted' in Morsink (n 161) 302, 308, 311, 312, 329. Compare the more pessimistic assessments in Morsink (n 158) 322–325, 334; Jan Mårtenson, 'The Preamble of the Universal Declaration of Human Rights and the United Nations Human Rights Programme' in Asbjörn Eide, Göran Melander, Lars Adam Rehof, Allan Rosas, and Theresa Swineheart (eds), *The Universal Declaration of Human Rights: A Commentary* (Scandinavian University Press 1992) 19; and the more optimistic assessments in Albert Verdoodt, *Naissance et Signification de la Déclaration Universelle des Droits de l'Homme* (Éditions Nauwelaerts 1964) 44, 91, 270, 301–314; Torkel Opsahl and Vojin Dimitrijevic, 'Articles 29 and 30' in Alfredsson and Eide, *Universal Declaration of Human Rights* (n 160) 638.

[168] See William A Schabas, 'Preface' in Schabas, *Universal Declaration of Human Rights* (n 156) vol I, xxxviii; Schabas, 'Introductory Essay' (n 156) cxvii.

[169] For example, that the preamble reflects a right to resist otherwise recognized in customary international law, in Paust (n 119) 180 (fn 12); Paust (n 15) 560 (fn 63); Kälin and Künzli (n 82) 49, 51; Paust (n 76) 1. Compare Chemillier-Gendreau (n 33) 955 [5]–[7], [16]. That it is reflective of a general principle of international law see for example Sumida (n 38) 168.

analytical detail. Some have parsed the paragraph to suggest its recognition of customary 'rights of recourse' amounts to a right to resist.[170] Indeed, Goldstone links it to the Magna Carta concept of rights enforcement as a deterrent.[171] Others characterize its formulation instead as recognition of a valid complementary self-help remedy: not as a right, but as 'an ultimate alternative to be used in the absence of rights'.[172]

Yet such claims on its behalf are not without skeptics. While Cassese initially argues that the 'right to rebel' is recognized in the Universal Declaration preamble,[173] upon later reflection he accuses the Declaration of the 'emasculation' of this right.[174] Noting that 'the right to rebel against tyranny … has been much blunted' by its preambular formulation,[175] he concludes that the Declaration 'fails – except in a very indirect and convoluted fashion – to recognize the right of oppressed groups and peoples to take up arms against a despotic regime when there is no peaceful way to secure their human rights'.[176] He deplores this as among the Declaration's 'ambiguities and lacunae'.[177]

Compare its somewhat more ambiguous characterization in Joseph DiPiero, 'The Common Law of Rebellion' (2017) 48(2) *Georgetown Journal of International Law* 605, 605, 609–610.

170 This is the premise behind the 'Meeting of experts on the analysis of the basis and forms of individual and collective action by which violations of human rights can be combated, held at Freetown, Sierra Leone, 3–7 March 1981', with proceedings published as *Violations of Human Rights: Possible Rights of Recourse and Forms of Resistance* (UNESCO 1984). 'Recourse' in this sense is not intended to mean exclusively 'recourse to force', as in the law on 'use of force' or *jus ad bellum*. Rather, as with the traditional concept of the right to resist, it is intended to refer to inclusive means. See ibid 'Final Report' 221–227.

171 See Richard Goldstone, 'Twenty-First Century Magna Carta' in Nicholas Vincent (ed), *Magna Carta: The Foundation of Freedom 1215–2015* (Third Millennium Publishing 2015) 173. See also discussion of clause 61 of the 1215 Magna Carta in Chapter 5, Section 5.3.1.

172 James L Taulbee, 'Political Crimes, Human Rights and Contemporary International Practice' (1990) 4 *Emory International Law Review* 43, 47. See also Tranh Van Minh, 'Political and Juridical Sanctions against Violations of Human Rights' in *Violations of Human Rights: Possible Rights of Recourse and Forms of Resistance* (UNESCO 1984) 157–166, 158, 163.

173 Cassese, 'Human Rights and Humanitarian Law' (n 11) 946–947.

174 Cassese (n 163) 42–43. Similarly, see the contextual analysis in Emma Stone Mackinnon, 'Declaration as Disavowal: The Politics of Race and Empire in the Universal Declaration of Human Rights' (2019) 47(1) *Political Theory* 57.

175 Cassese (n 163) 41–42.

176 See ibid 47.

177 Ibid 40. See also M Glen Johnson, 'A Magna Carta for Mankind: Writing the Universal Declaration of Human Rights' in M Glen Johnson and Janusz Symonides (eds), *The Universal Declaration of Human Rights: A History of Its Creation and Implementation 1948–1998* (UNESCO Publishing 1998) 60; Martti Koskenniemi, 'The Preamble of the Universal Declaration of Human Rights' in Alfredsson and Eide (n 160) 27–39, 27, 37–38; Morsink (n 158) 322–325, 334; Saul (n 10) 82–84.

In addition, the position of the reference to the right in the preamble rather than as originally proposed as a substantive provision renders somewhat more doubtful claims that this could be the source of an enforceable customary right.[178] Honoré therefore concludes that the right therein is at most 'semi-formal'.[179] However, other theories do not rely on the preamble as representing a stand-alone recognition of the right, and these are potentially more persuasive.

6.4.3 *Theory of an Unenumerated Right Implied by Article 21(3) Right to Government Based on 'Will of the People'*

Article 21(3) of the Universal Declaration reads in part: 'The will of the people shall be the basis of the authority of government.'[180] Several scholars derive not only an implied right to resist and to rebel but also an implied right to revolution from reading this substantive right together with the third preambular paragraph reference to 'last resort' rebellion as a remedy against 'tyranny and oppression' – presumably by a government unconstrained by popular will.[181] Following that logic, this provision may also represent a material source of a broader customary right to resist in enforcement of the right to internal self-determination, supplementary to UN General Assembly Resolution 2625.[182]

6.4.4 *Theory of a Right Implied by the Lawful Limitation, Disclaimer, and Non-diminution Clauses at Articles 29 and 30*

According to article 29(2) and (3), while the Declaration rights 'may in no case be exercised contrary to the purposes and principles of the United Nations',[183] they 'shall be subject only to such limitations as are determined

[178] On the conclusion that the preamble constitutes customary international law, based on evidence of the widespread practice of incorporation of its elements into other instruments, see Van Aggelen (n 155) 132. Compare Schabas, who omits the theorized preambular right to resist from his list of those human rights he maintains are incontrovertibly recognized as customary international law. See Schabas (n 7).

[179] Honoré (n 5) 42–43.

[180] Universal Declaration of Human Rights (n 159) article 21.

[181] See Paust (n 119) 180 (fn 12); Paust, 'Human Right to Armed Revolution' (n 15) 560, 562–567; Eide (n 122) 41–42, 44; Allan Rosas, 'Article 21' in Alfredsson and Eide (n 160) 432, 442, 448, 449; Morsink (n 166) 308–309; Paust (n 76) 1, 6. See further discussion in Chapter 7, Section 7.2.1.

[182] Note however that not all are prepared to accept article 21 as constituting customary international law. See Hannum (n 155) 348.

[183] Universal Declaration of Human Rights (n 159) article 29(3).

by law solely for the purposes of securing due recognition and respect for the rights and freedoms of others and of meeting the just requirements of morality, public order, and the general welfare in a democratic society'.[184] There is no provision for derogation as a valid competing right of the state. As such, article 30 warns that '[n]othing in this Declaration may be interpreted as implying for any State, group or person any right to engage in any activity or to perform any act aimed at the destruction of any of the rights and freedoms set forth herein'.[185] Among the rights that cannot be restricted except on the limited grounds indicated at article 29(2) are the equality rights set out at articles 1, 2, 6, 7, and 18; the negative rights to be free from state oppression at articles 1–15 and 17; the ordinary political rights under articles 19 on freedom of opinion and expression, 20 on freedom of assembly and association, and 21 on the right to vote and to participate in democratic governance; as well as positive economic, social, and cultural rights at articles 16 and 22–27.[186] On this basis Paust argues that the limitation, disclaimer, and non-diminution clauses at articles 29 and 30, when read together with the implied right in the preamble, represent an important constraint on state derogation, the logical corollary of which is an implied right to resist such measures that do not conform with the Declaration standards, as a last resort.[187] This theory describes a customary right to resist for the purpose of human rights enforcement that is far broader in scope than the right derived from article 21, either alone or in tandem with UN General Assembly Resolution 2625.

6.4.5 *Theory of an Unenumerated Right Implied by the Article 28 Right to a 'Social and International Order for the Realization of Human Rights'*

The presumption that there is no right to revolution authorized within the international system because the right to resist is 'restricted to the limited possibilities made available by the UN Charter'[188] appears to ignore the substantive provision in article 28 of the Universal Declaration, and its interpretive potential when read together with the third preambular paragraph. Article 28 reads: 'Everyone is entitled to a social and international order in which the rights and freedoms set forth in this Declaration can be

184 Ibid article 29(2).
185 Ibid article 30.
186 Ibid articles 1–27.
187 Paust (n 119) 181–188; Paust (n 76) 6, 11 (fn 48). For Samnøy, however, article 30 acts only as a limitation on unenumerated rights. See Samnøy (n 160) 17.
188 Chemillier-Gendreau (n 33) 957 [18].

fully realized.'[189] While it is undoubtedly a stretch,[190] article 28 nevertheless may without unreasonable distortion lend itself to interpretation as corroborative of, or representing an implied recognition of, a right to revolution, provided this specific object and purpose.[191]

6.4.6 *Elements of the Theorized Right to Resist Recognized in the Universal Declaration*

Bringing the above theories together and applying the Chapter 4 analytical framework generates a clearer concept of what a customary right to resist, as implicitly recognized by the Universal Declaration, could be. The rights-holders would be all individuals or groups 'as human persons', provided the trigger conditions are met and the object and purpose of the resistance is consistent with human rights. The primary triggers would include disregard of the 'will of the people' under article 21 amounting to 'tyranny';[192] a pattern of

[189] Universal Declaration of Human Rights (n 159) article 28. On article 28's purpose as promoting the identification of 'root causes' of human rights violations and 'structural adjustment' of 'power relations' both 'within States ("social order") and between States ("international order")', in order to eliminate 'domination and exclusion' and to ensure 'equal enjoyment of human rights' for all, see Asbjörn Eide, 'Article 28' in Alfredsson and Eide (n 160) 597–598, 600, 602–604.

[190] For example, article 28 may not constitute customary international law, and may also lack sufficient precision 'to constitute an international legal norm'. Hannum (n 155) 349. See also Eide's caution that article 28 is not, in all aspects, fully justiciable and enforceable. Eide (n 189) 433–437, 439.

[191] For a theory grounded not only in the preamble and article 21 but also article 28, see Matthew Lippman, 'The Right of Civil Resistance under International Law and the Domestic Necessity Defense' (1990) 8 *Dickinson Journal of International Law* 349, 357–358. In general, see also theories of a right to resist an unjust international order, the role of resistance in reshaping international law as part of a 'counter-hegemonic' approach, and the symbiosis of 'revolutionary' and 'reform' approaches to this as described in, for example, Richard Falk, 'The Adequacy of Contemporary Theories of International Law: Gaps in Legal Thinking' (1964) 50 (2) *Virginia Law Review* 231, 248–249, 255–256, 260; Richard Falk, *Legal Order in a Violent World* (Princeton University Press 1968) ix–xi, 5–9, 36–38; Richard Falk, 'The Algiers Declaration of the Rights of Peoples and the Struggle for Human Rights' in Antonio Cassese (ed), *UN Law/Fundamental Rights: Two Topics in International Law* (Sijthoff and Noordhoff 1979); Richard Falk, Balakrishnan Rajagopal, and Jacqueline Stevens (eds), *International Law and the Third World: Reshaping Justice* (Routledge 2008); Richard Falk, *Achieving Human Rights* (Routledge 2009) 25–38. Compare Issa G Shivji, *The Concept of Human Rights in Africa* (CODESRIA Book Series 1989) 69–87, 93–106; Bhupinder Singh Chimni, 'Third World Approaches to International Law: A Manifesto' (2006) 8 *International Community Law Review* 3, 19–27.

[192] In the absence of a formal procedure in international law for this purpose, elections or a plebiscite can constitute the best method for determining the content of the 'will of the people'. Therefore, ignoring the result would likely constitute a violation of article 21, according to Simma et al (n 48) 60–61 C [49]–[51], [53].

human rights violations amounting to 'oppression' in relation to any one or a combination of the Declaration's substantive articles 1–27, contrary to articles 29 and 30;[193] or otherwise the existence of a 'social order' or 'international order' that obstructs 'the realization of human rights' under article 28.[194] As the third preambular paragraph amounts to a recognition of the 'last resort' standard,[195] this would constitute the secondary trigger. The only valid object and purpose is the enforcement of the Declaration's human rights standards, including but not limited to government based on the 'will of the people' – in other words, internal self-determination – or establishment of 'a social and international order for the realization of human rights' where such rights are guaranteed by rule of law. Provided all of these elements have been met, the permissible means are unspecified and therefore presumably inclusive, although subject to the traditional necessity and proportionality standards for the use of force in addition to any other applicable human rights standards. As with UN General Assembly Resolution 2625, the duty-bearers would be all Member States: acting either individually at domestic level with respect to their own population, or collectively through the United Nations institutions in accordance with the UN Charter.[196]

Given all this, Chemillier-Gendreau's claim for a UN Charter-based right seems plausible: the Universal Declaration could provide evidence of recognition of a broader Charter right to resist, complemented by the narrow more generally accepted Charter right acknowledged in UN General Assembly Resolution 2625. Indeed, at least some states proceeded under this impression. For example, in the drafting debates on the 'International Covenant on Human Rights', the Soviet delegate indicates on two occasions his view that the 'right of rebellion' is recognized or implied in the Universal Declaration.[197]

193 Kälin and Künzli suggest setting the trigger at 'serious and systematic violations', the criminality threshold for application of article 19 of the Draft Articles on State Responsibility, as these may also attract UN Security Council action under Chapter VII. See Kälin and Künzli (n 82) 51–53.

194 It therefore may well be that the Universal Declaration can act as the most appropriate interpretive starting point for the usage of 'tyranny' and 'oppression' as international legal terms.

195 Honoré (n 5) 43.

196 See ibid 43.

197 See 'Commission on Human Rights, Fifth Session, Summary Record of the Ninety-First Meeting Held at Lake Success, New York, On Wednesday, 18 May 1949, at 2.30 p.m.' UN Doc E/CN.4/SR.91 (31 May 1949) 4; 'Commission on Human Rights, Fifth Session, Summary Record of the Ninety-Eighth Meeting Held at Lake Success, New York, On Tuesday, 24 May 1949, at 2.30 p.m.' UN Doc E/CN.4/SR.98 (2 June 1949) 2–3.

Chemillier-Gendreau laments that despite persistently weak remedial mechanisms for human rights enforcement including violations of international criminal law, no specific mechanism to support the right to resist exists outside the UN Security Council with reference to the UN Charter.[198] This, however, ignores the potential relevance of the UN Human Rights Council in its interpretation and application of the Universal Declaration,[199] including the right to internal self-determination as set out in article 21 and the right to a social and international order for the realization of human rights under article 28, as well as the lawful application of the ordinary limitations and non-diminution clauses at articles 29 and 30, having regard to the third preambular paragraph. Theoretically, interpretation of a right to resist arising from those provisions as a general principle, or otherwise as customary international human rights law, could also potentially be relevant to adjudication or the rendering of advisory opinions in the International Court of Justice,[200] or a 'World Court of Human Rights' were this proposal ever to come to pass,[201] and also to adjudication in domestic courts and tribunals.

In addition to the preceding evidence of recognition of a customary international human right to resist arising from the UN Charter and its later interpretive instruments on human rights and self-determination, another source seems to indicate a customary international right-duty to resist, arising from international criminal law. That source is the Nuremberg Principles.

6.5 IMPLIED RECOGNITION OF A RIGHT-DUTY: THE NUREMBERG PRINCIPLES

As argued by Wright, the continuing absence of a prohibition on resistance, rebellion, or revolution per se in contemporary international law in general, and in international criminal law in particular, is another possible indicator of

[198] Chemillier-Gendreau (n 33) 957 [19]–[20].

[199] See Schabas, 'Introductory Essay' (n 156) lxxi, cxvii–cxix, cxxii–cxxiii; the terms establishing the mandate to make recommendations to the General Assembly regarding the further development of international law on human rights, in 'Human Rights Council' UNGA Res 60/251 (15 March 2006) UN Doc A/RES/60/251. The role of the UN Human Rights Council is discussed further in Chapter 7, Section 7.4.

[200] See *USA* v *Iran* (n 158) [91].

[201] See Julie Kozma, Manfred Nowak, and Martin Scheinin, *A World Court of Human Rights: Consolidated Draft Statute and Commentary* (Neuer Wissenschaflichter Verlag 2010) Part II Jurisdiction, article 5 on applicable law; article 6 on general principles 11–12. However, for critical analysis of the general initiative see Stefan Trechsel, 'A World Court for Human Rights?' (2004) 1(1) *Northwestern University Journal of International Human Rights* 3; Philip Alston, 'Against a World Court of Human Rights' (2014) 28(2) *Ethics and International Affairs* 197.

the existence of a customary recognition of a right to resist.[202] That this absence of prohibition arises from a customary law exception, expressly acknowledged in the UN General Assembly Definition of Aggression,[203] appears to be further corroborated by the International Court of Justice finding that 'aggression' is a 'state-only' crime,[204] as well as the non-inclusion of resistance, rebellion, or revolution – or even a further provision on 'terrorism' as a 'distinct crime' – in the Statute of the International Criminal Court-codified international crimes.[205] The question remains whether this absence of criminal or other prohibition amounts to an implied customary permission or 'freedom' to resist under certain conditions, and if so whether an enforceable positive 'right' to resist can also be derived from this.

In the context of this absence of prohibition and the possibility of a recognized customary exception, some propose a theory of a customary international law right-duty to resist in order to prevent or halt internationally criminal acts.[206] This means a right-duty to resist acts also

[202] See for example Wright (n 9) 121–124; Wright, 'Intervention and Cuba' (n 8) 3–4. See also Mégret (n 136) 173, 175; Frédéric Mégret, 'Should Rebels Be Amnestied?' in Carsten Stahn, Jennifer S Easterday, and Jens Iverson (eds), *Jus Post Bellum: Mapping the Normative Foundations* (Oxford University Press 2014) 537. On the absence also of a duty of obedience imposed by customary international law, see Longobardo (n 112) 135–141.

[203] See UNGA Res 3314 (n 91) articles 6, 7.

[204] See *Legal Consequences of the Construction of a Wall in the Occupied Palestinian Territory* (n 96) [138]–[141]. See also the Rome Statute of the International Criminal Court (adopted 17 July 1998, entered into force 1 July 2002) 2187 UNTS 3 (as amended 2010) article 8 bis, the sole 'state-only' crime within the Rome Statute. Its definition is 'lifted word-for-word from the General Assembly Definition of Aggression' and article 22(2) of the Statute requires strict construction and prohibits extension by analogy. See Dinstein, *War, Aggression and Self-Defence* (n 111) 146–149.

[205] See William A Schabas, *An Introduction to the International Criminal Court* (2nd edn, Cambridge University Press 2004) 26, 34–35, 46; ibid (5th edn, 2017) 53, 75–76, 83–84, 101, 383, reasoning that that since comparable levels of impunity do not arise for 'terrorist' crimes its exclusion is appropriate. However compare Antonio Cassese, 'Terrorism is also Disrupting Some Crucial Legal Categories of International Law' (2001) 12(5) *European Journal of International Law* 993, 994, attributing the omission to Non-Aligned Movement states' aversion to conflating 'terrorism' with 'wars of national liberation' and other instances where the international right of resistance applies. See further discussion in Section 6.6.4.

[206] See for example Richard Falk, 'Nuremberg: Past, Present and Future' (1971) 80 *Yale Law Journal* 1501, 1516 fn 50; Richard Falk, 'The Nuremberg Defense in the Pentagon Papers Case' (1974) 13 *Columbia Journal of Transnational Law* 208, 208–210, 212–213, 226, 229, 232–233, 235–238; Richard Falk, 'Introduction' in Francis A Boyle, *Defending Civil Resistance under International Law* (Transnational 1988); Richard Falk, 'Telford Taylor and the Legacy of Nuremberg' (1998) 37 *Columbia Journal of Transnational Law* 693, 698–699; Boyle (n 206); Francis A Boyle, *Protesting Power: War, Resistance, and Law* (Rowman and Littlefield 2008); Matthew Lippman, 'Nuremberg and American Justice' (1991) 5 *Notre Dame Journal of Ethics, Law and Public Policy* 951; Kälin and Künzli (n 82) 55. See also Nicholas N Kittrie, *Rebels with a Cause: The Minds and Morality of Political Offenders* (Westview 2000)

amounting to violations of *jus cogens* norms – 'crimes against peace' or crimes of aggression, war crimes, genocide, and crimes against humanity which would also include apartheid, slavery, and torture in its scope[207] – and possibly any other acts internationally criminalized in future, such as 'ecocide'.[208] Consistent with this is the narrower right-duty to disobey internationally criminal orders, and thereby to individually uphold and enforce international law by avoiding complicity in, and therefore liability for, such crimes.

This hypothesized right-duty to resist is derived from the now customary 'Principles of International Law Recognized in the Charter of the Nürnberg Tribunal and in the Judgment of the Tribunal' (Nuremberg Principles).[209] Usually characterized as 'general principles' of customary international criminal law and as such binding on all states, the Nuremberg Principles are reflected in nearly all subsequent statutory codifications of international criminal law and have been treated as customary international law by domestic and international courts and tribunals.[210]

Proponents of this theory argue an implied duty to resist, and therefore an implied corollary right to resist, indicated in Nuremberg Principle VII. Principle VII designates as liable to criminal punishment, pursuant to Principle I, any 'complicity' in the commission of the crimes set out in Principle VI – being crimes against peace, war crimes, or crimes against humanity – even despite absence of specific penalty in law according to Principle II and regardless of superior orders according to Principle IV.[211] Logically, avoiding complicity will at the very least imply individual

342–344, 350, where it is implicit in his proposed 'Bill of Rights on Just Resistance' articles 1–2, 8–9, 15, and 'Typology of Political Offences' E1–F5.

[207] International Law Commission, 'Draft Conclusions on Identification and Legal Consequences of Peremptory Norms of General International Law' (n 27) Conclusion 23(a)–(g).

[208] See Independent Expert Panel for the Legal Definition of Ecocide, 'Commentary and Core Text' (Stop Ecocide Foundation, June 2021).

[209] See International Law Commission, 'Principles of International Law Recognized in the Charter of the Nürnberg Tribunal and in the Judgment of the Tribunal' (1950) UN Doc A/CN.4/SER.A/1950/Add.1.

[210] See 'Affirmation of the Principles of International Law recognized by the Charter of the Nürnberg Tribunal' UNGA Res 95(I) (11 December 1946); 'Formulation of the Nürnberg principles' UNGA Res 488(V) (12 December 1950); 'Affirmation of the Principles of International Law Recognized by the Charter of the Nürnberg Tribunal: General Assembly Resolution 95(I)' (United Nations Audiovisual Library of International Law 2008) 2; Antonio Cassese, 'Affirmation of the Principles of International Law Recognized by the Charter of the Nürnberg Tribunal' (United Nations Audiovisual Library of International Law 2009) 1–2, 4–7.

[211] See Nuremberg Principles (n 209) Principles I, II, IV, VI, and VII.

disobedience to internationally criminal orders.[212] In its more expansive version, avoiding effective complicity through inaction may in some circumstances require other acts of resistance beyond such direct disobedience. In either case, such theories propose that if there is a duty to resist consequently implied, this in turn implies a corollary right to resist, and that such acts of resistance should be immune from punishment and otherwise protected by law. Moreover, it is significant for this theory that the Nuremberg Principles use the term 'any person' in relation to duty-bearers, thus lacking the exclusive emphasis on the duty of superiors to prevent such crimes committed by subordinates that is found in some instruments.[213] The theory therefore effectively amplifies the International Military Tribunal holding that 'the very essence of the [IMT] Charter is that individuals have international duties [to prevent atrocities] which transcend the national obligations of obedience imposed by the individual state'.[214]

If the Nuremberg Principles do indeed constitute a material source of an implied customary right-duty to resist, applying the analytical framework from Chapter 4, all persons would be duty-bearers and therefore rights-holders. The object and purpose would be the prevention of international crimes and thereby the enforcement of 'higher' international criminal law. The full spectrum of means would be contemplated as permissible, provided compliance with necessity conditions and proportionality limitations as well as any others imposed by international criminal law. The main question is one of scope regarding triggers. For example, it is unclear whether the relevant elements of those crimes actually need to be met before the right could be triggered or whether preventive action is permissible and, if so, the appropriate

[212] See for example Dannenbaum's detailed rationale and proposals for recognition of a highly limited right to disobey orders to fight in criminal wars, claimable at the *jus ad bellum* stage. Dannenbaum (n 111) 'The Duty to Disobey Illegal Orders' 20–24, 'The Timing of Disobedience Protection' 272–276, 'A Limited Right to Disobey Orders to Fight in Illegal Wars' 292–299, 'The *Jus ad Bellum* and the Human Rights of Rights Defenders' 322–328. See also Tom Dannenbaum, 'The Criminalization of Aggression and Soldiers' Rights' (2018) 29 (3) *European Journal of International Law* 859.

[213] For example, articles 2(c) and 6 of the International Law Commission's ultimate 'Draft Code of Crimes against the Peace and Security of Mankind' (1996) [1996] *Yearbook of the International Law Commission* vol II. Regarding the customary right-duty that applies to all military personnel, see International Committee of the Red Cross, 'Rule 154: Every combatant has a duty to disobey a manifestly unlawful order' (International Committee of the Red Cross Customary IHL Database updated December 2017). For discussion of the equivalent corollary implied right-duty of disobedience to the crimes encoded in the Rome Statute, see Chapter 7, Section 7.2.3.

[214] See *France et al* v *Göring et al* (1946) 22 IMT 203, 13 ILR 203, 41 *American Journal of International Law* 172; *Trial of the Major War Criminals before the International Military Tribunal* (Official Documents 1947) vol I, 223.

indicators.[215] It is possible that other internationally unlawful but internationally non-criminal acts should be included in the scope of triggering conditions, with a view to prevention of atrocities. In these ways, this concept of a right-duty to resist could be partially analogous and possibly complementary to the third-party, late activating, 'responsibility to protect' duty on states and international organizations.[216]

This proposed customary international right-duty to resist internationally criminal acts has practical legal implications. It has been used as a criminal necessity defence in domestic courts,[217] with varying degrees of success.[218] It may also have specific *jus post-bellum* applications.[219] And it should be taken into account by current efforts to separately codify crimes against

[215] See for example the fourteen risk factors or indicators included in the UN 'Framework of Analysis for Atrocity Crimes' (n 71) 9–24.

[216] See Frédéric Mégret, 'Beyond the Salvation Paradigm: Responsibility to Protect (Others) vs the Power of Protecting Oneself' (2009) 40 *Security Dialogue* 575; Frédéric Mégret, 'Not "Lambs to the Slaughter": A Program for Resistance to Genocidal Law' in René Provost and Payam Akhavan (eds), *Confronting Genocide* (Springer 2011); Frédéric Mégret, 'Civilian Resilience in Syria: Helping the Syrians Help Themselves? The Ambiguities of International Assistance to the Rebellion' (2014) 3(1) *Stability: International Journal of Security and Development* 1.

[217] It operates as a 'justification' defence, under which necessity 'negates the wrongfulness of the criminal act' rendering it lawful. This involves a 'balancing that suggests that the overall benefits of the defendant's conduct outweigh the resulting harm caused' such that 'the defendant is rewarded for imposing harm' in order 'to improve the lot of a larger number of third parties'. Generally, the further elements of 'imminence' and 'proportionality' must also be met. See Ohlin and May (n 96) 141, 144–147, 149–151.

[218] See Falk, 'Nuremberg Defense' (n 206); Falk, 'Telford Taylor and the Legacy of Nuremberg' (n 206) 717–718. The availability of domestic necessity-based defences is jurisdictionally specific. For an example of jurisdictionally specific analysis of potentially relevant defences available as 'justification' – 'necessity' to 'prevent a greater imminent and immediate harm', 'self-defence', and 'defence of others', 'resisting unlawful arrest' – and their elements, see Matthew Lippman, *Contemporary Criminal Law Concepts, Cases and Controversies* (2nd edn, Sage Publications 2010) 216–239, 250–262. For jurisdictionally specific advice in mounting such defences, see Boyle, *Defending Civil Resistance* (n 206) 13–50 updated in Boyle, *Protesting Power* (n 206) 35–73. On a theory of 'public interest necessity' in defence of others and for human rights and international criminal law enforcement, relaxing the 'immediacy' requirement, see Lippman (n 191) 362–372. Acknowledging the value of the Nuremberg Principles for establishing a right-duty to resist but concluding they provide only a minimally viable criminal defence, compare Kittrie (n 206) 265–266, 274–276, 320–321; Hitomi Takemura, 'Disobeying Manifestly Illegal Orders' (2006) 18(4) *Peace Review: A Journal of Social Justice* 533, 537–539; Hitomi Takemura, *International Human Right to Conscientious Objection to Military Service and Individual Duties to Disobey Manifestly Illegal Orders* (Springer 2009) 1–2, 137–181. Regarding a specific anomaly identified with respect to the crime of aggression and consequent proposals, see Dannenbaum (n 111) 23–24, 273–276, 292ff.

[219] See Mégret (n 202).

humanity.[220] But it also suggests a more profound idea. If this right-duty to resist internationally criminal acts can be considered a form of international law enforcement, it raises the question of whether this norm can extend to self-help enforcement by individuals and groups regarding acts that are internationally unlawful, but fall short of international criminality – for example, to halt or prevent grave and irreversible environmental damage, pending recognition of an international crime of ecocide, or otherwise failure of states to uphold their climate change obligations.[221] At present, it is doubtful that recognition of a right-duty in customary international law stretches this far. However, this may not deter all individuals and groups from making such claims or attempting such defences. Nor need it hinder future developments in evolutive interpretation based on this principle.

Given their potential to change ideas about extrajudicial enforcement, the Nuremberg Principles may constitute the most intriguing of the three main sources of material evidence of recognition of a human right to resist in general or customary international law. However, the overall picture of the right's recognition status in general or customary international law would be incomplete without consideration of other sources that seem to corroborate customary recognition of this right.

6.6 CORROBORATIVE SOURCES INDICATIVE OF CUSTOMARY RECOGNITION

Certain sources of law are sometimes represented as 'sources' of an international right to resist, but are more accurately understood as indirect and corroborative rather than establishing. That is, they are indicative of customary recognition emanating from elsewhere, as discussed in the previous sections. Nevertheless, because these sources of law can provide practical benefits flowing from additional legal rights and impose practical constraints arising from other legal duties or areas of regulation under general international law

[220] For example, the corollary right-duty to resist internationally criminal orders and associated necessity defences are not addressed in the relevant provisions on 'Criminalization under national law', addressing superiors' duty of prevention, removing defences of superior orders and immunities grounded in official capacity. See International Law Commission, 'Draft Articles on Prevention and Punishment of Crimes against Humanity' (2019) [2019] *Yearbook of the International Law Commission* vol II, pt 2, article 6. In light of this, see also the Chapter 7, Section 7.4 discussion of the recently failed UN codification initiative that would have included specific provision for a right to resist crimes against humanity.

[221] Such obligations are subject of a forthcoming International Court of Justice Advisory Opinion. See 'Request for an Advisory Opinion of the International Court of Justice on the Obligations of States in Respect of Climate Change' UNGA Res 77/276 (4 April 2023).

related to the exercise of a right to resist in qualifying cases, they are worth brief consideration in this context. Note however, as established in the previous chapters, both historically and analytically the right to resist is the prior concept.

6.6.1 *The Customary Laws of Insurgency and Belligerency, Recognition, Responsibility*

For a cluster of rules in customary international law, their applicability depends entirely on the degree of success achieved by those employing forceful resistance. The law of insurgency and belligerency,[222] and the law of recognition of rightful authority or 'legitimacy',[223] regulate third-party treatment of comparatively successful groups. The law of state responsibility effectively applies exclusively to those 'state-like' parties whose success is complete, or nearly so.[224] All three confer some additional rights and/or

[222] On the traditional threefold classification rule by which 'rebels' are accorded neither recognition nor specific rights under international law; 'insurgents' may receive discretionary de facto recognition with some limited rights; and 'belligerents' receive limited de jure recognition as a 'state-like' entity with rights analogous to those available to a state including the right of self-defence under article 51 of the UN Charter, and for a critical analysis, see Falk (n 37) 194, 197–209, 223–239. See also Wilson (n 15) 23–27; Brad R Roth, *Governmental Illegitimacy in International Law* (Oxford University Press 2000) 173–184. On the virtual obsolescence of formal recognition of 'belligerency', the absence of clear conflict classification criteria despite its decisiveness for determining the applicable law and the legality of the use of force and intervention on invitation to assist by either side, and the rarity of either admission of civil war by states or determination as such by the UN Security Council, see Higgins (n 65) 170–172; Shaw (n 66) 1149–1151; Gray, *International Law and the Use of Force* (n 64) 81 (fn 70), 82–83, 86.

[223] On the traditional test for 'legitimate authority' either for the purposes of general recognition or specifically to use force, as a consequence of a 'state-like' status for which the traditional minimum criteria relates to the 'effectiveness' and 'representativeness' standards, involving 'effective control' over a 'substantial' portion of a population and territory, with administrative capacity to represent an entire people; and on an emerging doctrine of legitimacy that requires 'empirical manifestations of popular will', see Roth (n 222) 136, 226–233, 413, 419. This is a variation on Judge Ammoun's view of widespread resistance as an indicator of popular will 'more decisive than a referendum'. *Western Sahara* (n 106) Separate Opinion of Ammoun J [100]. This test is separate from, additional to, and potentially either complements or conflicts with, the test for a human 'right to resist'.

[224] On the customary rules establishing both state and 'state-like' responsibility under international law, whereby rebel groups may under certain circumstances be held liable for wrongful acts, see International Law Commission, 'Responsibility of States for Internationally Wrongful Acts' (n 28) articles 9–10. These rules also establish the applicable exceptions or 'circumstances precluding wrongfulness' ibid articles 20–25, and impose limitations on countermeasures against a state responsible for wrongful acts ibid articles 50–51. See also James Crawford, *The International Law Commission's Articles on State Responsibility: Introduction, Text and Commentaries* (Cambridge University Press 2002) 97 [9], 114–115 [1]–

duties,[225] elevating those qualifying into an elite category in international legal terms. However, the question of whether there is an actual human right to resist in such cases is entirely separate. Application of these rules is conditional on a rebel group's achievement of 'effectiveness' as an indicator of de facto authority.[226] Those who do not meet right to resist criteria could still achieve the status of official belligerents, recognized as 'legitimate' or 'responsible' insofar as they exert control over sufficient territory and people. Those that do have a valid right to resist but either fail, or have yet to achieve sufficiently, cannot access the same status. Nevertheless, the very fact of legal rules that facilitate rather than forbid comparatively favourable treatment of some rebel groups provided certain conditions are met has potentially corroborative implications for customary recognition of the human right to resist. Indeed, particularly in the absence of blanket suppression, these laws are considered by some as evidence that, together with the prohibition on intervention in civil wars, implies indirect recognition of a right to rebellion and right to revolution as an aspect of sovereignty underpinned by self-determination.[227]

Associated with but somewhat distinct from this cluster are the rules of insurgency/belligerency at sea.[228] These are separate from the law of piracy,[229]

[5], 116–120 [11]–[16]; Brownlie (n 6) 454–456. The law of state responsibility leaves open the question of whether and how a lawful right to resist on the part of a population could intersect with the question of prior state negligence or the requirement of 'due diligence' to prevent conflict-related damage.

225 For example, the law of recognition of rightful authority has the potential to confer obvious advantages and certain rights. Less obviously advantageous, the law of state responsibility when applied to rebel governments is nevertheless an indirect form of recognition. Recognition of 'insurgents' with 'intermediate status' opens the way for additional rights on a discretionary basis, while the formal status of 'belligerency' is associated with certain rights as well as duties and other legal consequences. See Higgins (n 65) 170; Shaw (n 66) 1149–1151. Conversely, where state-like subsidiary rights become available through belligerency, the UN Charter article 2(4) prohibition on the use of force also applies unless rebels have a valid claim to self-defence under the terms of article 51, or otherwise through UNGA Res 2625. See Gorelick (n 50) 72.

226 See for example Mégret (n 202) 535.

227 Compare for example Falk (n 37) 207, 219–220; Higgins (n 81) 2, 231.

228 For a partial account of its evolution as a discrete area within the law of the sea, see for example George Grafton Wilson, 'Insurgency and International Maritime Law' (1907) 1(1) *American Journal of International Law* 46, 50, 54–59.

229 On insurgent actions on the high seas as non-equatable to piracy due to its strict definition, the 'essence' of which is that 'it must be committed for private ends', but to which particular treaties such as the Convention on the Suppression of Unlawful Acts against the Safety of Maritime Navigation (1988) potentially apply, see Brownlie (n 6) 231; Shaw (n 66) 615; Malcolm D Evans, 'The Law of the Sea' in Malcolm D Evans (ed), *International Law* (3rd edn, Oxford University Press 2010) 667.

as is what may be considered an as yet inchoate doctrine of a right of resistance or rebellion at sea.[230] Again, determinations of a lawful right to resist or to rebel involve a separate evaluation from other issues arising specifically from the law of the sea.[231] Indeed, failure to also examine whether there is a right to resist under general or customary international law in cases involving the law of the sea can render a legal assessment incomplete at best.[232] Such assessments must also factor in that human rights apply equally on sea as on land.[233] While beyond the scope of this study, the under-explored relationship

[230] See for example the approach of the US Federal District Court of Connecticut in *US* v *Cinque et al* (1839) – which, having considered international law arguments, effectively found the captive Africans had the right of rebellion against slavery, hence were not guilty of piracy and murder – later affirmed by the United States Supreme Court in *United States* v *Schooner Amistad*, 40 US 518 (1841), 593–594, 595–597. See also Edward D Jervey and C Harold Huber, 'The Creole Affair' (1980) 65(3) *Journal of Negro History* 196, 206 citing the Opinion of the Law Lords, 29 January 1842 in Stanley to Cockburn, 31 January 1842, London, Public Records Office CO 24/22. Ibid 206 fn 55–58.

[231] Compare the contrary approach in *Institute of Cetacean Research et al* v *Sea Shepherd Conservation Society et al* DC No 2:11-cv-02043-RAJ (US Court of Appeals 9th Circuit 25 February 2013), where in making its 'piracy' finding the court deliberately disregards international law enforcement claims made by environmentalists in defence of their otherwise unlawful actions to stop whaling ships – thus ignoring the possibility or otherwise of a right to resist under customary international law. For an account of the respondent's claim of competence arising from section 21 of the UN World Charter for Nature, see Joseph Elliott Roeschke, 'Eco-Terrorism and Piracy on the High Seas: Japanese Whaling and the Rights of Private Groups to Enforce International Conservation Law in Neutral Waters' (2009) 20(1) *Villanova Environmental Law Journal* 99.

[232] For examples, see Glen Plant, 'Civilian Protest Vessels and the Law of the Sea' (1983) 14 *Netherlands Yearbook of International Law* 133; Glen Plant, 'International Law and Direct Action Protests at Sea: Twenty Years On' (2002) 33 *Netherlands Yearbook of International Law* 75; UN Human Rights Council, 'Report of the International Fact-Finding Mission to Investigate Violations of International Law, including International Humanitarian and Human Rights Law, Resulting from the Israeli Attacks on the Flotilla of Ships Carrying Humanitarian Assistance' UN Doc A/HRC/15/21 (27 September 2010) [53]–[60], [76], [79], [84], [99]–[104], [109], [113], [115]–[116], [137], [144], [149], [152]–[153], [163], [165], [276]–[277]; UN Secretary-General, 'Report of the Secretary-General's Panel of Inquiry on the 31 May 2010 Flotilla Incident' (September 2011) [133], Appendix 1 'The Applicable International Legal Principles' [72], [81]–[82]; International Criminal Court, 'Referral of the Union of the Comoros with respect to the 31 May 2010 Israeli raid on the Humanitarian Aid Flotilla bound for the Gaza Strip, requesting the Prosecutor of the International Criminal Court pursuant to Articles 12, 13 and 14 of the Rome Statute to initiate an investigation into the crimes committed within the Court's jurisdiction, arising from this raid' (14 May 2013) 1 [5], 7 [29], 9 [37], 11 [44]–[45]; *Situation of Registered Vessels of the Union of the Comoros, the Hellenic Republic of Greece and the Kingdom of Cambodia* ICC-01/13 (Final decision of the Prosecution concerning the 'Article 53(1) Report' (ICC-01/13-6-AnxA) dated 6 November 2014 with Public Annexes A–C, E–G and Confidential Annex D) (29 November 2017) Public Annex 1, [2], I.3(c) [88]–[93].

[233] See the fundamental principles derived from existing international legal obligations outlined in Human Rights at Sea, 'Geneva Declaration on Human Rights at Sea' (January 2022) 4.

between the customary right to resist and the law of the sea warrants a more detailed examination.

6.6.2 *The Customary International Humanitarian Law Recognition of* Levée en Masse *in the Hague Conventions and Regulation of 'Resistance Movements' and 'National Liberation Movements' by the Geneva Conventions*

As Longobardo describes, international humanitarian law does not prohibit resistance, nor does it directly confer a right to resist.[234] Instead, a second cluster of customary *jus in bello* rules regulate only that forceful resistance which has escalated to the point of 'armed conflict' – again ostensibly regardless of whether there is a recognized *jus ad bellum* 'right' to resist.[235] This customary international humanitarian law also contains complementary corroborative aspects that would seem to imply recognition of a right to resist elsewhere in customary international law.[236] Likewise, it confers some additional rights and duties – again, effectively elevating those qualifying into an elite category in international legal terms. For qualifying 'combatants' in cases of 'international armed conflict' it confers a 'privilege of belligerency', or 'right to participate directly in hostilities' without prosecution, which has a 'decriminalization effect'.[237] Such provisions may benefit a particular subset of those with a valid claim to a right to resist.

For example, the 1899 and 1907 Hague Regulations codify or formalize the customary international law recognition of the '*levée en masse*' as lawful participation. Common article 2 of these regulations stringently restricts this

[234] Longobardo (n 112) 141–150, 163–164. On this basis, arguing in favour of additional regulation, see Christopher J Finlay, 'The Perspective of the Rebel: A Gap in the Global Normative Architecture' (2017) 31(2) *Ethics and International Affairs* 213; and Christopher J Finlay, 'The Deadly Serious Causes of Legitimate Rebellion: Between the Wrongs of Terrorism and the Crimes of War' (2018) 12(2) *Criminal Law and Philosophy* 271.

[235] That *jus ad bellum* determinations are beyond the scope of international humanitarian law *jus in bello*, which applies its own independent criteria, see Mégret (n 136) 178–179; Mégret (n 202) 536. For more discussion on theories of the right to resist as *jus ad bellum*, see Chapter 3, Section 3.4.4. See also complementary analysis of shortcomings of both the traditional *jus ad bellum* and the *jus in bello* of international humanitarian law with respect to non-international armed conflicts, proposing solutions instead based in international human rights law in Eliav Lieblich, 'Internal Jus Ad Bellum' (2016) 67 *Hastings Law Journal* 687; Anthony Dworkin, 'Individual, Not Collective: Justifying the Resort to Force against Members of Non-State Armed Groups' (2017) 93 *International Law Studies* 476; Dannenbaum (n 73).

[236] Both Cassese and Chemillier-Gendreau classify it as corroborative only. Cassese (n 94) section 18.9, 374 fn 30; Chemillier-Gendreau (n 33) 956 [14]. See also Longobardo (n 112) 153–155.

[237] See Saul (n 10) 73, 76.

legal category to those residing in 'a territory which has not [yet] been occupied [by a foreign power's army] who, *on the enemy's approach*, spontaneously take up arms to resist the invading troops without having time to organize themselves in accordance with Article 1', provided they 'respect the laws and customs of war'.[238] Any assessment relying on this source and concept as the sole contemporary standard or rule for recognition of a right to resist in customary international law could only conclude that virtually no group ever qualifies.[239] Yet these regulations are not a direct or independent source of the right to resist, but instead merely constitute evidence relating to conditions for conferring or recognizing 'prisoner of war' status,[240] an additional and more specific right that is not interchangeable. Indeed, if not now virtually defunct as a legal concept, *levée en masse* is largely subsumed within and thus superseded by broader categories.[241]

Along similar lines, various provisions of the 1949 Geneva Conventions, universally ratified by all UN Member States, either reflect or at least corroborate an implied limited right to resist foreign invasion and occupation in customary international law.[242] These provide for recognition of the lawful combatant status of members of 'organized resistance movements, belonging to a Party to the conflict and operating in or outside their own territory, even if this territory is occupied', provided that they comply with the requirements of responsible command, carrying arms openly and having a 'fixed distinctive sign', as well as conducting operations 'in accordance with the laws and customs of war'.[243]

[238] Convention (II) with Respect to the Laws and Customs of War on Land (adopted 29 July 1899, entered into force 4 September 1900) 187 CTS 429 Annex: Regulations Respecting the Laws and Customs of War on Land (Hague Regulations 1899) article 2 [emphasis added]; Convention (IV) Respecting the Laws and Customs of War on Land (adopted 18 October 1907, entered into force 26 January 1910) 205 CTS 227 Annex: Regulations Respecting the Laws and Customs of War on Land (Hague Regulations 1907) article 2, which also includes the important additional condition of carrying arms openly.

[239] See Emily Crawford, 'Levée en masse: A Nineteenth Century Concept in a Twenty-First Century World' (2011) University of Sydney Law School, Legal Studies Research Paper No 11/31 (May 2011).

[240] See International Committee of the Red Cross, 'Practice Relating to Rule 106: Conditions for Prisoner of War Status' (Customary IHL Database updated December 2017).

[241] However, on this rule as uniquely constituting 'an existing, accepted law' legitimizing 'civilian participation in international armed conflict' in a hybrid civilian-combatant category, see Crawford (n 239).

[242] Regarding the customary law status of the Geneva Conventions themselves, see Jean-Marie Henckaerts and Louise Doswald-Beck (eds), *Customary International Humanitarian Law* (Cambridge University Press 2005) vol I 384–389.

[243] See article 13(2) of Geneva Convention (I) for the Amelioration of the Condition of the Wounded and Sick in Armed Forces in the Field (adopted 12 August 1949, entered into force

6.6.2.1 The Limited Immunity Available under Additional Protocol I to the Geneva Conventions

Additional Protocol I to the Geneva Conventions makes a similar provision for 'national liberation movements'. It specifies at article 1(4) that the Protocol applies to 'armed conflicts which peoples are fighting against colonial domination and alien occupation and against racist regimes in the exercise of their right of self-determination', with specific reference to the Declaration on Principles of International Law set out in UN General Assembly Resolution 2625. Article 43(2) further specifies that these are 'combatants' with a 'right to participate directly in hostilities', hence immunity from prosecution for participation and eligibility for prisoner of war status pursuant to article 44. However, article 4 cautions that the Protocol's application 'shall not affect the legal status of the Parties'.[244] This disclaimer is another way of confirming that Additional Protocol I is not an establishing source of the human right to resist.

Particularly given these provisions of Additional Protocol I, the scope of corroborative recognition for the sole purpose of the application of the Geneva Conventions is not as restricted as with the Hague Regulations. Nevertheless, it is still quite narrow. For example, as Cassese emphasizes, common article 3

21 October 1950) 75 UNTS 31; article 13(2) of Geneva Convention (II) for the Amelioration of the Condition of Wounded, Sick and Shipwrecked Members of the Armed Forces at Sea (adopted 12 August 1949, entered into force 21 October 1950) 75 UNTS 85; and article 4(2) Geneva Convention (III) Relative to the Treatment of Prisoners of War (adopted 12 August 1949, entered into force 21 October 1950) 75 UNTS 135.

244 See Protocol (I) Additional to the Geneva Conventions of 12 August 1949, and Relating to the Protection of Victims of International Armed Conflicts (adopted 8 June 1977, entered into force 7 December 1978) 1125 UNTS 3 articles 1(4), 4, 43(2), 44. On Additional Protocol I as elevating 'to the rank of international conflict' those wars 'in which an oppressed people is fighting for self-determination against a colonial or occupying power or a racist regime', with the consequence that the more favourable laws of inter-state war apply rather than the law of civil war, see Cassese (n 163) 178–180; Glazier (n 80) B.3[11]. Affirming the connection between Additional Protocol I article 1(4) and UNGA Resolution 2625 criteria, see Bruno Zimmermann, 'Article 1' in Yves Sandoz, Christophe Swinarski, and Bruno Zimmermann (eds), *Commentary on the Protocol Additional to the Geneva Conventions of 12 August 1949, and relating to the Protection of Victims of International Armed Conflicts (Protocol I)* (International Committee of the Red Cross-Martinus Nijhoff 1987) 41–56 [69]–[118], especially [81]–[85], [97], [100], [107], [110]–[116]; and Protocol I Reservations, Understandings and Declarations (RUDs) concerning article 1(4) and its relation to articles 44(3) and 96(3), including those of Australia, Belgium, Canada, France, Germany, Ireland, Japan, New Zealand, Republic of Korea, Spain, United Kingdom. See for example 'Spain's Declaration on Protocol Additional to the Geneva Conventions of 12 August 1949, and relating to the Protection of Victims of International Armed Conflicts (Protocol I), 8 June 1977' (1989).

to the four Geneva Conventions confers no such privileges in cases of 'armed conflict not of an international character'.[245] Nor is there any provision equivalent to Additional Protocol I articles 43(2) or 44 available under Additional Protocol II, applicable to 'non-international' armed conflicts. Indeed, article 6 of Additional Protocol II expressly provides for prosecutions of rebels for mere participation, subject to certain protections and procedural guarantees. Although article 6(5) encourages 'the broadest possible amnesty' for participation once the conflict is concluded, this is not an obligation per se.[246] While some treat this as corroborative evidence of definitive non-recognition of the right to resist in customary international law for such cases,[247] others arrive at more circumspect or even optimistic conclusions.[248]

As mentioned in Chapter 2, a common confusion seems to originate from conflating the concept of the right to resist and its legal sources with the recognition and non-recognition of combatant status for the purpose of regulation of armed conflict as engaged in by 'resistance movements', 'national liberation movements', and others, under the various sources of international humanitarian law. While 'privileged belligerency' and 'lawful combatant status' are complementary, they cannot substitute for the separate legal concept of the right to resist.[249] Indeed, these complementary rights have proven difficult to access in practice, even by those with the clearest-cut claims under

[245] Cassese (n 163) 178–179. Rather, common article 3 concerns obligations applying to all parties, extending certain protections to civilians and others 'hors de combat' and identifying prohibited acts, while specifically stipulating that its application 'shall not affect the legal status of the Parties to the conflict'. See Geneva Convention (I) (n 243) article 3; Geneva Convention (II) (n 243) article 3; Geneva Convention (III) (n 243) article 3; Geneva Convention (IV) Relative to the Protection of Civilian Persons in Time of War (adopted 12 August 1949, entered into force 21 October 1950) 75 UNTS 287 article 3.

[246] See Protocol (II) Additional to the Geneva Conventions of 12 August 1949, and Relating to the Protection of Victims of Non-International Armed Conflicts (adopted 8 June 1977, entered into force 7 December 1978) 1125 UNTS 609, article 6. For his critique of consequent scholarly proposals for automatic extension of the privilege of belligerency to qualifying Additional Protocol II rebel combatants – without addressing the need for a separate *jus ad bellum* assessment, see Mégret (n 202) 523, replying to Antonio Cassese, 'Should Rebels Be Treated as Criminals? Some Modest Proposals for Rendering Internal Armed Conflicts Less Inhumane' in Antonio Cassese (ed), *Realizing Utopia: The Future of International Law* (Oxford University Press 2012).

[247] See for example, Saul (n 10) 81–86; Bellal and Doswald-Beck (n 15) 21–22.

[248] Compare Frédéric Mégret, 'Beyond "Freedom Fighters" and "Terrorists": When, If Ever, Is Non-State Violence Legitimate in International Law?' (SSRN 2009); Mégret (n 136). Compare also Finlay (n 146) 87–124, 178–246.

[249] See Mégret (n 136) 179; Mégret (n 202) 536. On the problematic classification of the *jus in bello* 'privilege of belligerency' as a *jus ad bellum* 'right' given the 'functional specialization' of international humanitarian law, see Mégret (n 202) 521–522, 524–525, 529–537, 540. Compare Kälin and Künzli (n 82) 59–61.

the terms of UN General Assembly Resolution 2625.[250] Fundamentally, the more restricted application of the *jus in bello* regulations to some instances of the right's exercise does not directly constrict the right to resist itself – *jus ad bellum* or otherwise – though it may do so indirectly, as a byproduct.[251]

6.6.3 *The Political Offence Exception in Extradition Law*

The political offence exception in extradition law is another source of corroborative indirect recognition of the right to resist in customary international law.[252] Given its origins as a nineteenth-century protection from refoulement for those resisting 'tyranny and oppression', some suggest that the political offence exception is a logical corollary of a customary international law recognition of the right to resist, as the prior concept.[253]

Again, however, it is necessary to distinguish between the test for what is considered a 'political offence' for the purpose of extradition law, and the tests for evaluating a right to resist, as they are not interchangeable. Indeed, there is still no internationally agreed standard for the political offence exception.[254] Its discretionary and subjective definition and use by individual states has

[250] See Kubo Mačák, 'Wars of National Liberation: The Story of One Unusual Rule I' *OUP Blog* (23 July 2018); Kubo Mačák, 'Wars of National Liberation: The Story of One Unusual Rule II' *OUP Blog* (30 July 2018). As Mačák observes, the first such instance was by the Polisario Front in 2015, the Sahrawi people being possessed of an International Court of Justice Advisory Opinion affirming their right to self-determination. On the other hand, the apartheid-era African National Congress-*Umkhonto we Sizwe* was not able to access the right, despite its deposit of a Declaration under article 96(3) in 1980.

[251] Mégret's growing body of work on this subject represents a concerted effort to disentangle, and then locate the most appropriate points of intersection and symbiosis between, the *jus ad bellum, jus in bello*, and indeed *jus post-bellum* in relation to the right to resist and the right to rebel.

[252] Mégret (n 202) 183; Hessbruegge (n 135) 339. The exception is considered customary because virtually 'every extradition law and treaty contains the rule'. Christine Van den Wijngaert, 'The Political Offence Exception to Extradition: Defining the Issues and Searching a Feasible Alternative' (1983) 2 *Revue Belge de Droit International* 741, 741. However, on conceptual problems resulting in definitional discretion and thus inconsistent practice in implementation, contributing to doubts about its customary status, see Torsten Stein, 'Extradition' in *Max Planck Encyclopedia of Public International Law* (Oxford Public International Law online database 2011) C.3(b)(vii)[31].

[253] See Sibylle Kapferer, 'The Interface between Extradition and Asylum' (Department of International Protection, UN High Commissioner for Refugees 2003) 25–27, [70]–[73]. See also Taulbee (n 172) 44–45, citing Christine Van den Wijngaert, *The Political Offense Exception to Extradition: The Delicate Problem of Balancing the Rights of the Individual and International Public Order* (Kluwer 1980) 19; Kälin and Künzli (n 82) 63–65.

[254] On its status as 'both one of the most universally accepted and one of the most universally contested rules of international law', see Van den Wijngaert (n 252) 741, 743, 744–750; Bassiouni (n 76) 220; Stein (n 252) C.3(b)(vii)[31]–[33].

generated both doubt as to its contemporary utility and suggested alternatives or improvements for more reliable and standardized interpretive methods.[255] In this context, some propose that the right to resist concept could help establish a better test for application of the political offence exception than the most commonly used traditional tests for 'pure' and 'relative' political offences, either as a complementary test or as a substitute.[256]

6.6.4 *Persistent Non-equation with 'Terrorism'*

The final example that seems to corroborate the existence of general or customary international law recognition of the human right to resist is, perhaps counterintuitively, provided by the status of 'terrorism' in international law. There is an argument that the UN Charter-protected right has become 'confused' by the UN terrorism debates, which 'reveal the uncertainty of international law' when means of resistance exceed the *lex generalis*, even where a lawful right to resist is demonstrable.[257] Yet there is also credible legal scholarship that sharply distinguishes the right to resist concept from the concept of terrorism, argues against any tendency to conflation, and promotes the possibility of inter-conceptual coherence.[258]

Cassese in particular long insisted on separation of the right to resist as a *jus ad bellum* question, from the *jus in bello* question of criminally prohibited acts that may be characterized as 'terrorist'.[259] He also insisted that nothing prohibited by international criminal law is permitted by a right to resist, since the right to resist acts as an exception to the state monopoly on the lawful use of force but not as an exception to international criminal prohibitions.[260] This nuanced approach at first appears to contrast with his widely criticized attempt

[255] Compare, for example, Bassiouni (n 76); Van den Wijngaert (n 253); Van den Wijngaert (n 252). See also Stein (n 252) C.3(b)(vii)[31], [33].

[256] See the detailed proposals in Bassiouni (n 76) 254–257; Kittrie (n 206) 331–350. See also Kälin and Künzli (n 82) 53. Compare Taulbee (n 172) 48–51.

[257] See Chemillier-Gendreau (n 33) 957–958 [22]–[23].

[258] See for example Longobardo (n 112) 159–162. Such legal scholarship complements similar work in other disciplines, such as Finlay (n 146); Finlay, 'The Perspective of the Rebel' (n 234); Finlay, 'Deadly Serious Cases of Legitimate Rebellion' (n 234).

[259] See Cassese, 'Human Rights and Humanitarian Law' (n 11) 947–950; Cassese (n 205) 995.

[260] See Cassese, 'Human Rights and Humanitarian Law' (n 11) 946–950, 958; Antonio Cassese, *International Criminal Law* (Oxford University Press 2003) 120–131. See also Bassiouni (n 81) xii–xiv, xvi–xviii, xxi. Compare Saul (n 10) 69–128; Ben Saul, 'Defending "Terrorism": Justifications and Excuses for Terrorism in International Criminal Law' Legal Studies Research Paper No 08/122 (University of Sydney Law School, October 2008), concurring that those claiming a right to resist are not exempt from liability for internationally criminal conduct, but whose parallel approach does not involve recognition of a right to resist per se.

to establish a definition of terrorism as a crime in customary international law in the Special Tribunal for Lebanon Decision on the Applicable Law: Terrorism, Conspiracy, Homicide, Perpetration, Cumulative Charging.[261] The controversial aspect is not the contention of a *dolus specialis* element of the 'intent to spread fear', but rather its broadening clause 'or directly or indirectly coerce a national or international authority to take some action, or refrain from taking it',[262] which incorrectly trespasses on evaluation of right to resist legitimate object and purpose claims. Yet Cassese's involvement in the decision looks slightly different against the backdrop of his previously established positions on the right to resist and right to rebel in international law and his obvious desire to distinguish between the valid exercise of these rights and the use of 'terrorist' means.

Many scholars follow this traditional *jus ad bellum/jus in bello* distinction, firmly placing the right to resist in the former category, allowing international human rights law, international humanitarian law, and international criminal law to separately regulate the latter category, including 'terrorist' acts.[263] Yet others maintain that the 'terrorism' conceptual framework has both *jus ad bellum* and *jus in bello* components that operate in conditions short of armed conflict, with implications for whether and how they view the right to resist as an exception.[264]

In this context, the UN Sixth Committee Ad Hoc Committee/Working Group process to agree a Comprehensive Convention on International Terrorism, despite significant progress on numerous issues, remains effectively stalled after more than two decades.[265] One of the main barriers to agreement

[261] *Decision on the Applicable Law: Terrorism, Conspiracy, Homicide, Perpetration, Cumulative Charging* (Interlocutory Decision) STL-11-01/I/AC/R17bis Appeals Chamber (16 February 2011) [83]–[85], [102], [110]–[111]. On the questionable legal basis of this decision given the incomplete 'process of formulating an internationally applicable definition' and persisting disagreement over its status and elements as an 'international crime', despite 'proscription of terrorism' as a 'settled norm' of international law, see Nidal Nabil Jurdi, 'The Crime of Terrorism in Lebanese and International Law' in Amal Alamuddin, Nidal Nabil Jurdi, and David Tolbert (eds), *The Special Tribunal for Lebanon: Law and Practice* (Oxford University Press 2014) 82, 86.

[262] *Decision on the Applicable Law: Terrorism, Conspiracy, Homicide, Perpetration, Cumulative Charging* (n 261) [emphasis added].

[263] See for example, Bassiouni (n 81) xi–xxii.

[264] Compare the differing approaches in Saul (n 10) 59–66, 70–71, 74–75, 81–84, 94–95, 105–120, 128; Saul (n 260); Frédéric Mégret, '*Jus in Bello* as *Jus ad Bellum*' (2006) *Proceedings of the American Society of International Law* 121; Mégret (n 248); Mégret (n 136) 172; Finlay (n 146) 3–8, 87–124, 247–285.

[265] See 'Measures to Eliminate International Terrorism' UNGA Res 51/210 (17 December 1996); 'Measures to Eliminate International Terrorism' UNGA Res 71/151 (20 December 2016). Despite annual resolutions renewing intent, agreement on a comprehensive convention and

has been negotiators' continued use of an over-inclusive definition whose exceptions do not fully account for the right to resist,[266] and failure to develop a satisfactory alternative in light of a persistent refusal by many states to equate exercise of the right to resist with 'terrorism'.[267] This would seem to indicate that acknowledgment of a customary right to resist is something that the customary international law of terrorism must grapple with before it can finally settle.

Arguably 'terrorism' as a legal concept is unhelpful at best, more often abused by conflation and inconsistency than applied with precision, despite concerted scholarly and diplomatic efforts over many decades. Indeed, its separate codification could prove problematic in the absence of an equivalent codified provision for the right to resist, potentially narrowing the interpretive space. Nevertheless, some insist that the right to resist concept and 'anti-terrorist' measures are not necessarily mutually exclusive, and even potentially complementary, although this requires distinguishing between their respective legal regimes.[268] This harmonization idea has potential implications for responsible UN agencies such as the UN Office on Drugs and Crime, which should be taking account of the legal concept of the human right to resist, inter alia, when interpreting its 'terrorism-prevention' mandate and applying the relevant legal instruments and UN Security Council resolutions. Indeed, the drug control and human rights 'parallel universes', as described by Lines, provide a useful comparison in this regard, as does his proposed dynamic interpretation solution.[269] Further examination of this particular aspect would be appropriate but is beyond the scope of this study.

'generic' definition remain outstanding at time of writing. See the account in Ben Saul, 'Attempts to Define "Terrorism" in International Law' (2005) LII *Netherlands International Law Review* 57, 76–83.

[266] See the working definition in UN General Assembly, 'Report of the Ad Hoc Committee established by General Assembly resolution 51/210 of 17 December 1996, Sixth Session (28 January–1 February 2002)' UN Doc A/57/37 annex II article 2.1, annex IV article 18. Draft article 14 proposes to exclude these offences from the political offence exception to extradition. See Saul (n 265) 77–83.

[267] The main disagreement concerns the scope of the exceptions. Saul (n 10) 69–70. See the account of early UN debates in ibid 71–74; Saul (n 260) 69. Specialist scholars have also long avoided such equation. See Bassiouni' (n 81) xi–xxii.

[268] See for example Bassiouni (n 81) xi–xxii; Georg Gesk, 'Right to Resistance and Terrorism – The Example of Germany' (2012) 13 *German Law Journal* 1075, 1076–1077, 1094. See also, generally, Mégret (n 136). Compatibility is also the implication of Saul's proposed alternative to the 'right' as such in Saul (n 10) 70–71, 75, 116–120, 128; Saul (n 260).

[269] See Richard Lines, *Drug Control and Human Rights in International Law* (Cambridge University Press 2017) 1–15, 126–172.

6.7 CONCLUSION

As the preceding evidence shows, determining the status of the right to resist in general or customary international law is not straightforward. However, given that such norms 'do not . . . ever have textual determinacy, nor necessarily a coherent and consistent content' unless also 'codified or embedded in authoritative decisions',[270] this is a problem common to the source category rather than exclusive to the particular concept.

Yet reasonable theories regarding implied rights to resist deriving from three separate formal declarations of general principles of international law are offset by decades-long patterns of state practice and *opinio juris* that are inconsistent, at least as to the concept's content and application, and an apparent disjuncture between the evidence of *opinio juris* and that of practice by particular states – that is, between what they say and what they do. While establishment of custom does not require uniformity,[271] these features appear at first to undermine the right's potential status as 'settled' customary international law. However, such inconsistency and disjuncture are also not uncommon even where customary norms are considered not only settled but *jus cogens*.[272]

The question regarding the current status of the human right to resist in general or customary international law raises three possibilities. The first is that, in this contemporary United Nations period, the norm continues in its uneven stop–start development that is a normal part of the 'struggle for law' that constitutes the gradual emergence and refinement of custom,[273] during which there exists a formation 'continuum' or 'sliding scale of normativity' between general practice and *opinio juris*, exhibiting high *opinio juris*–low practice, or vice versa.[274] The second – least persuasive – possibility is that the norm, previously established, has gradually fallen into obsolescence and therefore desuetude in the early twenty-first century, consistent with the incremental reduction of clear-cut cases within a narrow band of settled recognition.[275] The third possibility is that its position as a customary norm is actually more secure than it first appears, despite its partially unsettled

[270] Bederman (n 6) 164.

[271] Ibid 147.

[272] Ibid 149.

[273] See ibid 145, 165. See in particular Bederman's dynamic process theory of customary norm formation involving competing ideas. Ibid 150–151.

[274] Ibid 145.

[275] For example, as argued by scholars who acknowledge recognition of the right but make claims that only particular past cases of resistance – against Second World War aggression; colonialism; the South African apartheid regime – qualify.

nature, as a consequence of the lack of its replacement by 'contrary consistent state practice and *opinio juris*'.[276] This is in part because customary norm termination may require higher levels of 'uniformity, consistency, and volume of state practice' than for norm creation, and must amount to clear evidence of new practice patterns and of rejection of the previous norm as law.[277] While a more forensic analysis of the evidence of all state and international organization practice and *opinio juris* might yield a firmer conclusion, such is beyond the scope of this present study.

The above militates against a decisive conclusion on whether non-prohibition implies recognition of a pre-existing customary right to resist, in the absence of formal findings by way of judicial interpretation by international courts or tribunals. However, competing theories that the right to resist is either beyond subject matter jurisdiction, or *non liquet* because international law cannot take any position on it, have likely been superseded by subsequent legal developments such as the series of UN clarifications of agreed principles of international law discussed above. Likewise, while the theory that only the internal aspect of the right to resist is *non liquet* has superficial merit attributable to ongoing legal uncertainty, so does the opposite theory that the internal aspect is not *non liquet* but rather consistently implied across numerous sources and therefore capable of evolutive interpretation and progressive development. Again, which perspective is actually correct may be impossible to determine in the absence of judicial findings, other formal outcomes, or greater consistency in state practice and *opinio juris*. Nevertheless, while the law may not be entirely settled on international recognition of a right to resist for internal self-determination or other human rights enforcement, the evidence does suggest sufficient scope to extend this through interpretive means including analogy, without the need for legal fiction.

Therefore, even with these qualifications, it is not unreasonable to conclude that under certain conditions there is a limited right to resist recognized as a general principle of international law, grounded in the obligation of respect for human rights including, but not necessarily limited to, the right to self-determination. Furthermore, as Charter law, it is potentially amenable to evolutive interpretation and subject to further progressive development as needed. From this principle of international law arises the associated international 'conduct rule' of exception to the general law of intervention and the

[276] This is distinct from 'general acquiescence' or 'consent through silence'. See Bederman (n 6) 153–155, 160.

[277] Ibid 160–161.

use of force, which includes a third-party obligation on the United Nations and its Member States to either assist within the limits of international law, or otherwise not obstruct that resistance, in cases where a valid right to resist is a factor. The latter amounts to a further ground for prohibition on providing assistance to a rights-abusing requesting state. The former potentially amounts to a further ground for activating UN-authorized assistance supplementing the 'responsibility to protect'.

If states appear to recognize the human right to resist as a general idea, there remains considerable disagreement about its contemporary application to particular circumstances. The lack of express general international law provision in the manner originally suggested by Humphrey and Cassin facilitates self-contradiction by states and enlarges the scope for abuse as an express or implied justification for unlawful intervention. Arguably, codification of this right within the UN human rights system would have potential clarification and increased certainty benefits at both the international level and at the level of individual cases in domestic legal systems. Yet as shown in the next chapter, twenty-first-century attempts to resurrect the project of express provision at the UN level through international legal codification proved equally unsuccessful, while express provision at the regional level remains limited and uneven. All of this has bearings on the practical – as opposed to theoretical – enforceability of the human right to resist and hence its value at international level.

7

Provision in Treaty Law and Other International Codification

7.1 INTRODUCTION

It is not hard to understand the lack of focus by contemporary international legal scholarship on the human right to resist. Its international codification is weak compared to its domestic codification. Its recognition and protection in international human rights treaties is considerably thinner than that afforded many other fundamental rights. That is, only two human rights treaties include express provisions. These have yet to be litigated. Its recognition is 'fragmented' in the regional human rights systems, reflecting a divide in perspective on the concept. It is at best 'submerged' in the universal human rights system. The most recent codification efforts at the UN ultimately did not succeed. Thus the overall status of the right in conventional law generally suggests marginality.

Yet the context for this is an absence of effort specifically devoted to clarifying and enhancing the legal status of the human right to resist in international law through codification. Twice previously it has been under active consideration for 'soft law' codification, often an important first step in the process of international norm development.[1] However, on both occasions it has constituted only one proposal among many, and its survival or demise has therefore depended on an overall package. Negotiators either conceded more ambiguous language or bargained it away as a line item, in order to salvage the whole. This suggests that even if prospects of success are limited, it

[1] See Alan Boyle, 'Soft Law in International Law Making' in Malcolm D Evans (ed), *International Law* (3rd edn, Oxford University Press 2010); Dinah Shelton, 'International Law and "Relative Normativity"' in ibid 141, 164–166.

cannot be ruled out that a more concerted approach could potentially improve outcomes in future codification efforts.

Alternatively, with sufficient will to do so – and as with general or customary international law discussed in the previous chapter – there may be enough interpretive room to enhance recognition of the human right to resist using the law as it stands. A reconsideration of the right's status in treaty law reveals a possible interpretive method relying on the 'principle of integration'.[2] This involves reference to disclaimer and non-diminution clauses in the human rights treaties to buttress absent or ambiguous provision in treaty law with somewhat firmer albeit limited recognition in customary international law.[3]

This chapter considers the hypothesized, actual, and proposed provisions for the human right to resist in international treaty law and in 'soft law' declarations as another form of international codification, and applies the Chapter 4 analytical framework. Section 7.2 assesses theories of implied recognition in the 'universal' human rights system, including corroborative sources of indirect provision related to complementary or subsidiary rights. Section 7.3 analyzes its status in the regional human rights systems – where express provision is present in the African and the Arab systems and absent from the European and Inter-American systems. Section 7.4 reviews the most recent failed codification, its proposed inclusion in but ultimate exclusion from the UN Declaration on the Human Right to Peace adopted in 2016. The conclusion at Section 7.5 assesses the implications of the legal fissures between systems, evaluates prospects for firmer recognition through dynamic interpretation, and briefly identifies factors that could improve chances of success in future codification efforts.

[2] See Ian Brownlie, *Principles of Public International Law* (7th edn, Oxford University Press 2008) 631–637. This requires interpretation of provisions in the context of the treaty as a whole, and 'in light of its object and purpose', pursuant to the general rule of interpretation at article 31(1) and (2) of the Vienna Convention on the Law of Treaties (adopted 22 May 1969, entered into force 27 January 1980) 1155 UNTS 331.

[3] The general rule of interpretation also requires taking account of 'any relevant rules of international law applicable in the relations between the parties' external to the treaty, including general principles or rules of customary international law. See Vienna Convention on the Law of Treaties (n 2) article 31(3)(c). On the consequent doctrine of 'dynamic' or 'evolutive' interpretation or construction of concepts in light of current conditions, applied most often in human rights treaties via non-diminution clauses, see Richard Gardiner, *Treaty Interpretation* (Oxford University Press 2008) 243, 251–252, 254, 256. See also International Law Commission, 'Conclusions of the Work of the Study Group on the Fragmentation of International Law: Difficulties Arising from the Diversification and Expansion of International Law' (2006) [2006] *Yearbook of the International Law Commission* vol II, pt 2 [17]–[23]. On the extent of recognition of the right to resist in customary international law, see Chapter 6. On the possibility that it constitutes a general principle of law, see Chapter 3, Section 3.3.2 and Chapter 6, Sections 6.2.1, 6.2.3, 6.3, 6.4, and 6.5.

7.2 SUBMERSION IN THE UNIVERSAL HUMAN RIGHTS SYSTEM

The apparent ambiguities of the Universal Declaration of Human Rights and UN General Assembly Resolution 2625 discussed in Chapter 6 are not immediately clarified by the human rights treaties of the universal system, where there is still no express provision guaranteeing the right to resist. Nevertheless, some suggest that its recognition is implied in several multilateral treaties: the International Covenant on Civil and Political Rights as the source of an unenumerated right; the Refugee Convention as providing a corroborative subsidiary individual right of protection from refoulement; and the Rome Statute of the International Criminal Court as a source corroborating a narrower, specific form of the customary right-duty to resist internationally criminal acts.

7.2.1 *International Covenant on Civil and Political Rights: The Theory of Articles 1, 25, and 2(3)(a)*

An express provision for the right to resist does not appear in the International Covenant on Civil and Political Rights. Yet some highly credible scholars maintain that, in part as a consequence of constructive ambiguity, an unenumerated right to resist is latent in that treaty.[4]

[4] See Manfred Nowak, *UN Covenant on Civil and Political Rights – CCPR Commentary* (NP Engel 1993) 23 [34] and Manfred Nowak, *UN Covenant on Civil and Political Rights – CCPR Commentary* (2nd edn, NP Engel 2005) 24 [34]; Allan Rosas, 'Article 21' in Gudmundur Alfredsson and Asbjörn Eide (eds), *The Universal Declaration of Human Rights: A Common Standard of Achievement* (Martinus Nijhoff 1999) 432, 441–442, 449, 451; Allan Rosas, 'Internal Self-Determination' in Christian Tomuschat (ed), *Modern Law of Self-Determination* (Martinus Nijhoff 1993) 242–244, 249; Bruno Simma, Hermann Mosler, Albrecht Randelzhofer, Christian Tomuschat, Rüdiger Wolfrum, Andreas Paulus, and Eleni Chaitidou (eds), *The Charter of the United Nations: A Commentary* (2nd edn, Oxford University Press 2002) B [15] 52, C [40] 58. See also Jordan J Paust, 'Political Oppression in the Name of National Security: Authority, Participation, and the Necessity within Democratic Limits Test' (1982) 9(1) *Yale International Law Journal* 178, 181–191; Matthew Lippman, 'The Right of Civil Resistance under International Law and the Domestic Necessity Defense' (1990) 8 *Dickinson Journal of International Law* 349, 358–359; Jordan J Paust, 'International Law, Dignity, Democracy and the Arab Spring' (2013) 46 *Cornell International Law Journal* 1, 4–6, 11 (fn 48), 15 (fn 62); and the suggestion in Asbjörn Eide, 'The Right to Oppose Violations of Human Rights: Basis, Conditions and Limitations' in *Violations of Human Rights: Possible Rights of Recourse and Forms of Resistance* (UNESCO 1984) 41–42, 44; Richard Falk and Burns H Weston, 'The Relevance of International Law to Palestinian Rights in the West Bank and Gaza: In Legal Defense of the Intifada' (1991) 32(1) *Harvard International Law Journal* 129, 156–157.

According to such theories, the International Covenant right to resist derives primarily from the human right to political and economic self-determination, guaranteed to the whole people of a state, affirmed in article 1 common to the International Covenant on Civil and Political Rights and International Covenant on Economic, Social and Cultural Rights.[5] If so, this would be consistent with the UN Charter-implied right to resist for enforcement of the right to self-determination, a right at least partly exercisable through resort to force under limited conditions in customary international law.[6] While the internal dimension of this right to self-determination is not adequately addressed in UN General Assembly Resolution 2625,[7] the International Covenant on Civil and Political Rights includes, in addition to the article 1 affirmation, a substantive internal self-determination right in the form of the article 25 individual right to political participation.[8] Article 25 of the International Covenant is in turn consistent with, and expands upon, the internal self-determination 'will of the people' provision at article 21 of the Universal Declaration of Human Rights.[9] If a right to resist for enforcement of self-determination is implied under article 1 of the International Covenant it would also thereby extend to the right to internal self-determination exercised

5 See International Covenant on Civil and Political Rights (adopted 16 December 1966, entered into force 23 March 1976) UNGA Res 2200A (XXI) UN Doc A/6316 (1966) article 1; International Covenant on Economic, Social and Cultural Rights (adopted 16 December 1966 entered into force 3 January 1976) UNGA Res 2200A (XXI) UN Doc A/6316 (1966) article 1.

6 See Simma et al (n 4) B [15] 52, B [19] 53, B [20] 53, C [40] 58; see also discussion in Chapter 6, Sections 6.2.3, 6.3, and 6.5. Affirming the interrelationship between the UN Charter right and article 1, see UN Human Rights Committee, 'General Comment 12 – Article 1: The Right to Self-Determination of Peoples' (1984) UN Doc A/39/40 [1]–[2].

7 See discussion in Chapter 6, Section 6.3.

8 See International Covenant on Civil and Political Rights (n 5) article 25. Affirming the interrelationship between article 25 and article 1, and affirming article 25 as an important reinforcement of the 'internal' aspect of the right to self-determination in article 1, which 'lies at the core of democratic government based on the consent of the will of the people', see UN Human Rights Committee, 'General Comment 12' (n 6) [4]; UN Human Rights Committee, 'General Comment 25 – Article 25: The Right to Participate in Public Affairs, Voting Rights and the Right of Equal Access to Public Service' (1996) UN Doc A/51/40 vol 1, 98 [1]–[2].

9 See also corresponding discussion on article 21 of the Universal Declaration in Chapter 6, Section 6.4, in particular Section 6.4.3. On article 21 of the Universal Declaration having informed the drafting of Covenant article 25 see Marc J Bossuyt, *Guide to the 'Travaux Préparatoires' of the International Covenant on Civil and Political Rights* (Martinus Nijhoff 1987) 469. On the theory of a linkage between articles 1 and 25 and Universal Declaration article 21 as customary law establishing a right to democratic governance, violations of which give rise to an implied right of resistance when read together with the Universal Declaration preamble, see Rosas, 'Article 21' (n 4) 432, 441–442, 449, 451; Rosas, 'Internal Self-Determination' (n 4) 239, 241–249.

by virtue of article 25. The general premise of these theories is that the ability to enforce the article 1 right to political and economic self-determination matters because it is 'essential for the enjoyment of all other rights' and is one 'on which all other rights depend'.[10] As Nowak puts it, the internal dimension of article 1 'contains the seeds of a right of revolution against dictatorships that systematically and grossly violate human rights'.[11]

In this context, an even broader right to resist may be further implied by the International Covenant's provision for the right to an effective remedy for human rights violations at article 2(3)(a), since this is not limited to legal, judicial, or administrative remedies and therefore does not rule out self-help.[12] However, article 2(3)(a) is 'not a free-standing right' but rather a 'supporting guarantee', and breach can only be found 'in conjunction with' another 'substantive right'.[13] Yet combined with the lack of an express prohibition on resistance in the treaty itself or in general or customary international law,[14] and a UN Charter right that may include a customary right to resist human rights violations implied in the Universal Declaration of Human Rights, the open formulation of article 2(3)(a) reinforces the possibility that the aforementioned provisions taken together could indicate an unenumerated right to resist as an implied secondary enforcement right and effective remedy for human rights violations, deriving from the three documents that constitute the 'International Bill of Human Rights'.[15] Thus the theory of an unenumerated Covenant right to resist really balances on article 2(3)(a), and the idea that denial of effective legal remedy should trigger permissibility of self-help

[10] Affirming the interrelationship between article 1 and other International Covenant rights, see UN Human Rights Committee, 'General Comment 12' (n 6) [1]–[2]. See also Bossuyt (n 9) 25; Daniel Thürer and Thomas Burri, 'Self-Determination' in *Max Planck Encyclopedia of Public International Law* (Oxford Public International Law online database 2008) B.2 [10]. In other words, if the right to resist is considered the 'ultimate' human right, then the right to self-determination is the 'penultimate' one.

[11] Nowak (2nd edn) (n 4) 24 [34].

[12] See International Covenant on Civil and Political Rights (n 5) article 2(3)(a); UN Human Rights Committee, 'General Comment 3 – Implementation at the National Level: Article 2' (1981) UN Doc 29/07 replaced by 'General Comment 31 [80]: The Nature of the General Legal Obligation Imposed on States Parties to the Covenant' (2004) UN Doc CCPR/C/21/Rev.1/Add.13. Neither the content of 'effective remedy' nor the issue of extralegal remedies were discussed in the drafting debates. See Bossuyt (n 9) 64–67.

[13] See Sarah Joseph and Melissa Castan, *The International Covenant on Civil and Political Rights: Cases, Materials and Commentary* (3rd edn, Oxford University Press 2013) 869–870 [25.07]–[25.08], 872 [25.13], 882 [25.30].

[14] See discussion in Chapter 6, Section 6.2.

[15] These being the Universal Declaration of Human Rights, the International Covenant on Civil and Political Rights, and the International Covenant on Economic, Social and Cultural Rights.

extrajudicial remedies for the denial of the right to internal self-determination, or other human rights violations, as an exception.

None of the theorists who have suggested this hypothesized unenumerated International Covenant right have fully elaborated its elements or described how it might work. Application of the Chapter 4 analytical framework could assist clarification in this regard.

7.2.1.1 Elements of the Theorized Unenumerated International Covenant Right to Resist

For the purpose of a claim based at least in part on article 1, the rights-holders would be the whole 'people' or 'peoples' of a state, or a whole 'people' within that state experiencing violation of its internal right to self-determination,[16] where that state is party to the Covenant. For a claim based on article 25, article 2(3)(a), and any other Covenant article in conjunction with these, the rights-holders could also be individuals and groups.

It remains to be clarified exactly what type of violations would constitute a primary trigger,[17] though presumably virtually no single-instance violations would qualify unless exceptionally egregious. The primary triggers would otherwise consist of a pattern of violations related to the substantive Covenant guarantees: particularly internal self-determination pursuant to articles 1 and 25,[18] but also potentially violations of other civil and political rights where the secondary trigger condition is met.

The secondary trigger in all cases is the same: denial of the article 2(3)(a) right to an effective remedy for the primary trigger violations, by judicial or other legal means.[19] Whether other means of effective remedy must be

[16] Simma et al (n 4) B [21] 53–54.

[17] Nowak (n 4) sets the trigger for the Covenant 'right of revolution' at 'systematic' and 'gross' violations. Simma et al (n 4) suggest a trigger of 'brutal oppression' for the Covenant 'right to resist', presumably involving use of force against the population.

[18] On internal self-determination as essentially a 'right of meaningful political participation' that is an entitlement of all 'peoples' of a state, even if they are not entitled to external self-determination, see Simma et al (n 4) [7.13], [7.15]–[718] 160–161.

[19] On 'remedies' involving a 'range of measures' responding to 'an actual or threatened violation of human rights', including both 'remedial institutions and procedures' and 'substantive redress' that is 'capable of redressing the harm', whose purpose may be 'compensatory', 'condemnatory', 'deterrent', or 'restorative'; and on the 'effective remedy' standard being 'timely, adequate and effective' and, in the case of the International Covenant right specifically, potentially 'non-judicial', see Dinah Shelton, *Remedies in International Human Rights Law* (2nd edn, Oxford University Press 2005) 8–16, 114. See also UN Human Rights Committee, 'General Comment 31' (n 12) [15]–[17], [20].

demonstrably 'exhausted' or just not 'reasonably available' to trigger the exception also remains to be determined.

Where primary and secondary triggers are present, permissible means are unspecified but presumably additional to those allowable under ordinary political rights guarantees at articles 19 and 21 with their applicable lawful limitations. Therefore, permissible means are 'otherwise unlawful' and inclusive of peaceful or forceful means, though subject to relevant proportionality restrictions.[20]

The object and purpose of any claim to an International Covenant right to resist would have to be consistent with Covenant-guaranteed human rights generally. The purpose of article 1 claims would be either enforcement of external self-determination as also recognized elsewhere in customary international law or enforcement of internal self-determination and made in conjunction with enforcement of article 25 political rights – though presumably article 25 enforcement claims could also be made independently of article 1. The purpose of article 2(3)(a) claims would be enforcement of the secondary right to an effective remedy for violations of other specific Covenant-guaranteed primary rights.

Finally, the duty-bearers would be the States Parties to the treaty, whose principal correlated duties are not only to respect these Covenant rights in the first instance, but also to provide effective judicial and other legal remedies for violations so as to not to trigger the right to resist exception, rendering the right's exercise unnecessary. As Paust argues,[21] the right to resist as a principle of general international law provides additional guidance for evaluation of a state's application of the ordinary limitations clauses and compliance with article 4 on derogations under emergency conditions which, inter alia, must not be 'inconsistent with other obligations under international law'.[22] This would include the obligation to 'assist or not obstruct' valid claimants to an international right to resist as recognized in customary international law.[23]

[20] See discussions of 'proportionality' in Chapter 4, Section 4.7.2 and Chapter 6, Section 6.3.1.5.

[21] See Paust, 'Political Oppression' (n 4) 181–191; Paust, 'International Law, Dignity, Democracy' (n 4) 11 (fn 48).

[22] See International Covenant on Civil and Political Rights (n 5) article 4(1); American Association for the International Commission of Jurists, 'Siracusa Principles on the Limitation and Derogation Provisions in the International Covenant on Civil and Political Rights' (1985); UN Human Rights Committee, 'General Comment 29 – States of Emergency (Article 4)' (2001) UN Doc CCPR/C/21/Rev.1/Add.11 replacing 'General Comment 5 – Article 4 (Derogations)' (1981) UN Doc CCPR/GEC/4717/E.

[23] See Chapter 6, Section 6.3.1.6.

7.2.1.2 Considerations Relevant to Interpretation

Since no right to resist claims relying on the International Covenant have been tested at the UN Human Rights Committee or International Court of Justice to date,[24] whether these theories would withstand scrutiny remains debatable. For example, the International Covenant's *travaux préparatoires* shed no real light on this issue.[25] They provide only evidence of non-discussion and non-inclusion of the right to resist,[26] although as such they also appear to leave the possibility open. None of the UN Human Rights Committee General Comments on the relevant provisions address this question.[27] The Committee's case law to date suggests that recognition of such an unenumerated right could face considerable obstacles, given that it has often taken a restrictive view of even the ordinary 'right to protest' implied in the Covenant's protection of *lex generalis* political rights under articles 19 and 21,[28] treating even peaceful methods unfavourably where these are 'otherwise unlawful' or obstruct the rights of others to ostensibly lawful conduct.[29]

24 Nor has the International Court of Justice been asked to render an advisory opinion relating to this question.

25 Pursuant to Vienna Convention on the Law of Treaties (n 2) article 32, preparatory works are not determinative but may however be used as 'supplementary means of interpretation' where the application of the article 31 general rule 'leaves the meaning ambiguous or obscure' or 'leads to a result which is manifestly absurd or unreasonable'.

26 Proposals for an express right to resist in the Universal Declaration, discussed in Chapter 6, Section 6.4.1, were not resurrected during the International Covenant drafting process. The only response to concerns that article 1 could be 'wrongly' used by minority groups to claim a 'right of secession' was a pragmatic decision not to further specify its content, scope, or beneficiaries. See Bossuyt (n 9) 24 [32], 35.

27 See UN Human Rights Committee, 'General Comment 3' (n 12); UN Human Rights Committee, 'General Comment 31' (n 12); UN Human Rights Committee, 'General Comment 12' (n 6); UN Human Rights Committee, 'General Comment 25' (n 8).

28 For the *lex generalis* provisions and their limitations clauses see International Covenant on Civil and Political Rights (n 5) articles 19, 21. For the interpretation of the interrelationship between these clauses and the ordinary 'right to protest' see John P Humphrey, 'Political and Related Rights' in Theodor Meron (ed), *Human Rights in International Law: Legal and Policy Issues* (1984) vol I, 188 cited and concurred with in Comm 412/1990 *Kivenmaa* v *Finland* (10 June 1994) UN Doc C/50/D/412 [6.2], [9.3], Dissenting Opinion of Kurt Herndl [3.1]–[3.5]; Nowak (n 4) 477, 485–487; UN Human Rights Committee, 'General Comment 34 – Article 19: Freedoms of Opinion and Expression' (2011) UN Doc CCPR/C/GC/34 [4], [20], [28], [30], [37], [38], [46]; Comm 1790/2008 *Govsha, Syritsa and Mezyak* v *Belarus* (27 July 2012) UN Doc CCPR/C/105/D/1790/2008 [9.4]; UN High Commissioner for Human Rights, 'Report on Effective Measures and Best Practices to Ensure the Protection and Promotion of Human Rights in the Context of Peaceful Protests' UN Doc A/HRC/22/28 (21 January 2013) [4], [6].

29 See Comm 347/1988 *SG* v *France* (1 November 1991) UN Doc C/43/D/347/1988; Comm 384/1989 *GB* v *France* (1 November 1991) UN Doc C/43/D/348/1989 [5.2]; Comm 628/1995

However, that approach may be changing in light of the new dedicated General Comment 37 providing a more expansive and protective interpretation.[30] That said, even robust recognition of the ordinary right to protest is not sufficient in itself, and is only indirectly helpful since that right is not interchangeable with the right to resist.[31] In addition, there is the matter of states' potentially competing obligations under the Covenant. In particular, where exercise of the right to resist may threaten the right to life of others, state obligations to protect the right to life under article 6(1) may extend to preventative and punitive measures against that resistance. In any rights-balancing exercise by a state, it is admittedly difficult to imagine an unenumerated right to resist prevailing over its article 6(1) rights and obligations.

These are among the reasons why, in order to succeed, the theory of an unenumerated *lex specialis* International Covenant right to resist demands a muscular approach to evolutive or dynamic interpretation of the relevant provisions in conjunction with recognitions elsewhere in customary international law. Failing this, it is unlikely that such claims would even be considered admissible.

Crucial for dynamic interpretation of, but also as a source of applicable limitations on, the hypothesized unenumerated exceptional right are the Covenant's article 5 disclaimer and non-diminution clauses. Article 5(1) cautions that none of the Covenant's provisions 'may be interpreted as implying for any State, group or person any right to engage in any activity or perform any act aimed at the destruction of any of the rights and freedoms recognized herein or at their limitation to a greater extent than is provided for' therein.[32] Any claimed right to resist relying on the Covenant would need to comply with this requirement. However, insofar as it prohibits any acts whose object and purpose is not merely inconsistent with, but actually 'aimed at the destruction' or otherwise excessive limitation of Covenant rights, the article 5(1) restriction is narrower than it first appears.[33] Indeed, it is article 5(2) that

Tae Hoon Park v *Republic of Korea* (3 November 1998) UN Doc C/64/D/628/1995 [2.4], [9.3], [10.3]; Nowak (n 4) 439, 445, 487–488, 494; UN High Commissioner for Human Rights, 'Report on Effective Measures and Best Practices' (n 28) [10], however compare [12]. On the general scarcity and weakness of relevant Committee jurisprudence, see Joseph and Castan (n 13) 664–665 [19.36]–[19.37].

30 UN Human Rights Committee, 'General Comment 37 – On the Right of Peaceful Assembly (article 21)' (2020) UN Doc CCPR/C/G/37.

31 See discussion of the right to resist as a *lex specialis* exception to the *lex generalis* limitations on the ordinary 'right to protest' in Chapter 2, Section 2.6.1 and Chapter 3, Section 3.4.5.

32 International Covenant on Civil and Political Rights (n 5) article 5(1) [emphasis added].

33 The debate on article 5(1) focused on prevention of totalitarianism not rebellion prevention. See Bossuyt (n 9) 105.

is the fulcrum for dynamic interpretation purposes. It warns against 'restriction upon or derogation from any of the fundamental human rights recognized or existing in any State Party to the present Covenant pursuant to law, conventions, regulations or custom on the pretext that the present Covenant does not recognize such rights or that it recognizes them to a lesser extent'.[34] This opens the way for arguments that the Covenant cannot be used for 'restriction or derogation' related to the right to resist to the extent that it is 'recognized or existing' in the constitutional law of a State Party,[35] or otherwise in general or customary international law applying to all States Parties.[36]

In that context, it is worth noting the UN Human Rights Committee position that it can generally only interpret article 1 in relation to violations of other Covenant rights such as article 25, and cannot make direct or exclusive article 1 determinations.[37] In such cases, it refers to the relevant interpretive instruments, 'in particular' UN General Assembly Resolution 2625 discussed in Chapter 6, meaning that article 1 'accords with the international legal meaning' of the right.[38] This would suggest two things. First, the merits of such claims cannot be interpreted in a way that ignores the UN Charter right to resist for enforcement of the right to self-determination. Second, the UN Declaration on the Rights of Indigenous Peoples, another interpretive instrument elaborating aspects of the right to self-determination, could also be relevant to interpretation of the elements of an implied unenumerated right in certain cases.[39]

34 International Covenant on Civil and Political Rights (n 5) article 5(2) [emphasis added].

35 See Chapter 5, Section 5.5.

36 See Chapter 6, Sections 6.2.1, 6.2.3, 6.3, 6.4, and 6.5.

37 See Comm 167/1984 *Ominayak* v *Canada* (26 March 1990) ICCPR A/45/40 vol 2 [32.1]; Comm 760/97 *Diergaardt et al* v *Namibia* (25 July 2000) ICCPR A/55/40 vol 2 [10.3]; Comm 932/2000 *Gillot* v *France* (15 July 2002) ICCPR A/57/40 vol 2 270 (CCPR/c/75/D/932/2000) [13.4]. On the consequent lack of effective remedy for article 1 violations provided for under the Covenant itself, despite the general guarantee under article 2(3)(a), see Antonio Cassese, *Self-Determination of Peoples: A Legal Reappraisal* (Cambridge University Press 1995) 142–143. On this and other shortcomings of the Committee jurisprudence, see Joseph and Castan (n 13) 154 [7.03], 164–165 [7.24]–[7.26].

38 See UN Human Rights Committee, 'General Comment 12' (n 6) [7]; Joseph and Castan (n 13) 154 [7.05].

39 See the United Nations Declaration on the Rights of Indigenous Peoples, UNGA Res 61/295 (13 September 2007), most clauses of which are relevant to the human right to self-determination, in one way or another. This document, while not legally binding in and of itself, is nevertheless legally significant insofar as it represents the largely agreed interpretation of the application of UN human rights treaties to indigenous peoples, and is as such 'heavily grounded' in established international human rights law. Sylvanus Gbendazhi Barnabas, 'The Legal Status of the United Nations Declaration on the Rights of Indigenous Peoples (2007) in

In addition, the UN Human Rights Committee's General Comment 37 on the *lex generalis* right to protest not only represents a significant interpretive advance regarding the scope of article 21 of the Covenant, it may also in turn help clarify the triggering and other elements of its unenumerated *lex specialis* right to resist, because exercise of the ordinary right will generally precede triggering and exercise of the exceptional right. For example, General Comment 37 clarifies what constitutes 'peaceful' and therefore protected action,[40] affirming that the range of actions that should be protected by the *lex generalis* extends to peaceful actions that cause disruption, including economic disruption[41] and acts of 'civil disobedience'.[42] Therefore, preventing the use of such means, thus rendering them unavailable, may in some instances act as either a primary violation trigger or a secondary necessity trigger for the right to resist. It also extensively clarifies what constitutes lawful and unlawful restrictions or violations of article 21 rights, by way of limitation and derogation,[43] providing further indications of what might constitute primary or secondary triggers. While the article 20 restrictions on propaganda for war and incitement to hatred and racist violence continue to apply, neither these nor the other limits applicable to article 19 and 21 can be lawfully used to restrict expression of 'opposition to government, challenges to authority . . . calls for democratic changes to government, the constitution or the political system, or the pursuit of self-determination'.[44] In addition, legal definitions for the purpose of criminalizing terrorism 'must not be overbroad or discriminatory' or used to curtail the right to protest peacefully.[45] Therefore, patterns of violations or unlawful restrictions rendering lawful and peaceful means unavailable can provide evidence of primary violation triggers and secondary necessity triggers. This is so whether applying the Covenant's limitation or derogation regimes and, more importantly, where its derogation regime requirements are ignored. By clarifying what constitutes 'violent' action falling outside protection of the *lex generalis*,[46] including damage to property,[47]

Contemporary International Human Rights Law' (2017) 6 *International Human Rights Law Review* 242, 252–256.

40 UN Human Rights Committee,' General Comment 37' (n 30) [15]–[20].

41 Ibid [7], [31], [47].

42 Ibid [16].

43 Ibid [36]–[69]. For a full picture of what constitutes violations, these clauses should be read together with the 'Siracusa Principles' (n 22) 5–16, 44, as well as UN Human Rights Committee, 'General Comment 29' (n 22) on the Covenant's article 4 derogation clause.

44 UN Human Rights Committee, 'General Comment 37' (n 30) [49]–[50].

45 Ibid [68].

46 Ibid 37 [15], [17]–[20].

47 Ibid [43].

it indicates the type of 'otherwise unlawful' but potentially permissible means captured by the scope of the exceptional right to resist. Finally, it affirms that, in common with the other political rights under discussion in this chapter, the ordinary right to protest is essential for advancing other human rights.[48] This would be no less true for a Covenant right to resist. All of these clarifications should be brought to bear on analysis of any particular claims regarding an unenumerated right under the Covenant. In this sense, General Comment 37 becomes a potentially important interpretive tool.

7.2.1.3 Prospects for Application

While undoubtedly challenging to make the case for an unenumerated right, it cannot be automatically ruled out. For example, the UN Human Rights Committee has not specified that what constitutes an effective remedy under article 2(3)(a) of the Covenant is limited to legal remedies.[49] Peaceful but otherwise illegal or even forceful self-help action on the part of individuals and groups for this remedial purpose is not expressly prohibited. Moreover, the Committee has been careful to point out that Covenant prohibitions on propaganda for war 'do not prohibit advocacy of the sovereign right of self-defence or the right of peoples to self-determination and independence in accordance with the Charter of the United Nations'.[50] It has also indicated that restrictions on ordinary Covenant political rights 'may not put in jeopardy the right itself'.[51] At the same time, the Committee's more restrictive article 19 and 21 jurisprudence on the 'right to protest' has also generally avoided relevant questions related to context or availability of equally effective remedy – under conditions of 'oppression', for example – elements that relate to the primary and secondary triggers for an exceptional right to resist as *lex specialis*.[52] Such

48 Ibid [1]–[2], [4], [9], [49], [98]–[102].

49 See UN Human Rights Committee, 'General Comment 3' (n 12) [1]. Likewise, the more detailed 'replacement' 'General Comment 31' (n 12) [80] neither specifically addresses nor forecloses extrajudicial remedies.

50 UN Human Rights Committee, 'General Comment 11 – Article 20: Prohibition of Propaganda for War' (1983) UN Doc A/38/40 [2].

51 See for example UN Human Rights Committee, 'General Comment 10 – Freedom of Expression (art 19)' (1983) UN Doc A/29/06/83 [4] and its replacement 'General Comment 34' (n 28) [1], [21], both citing in particular the non-diminution obligation at article 5(1). See also the 'Siracusa Principles' (n 22) 6 IA[2]; and in general UN Human Rights Committee, 'General Comment 29' (n 22); UN Human Rights Committee, 'General Comment 37' (n 30).

52 See for example Comm 386/1989 *Koné* v *Senegal* (27 October 1994) UN Doc C/52/D/386/1989 [2.1], [2.3], [3], [6.8], [7.4], [7.7], [8.5]; Comm 518/1992 *Sohn* v *Republic of Korea* (3 August 1995) UN Doc C/54/D/518/1992 [7.1]-[7.2], [8.1], [9.1], [9.3], [10.2]; Comm 1014/2001 *Baban* v *Australia* (18 September 2003) UN Doc C/78/D/1014/2001 [3.4], [4.5], [6.7].

questions therefore remain open in the interpretation of International Covenant rights.

Notwithstanding the above, it is likely that the absence of an express right to resist denotes overall ambivalence rather than either acceptance or rejection within the UN human rights system, at least at this point. In other words, if the right is there, for now it remains submerged. However, if it can be established that the human right to resist is an unenumerated *lex specialis* exception implicitly protected as a political right under the International Covenant, this opens the possibility that the right is therefore also implicitly available as an effective self-help remedy, provided all relevant conditions can be met, for the enforcement of the other human rights enshrined under the major UN human rights treaties – which also neither expressly protect nor prohibit the right to resist violations relevant to their provisions.[53] As such, the International Covenant on Civil and Political Rights as a source of treaty law on the right to resist awaits construction.

7.2.2 *Corroboration in the Refugee Convention: The Doctrine of Protected Political Activity Implied under Article 1F(b)*

Another source of corroboration of the human right to resist is the implicit doctrine of 'protected political activity', which emerges from international refugee law jurisprudence as a consequence of states adjudicating application of the exclusion clauses under article 1F of the Convention Relating to the

[53] This would include those already covered at least in part by the customary right to resist, as discussed in Chapter 6, Sections 6.2.3, 6.3, and 6.5: Slavery Convention (1926 as amended by Protocol 1953, entered into force 7 July 1955) 212 UNTS 17; Supplementary Convention on the Abolition of Slavery, the Slave Trade, and Institutions and Practices Similar to Slavery (adopted 7 September 1956, entered into force 30 April 1957) 266 UNTS 3; Convention on the Prevention and Punishment of the Crime of Genocide (adopted 9 December 1948, entered into force 12 January 1951) 78 UNTS 277; Convention on the Elimination of All Forms of Racial Discrimination (adopted 21 December 1965, entered into force 4 January 1969) 660 UNTS 195; International Convention on the Suppression and Punishment of the Crime of Apartheid (adopted 30 December 1973, entered into force 18 July 1976) 1015 UNTS 243. However, it would also include violations of those likely not otherwise covered, such as the International Covenant on Economic, Social and Cultural Rights (n 5); Convention on the Elimination of All Forms of Discrimination Against Women (adopted 18 December 1979, entered into force 3 September 1981) UNGA Res 34/180, UN Doc A/34/46; Convention Against Torture and Other Cruel, Inhuman or Degrading Treatment or Punishment (adopted 10 December 1984, entered into force 26 June 1987) 23 ILM 1027; Convention on the Rights of the Child (adopted 20 November 1989, entered into force 2 September 1990) 1577 UNTS 3; International Convention on the Protection and Promotion of the Rights and Dignity of Persons with Disabilities (adopted 13 December 2006, entered into force 3 May 2008) UNGA Res 61/106 Annex 1, UN Doc A/RES/61/106 (2006).

Status of Refugees.[54] It derives primarily from the process of defining 'political' against 'non-political' crimes when assessing cases proposed for exclusion from refugee protection under article 1F(b) of the Refugee Convention.[55] Kälin and Künzli connect this doctrine to the right of resistance in customary international law.[56]

Convention refugee claim determinations are decentralized to states, and there are no universally obligatory definitions of either 'serious non-political crimes' for the purpose of exclusion or the inverse: 'political crimes' for the purpose of inclusion.[57] Exclusion law has therefore often borrowed and adapted the customary 'political offence exception' from extradition law.[58] This uses certain concepts, principles, and tests to establish what is 'political'

[54] Convention Relating to the Status of Refugees (adopted 28 July 1951, entered into force 22 April 1954) 189 UNTS 137 article 1F; Protocol Relating to the Status of Refugees (adopted 31 January 1967, entered into force 4 October 1967) 606 UNTS 267. All references to 'the Refugee Convention' mean both Convention and Protocol.

[55] To prevent abuse of the international refugee regime for the purpose of avoiding legitimate prosecution, a person can be excluded from protection if he or she is found 'undeserving' of protection on the basis of his or her own actions, if they constitute a violation of international humanitarian or international criminal law under article 1F(a), an 'act contrary to the principles and purposes' of the UN under article 1F(c), or a 'serious non-political crime' under article 1F(b). See UN High Commissioner for Refugees, 'UNHCR Guidelines on International Protection No 5 – Application of the Exclusion Clauses: Article 1F of the 1951 Convention Relating to the Status of Refugees' UN Doc HRC/GIP/03/05 (4 September 2003) in *UNHCR Handbook and Guidelines on Procedures and Criteria for Determining Refugee Status under the 1951 Convention and 1967 Protocol Relating to the Status of Refugees* (3rd edn, UN High Commissioner for Refugees 2011) 116 [2].

[56] See Walter Kälin and Jorg Künzli, 'Article 1F(b): Freedom Fighters, Terrorists and the Notion of Serious Non-Political Crime' (2000) 12 supp *International Journal of Refugee Law* 46. See also DJ Steinbock, 'Interpreting the Refugee Definition' (1998) 45 *University of California Los Angeles Law Review* 733, 737 fn 85, 744; Amar Khoday, 'Protecting Those Who Go beyond the Law: Contemplating Refugee Status for Individuals Who Challenge Oppression through Resistance' (2012) 25 *Georgetown Immigration Law Journal* 571. Compare Jan Arno Hessbruegge, *Human Rights and Personal Self-Defense in International Law* (Oxford University Press 2017) 339–340.

[57] On the need for a narrow construction of the term 'serious non-political crimes', see *UNHCR Handbook and Guidelines* (n 55) 28–29 [140], [149], 30 [155], 35 [176]–[177], [179]–[180]; James C Hathaway and Michelle Foster, *The Law of Refugee Status* (2nd edn, Cambridge University Press 2014) 537–538, 541.

[58] On the relationship between the two distinct types of adjudication, which consider exceptions from a different rule, see Kälin and Künzli (n 56) 69–71; Sibylle Kapferer, 'The Interface between Extradition and Asylum' (Department of International Protection, UN High Commissioner for Refugees 2003) 103 [316], 104 [318], 105 [323]. Convention refugees are also protected from extradition if they are not excludable by virtue of article 1F(b), which in turn imposes a requirement of 'extraditable criminality'. See Executive Committee Conclusion No 17 (XXXI) (1980) in UN High Commissioner for Refugees, 'A Thematic Compilation of Executive Committee Conclusions' (7th edn, UN High Commissioner for Refugees 2013) 214; James C Hathaway and Colin J Harvey, 'Framing Refugee Protection in

activity and therefore protected and, conversely, what is 'criminal' activity and therefore 'non-political' and excluded from protection.[59] While there are also no common rules for applying the political offence exception, influential general principles have developed from the jurisprudence of English-speaking common law reception jurisdictions, as well as the authoritative opinions of the UN High Commissioner for Refugees and leading commentators.[60] In general, for an otherwise unlawful act to qualify as 'political' and thus 'protected', it must be genuinely politically motivated, committed in a context of political 'struggle' and constitute an incident in that struggle,[61] demonstrate a direct causal link between the act and the political purpose, and be proportional to that purpose. The UN High Commissioner for Refugees Guidelines on Exclusion identify an additional requirement that political objectives must be consistent with international human rights law as a basic threshold for whether a crime will be considered 'political'.[62] In other words, protection may theoretically apply to resistance in pursuit of all causes whose object and purpose is consistent with international human rights law, so long as the actions in question do not fall afoul of international criminal law or otherwise fundamentally offend the purposes and principles of the UN,[63] and can meet

the New World Disorder' (2001) 34 *Cornell International Law Journal* 257, 273–275, 282, 285.

59 On the four categories of 'political offences' subject to the exception – 'absolute' or 'pure', 'relative', 'compound', and 'connected' – and on those automatically disqualified as 'political' because they violate *jus cogens* norms and are specifically prohibited under international criminal law, such as genocide or torture, see Kapferer (n 58) 27–29 [75]–[77].

60 See *UNHCR Handbook and Guidelines* (n 55) 30–31 [152], [157]; Hathaway and Foster (n 57) 7.2, 555. See also *T* v *Secretary of State for the Home Department* (HL) [1996] 2 WLR 766 [1996] 2 All ER 865 and *Immigration and Naturalization Service* v *Aguirre-Aguirre*, 526 US 415 (1999) 119 S. Ct. 1439, cited as 'seminal' cases in 'UNHCR Compilation of Case Law on Refugee Protection in International Law' (UN High Commissioner for Refugees March 2008) s 5.2, 19–20. For a more thorough treatment of the relevant article 1F(b) case law from multiple jurisdictions see Hathaway and Foster (n 57) 537–566.

61 The more general term 'struggle' is used because the higher 'armed conflict' thresholds applicable to additional protections under international humanitarian law do not apply here.

62 'UNHCR Guidelines on Application of the Exclusion Clauses' (n 55) 118 [15]; UN High Commissioner for Refugees, 'Background Note on the Application of the Exclusion Clauses: Article 1F of the 1951 Convention Relating to the Status of Refugees' UN Doc HRC/GIP/03/05 (4 September 2003) 16 [43].

63 Where actions do violate international criminal prohibitions, they would be excludable under article 1F(a). Article 1F(c) may be applied to 'terrorism' cases, but only 'in extreme circumstances', where 'the resulting acts have the requisite serious effect on international peace, security, and peaceful relations between states' and are of a 'comparably egregious character' to acts excludable under article 1F(a), 'such as sustained human rights violations and acts which have been clearly identified and accepted by the international community as being contrary to the purposes and principles of the United Nations'. See *Al-Sirri* v *Secretary of State for the Home Department* [2012] UKSC 54 [13]–[14], [37]–[38], [40].

the established 'nexus', 'clear and direct purpose', 'predominance', and 'proportionality' tests.[64] Attempts to create more rigid determination standards through adoption of 'depoliticization' lists of 'terrorist' acts to be automatically considered as 'non-political', linked to the requirements of other international or regional treaties, resolutions, or legal regulations,[65] have not eliminated the 'political offence exception' as some predicted.[66] However, such efforts have undoubtedly narrowed its application in both extradition and exclusion law,[67] with the potential to also undermine the right to resist through oversimplification that casts too broad a net.

As with the test for applying the political offence exception under extradition law,[68] reference to the right to resist as a principle of general or customary international law could improve guidance for the application of the 1F clause in exclusion hearings.[69] What is needed is authoritative guidance in the form of principles to prevent misapplication of article 1F(b) where a customary right to resist is implicitly recognized, along the lines of that developed for article 1F(a) by Hathaway.[70] In this regard, the Chapter 4 analytical framework may help clarify a more reasonable basis for positively identifying a 'political crime' or political activity deserving of protection, to which article 1F(b) of the Refugee Convention therefore does not apply. This approach would seem to be reinforced by the specification that 'motivation, context, methods and proportionality of a crime to its objectives are important factors

64 See for example *McMullen* v *Immigration and Naturalization Service*, 658 F 2d 1312 (9th Cir. 1981) as confirmed by *INS* v *Aguirre-Aguirre* (n 60); *Gil* v *Canada* (MEI) (A-375-92) (Court of Appeal 21 October 1994); *T* v *SSHD* (n 60).

65 See Hathaway and Harvey (n 58) 282–284; Kapferer (n 58) 30–31 [81]–[84].

66 Extradition treaty designation of particular acts will be significant but 'not conclusive in itself', nor will membership of an organization on a proscription list in itself constitute sufficient evidence in making a determination under article 1(F)(b). See 'UNHCR Guidelines on Application of the Exclusion Clauses' (n 55) 119–121, [15], [19]–[20], [25]–[27]; UN High Commissioner for Refugees, 'Guidance Note on Extradition and International Refugee Protection' (UN High Commissioner for Refugees 2008) 4 [3], [5], 12 [23], 18 [42].

67 See Kapferer (n 58) 32 [86]; Hathaway and Foster (n 57) 560.

68 See discussion in Chapter 6, Section 6.6.3.

69 See Kälin and Künzli (n 56) 46–47, 53, 55, 58–59, 76–78. See also the 'typology of political offences' and corresponding legal protections extrapolated from international standards and derived 'jurisprudential principles' for a proposed 'Bill of Rights for Just Resistance' intended as a basis for international codification regulating internal conflict in Nicholas N Kittrie, *Rebels with a Cause: The Minds and Morality of Political Offenders* (Westview 2000) 319–320, 322–327, 331–348, Appendix A 350. See also Khoday (n 56).

70 See James C Hathaway, 'Michigan Guidelines on the Exclusion of International Criminals' (2013) 35(4) *Michigan Journal of International Law* 5.

in evaluating its political nature', and that article 1F(b) does not apply to the 'legitimate exercise of human rights'.[71]

The potential rights-holders would be refugee claimants not falling under the international criminality exclusions pursuant to article 1F(a) and (c) – that is, those whose alleged offence, committed in pursuit of an object and purpose consistent with international human rights law in general, does not amount to conduct prohibited under international criminal law. In the absence of trigger conditions specific to the Refugee Convention, the appropriate test would be determined by those associated with the relevant source of customary international law. For claims involving trigger violations of the right to external self-determination, the primary and secondary triggers would be those associated with the UN Charter as set out in UN General Assembly Resolution 2625.[72] For claims involving primary trigger violations of the right to internal self-determination or other human rights violations in a context where judicial or other effective legal remedies are not reasonably available, the secondary trigger associated with the Universal Declaration of Human Rights – 'last resort' – would apply.[73] In either case, permissible means would be determined by meeting appropriate tests for proportionality.[74] The customary Nuremberg right to disobey manifestly unlawful orders or resist other internationally criminal conduct should also lead to augmentation of existing protection from refoulement on this basis.[75] The duty-bearers are receiving states, with non-exclusion and non-refoulement the correlated duties.

Ultimately, the implied doctrine of protected political activity under refugee law is a source of indirect recognition of the right to resist, corroborative and subsidiary only. Its practical effect is limited to shielding associated individuals from risk of persecution as a result of refoulement. While this helps ensure the lives and security of those involved, it does not necessarily protect their right to resistance as such.[76] Indeed, expulsion under articles 32 and 33(2) of the Refugee Convention may nevertheless apply after a

[71] See 'UNHCR Guidelines on Application of the Exclusion Clauses' (n 55) 118 [14]–[15].

[72] See discussion in Chapter 6, Sections 6.3.1.3 and 6.3.1.4.

[73] See discussion in Chapter 6, Section 6.4.6.

[74] See discussion in Chapter 6, Section 6.3.1.5.

[75] See discussion in Chapter 6, Section 6.5. See also 'Chapter V: Special Cases – B. Deserters and Persons Avoiding Military Service' in *UNHCR Handbook and Guidelines* (n 55) 33–34 [170]–[173], which does not directly address this aspect.

[76] See for example UN High Commissioner for Refugees Executive Committee Conclusion No 94 (LIII) (2002), which calls for 'special procedures' under article 1F in the case of former combatants, requiring them also to 'genuinely and permanently renounce military activities' as a condition of initial claim consideration. 'Thematic Compilation' (n 58) 214.

positive determination of refugee status, consequent on their political activity in their reception country.[77]

7.2.3 *Corroboration in the Rome Statute: The Theory of an Implied Right-Duty to Disobey Internationally Criminal Orders as a Corollary of Article 33*

There is absolute legal clarity that certain acts are always in violation of international criminal law, regardless of perpetrator or motivation. Rebels who are either citizens of States Parties or are operating on the territory of States Parties can be internationally prosecuted for committing acts prohibited under the Rome Statute of the International Criminal Court since July 2002 as genocide, crimes against humanity, or war crimes.[78] The Rome Statute therefore acts primarily as a source of constraint upon the scope of action in the exercise of resistance and rebellion. However, the customary international law right-duty to disobey orders to commit international crimes, or equivalent laws,[79] is also corroborated by article 33 of the Rome Statute, which affirms the unavailability of a defence of 'superior orders' or 'prescription of law' where such are 'manifestly unlawful'.[80] This logically implies a right-duty to

[77] Prakash Shah, 'Taking the "Political" Out of Asylum: The Legal Containment of Refugees' Political Activism' in Frances Nicholson and Patrick Twomey (eds), *Refugee Rights and Realities: Evolving International Concepts and Regimes* (Cambridge University Press 1999).

[78] See Rome Statute of the International Criminal Court (adopted 17 July 1998, entered into force 1 July 2002) 2187 UNTS 3 (as amended 2010) articles 6, 7(2)(a), 8(2)(a)–(c), and (e); William A Schabas, 'Punishment of Non-State Actors in Non-International Armed Conflict' (2002) 26(4) *Fordham International Law Journal* 907, 914–922. In contrast, the crime of aggression as codified in the Rome Statute as amended, under provisions at articles 8 *bis* and 15 *bis-ter*, is exclusively a state crime.

[79] For example, International Committee of the Red Cross, 'Rule 154: Every combatant has a duty to disobey a manifestly unlawful order' (Customary IHL Database updated December 2017); Hitomi Takemura, 'Disobeying Manifestly Illegal Orders' (2006) 18(4) *Peace Review: A Journal of Social Justice* 533; Hitomi Takemura, *International Human Right to Conscientious Objection to Military Service and Individual Duties to Disobey Manifestly Illegal Orders* (Springer 2009). On the hypothesized broader customary right to resist internationally criminal acts, see discussion in Chapter 6, Section 6.5 and Section 7.4.

[80] See Rome Statute (n 78) article 33, and related articles 25, 27, 28, 31. Demonstrating that there is no meaningful distinction between this provision and the rule of absolute liability for international crimes under customary international law, see Paola Gaeta, 'The Defence of Superior Orders: The Statute of the International Criminal Court versus Customary International Law' (1999) 10 *European Journal of International Law* 172. For a review of the literature on and criticisms of the provision and its 'manifest illegality standard' see Lydia Ansermet, 'Manifest Illegality and the ICC Superior Orders Defense: Schuldtheorie Mistake of Law Doctrine as an Article 33(1)(c) Panacea' (2014) 47 *Vanderbilt Journal of Transnational Law* 1425, 1446–1456.

resist 'manifestly unlawful orders' as a corollary of article 33.[81] This implied right-duty under article 33 would impose a correlated obligation upon the States Parties to make available within their domestic law provision for non-prosecution, a defence, and/or mitigation for those who disobey or otherwise resist 'manifestly unlawful orders'.[82] Thus, while not a source of direct recognition of or provision for the right to resist per se, the Rome Statute should nevertheless yield to the citizens of States Parties a subsidiary right to protection from prosecution or punishment for such disobedience or other resistance as it relates to crimes codified under the Statute: against orders to commit – or laws otherwise leading or contributing to – genocide, crimes against humanity, war crimes, or the crime of aggression.[83]

Separately, certain specialists have raised concerns that a number of factors have led to a questionable overemphasis on the international prosecution of rebels at the International Criminal Court.[84] Given that the Special Court for Sierra Leone sometimes strayed into implicit denial of the right to resist despite the continuing absence of the criminalization of resistance, rebellion, or revolution as such in international criminal law,[85] this is a risk that should

[81] Kälin and Künzli (n 56) 55.

[82] This could of course include, inter alia, legislative provision for a recognized right to 'selective' as well as 'absolute' conscientious objection, as suggested by Takemura, 'Disobeying Manifestly Illegal Orders' (n 79) 539–540; Takemura, *International Human Right to Conscientious Objection* (n 79) 137–181. On the subordinate cognate 'right to conscientious objection', see brief reference in Section 7.4.

[83] For a more complete argument specifically regarding the crime of aggression, see Tom Dannenbaum, *The Crime of Aggression, Humanity, and the Soldier* (Cambridge University Press 2018) 'The Duty to Disobey Illegal Orders' 20–24; 'The Timing of Disobedience Protection' 272–276, 'A Limited Right to Disobey Orders to Fight in Illegal Wars' 292–299, 'The *Jus ad Bellum* and the Human Rights of Rights Defenders' 322–328.

[84] See William A Schabas, 'Prosecutorial Discretion v Judicial Activism at the International Criminal Court' (2008) 6 *Journal of International Criminal Justice* 731, 750–753, 760–761; William A Schabas, '"Complementarity" in Practice: Some Uncomplimentary Thoughts' (2008) 19 *Criminal Law Forum* 5, 6, 8, 19, 22, 33; William A Schabas, 'State Policy as an Element of International Crimes' (2008) 98(3) *Journal of Criminal Law and Criminology* 953, 974, 982. On the empirical and normative bases of these objections, finding that 60–80 per cent of proceedings concern 'non-state actors', meaning current or former rebel groups, and concluding that such groups are indeed now 'more vulnerable' to international prosecution regardless of disparity in scale and gravity of offences when compared to state actors, see Frédéric Mégret, 'Is the ICC Focusing Too Much on Non-State Actors?' in Diane Marie Amann and Margaret deGuzman (eds), *Arcs of Global Justice: Essays in Honor of William A Schabas* (Oxford University Press 2017) 177, 178.

[85] See William A Schabas, *The UN International Criminal Tribunals – The Former Yugoslavia, Rwanda and Sierra Leone* (Cambridge University Press 2006) 309–314, 312; Simon M Meisenberg, 'Joint Criminal Enterprise and the Special Court for Sierra Leone' in Charles Chenor Jalloh (ed), *The Sierra Leone Special Court and Its Legacy: The Impact for Africa and International Criminal Law* (Cambridge University Press 2013).

be avoided in other international criminal proceedings. Indeed, a clearer understanding of the applicable law of the right to resist as a *jus ad bellum* exception could assist in distinguishing between internationally criminal and internationally non-criminal 'common purposes' under article 25(3)(d) of the Rome Statute in appropriate cases regarding the use of force, so as not to wrongly conflate simple participation with actual violation of international criminal law.[86] Additionally, in the application of the Rome Statute, the fact that participation in resistance and rebellion are not, in themselves, international crimes demands particular adherence to the requirement of strict construction of crimes under article 22(2) prohibiting extension by analogy.[87]

7.3 FRAGMENTATION IN THE REGIONAL HUMAN RIGHTS SYSTEMS

In the regional human rights systems, the right to resist has a mixed record of recognition. The African and Arab systems make express treaty provision for this right. In contrast, the European and Inter-American systems contain no such provision, nor do they appear to afford implied recognition. Indeed, certain aspects of the European and Inter-American treaties suggest the opposite. The result is a 'fragmentation' effect.[88]

7.3.1 *Recognition in the African and Arab Systems*

By making express provision for the right to resist, the African and Arab human rights treaties represent a significant departure from all the other main human rights treaties, and a challenge to those who maintain that international codification of this right is not possible. However, since these two provisions have not yet been subject to either judicial or thorough scholarly analysis, and

86 To attract liability for 'common purpose complicity' the 'common purpose' must involve 'the commission of a crime within the jurisdiction of the Court'. That is, it must amount to an internationally criminal act or purpose. See Rome Statute (n 78) article 25(3)(d). See also Marco Sassòli, 'Taking Armed Groups Seriously: Ways to Improve Their Compliance with International Humanitarian Law' (2010) 1 *International Humanitarian Legal Studies* 5, 44–45.

87 See Rome Statute (n 78) article 22(2). See also Schabas (n 78) 932; Schabas, 'Prosecutorial Discretion' (n 84) 755–756; William Schabas, *Introduction to the International Criminal Court* (5th edn, Cambridge University Press 2017) 215–216.

88 For a general statement of this phenomenon see International Law Commission, 'Fragmentation of International Law: Difficulties Arising from the Diversification and Expansion of International Law – Report of the Study Group of the International Law Commission, finalized by Mr Martti Koskenniemi' UN Doc A/CN.4/L.682 and Add 1 (13 April 2006) [5]–[55] 10–18.

are also to an extent dependent on other sources of international law for their interpretation, the full scope of these rights to resist has yet to be determined.

7.3.1.1 African Charter on Human and Peoples Rights: Article 20(2) and (3) Provisions

The African Charter on Human and Peoples Rights is the first international human rights instrument to expressly codify the right to resist. As the sole internationally codified 'right to resist oppression' it represents a significant progressive legal development.[89] Within the context of article 20 on the right to self-determination, article 20(2) of the African Charter asserts the right to resist. It states that '[c]olonised or oppressed peoples shall have the right to free themselves from the bonds of domination by resorting to any means recognised by the international community'.[90] Article 20(3) goes further, providing that '[a]ll peoples shall have the right to the assistance of the States Parties ... in their liberation struggle against foreign domination, be it political, economic or cultural'.[91]

ELEMENTS OF THE AFRICAN CHARTER RIGHT TO RESIST Applying the Chapter 4 analytical framework, the lawful object and purpose of the African Charter right to resist is, in particular, enforcement of the right to self-determination, in both its external and internal forms, but also enforcement of human rights in general. The potential rights-holders are all 'peoples' of Africa, however that term is legally understood within the context of the African Charter. The trigger conditions are 'colonization' or other 'oppression', however the latter term is legally understood within the context of the African Charter. Provided one or both of these conditions pertains, it appears from the text that no secondary trigger is required. By employing the euphemism 'the right to free themselves ... by resorting to any means', this indicates that permissible means of self-help are inclusive of peaceful and forceful means, albeit otherwise limited by international law as stated. The duty-bearers are the Member States of the African Union. Hence the

[89] For a more complete but also earlier version of this analysis see Shannonbrooke Murphy, 'Unique in International Human Rights Law: Article 20(2) and the Right to Resist in the African Charter on Human and Peoples' Rights' (2011) 11(2) *African Human Rights Law Journal* 465, 467, 473–494.

[90] African Charter on Human and Peoples' Rights (adopted 27 June 1981, entered into force 21 October 1986) (1982) 21 ILM 58 article 20(2) [emphasis added].

[91] Ibid article 20(3).

analytical framework helps identify three distinctive elements of the African Charter right to resist.

Firstly, article 20(2) is a broad formulation that extends the right to all 'oppressed' peoples in Africa.[92] Certainly, it is a right to enforce the right to external self-determination in cases of foreign 'domination', including invasion and occupation, or other intervention, or colonization. But it is also a right to enforce the right to internal self-determination, not only by resisting the imposition of racist rule, but also in cases of otherwise violative domestic regimes.[93] While the Charter concept of 'oppression' as a trigger condition remains to be defined by the African Commission or African Court of Human and Peoples' Rights, no claim under article 20(2) can succeed without meeting this element, since oppression is also inherent to colonization. Where 'oppression' cannot be established, there will be no African Charter right to resist.[94] Given the specific context of article 20 as a peoples' right, presumably it refers not to single or even multiple instances of violations against an individual or group of individuals, but rather systematic and serious violations of the rights of a people as a whole, even if that is a minority people within a state. Beyond this, the term is unqualified and therefore arguably a broad rather than narrow concept, and otherwise remains open to interpretation. 'Oppression' would surely include massive violations such as crimes against humanity or other international crimes. It could also include

[92] See Murphy (n 89) 482–483, 489–492.

[93] Edem Kodjo, 'The African Charter on Human and Peoples' Rights' (1990) 11(1–2) *Human Rights Law Journal* 271, 272–274, 281–282; Fatsah Ouguergouz, *The African Charter on Human and Peoples' Rights: A Comprehensive Agenda for Human Dignity and Sustainable Democracy in Africa* (Martinus Nijhoff 2003) 203–269, 261–269. See also Paust (n 4) 18.

[94] Compare the Commission's *obiter dictum* that article 20 'has a particular historical context ... aimed at addressing the situation of Africans who remained under colonial domination', consequently 'the right to self-determination, the right of colonised and oppressed people to free themselves from domination and the right to assistance in liberation struggle are reserved for colonised peoples'. See Comm 328/06 *Front for the Liberation of the State of Cabinda* v *Angola* (5 November 2013) (2013) ACHPR (54th Ordinary Session) [124]–[125] [emphasis added]. This contradicts the actual wording of the provision, which uses 'colonised or oppressed', and furthermore it conflates the broader scope of article 20(1) and (2) with the narrower scope of article 20(3). It also ignores confirmation by then-Organization of African Unity Secretary General that the Charter was also intended to address proliferation of post-colonial human rights violating regimes and African dictatorships, and African expert opinion as to the provision's proper scope. See Kodjo (n 93) 272–274, 281–282; Ouguergouz (n 93) 261–269. Therefore, since no claim was made under article 20(2) or (3) and none of the relevant paragraphs concerning the article 20(1) aspect of the claim otherwise define 'oppression', the term remains undefined by the Commission as to its meaning under Charter article 20(2). See *Front for the Liberation of the State of Cabinda* v *Angola* (n 94) [120]–[126]. The African Court of Human and Peoples' Rights has neither considered an article 20(2) case, nor specifically defined 'oppression' in a broader article 20(1) case at the time of writing.

coups and other unconstitutional rule or unlawful exercise of power amounting to systematic violations falling short of the crimes against humanity threshold. It could include systematic discrimination against and exclusion of minority peoples, either meeting or falling outside of the 'apartheid' threshold for racist regimes.[95] In addition, it could include situations of foreign economic domination amounting to interference with the right to economic self-determination, as well as other systematic violations of economic and social rights amounting to economic 'oppression'.[96]

Secondly, article 20(2) provides that those resisting oppression may have recourse to 'any means' provided these are 'recognized by the international community'.[97] This has the positive effect of ensuring that exercise of the right is consistent with international norms and subject to regulation by international human rights law, international humanitarian law, and international criminal law. Unfortunately, it also makes the provision dependent on the legal status of the right to resist elsewhere, and thus impossible to interpret from the African Charter alone.[98] The permissible means clearly extend beyond the African Charter's *lex generalis* political rights and the exclusively peaceful means otherwise protected in this and the other systems. However, its 'dependent formulation' means that the available latitude is not unlimited.[99] That is, interpreting permissible means in any given case is hampered by the lack of clear permissions in established customary international law on the right to employ force to resist domestic oppression,[100] as well as the right to use peaceful but otherwise illegal means short of force,[101] or 'mid-spectrum cases – where the means employed are neither entirely peaceful nor involve armed force [but involve] physical confrontation or property destruction without munitions'.[102] This is a consequence not only of apparent 'gaps' in the law but also adjudicative bodies' limited findings regarding political rights outside *lex generalis* conditions. It thus depends on the degree of normative clarification outside the African system, potentially reducing the chance of making the right meaningful in practice. However, this also means that there is some interpretive scope, particularly where ambiguities remain regarding

95 See discussion in Chapter 6, Sections 6.3.1.2 and 6.3.1.3.
96 See Murphy (n 89) 482–483, 489–492. See also further discussion of the concept of 'oppression' in Chapter 4, Section 4.2.2.
97 Regarding such means, see previous sections of this chapter and Chapter 6, Sections 6.3.1.5, 6.4.6, and 6.5.
98 See Murphy (n 89) 483–489.
99 See ibid 473–476, 483–489.
100 See discussion in Chapter 6 generally; Murphy (n 89) 484–485.
101 See discussion in Section 7.2.1 above. See also Murphy (n 89) 485–488.
102 Ibid 475.

peaceful but otherwise unlawful means, and in general under the *lex specialis* or law applicable under the exceptional circumstances of oppression.[103] The basic requirement of general international human rights law appears to be that, under otherwise normal conditions at least, resistance actions must be peaceful. Therefore, at such time as actions employ force of any kind, at present they fall outside the scope of protection of the general law. However, the African Commission or Court could come to a different conclusion that still respects the overarching framework of the law – but only if it can be established that the balance of competing rights favours the fundamental rights of the claimants in a clear context of oppression where no other effective remedy exists, with the possible additional requirement that the actions taken in resistance are both necessary and proportionate to remedy the violations resisted by such means. In the specific context of oppression of a people, African adjudicators may elect not to accord the ordinary right to property, for example, the same weight as the competing fundamental rights of peoples. Such an approach would be justified, as the UN Human Rights Committee considers these ordinary political rights in a treaty instrument without a clear law of exception in the form of an express right to resist equivalent to the African Charter. So long as the reasoning is generally consistent with its jurisprudence, the Committee's approach should therefore not unduly restrict the interpretation of article 20(2). Thus, the overall interpretive effect of the dependent formulation is constraint but not total paralysis.[104] Indeed, articles 60 and 61 of the African Charter on applicable principles, standards, and sources can help with the decoding. They specify that applicable principles can include the UN Charter and Universal Declaration, the Charter of the Organization of African Unity, other UN and African regional instruments, as well as 'customs generally accepted as law, general principles of law ... legal precedents and doctrine'.[105] Furthermore, the African Charter provisions generally provide ample room for dynamic interpretation, both as a matter of intent and as the net effect of the simplicity bordering on vagueness of their framing, and also because the 'incomplete and cursory' *travaux préparatoires* provide little or no interpretive guidance. Thus, the meaning of the provisions can also evolve over time.[106]

103 Ouguergouz (n 93) 208 fn 694.

104 Murphy (n 89) 475.

105 See African Charter on Human and Peoples' Rights (n 90) articles 60, 61.

106 See Frans Viljoen, 'The African Charter on Human and Peoples' Rights: The *Travaux Préparatoires* in the Light of Subsequent Practice' (2004) 25 *Human Rights Law Journal* 313, 315–316, 325. See also Nasila S Rembe, *The System of Protection of Human Rights under the African Charter on Human and Peoples' Rights: Problems and Prospects* (Institute of Southern

Thirdly, the express right to assistance from other African states under article 20(3) also constitutes a correlated third-party duty, though this is specifically restricted to those resisting 'foreign domination', meaning that most of those resisting oppression by a domestic power probably do not share this supplementary right.[107] Prior positive findings on both article 20(1) and article 20(2) claims would likely be necessary but not sufficient to validate any separate or concurrent claim for assistance made under article 20(3), which would need to be subject to a separate assessment last in the sequence, to ensure among other things that the 'foreign political, economic or cultural domination' criterion is also met. Just as not all claimants who as a 'people' qualify for self-determination rights under article 20(1) will also qualify for the further right to resist under article 20(2),[108] not all claimants who qualify under article 20(2) will also qualify for the further right to assistance under article 20(3).

While there are no limits internal to the provision, or a derogation regime provided under the African Charter, the article 20(2) right is further shaped and potentially constrained by provisions at articles 23 and 27(2).[109] Article 27 (2) is a general clause requiring that all Charter rights are exercised with 'due regard to the rights of others' as well as collective security and common interest,[110] although the African Commission has insisted that any limitations deriving from this clause must be necessary and proportionate and also not negate the right in question.[111] Article 23 is a right to peace including domestic peace,[112] which also prohibits intervention in the form of subversion

African Studies, National University of Lesotho 1991) 4–5; Bertrand G Ramcharan, 'The *Travaux Préparatoires* of the African Commission on Human and Peoples' Rights' (1992) 13 *Human Rights Law Journal* 307.

107 See Murphy (n 89) 489.

108 Notwithstanding the African Commission's apparent suggestion to the contrary in Comm 266/03 *Kevin Mgwanga Gunme et al* v *Cameroon* (27 May 2009) [2009] ACHPR 99 [197], it is technically possible to make an article 20(1) claim without making any further claim as to rights under articles 20(2) or 20(3). For a critical analysis of the Commission's reasoning see Murphy (n 89) 480–481.

109 See ibid 476–478.

110 See African Charter on Human and Peoples' Rights (n 90) article 27(2).

111 See Comms 105/93–128/94, 130/94–152/96 *Nigeria Media Rights Agenda and Others* v *Nigeria* (31 October 1998) (2000) AHRLR 200 [65]–[70].

112 See African Charter on Human and Peoples' Rights (n 90) article 23(1). On this meaning that 'both the people of a State taken as a whole, and its different … components taken individually, have the right to peace and security domestically', see Ouguergouz (n 93) 353. On article 23 as a right of peoples against states see Clive Baldwin and Cynthia Morel, 'Group Rights' in Malcolm Evans and Rachel Murray (eds), *The African Charter on Human and Peoples' Rights: The System in Practice, 1986–2006* (Cambridge University Press 2008) 279–282.

against another state,[113] placing limits on provision of support for anti-government rebels from another jurisdiction, similar to those found in customary international law.[114] Yet Ouguergouz warns against misconstruction: article 23 must be read in light of article 20(2) and (3), not the reverse.[115] Ultimately, neither article 27(2) nor article 23 necessarily trump article 20(2)–(3).[116]

JURISPRUDENCE RELEVANT TO INTERPRETATION OF ARTICLE 20(2) AND (3) Despite its unique place in international human rights law, with the notable exception of Ouguergouz, the right to resist oppression at article 20(2) and (3) of the African Charter has received mostly cursory consideration from commentators.[117] This may be at least partially explained by the fact that the African Commission and African Court have yet to consider any article 20 (2) claims.[118] However, the Commission's three key article 20(1) cases all make findings relevant to its future interpretation,[119] as does the Court's key article 20(1) and (3) case.[120]

113 See African Charter on Human and Peoples' Rights (n 90) article 23(2).

114 See Comm 227/99 *Democratic Republic of the Congo* v *Burundi, Rwanda and Uganda* (29 May 2003) (2004) AHRLR 19 [76]–[77]. See also discussion in Chapter 6, Sections 6.2 and 6.3.

115 In particular, article 23 must be construed in a manner consistent with respect for human rights in general and especially self-determination rights as a precondition to peace, as reflected in the UN Charter and Universal Declaration. See Ouguergouz (n 93) 334–335, 345, 353. In other words, a well-regulated and responsibly exercised right to resist could even under certain conditions actually be necessary for the realization of the right to peace in the medium to longer term, or else the only available form of effective remedy for violations of this right in the short-term. Murphy (n 89) 477.

116 Murphy (n 89) 478.

117 Compare Ouguergouz (n 93) 215–265, 267; U Oji Umozurike, *The African Charter on Human and Peoples' Rights* (Martinus Nijhoff 1997) 126; Christof Heyns, 'Civil and Political Rights in the African Charter' in Evans and Murray, *The African Charter on Human and Peoples' Rights* (n 112); Baldwin and Morel (n 112) 279–282; Rachel Murray, *The African Charter on Human and Peoples' Rights: A Commentary* (Oxford University Press 2019) 504–507.

118 See Murphy (n 89) 479–481; Murray (n 117) 506. The *Cabinda* case before the African Commission was not a right to resist claim under article 20(2) or (3), but rather only a general claim to self-determination under article 20 and a specific claim for economic self-determination under article 20(1). See *Front for the Liberation of the State of Cabinda* v *Angola* (n 94) [54]. Similarly, see Comm 276/03 *Centre for Minority Rights Development and Another* v *Kenya* (25 November 2009) [2009] ACHPR 102 and *African Commission on Human and Peoples' Rights* v *Kenya* (2017) 28 AFCHPR 60, which also make no direct findings on article 20(2) or (3).

119 For case synopses and more extensive analysis see Murphy (n 89) 479–481.

120 *Mornah* v *Republic of Benin* [2022] AFCHPR 22 makes article 20(1) and (3) findings, but no article 20(2) findings.

Gunme et al v *Cameroon* establishes the definition of a 'people' as a rights-holder within the meaning of the African Charter, determinative of eligibility to make an article 20 claim and therefore potentially also an article 20(2) claim. According to the *Gunme et al* findings, collective rights in general can at least in theory be exercised by 'a people bound together by their historical, traditional, racial, ethnic, cultural, linguistic, religious, ideological, geographical, economic identities and affinities or other bonds'.[121] Indeed, a claim to be a 'people' need not require manifestation of all but rather only some of the 'identified attributes' – among which are ideological or economic identity and the totally open category of 'affinities or other bonds' – and need not necessarily be ethnically or otherwise anthropologically distinct to qualify.[122] The African Commission thus not only adopts a broad and inclusive definitional approach, but finds that sovereignty and territorial integrity do not provide an absolute shield against self-determination claims of a minority people.[123] Hence *Gunme* is also the leading case for a minority right to resist claim.[124]

Katangese Peoples' Congress v *Zaire* establishes that article 20 claims in general cannot be adjudicated independently of article 13.[125] That is, finding a violation of the article 20(1) right to self-determination – which could trigger

[121] See *Gunme et al* v *Cameroon* (n 108) [169], [171], [174].

[122] Ibid [178]. For African indigenous peoples, the *Gunme* elements are supplemented somewhat by criteria set out in *Centre for Minority Rights Development and Another* v *Kenya* (n 118) [150]–[151], specifying 'occupation and use of a specific territory'; 'voluntary perpetuation of cultural distinctiveness'; 'self-identification as a distinct collectivity'; 'recognition by other groups'; 'experience of subjugation, marginalisation, dispossession, exclusion or discrimination'; and, as a '*key characteristic*', that '*survival of their particular way of life depends on access and rights to their traditional lands and the natural resources thereon*' [emphasis in original].

[123] On the state obligation to address such claims using African or other international dispute resolution mechanisms if necessary, giving systemic preference to internal self-determination remedies but not ruling out a 'right to secession', see *Gunme et al* v *Cameroon* (n 108) [181], [188], [190]–[191], [194], [199]–[200] citing Comm 75/92 *Katangese Peoples' Congress* v *Zaire* (22 March 1995) (2000) AHRLR 72 [4], [6]. See also *Front for the Liberation of the State of Cabinda* v *Angola* (n 94) [126].

[124] See Murphy (n 89) 479–481. Note that the African Court of Human and Peoples' Rights, in considering what may constitute a 'people' within the meaning of the Charter, does not refer to, and therefore neither accepts nor refutes, the Commission's earlier conclusion in *Gunme et al*, instead observing that the Charter's non-definition was a deliberate effort to assure interpretive flexibility, and affirming that minority peoples of a state may have a right to internal self-determination, even where they may not exercise a right to external self-determination amounting to a right to secession. See *ACHPR* v *Kenya* (n 118) [196]–[201]. For its part, the Commission also does not explain why it did not apply its own existing *Gunme* test to arrive at its negative finding on the article 20 claim in *Front for the Liberation of the State of Cabinda* v *Angola* (n 94) [120]–[126].

[125] *Katangese Peoples' Congress* v *Zaire* (n 123) [6]. See African Charter on Human and Peoples' Rights (n 90) article 13. See also Murphy (n 89) 479–480.

an article 20(2) claim – requires a prior finding of violation of the article 13 right to political participation.[126] This 'Katanga test' can likewise apply to a whole people or a minority people.[127]

Jawara v *the Gambia* establishes that a coup even without force is a 'grave violation' of the article 20(1) right to self-determination.[128] Hence *Jawara* is the leading case for a right to resist claim by a majority or a people of a state as a whole. Furthermore, it finds that where a regime creates 'generalized fear' through repression there is no requirement to pursue a remedy through the courts, as such a remedy can only be effective where there is some prospect of success.[129]

The African Charter case law to date thus generates a multi-part test for establishing valid grounds for a right to resist in cases other than, and in addition to, colonization or foreign occupation cases.[130] As the first hurdle, claimants must establish they are rights-holders as a 'people' meeting the elements of the *Gunme* definition. Then they must establish necessity in a three-part trigger test. That is, they must provide evidence of denial of the article 13 right to political participation pursuant to the Katanga test. Next, they must show that conditions constitute 'oppression' amounting to denial of the right to internal self-determination, either because the regime is inherently oppressive as a consequence of unconstitutional or corrupt rule, or as the result of unlawful seizure of power, or through a pattern of abuse of power and primary Charter rights that is systematic and at least 'serious'.[131] Additionally they must show that there is no other prospect of 'available, effective and sufficient' remedy pursuant to the Jawara test. Meeting these criteria grounds a valid claim under 20(2), provided that the final test for a valid object and

[126] See also Comm 102/93 *Constitutional Rights Project and Another* v *Nigeria* (31 October 1998) (2000) AHRLR 191 [51]–[53]. However, compare the African Court's approach in a seizure of unconstitutional powers case concerning the internal right to self-determination of the people as a whole, in which the Court declined to consider the article 20(1) dimension of the claim, as it considered the article 13 aspect to cover this sufficiently. *Belguith* v *Republic of Tunisia* [2022] AFCHPR 35 [108]–[109]. Article 20(2) and (3) were not raised.

[127] See *Katangese Peoples' Congress* v *Zaire* (n 123) [4], [6] affirmed in *Front for the Liberation of the State of Cabinda* v *Angola* (n 94) [122], [123], [126]. Since an article 13 violation was not even alleged by the complainant in the latter case, this automatically undermined its article 20 claim at the outset.

[128] Comm 147/95–149/96 *Sir Dawda K Jawara* v *the Gambia* (11 May 2000) (2000) AHRLR 107 [72]–[73].

[129] Ibid [28]–[40]. See also Murphy (n 89) 481. The African Commission followed this rule in *Front for the Liberation of the State of Cabinda* v *Angola* (n 94) [49], [51]–[52].

[130] This is a variation on the test originally proposed in Murphy (n 89) 490–491.

[131] As noted, the African Commission and Court have yet to establish a definition or test for 'oppression'.

purpose under article 27(2) of the Charter is also met. Note that establishing permissible means involves a separate test, pursuant to the dependent formula.

Mornah v *Republic of Benin*, the first direct examination of the African Charter's article 20(3)-correlated third-party duty to assist, affirms that this further right to assistance requires not only meeting requirements for a valid claim under article 20(1), being status as a people with a right to self-determination, but also specific trigger conditions of foreign political, economic, or cultural 'domination' which are an independent additional requirement of this provision. Where these conditions are the consequence of incomplete decolonization or foreign occupation, this is more straightforward, and prior formal recognition as such provides helpful corroboration.[132] The African Court describes the article 20(3) third-party duty as arising from the *jus cogens* and *erga omnes* nature of the right to self-determination, having a positive dimension which includes assistance to those with a valid right, and a negative dimension which includes abstaining from acts that can have adverse effects. This implies an obligation on all African states towards all African peoples not to assist the foreign dominating state or recognize as lawful the situation it creates that deprives a people of the right to external self-determination.[133] In considering whether failure to assist qualifying claimants – either by doing nothing or by not taking certain available actions that could assist – constitutes conduct in violation of article 20(3), the Court applies customary international law criteria regarding attribution of a violation causing damage and the circumstances precluding state responsibility.[134] It concludes that article 20(3) does not require specific assistive actions but rather permits discretion in this regard. Furthermore, ineffective actions or inability to assist may amount to failure to assist, but not necessarily a violation of article 20(3) or an internationally wrongful act as such.[135]

PROSPECTS FOR APPLICATION OF THE AFRICAN CHARTER RIGHT TO RESIST As a secondary right, article 20(2) could be litigated in at least

[132] See the Court's affirmative findings with respect to the Sahrawi people's article 20(1) and 20(3) rights in *Mornah* v *Republic of Benin* (n 120) [285]–[286], [289]–[299], [301]–[303], [307], [314], [323]. Note that while article 20(2) is briefly referred to, the Court does not take the opportunity to interpret it or assess its applicability in this case.

[133] Ibid [297]–[299], [305].

[134] Ibid [304]. See International Law Commission, 'Responsibility of States for Internationally Wrongful Acts' (2001) annexed to UNGA Res 56/83 (12 December 2001) articles 1–4 concerning attribution, articles 12–15 concerning identification of a breach of international obligation, articles 16–18 regarding responsibility of a state connected to acts of another state, and articles 20–26 regarding circumstances precluding wrongfulness.

[135] *Mornah* v *Republic of Benin* (n 120) [304], [308], [314]–[315], [318].

two ways.[136] It could be raised concurrently as part of a broader complaint before the African Commission or African Court regarding violations of primary rights, seeking affirmation that other forms of remedy are not available or unlikely to succeed, thereby pre-authorizing resort to the exceptional secondary right for the purpose of primary rights enforcement. On a practical level, a finding validating a claim to this secondary right could act as a deterrent signal to a regime, a form of 'cease and desist' with a view to encouraging de-escalation, negotiation, or other positive engagement on the part of a state. Alternatively, a separate consecutive complaint could be raised regarding violation of the secondary right itself, following findings on the primary violation/s, concerning the validity of specific laws or prosecutions, or challenging obstructive actions.

If article 20(3) applies, the initial case law suggests that while it may be possible to achieve an affirmative finding on a claim to this right, provided the necessary rights-holder and trigger criteria are met, it may also prove difficult to successfully claim failure to assist by other states or by the African Union itself as a violation, where this results from inaction or ineffective action alone. For this, the African Court has made it clear that responsibility for internationally wrongful acts will also need to be established, in tandem. Therefore, a challenge involving active obstruction or refusal of a specific request for assistance may prove more effective than one based on failure to assist.

Domestically, article 20(2) could in appropriate cases reinforce a defence against prosecution, or buttress arguments for invalidation of certain laws either generally or in their specific application. For example, particular proceedings in relation to sedition or treason or even the laws themselves depending on their framing could be shown to be fundamentally incompatible, or else require interpretation or amendment to provide a defence if it can be shown that the accused was acting within internationally lawful means, as part of a people resisting oppression or other domination within the meaning of the African Charter.[137] Of course, any domestic constitutional right to resist

[136] Murphy (n 89) 478.

[137] Unfortunately, there is no guidance on this provided by Charter jurisprudence to date. The one attempt to challenge a prosecution for high treason via claim under article 20(1) was dismissed due to insufficient submissions in Comm 144/95 *William A Courson* v *Equatorial Guinea* (22 November 1997) (2000) AHRLR 93 [17]–[19]. However, in the matter of S v *Okah* before the South African Constitutional Court, see the Southern Africa Litigation Centre written submissions as *amicus curiae*, including analysis on whether Okah's proposed application of a section 1(4) exception to the South African Terrorism Act was in fact compliant with article 20(2) of the African Charter, using the 'Murphy test' in Murphy (n 89). 'Written Submissions for the *Amius Curiae* Southern Africa Litigation Centre ("SALC")', *State* v *Henry Eomotimi Okah*, Case No CCT315/16 & CCT 193/17, Constitutional Court of

provision of an African Union Member State must be interpreted in a manner compatible with the African Charter right to resist provision, as well as with the Charter as a whole.[138]

In instances where a positive article 20(2) finding would give rise to a state duty under article 20(3), this would validate and mandate compliance with requests for assistance. In certain instances, it could possibly oblige the African Union or individual Member States to request additional assistance of third parties thus authorized under international law, such as the UN Security Council.

The African Charter provision also has implications for the broader African Union system. All African Union instruments must be interpreted in harmony with, and potentially conflicting provisions construed in light of, the African Charter guarantees.[139] This includes its right to resist provision. This would have particular effect on the interpretation and application of the African Union Charter on Democracy, which bans 'unconstitutional' change of government thereby essentially stipulating elections only, without internally providing for human rights-based exceptions in cases where an African Charter right to resist oppression can be established.[140] The article 20(2) provision must also guide assessments leading to any intervention or other action on the part of the African Union pursuant to the African Union Constitutive Act;[141] the African Union Peace and Security Protocol;[142]

South Africa, 24 November 2017 [38]–[71]. See the Court's concurring assessment in its judgment, S v *Okah* [2018] ZACC 3 [44]–[52], in particular the unanswered questions at [46] and conclusions at [47]–[48].

138 African Charter on Human and Peoples' Rights (n 90) article 45 and Protocol to the African Charter on Human and Peoples' Rights on the Establishment of an African Court of Human and Peoples Rights (9 June 1998) OAU Doc OAU/LEG/EXP/AFCHPR/PROT (III) articles 3–5 mandate the African Commission and Court to provide guidance to Member States in this regard. For the African states concerned, see Chapter 5, Section 5.5.

139 See Constitutive Act of the African Union (adopted 7 November 2000, entered into force 26 May 2001, as amended by the Protocol on Amendments to the Constitutive Act of the African Union adopted 13 July 2003, entered into force 25 April 2012) article 3(h).

140 See African Charter on Democracy, Elections and Good Governance (adopted 30 January 2007, entered into force 15 February 2012) OAU Doc Assembly/AU/Dec.147 (VIII) article 2 (4) and 'Explanatory Note'. Similarly, see Protocol on Democracy and Good Governance (adopted 21 December 2001) ECOWAS A/SP1/12/01 article 1(b) and (c). Unfortunately, the African Commission also overlooked making necessary provision for the article 20(2) exception regarding conditions of oppression in its 'Resolution on Unconstitutional Changes of Government in Africa' ACHPR Res 515(LXX) (25 March 2022).

141 See Constitutive Act of the African Union (n 139) articles 3(g), 4(j), 4(h) (as amended), 4(p) and 30.

142 See Protocol Relating to the Establishment of the Peace and Security Council of the African Union (adopted 9 July 2002, entered into force 26 December 2003) article 7(1)(g).

Declaration on a Framework for an OAU Response to Unconstitutional Changes of Government;[143] and chapter 8 of the African Union Charter on Democracy concerning 'Sanctions in Cases of Unconstitutional Changes of Government'.[144] All of these may provide for African Union intervention in the event of a 'coup' by dissident military or rebel forces, but their application is also broader, with the potential to support a people's African Charter right to resist or otherwise, through multilateral obstruction, to trespass on situations where a right to resist could apply. As a consequence of the African Charter provision, a distinction must be made between an unlawful 'coup' and an exercise of internal or external self-determination involving otherwise internationally lawful forcible means where right to resist elements are met, including in particular the trigger condition of 'oppression', provided also that enforcement of self-determination in particular and human rights in general constitute the object and purpose.[145] Likewise, the African Criminal Chamber must also take account of the African Charter right to resist when determining whether unconstitutional change of government amounts to a crime under its jurisdiction.[146]

7.3.1.2 Arab Charter on Human Rights: Article 2(4) Provision

The Arab Charter on Human Rights is the source of the second express codification of the right to resist in an international human rights treaty. According to article 2(4), in the context of a general provision on the right

143 See Declaration on the Framework for an OAU Response to Unconstitutional Changes of Government OAU AHG/Decl.5 (XXXVI) (10–12 July 2000) (Lome Declaration) preamble, principles [viii]–[ix], definition [iii].

144 See African Charter on Democracy (n 140) chapter 8, articles 23(3), 24, 25, 46.

145 For a critical analysis of past African Union interventions related to 'unconstitutional changes of government', in some cases undermining the right to resist for self-determination and to enforce human rights guarantees, see Eki Yemisi Omorogbe, 'A Club of Incumbents? The African Union and Coups d'État' (2011) 44 *Vanderbilt Journal of International Law* 123, 138, 154. See also for example Simon M Waldehaimanot, 'African Law of Coups and the Situation in Eritrea: A Test for the African Union's Commitment to Democracy' (2010) 54(2) *Journal of African Law* 232, 252; Lydia A Nkansah, 'The Right of Resistance and the Defence of Ghana's Fourth Republican Constitution' (2014) 6 *Kwame Nkrumah University of Science and Technology Law Journal* 129, 146–147, 155 (fn 94)–157. Proposing a consequent African right to resist 'gross undemocratic practices', see Pacifique Manirakiza, 'Towards a Right to Resist Gross Undemocratic Practices in Africa' (2019) 63(1) *Journal of African Law* 81.

146 See Harmen Van der Wilt, 'Unconstitutional Change of Government: A New Crime within the Jurisdiction of the African Criminal Court' (2017) 30(4) *Leiden Journal of International Law* 967.

to self-determination, 'All peoples have the right to resist foreign occupation'.[147]

ELEMENTS OF THE ARAB CHARTER RIGHT TO RESIST Applying the Chapter 4 analytical framework, the potential rights-holders are all 'peoples' of the Arab world. However, article 2(4)'s object and purpose relate not to enforcement of the general right to self-determination, but the more specific right to self-defence against external aggression. Thus, unlike the African Charter right, this provision is drawn more narrowly than even the UN Charter right, addressing only one of the primary triggers otherwise recognized in general or customary international law.[148] No 'last resort' necessity or similar secondary trigger is specified, so therefore appears not required under the Arab Charter. Permissible means are also unspecified, thus presumably inclusive. However, under any requirement of consistent interpretation with other international law obligations, permissible means would be subject to the standard necessity and proportionality constraints otherwise imposed by customary international law,[149] as well as further regulation under international criminal law and international humanitarian law as applicable. The duty-bearers would be the League of Arab States and its members, that have the obligation to assist or not obstruct those validly exercising the right.

It is not immediately clear whether or to what extent the Arab Charter's own non-diminution clause permits interpretive broadening of article 2(4) to take account of the right as established in customary international law. Pursuant to article 43, 'Nothing in the present Charter shall be interpreted as impairing the rights and freedoms protected by the State Parties' own laws, or as set out in international or regional instruments of human rights that the State Parties have signed or ratified'.[150] As far as 'international human rights instruments', and as discussed in Chapter 6 and earlier in this chapter, implicit recognition

[147] Arab Charter on Human Rights (adopted 23 May 2004, entered into force 15 March 2008) article 2(4), reprinted in (2005) 12 *International Human Rights Reports* 893. Note that the right to resist was not included in the previous now discarded version. See Arab Charter on Human Rights (adopted 15 September 1994, not in force) article 2 (1997) 18 *Human Rights Law Journal* 151.

[148] See discussion in Chapter 6, Section 6.3.1.3. Identifying the interpretation of article 2(4) as an area of concern in light of its perceived non-alignment with international treaty law on the right to self-determination, see Mervat Rishmawi, 'The Revised Arab Charter on Human Rights: A Step Forward?' (2005) 5(2) *Human Rights Law Review* 361, 375–376. She does not however assess it against the right to resist in customary international law, pursuant to the UN Charter.

[149] See discussion in Chapter 6, Section 6.3.1.5.

[150] Arab Charter on Human Rights (n 147) article 43. For example, all but four members of the League of Arab States have either signed or ratified the International Covenant. Regarding a

of the right to resist is only theorized in the Universal Declaration and International Covenant. Possibly an argument could be made on behalf of the UN Charter right, provided this is characterized and accepted as a 'human rights instrument'. However the question remains open at present, as it appears that the right to resist under the Arab Charter has not yet been subject to interpretation by the Arab Human Rights Committee.[151] While this supervisory body lacks enforcement powers and does not consider individual complaints,[152] the Statute of the Arab Court of Human Rights adopted in 2014 will permit inter-state litigation, following sufficient ratifications.[153] Thus, although the revised Arab Charter, the Arab Human Rights Committee, and the proposed Arab Court of Human Rights have been criticized for their various other shortcomings,[154] it is nevertheless now a possibility that the article 2(4) right to resist could become the subject of interpretation and litigation in future.[155]

7.3.2 *Apparent Non-recognition in the European and American Systems*

In contrast to its recognition through express provision in the African and Arab systems, the European and Inter-American regional human rights treaties appear not to recognize the right to resist. As with the International Covenant discussed above, while all other 'ordinary' political rights short of resistance – freedom of expression, freedom of peaceful assembly, freedom of

Member State's 'own laws', as indicated in Chapter 5, Section 5.5, only Algeria has recognized a constitutional right to resist.

151 This conclusion is necessarily qualified by the scarcity of documentation of the Committee's work available in translation and scholarly comment on its work available in English.

152 See Mervat Rishmawi, 'The Arab Charter on Human Rights and the League of Arab States: An Update' (2010) 10(1) *Human Rights Law Review* 169, 174. However, its Rules of Procedure adopted in 2014 confirm that it does have the authority to interpret the Charter. See Mervat Rishmawi, *The League of Arab States Human Rights Standards and Mechanisms – Towards further Civil Society Engagement: A Manual for Practitioners* (Open Society Foundations and Cairo Institute for Human Rights Studies 2015) 41.

153 See Statute of the Arab Court of Human Rights (adopted 7 September 2014, not yet entered into force) article 16, in Mohammed Amin Al-Midani, 'Statute of the Arab Court of Human Rights, Non-official English Translation' (Arab Center for International Humanitarian Law and Human Rights Education 2018).

154 See for example Rishmawi (n 148); Mohammed Amin Al-Midani, 'Arab Charter on Human Rights 2004' (2006) 24 *Boston University International Law Journal* 147, 147–149; Rishmawi, 'Arab Charter on Human Rights' (n 152) 172–175; International Commission of Jurists, 'The Arab Court of Human Rights: A Flawed Statute for an Ineffective Court' (International Commission of Jurists 2015).

155 The Arab Charter should be taken seriously as it has the potential to affect more than 395 million people. Rishmawi, 'Arab Charter on Human Rights' (n 152).

association, and the right to participation in the political process – get explicit albeit limited protection,[156] there is no express provision on the right to resist in the European Convention for the Protection of Human Rights and Fundamental Freedoms or in the American Convention on Human Rights.[157] Yet despite this apparent similarity, the European and Inter-American systems depart from the UN system in three important ways.

First, there is no analogous right to self-determination in these regional instruments. Second, in contrast to the International Covenant's open-ended provision on the right to an effective remedy, the European Convention and American Convention clauses are specifically limited to a remedy provided by the state.[158] Third, in this different context, the express right of the state to use lethal force against resistance with force where 'absolutely necessary' under article 2(2)(c) of the European Convention and the American Convention's explicit specification at article 15 that the right to assembly must be exercised 'without arms' suggest instead an apparent position that the state has an absolute monopoly on exceptional measures including force. This amplifies the codified albeit limited and conditional right of the state under the derogation regimes at article 15 of the European Convention and article 27 of the American Convention, but is not necessarily implied in the International Covenant despite its own derogation provision at article 4.[159] All of the above, taken together, make a convincing prima facie case that even

[156] These provisions are, respectively: Convention for the Protection of Human Rights and Fundamental Freedoms (1950) (adopted 4 November 1950, entered into force 3 September 1953) ETS 5 as amended by Protocol 11 (entered into force 1 November 1998) ETS 155 and Protocol 14 (entered into force 1 June 2010) ETS 2194 (European Convention on Human Rights or European Convention) articles 10, 11 and Protocol 1 to the European Convention for the Protection of Human Rights and Fundamental Freedoms (adopted 20 March 1952, entered into force 18 May 1954) ETS 9 article 3; American Convention on Human Rights (adopted 22 November 1969 entered into force 18 July 1978) OASTS 36 (1979) 9 ILM 673 (1970) (American Convention or Inter-American Convention) articles 13, 15, 16, 23. See also the American Declaration of the Rights and Duties of Man (1948) OEA/Ser L/V/11.71 at 17 (1988) articles 4, 20, 21, 22, and its unique article 24 'right of petition' and article 32 'duty to vote'.

[157] Nor for that matter is there an express provision for the right to resist in the American Declaration on the Rights and Duties of Man, despite its presence in the antecedent documents referenced in its title. See Chapter 5, Sections 5.4.1 and 5.4.2.

[158] See European Convention on Human Rights (n 156) article 13; American Convention on Human Rights (n 156) article 25.

[159] Under all these derogation regimes the state may suspend certain rights, provided the state complies with the other conditions. In the International Covenant on Civil and Political Rights (n 5) article 4 and European Convention on Human Rights (n 156) article 15 the 'derogable' rights include the full cluster of political rights. However, article 27(2) of the American Convention on Human Rights (n 156) makes the right to vote non-derogable.

if there may be room for an implied unenumerated or latent right to resist in an ambivalent and ambiguous UN system, at the very least there is no implied right to resist protected by either the European or Inter-American regional human rights systems. More likely, the European and Inter-American systems have foreclosed the possibility under an indirect but discernible doctrine of disavowal.[160]

Even so, upon closer examination there may nevertheless still be just enough room to neutralize the restrictions by preventing misuse of the European and American human rights systems as an obstacle. In each case, this would rely not on dynamic or evolutive interpretation of ambiguous substantive provisions internal to the instrument, but rather on the non-diminution clauses that demand respect for the right as otherwise recognized in general or customary international law.[161]

7.3.2.1 European Convention on Human Rights: Article 2(2)(c) Restriction versus Article 2(2)(a) Exception, Article 15(1) Condition, and Article 53 Non-diminution Clause

The space for constructing a right to resist cognizable under the European Convention seems non-existent, for five reasons. First, while the article 2(2)(c) express permission for the state to use lethal force to suppress 'riots' or 'insurrections' is conditioned on 'lawfulness', necessity, and proportionality, no exceptions are indicated.[162] The logical corollary is that no right to resist could be acknowledged if the resistance involves the use of force, however organized or disorganized. Second, the European Court of Human Rights

[160] It is this more conservative and ostensibly less flexible Euro-American position – and not the more ambiguous International Bill of Human Rights position – that the UN Declaration on Human Rights Defenders consolidates at articles 12 and 13. See Shannonbrooke Murphy, 'The Right to Resist Reconsidered' in David P Keane and Yvonne McDermott (eds), *The Challenge of Human Rights: Past, Present and Future* (Edward Elgar 2012) 92–95.

[161] See Chapter 6, Sections 6.2.3, 6.3, 6.4, and 6.5.

[162] This is a qualification of the right to life protected under the European Convention on Human Rights (n 156) article 2. What is permissible is not 'intentional killing' by the state, but rather 'deprivation of life as an unintended outcome' in a law enforcement context. While the European Court of Human Rights has confirmed that repressing secessionist resistance is among the 'legitimate purposes' under article 2(2)(c), it has yet to exhaustively define these, or to consider whether the right to resist in general or customary international law is among their limits. See William A Schabas, *The European Convention on Human Rights: A Commentary* (Oxford University Press 2015) 122, 147, 152–158. While the jurisprudence generally strongly favours state actions intended to uphold right to life obligations, the scope for lawful state use of force in pursuit of this objective is not unlimited. See European Court of Human Rights, *Guide on Article 2 of the European Convention on Human Rights – Right to Life* (Council of Europe 2020).

'right to protest' jurisprudence is not only strict on the inapplicability of Convention protections to assemblies intending or inciting any form of force, but also often unfavourable to 'otherwise unlawful' protest actions, even where these do not involve the use of force and would thus comply with the 'peacefulness' requirement.[163] Third, the Protocol 1 article 3 right to political participation in the electoral process and related article 11 right to association for this purpose also face potentially significant restrictions, for example if the political party advocates resistance for any reason – including for the purpose of enforcing the right to self-determination of a 'people' in a state.[164] Fourth, the more limited right to a remedy for violations seems to rule out self-help enforcement.[165] Fifth, this restrictiveness is reinforced by the notoriously strong 'margin of appreciation' doctrine the Court has applied to the article 15 derogation regime permitting a state to use special measures to suppress resistance.[166]

There are, however, several narrow possibilities for construction. First, it is possible to read a narrow right to resist in self-defence against unlawful state violence deriving from the article 2(2)(a) exception to the right to life permitting 'defence of any person from unlawful violence' provided this involves 'no more force than is absolutely necessary', a limitation that would be consistent with the concept of a right to resist in self-defence.[167] Second, it is possible that where a valid right to resist under customary international law can be established,[168] the article 15(1) requirement of compliance with other international obligations would include the obligation not to obstruct those with such a right and thereby foreclose derogation by the state.[169] Third, it is possible that the non-diminution and disclaimer clauses, in particular article

[163] See European Court of Human Rights (n 162) 495–498. For a comprehensive study of the European Convention jurisprudence on the ordinary right to protest, see David Mead, 'The Right to Peaceful Protest under the European Convention on Human Rights: A Content Study of Strasbourg Case Law' (2007) 4 *European Human Rights Law Review* 345; David Mead, *The New Law of Peaceful Protest: Rights and Regulation in the Human Rights Act Era* (Hart 2010) 2, 11–12, 57–117, 400–401.

[164] See Schabas (n 162) 499, 504–505, 513–514, 517–521, 1018–1020, 1023–1025, 1030.

[165] See ibid 550–551.

[166] See ibid 82–83, 596, 599.

[167] See European Convention on Human Rights (n 156) article 2. While the European Court case law on article 2(2)(a) has generally concerned the actions of state forces, including where the state claims self-defence in the context of conflicts with rebels and insurgents, this exception is not actually 'confined to a law enforcement context' or to state forces. See Schabas (n 162) 147–150. See also the discussion of the right to resist in self-defence concept in Chapter 4, Section 4.6.1.2.

[168] See Chapter 6, Sections 6.2.3, 6.3, and 6.5.

[169] See European Convention on Human Rights (n 156) article 15.

53, could offset the ability of a state to use the European Convention as legal grounds to obstruct or otherwise deny the customary or constitutional right to resist where validly exercised. The article 53 'safeguard for existing human rights' provides that '[n]othing in this Convention shall be construed as limiting or derogating from any of the human rights and fundamental freedoms which may be ensured under the laws of any High Contracting Party or under any other agreement to which it is a Party'.[170] This would particularly apply to those states that have made constitutional provision for the right to resist.[171] Ultimately it would apply to all European Convention States Parties as also parties to the UN Charter in particular – an 'other agreement' under which a limited implied right to resist has been recognized.[172] The latter is the most likely option for constructing a right to resist that could be acknowledged in the course of interpretation of the European Convention – albeit most likely not directly judicially cognizable thereunder by the European Court.[173]

At a minimum, therefore, as with the International Covenant, the right to resist as a principle of general international law or as recognized in customary international law should provide guidance to the Court in evaluating the application of the derogation clause, insofar as the concept can help analyze where lawful derogations could apply as there is no valid claim to a right to resist and vice versa. Likewise it could assist in differentiating between where limitations that are lawful under ordinary democratic conditions apply, and those conditions where the *lex generalis* ceases to apply due to the presence of primary and secondary triggers for the customary *lex specialis* right to resist exception described in Chapter 6. That said, especially given the Court's frequent presumption in favour of Member State discretion in suppressing resistance, the fact that it would likely require both an unusually persuasive set of facts and an element of determined 'judicial creativity' probably reduces the prospects of the Court adopting an interpretation of state abuse of rights under article 17,[174] abuse of power under

[170] See ibid articles 17, 18, 53. Article 53 is addressed 'to courts and tribunals at the domestic or international level where the Convention is enlisted in support of arguments aimed at restricting rights ... secured by other legal instruments'. Schabas, European Convention on Human Rights (n 162) 904.

[171] See Chapter 5, Section 5.5.1.1.

[172] See Chapter 6, Sections 6.2.3 and 6.3.

[173] On the European Court's application of the general rule of interpretation in article 31(3)(c) of the Vienna Convention on the Law of Treaties, requiring it to also 'take into account' the rules and principles of 'general international law', see Schabas (n 162) 33, 35, 37–42, 65.

[174] Article 17 'operates as a principle of interpretation' ostensibly used to help assess the margin of appreciation, necessity, and proportionality of rights restrictions, and is intended to prevent exploitation and misuse of the Convention including by states. See ibid 616–617, 620.

article 18,[175] or unlawful diminution contrary to article 53,[176] premised on recognition of a right to resist under general or customary international law.[177]

7.3.2.2 American Convention on Human Rights: Article 15 Restriction versus Article 29 Non-diminution Clause

There also appears to be negligible interpretive room for constructing a right to resist cognizable under the American Convention, for four reasons. First, that article 15 expressly rules out Convention protection of assembly with arms, without indicating any exception,[178] at a minimum suggests no possibility of Convention recognition of a right to resist using force, even for self-defence.[179] Second, article 25 narrows the scope of the right to a remedy down to a 'right to judicial protection',[180] which therefore expressly does not cover self-help remedies – even if short of force. Third, article 32(2) limits all rights not only by 'the rights of others' but also 'by the security of all', a provision that appears to augment the right of a state to restrict even ordinary political rights whether or not applying the Convention's derogation regime.[181] Finally, the apparent disavowal doctrine is reinforced by a drafting history which resulted in non-inclusion of a codified right to resist despite a specific Cuban proposal.[182] Indeed, elsewhere the Inter-American system

[175] Article 18 case law is 'exceedingly sparse' with only 'a handful' of breach determinations. This may be at least in part because '"the whole structure of the Convention rests on the general assumption that public authorities in the member States act in good faith"'. See ibid 624, 626.

[176] Article 53 is 'rarely referenced' by the Court and there are 'almost no citations' in its jurisprudence. See ibid 903–904.

[177] Yet on the Court's record of 'judicial law-making' through 'dynamic and evolutive' interpretation, see ibid 47–49.

[178] On the application and interpretation of article 15 see Laurence Burgorgue-Larsen and Amaya Úbeda de Torres, *The Inter-American Court of Human Rights: Case Law and Commentary* (Oxford University Press 2011) 589–612.

[179] Note that unlike the European Convention provision discussed above, the American Convention's article 4 'right to life' does not contain a self-defence or defence of others exception. See American Convention on Human Rights (n 156) article 4.

[180] See ibid article 25. However, on the Convention having provided important judicial remedies against patterns of 'gross violations' arising from what had been a regional prevalence of 'tyranny' or 'dictatorship', see Robert K Goldman, 'History and Action: The Inter-American Human Rights System and the Role of the Inter-American Commission on Human Rights' (2009) 31 *Human Rights Quarterly* 856, 871–874; Cecilia Medina, *The American Convention on Human Rights: Crucial Rights and Their Theory and Practice* (Instersentia 2014) vii–ix.

[181] See American Convention on Human Rights (n 156) article 32(2). See also ibid articles 13, 15, 16, 23.

[182] For brief reference to the Cuban proposal for an express right to resist 'manifest acts of oppression and tyranny', rejected because it was 'not yet recognized in the international juridical order' due to lack of means for its enforcement, see Alwyn V Freeman, 'The First

recognizes a converse 'duty to obey the law and other legitimate commands' under article 33 of the American Declaration, and its article 34 'duty to serve the community and the nation' is defined exclusively as civil and military service or public office.[183]

Again, however, there are narrow possibilities for construction relying on the article 29 disclaimer and non-diminution clause, primarily to prevent the American Convention being used to obstruct or deny the right to resist since, according to articles 1(1) and 62(3) only Convention rights are directly protected. Notwithstanding this, article 29 states that nothing in the Convention 'shall be interpreted as … (b) restricting the enjoyment or exercise of any right or freedom recognized by virtue of the laws of any State party or by virtue of another convention to which one of the said states is a party'. Nor shall it be interpreted as '(c) precluding other rights or guarantees that are inherent in the human personality or derived from representative democracy as a form of government' or '(d) excluding or limiting the effect that the American Declaration of the Rights and Duties of Man and other international acts of the same nature may have'.[184] Clause 29(b) would therefore apply where a State Party has made provision for a constitutional right to resist,[185] but would also ultimately apply to all States Parties as also States Parties to the UN Charter, and to this extent could be interpreted as indirectly recognizing a limited customary right to resist that cannot be interfered with.[186] Clauses 29(c) and 29(d) potentially open the way for constructions that take account of the concept of a human right to resist

Meeting of the Inter-American Council of Jurists' (1950) 44(2) *American Journal of International Law* 374, 375; DJ, 'The Inter-American Council of Jurists' (1951) 4(4) *International Law Quarterly* 521. On the unsatisfactory level of detail available from the *travaux préparatoires* see Medina (n 180) vii. For an overview of the drafting history see Goldman (n 180) 858–865.

[183] See American Declaration of the Rights and Duties of Man (n 156) articles 33, 34 [emphasis added].

[184] American Convention on Human Rights (n 156) article 29 [emphasis added]. Pursuant to article 29 the Inter-American Court '"can observe that certain acts or omissions … violate human rights"' pursuant to treaties outside the Court's subject matter jurisdiction, which '"may be taken into consideration as elements for the interpretation of the American Convention"'. See Burgorgue-Larsen and Torres (n 178) 56–71, 69.

[185] See Chapter 5, Section 5.5.1.1. On developments in Latin American constitutional case law suggesting the possibility of indirect recognition of an exceptional, limited, and conditional right to resist in countries lacking express constitutional provision, achieved through dynamic interpretation of the right to freedom of expression, see Roberto Gargarella and Ramiro Alvarez Ugarte, 'Freedom of Expression and Social Protest' in Juan F Gonzalez-Bertomeu and Roberto Gargarella (eds), *The Latin American Casebook: Courts, Constitutions, Rights* (Routledge 2016).

[186] See Chapter 6, Sections 6.2.3 and 6.3.

implicit in the Universal Declaration of Human Rights, as both declaratory instrument 'of the same nature' as the American Declaration and source of codification of 'inherent' human rights, now indicating customary international law.[187] Therefore, the most likely option for constructing a right to resist that could be acknowledged in the course of interpretation of the American Convention – albeit most likely not directly judicially cognizable thereunder by the Inter-American Court – would rely upon reference to other sources such as constitutions, treaties, customary international law, or soft law, combined with the non-diminution obligation in article 29(b), (c), and (d).[188]

As with the International Covenant and European Convention, at a minimum the right to resist as a principle of general international law or as recognized in customary international law should provide guidance to the Inter-American Court in the evaluation of whether ordinary limitations clauses apply under the *lex generalis* or instead the customary right to resist as a *lex specialis* exception. It also provides similar guidance in the interpretation of the article 27(1) clause in the Inter-American derogation regime, under which a state may not employ measures that are 'inconsistent with its other obligations under international law'[189] which would include a duty to not obstruct those validly exercising a customary right to resist. As discussed in Section 7.2 above and in Chapter 6, the right to resist concept could also potentially provide guidance in the application of certain corroborative protections for political offenders under the American Convention that are similar to the customary corroborative right to protection from extradition or refoulement for political offences.[190]

In addition, the right to resist as recognized in customary international law can provide direction as to interpretation of certain provisions of other instruments within the Inter-American system, pursuant to the non-diminution clause regarding UN Charter rights and obligations at article 102 of the Charter of the Organization of American States.[191] Indeed, the commitment to democracy promotion while respecting the principle of non-intervention as a 'purpose' of the Organization could be interpreted as tacitly recognizing the

187 Gargarella and Ugarte (n 185).

188 Since the Inter-American Court's subject matter jurisdiction is restricted to provisions in the American Convention itself, it can use other treaties, customary law, and 'soft law' including declaratory instruments in an 'advisory capacity' to interpret the Convention but cannot apply them directly. See Burgorgue-Larsen and Torres (n 178) 57–58, 63, 68, 70–71.

189 See American Convention on Human Rights (n 156) article 27.

190 Ibid articles 4, 22.

191 See Charter of the Organization of American States (adopted 30 April 1948, entered into force 13 December 1951) 119 UNTS 3, article 102.

necessity of self-help and the right to resist under certain conditions.[192] As a consequence of article 102 of its Charter, in the application of its Resolution on 'Representative Democracy' distinction must be made between an 'interruption' amounting to an unlawful military coup and forcible exercise of internal or external self-determination where customary right to resist elements are met.[193] Likewise, the customary right to resist – or the constitutional right to resist in a Member State where relevant – must inform the application of the 'pro-democratic' or 'anti-coup' clauses permitting and regulating certain limited forms of intervention by the Organization of American States under articles 17–21 of the Inter-American Democratic Charter,[194] premised on the recognition of a peoples' 'right to democracy' pursuant to article 1 of that Charter.[195] Indeed, such applications and constructions of a right to resist for the self-help enforcement of internal self-determination under the broader Inter-American system seem potentially more promising than the highly restricted interpretive opportunities provided by the American Convention.[196]

7.4 'SOFT LAW' CODIFICATION: DRAFT ARTICLE 7 OF THE DRAFT UN DECLARATION ON THE RIGHT TO PEACE

Chapter 6 reviewed the process by which UN codification of a right to resist was first considered during the course of drafting the Universal Declaration of Human Rights. Ultimately such proposals were withdrawn in the absence of consensus. This pattern recently repeated itself at the UN Human Rights Council, which considered a proposed codification of the right to resist as a substantive provision in a draft 'UN Declaration on the Right to Peace'. Its recommended inclusion survived most stages of a ten-year hybrid civil society–UN drafting process,[197] but it was ultimately excluded prior to the final version

[192] See Resolution on 'Representative Democracy' OAS GA Res 1080 (XXI-0/91) (5 June 1991) preamble; Inter-American Democratic Charter (adopted 11 September 2001) OAS GA Res 1, OAS Doc OEA/SerP/res.1 (2001) 40 ILM 1289 preamble.

[193] That is, the OAS General Assembly commits to 'adopt any decisions deemed appropriate, in accordance with the [OAS] Charter and international law'. See Resolution on 'Representative Democracy' (n 187) [1]–[2].

[194] See Inter-American Democratic Charter (n 192) articles 17–21.

[195] See ibid article 1.

[196] Yet two Inter-American Court practices signal potential to take account of a human right to resist as recognized under general or customary international law, on the basis of the UN Charter: evolutive interpretation and use of compromissory clauses to extend the scope of its subject matter jurisdiction. See Medina (n 180) ix–x; Burgorgue-Larsen and Torres (n 178) 57–58, 62–65, 67, 70.

[197] This UN process was initiated by 'Promotion of the Right of Peoples to Peace' UNHRC Res 8/9 (18 June 2008) [1], [10(a)]. The Council subsequently referred the matter to the UN

adopted by the UN General Assembly in 2016.[198] Had it succeeded, draft article 7 would have represented the broadest express provision for the right to resist in international law to date and the most detailed statement of how the right is understood in the universal system, legally significant even though as a declaration the instrument itself would not be binding on states. This is because such non-binding instruments, often known as 'soft law', have an acknowledged role both in the process of formation of customary international law and its evolution into codified law through treaties.[199]

The UN Human Rights Council process originated in a civil society-led UN codification campaign initiative ultimately endorsed by an international coalition of hundreds of non-governmental organizations, launched by the Spanish Society for International Human Rights Law in 2006 with the 'Luarca Declaration on the Human Right to Peace' and later endorsing a revised 'Santiago Declaration on the Human Right to Peace'.[200] Both declarations contained provisions on the right to resist that would become the basis for the later UN draft version.[201] The campaign successfully persuaded the expert-led UN Human Rights Council Advisory Committee of the merit of including the right,[202] and an express formulation of the right to resist was later advanced by

Human Rights Council Advisory Committee, requesting preparation of a draft Declaration. See 'Promotion of the Right of Peoples to Peace' UNHRC Res 14/3 (23 June 2010) [15]. On the civil society-led process that preceded this, see below n 200.

198 'Declaration on the Right to Peace' UNGA Res 71/189 (19 December 2016). Since this was not adopted by consensus it is unlikely to be considered declarative of customary international law.

199 See for example Boyle (n 1); Shelton (n 1) 141, 164–166.

200 For a fuller account of the civil society campaign process see David Fernández Puyana, 'World Campaign on the Human Right to Peace' in Carlos Villán Durán and Carmelo Faleh Pérez (eds), *Contribuciones regionales para una declaración universal del derecho humano a la paz* (Asociación Española para el Derecho Internacional de los Derechos Humanos 2010). For an inside account of the UN drafting and negotiation process, see Christian Guillermet-Fernández and David Fernández Puyana, 'The General Assembly Adopts the Declaration on the Right to Peace: An Opportunity to Strengthen the Linkage between Peace, Human Rights and Development in the New Millennium' (2017) 2(3) *Eruditio* 39; Christian Guillermet-Fernández, David Fernández Puyana, and Miguel Bosé, *The Right to Peace: Past, Present and Future* (UN Educational, Scientific and Cultural Organization, University for Peace 2017).

201 See Spanish Society for the Advancement of International Human Rights Law, 'Luarca (Asturias) Declaration on the Human Right to Peace' (2006) article 6; International Congress on the Human Right to Peace, 'Santiago Declaration on the Human Right to Peace' (2010) article 6.

202 UN Human Rights Council Advisory Committee Drafting Group, 'Progress Report on the Right of Peoples to Peace' UN Doc/A/HRC/AC/6/CRP.3 (22 December 2010) 5 [22(d)], 12 Part VII [42]–[44](a)–(b) describes it as 'an important element of peoples' right to peace' and 'essential to achieving and maintaining a just peace'.

the Advisory Committee as draft article 7.[203] However, the right to resist provision did not survive the UN Human Rights Council's Open-Ended Inter-governmental Working Group subsequently tasked with agreeing a declaration text to bring before the Council.[204] It does not appear in the final resolution endorsed by the Human Rights Council ultimately proposed and adopted by the United Nations General Assembly in 2016 as a new 'UN Declaration on the Right to Peace'.[205] Yet despite its failure and certain shortcomings in its formulation, draft article 7 nevertheless deserves closer analysis as the most comprehensive proposed codification of the right to resist yet formally considered for adoption at international level.

7.4.1 *Elements of the Draft Article 7 Provision: The Right of 'Resistance and Opposition to Oppression'*

The final version of draft article 7(1) as recommended by the UN Human Rights Council Advisory Committee provided that 'All peoples and individuals have the right to resist and oppose oppressive colonial, foreign occupation or dictatorial domination (domestic oppression)'. Draft article 7(2) provided that 'Everyone has the right to oppose aggression, genocide, war crimes and crimes against humanity, violations of other universally recognized human rights, and any propaganda in favour of war or incitement to violence and violations of the right to peace'.[206] Using the Chapter 4 analytical framework, it is possible to identify the elements of draft article 7 and evaluate it against the current state of the right in international law.

The rights-holders are clearly stated as 'all peoples and individuals'. While the provision does not specify any secondary trigger conditions such as 'necessity' or 'last resort', it identifies four distinct sets of conditions sufficient

[203] See 'Progress Report of the Human Rights Council Advisory Committee on the Right of Peoples to Peace' UN Doc A/HRC/17/39 (1 April 2011) section D 'Proposed Standards' 9–10 [35]–[37]; 'Report of the Human Rights Council Advisory Committee on the Right of Peoples to Peace' UN Doc A/HRC/20/31 (16 April 2012) annex 'Draft Declaration on the Right to Peace' article 7.

[204] Its initial mandate specified negotiations 'on the basis of the draft submitted by the Advisory Committee'. See 'Promotion of the Right to Peace' UNHRC Res 20/15 (17 July 2012) [1].

[205] See UN Human Rights Council 'Declaration on the Right to Peace' UN Doc A/HRC/32.L.18 (24 June 2016); 'Declaration on the Right to Peace' UNHRC Res 32/28 (18 July 2016).

[206] 'Report of the Human Rights Council Advisory Committee on the Right of Peoples to Peace' (16 April 2012) (n 203) 'Draft Declaration on the Right to Peace' article 7. The legal basis relied upon was the preamble of the Universal Declaration of Human Rights and the relevant text from UNGA Res 2625. See UN Human Rights Council Advisory Committee Drafting Group, 'Progress Report on the Right of Peoples to Peace' (22 December 2010) (n 202) 12 Part VII [42]–[44](a)–(b).

to act as a trigger. The first set of trigger conditions under article 7(1) includes foreign occupation and colonization as well as 'domestic oppression' – the latter also styled as 'dictatorial domination' – all of which conceptually relate to the right to external and internal self-determination. This therefore appears to affirm and clarify or extend the customary international right implied under the UN Charter and its interpretive 'Declaration of Principles of International Law' discussed in Chapter 6, and confirm the theorized latent unenumerated right in the International Covenant discussed in Section 7.2.1. It thus represents a long overdue progressive clarification of the right to resist as it relates to 'internal' self-determination, on which the law is presently ambiguous at best. The second set of triggers under article 7(2) relate to any of the acts now codified as internationally criminal – aggression, war crimes, genocide, and crimes against humanity. This appears to formalize and clarify or extend the implied customary international right arising from the 'Nuremberg Principles' discussed in Chapter 6 and implicitly corroborated in the Rome Statute, as discussed in Section 7.2.3. Indeed, this is also reinforced and further clarified by the inclusion of a complementary more limited article 5(2) 'right to disobey' manifestly unlawful orders, an implied corollary right consistent with customary international criminal law.[207] The third and broadest set of trigger conditions under article 7(2) relate to 'violations of other universally recognized human rights'. This appears to formalize the implied customary right pursuant to the Universal Declaration of Human Rights discussed in Chapter 6 and the latent unenumerated right theorized in the International Covenant discussed earlier. It would have not only vindicated the various theories about an implied right to resist in international human rights law, but would have both clarified and generously expanded the conditions and violations which could be lawfully resisted. It imposes only two preconditions. First, the right in question must already be recognized somewhere in international human rights law, meaning either in a treaty or in customary international law, and therefore the right to resist cannot be used to assert 'new' rights. Second, there must be a violation. However, it is not specified that this violation need already have occurred and so it may involve only a risk of violation. Nor must a certain threshold of violation be met before resistance can be considered lawful. As such, it potentially represents a very significant new tool for both preventive and remedial action in human rights. The final – and least clear – set of trigger conditions under article 7(2) relate to war

[207] See 'Report of the Human Rights Council Advisory Committee on the Right of Peoples to Peace' (16 April 2012) (n 203) 'Draft Declaration on the Right to Peace' article 5 'the right to conscientious objection to military service'.

propaganda or other incitement. Permissible means are not specified, and therefore presumed both inclusive and subject to the customary limitations including proportionality, and otherwise regulation imposed by international human rights law and international criminal law, as discussed in Chapter 6.[208]

The duty-bearers are not only all states and the UN General Assembly, Security Council, and Human Rights Council, but also 'every individual and every organ of society', pursuant to the general provision at draft article 13.[209] The obligation is one of 'preservation, promotion and implementation' for 'effective and practical realization of the right' by 'progressive measures' to 'secure its universal and effective recognition and observance'.[210] Draft article 14(3) imposes an additional obligation of implementation on Member States 'by adopting relevant legislative, judicial, administrative, educational or other measures to promote [the Declaration's] effective realization',[211] and draft article 13(6) empowers the Human Rights Council to monitor implementation and 'report to relevant United Nations bodies'.[212]

As to its object and purpose, the provision is apparently intended as a *lex specialis* exception operating as a lawful means of enforcement of the right to peace. On the one hand, it is understood as contributing to conflict prevention, in the form of a deterrence clause aimed at those who would use state power to abuse human rights. On the other, it is understood as contributing to restoration of peace by providing a means of removing a human rights-abusing regime when other lawful methods – such as elections, litigation or judicial review, peaceful protest, appeals to the international community for assistance – fail.

The potential to authorize engagement in human rights violations on the basis of a confirmed right to resist is clearly excluded by the internal limitations under the disclaimer and non-diminution clauses. These are not specific to the right itself, but rather are found in the generally applicable Final Provisions at draft article 14(1) and (2). The application of the interpretation clause at article 14(1) ensures against the intentional abuse of the provision by obviously non-qualifying groups or by states using either qualifying or

208 Suggesting the addition of express limits on permissible means and an alternative formulation that includes a reference to 'last resort' to force exclusively in self-defence, see Gloria María Gallego García, 'El amplio derecho a la resistencia en la Declaración de Luarca: Objeción de conciencia, desobediencia civil y resistencia contra la opresión y la barbarie' in Durán and Pérez (n 200) 175–213, 210–212.

209 See 'Report of the Human Rights Council Advisory Committee on the Right of Peoples to Peace' (16 April 2012) (n 203) 'Draft Declaration on the Right to Peace' article 13(1)–(5).

210 See 'Draft Declaration on the Right to Peace' (ibid) article 13(1), (3), (4), (5).

211 See ibid article 14(3).

212 See ibid article 13(6).

non-qualifying groups unlawfully as an instrument of intervention or aggression. The article 14(2) interpretation clause effectively 'limits the limitation' in an appropriate way, providing a safeguard against the risk of ungenerous interpretation – whether out of excessive formalism or bias even if unintentional.[213] Importantly, the draft article 7 right to resist is not subject to derogation. Rather, it is precisely constructed as a device to insure against the abuse of derogation by states.

On the basis of these elements, draft article 7 therefore would have generally constituted codified affirmation, clarification, and progressive development of the current customary international law recognizing the right to resist. In particular, it had the potential to contribute substantive legal value by way of its express recognition of the right to resist domestic oppression and crimes against humanity. This would have helped redress persistent and vexing ambiguities in the customary international law regarding the right to resist or to rebel against one's own abusive government. Specifically, it would clarify customary international law as expressed in the fifth paragraph of the fifth principle of UN General Assembly Resolution 2625, which is in the form of an indirect or implied right to resist forcible deprivation of the right to self-determination. It would clarify that there is also a right to resist in defence or in pursuit of the 'internal' dimension of self-determination that extends beyond the case of racist regimes, and that in some such cases there may be more than an obligation on the UN and its Member States not to obstruct. Article 7 or a similar codification could have provided corroborative grounds for evolutive interpretation of the Universal Declaration of Human Rights and International Covenant, in a manner suggested by the theories that these instruments contain an implied or latent right to resist. In particular, the affirmation of a right to resist 'violations of other universally recognized human rights' would not only represent a significant substantive advance in the law of the right to resist, it could also provide an important new tool for human rights defenders, with practical potential for expanding the scope of internationally lawful preventive and remedial action. Furthermore, an express codification of this nature could also clarify the scope and application of the article 20(2) right to resist oppression in the African Charter which, as discussed, is presently difficult to determine without reference to the legal regime of the universal system due to its dependent formulation.

That said, the article is not without drafting deficiencies. Firstly, it is not obvious what its use of the additional cognate term 'right to oppose' in the heading and both clauses intends. As discussed in Chapter 2, the term used

[213] See ibid article 14(1)–(2).

here as supplementary is probably redundant – adding nothing conceptually to either the 'right to resist' or to 'the right to protest' under ordinary conditions already protected by political rights guarantees of the *lex generalis*. Used interchangeably, it likewise adds no value. For the sake of clarity and certainty, this term should be avoided in future formulations. Secondly, while a right to resist racist regimes is certainly implied in both clauses of article 7, it is not expressly stated as it was in earlier drafts. Given the establishment of this form of the right in customary international law, there is probably no harm in restating it for future avoidance of doubt that this not only constitutes a potential trigger for the exercise of the right to resist but also validates external self-determination remedies if internal forms prove unavailable or ineffective and the secondary forcible deprivation trigger condition is present. Thirdly, it is not clear from the *travaux préparatoires* or other literature what a 'right to resist propaganda or incitement' would consist of, or how it would add to the right as otherwise defined in the two clauses. If this cannot be explained, it should be excluded from future formulations as redundant, since propaganda for war and incitement to hatred and violence are already prohibited under the International Covenant.[214] Fourthly, the initial use of the modifier 'oppressive' to describe situations of colonization and foreign occupation is presumably intended to indicate that this brings them under the 'right to resist oppression' concept. However, it is probably not helpful, as its insertion implies that there may be situations of colonization and foreign occupation that are not oppressive, thereby potentially unnecessarily adding a required element to establish trigger conditions that does not fully align with the customary right's secondary trigger condition. Additionally, the use of the florid term 'dictatorial domination' in addition to the more explanatory 'domestic oppression' is not only redundant but potentially creates an unnecessary additional conceptual hurdle best avoided in future formulations. This is important because not all regimes abusive of human rights would necessarily fit a 'dictatorial' definition. Finally, the earlier civil society drafts of the complementary right of disobedience were probably more useful in clarifying the customary cognate right derived from the Nuremberg Principles, though these drafts aspire beyond codification of existing custom, with certain aspects amounting to ambitious progressive development.[215]

[214] See International Covenant on Civil and Political Rights (n 5) article 20.

[215] Compare the significantly broader 'Luarca Declaration' (n 201) article 5 'right to disobedience and conscientious objection', and even more detailed seven clause provision in the 'Santiago Declaration' (n 201) article 5.

7.4.2 *Prospects after the Second Failure to Codify the Right to Resist in a UN Human Rights Instrument*

Ultimately, no matter how appealing the idea, the new UN Declaration on the Right to Peace was probably not the best place to codify the right to resist. According to the Inter-governmental Working Group Chairperson-Rapporteur's account, not even the final compromise declaration adopted could achieve consensus among states and regional groupings 'because of the lack of agreement on the title and Article 1', which is to say that the characterization of 'peace' as a 'right' remains disputed.[216] In this context, the right to resist was an obvious candidate for negotiated exclusion, given its own controversial nature and marginality to a core 'right to peace' concept contentious in itself.[217] Indeed, in the first session of the Inter-governmental Working Group draft article 7 was immediately identified as too 'controversial' and 'ambiguous' and proposed for deletion, or amendment to essentially reflect current well-established customary law in the elements of UN General Assembly Resolution 2625,[218] but with a peaceful means stipulation.[219] It appears from the available documentation that while only one Member State made a substantive argument in opposition to article 7, none submitted a formal position in its support.[220] Thus the significantly revised 'Guillermet draft' text dropped draft article 7, along with most of the other draft substantive provisions.[221]

216 See Guillermet-Fernández and Puyana (n 200) 54.

217 Those in favour were largely 'Non-Aligned Movement' states. Those opposed were largely European states. For patterns of support for and opposition to the initiative and its core concept among UN Member States, as well as the voting patterns on various drafts and the final Declaration see ibid; Guillermet-Fernández et al (n 200) 143–183, 289–302.

218 See Chapter 6, Section 6.3.

219 See 'Report of the Open-Ended Inter-governmental Working Group on the Draft United Nations Declaration on the Right to Peace' [First Session] UN Doc A/HRC/WG.13/1/2 (26 April 2013) [60]–[61].

220 See 'Open-Ended Intergovernmental Working Group on a Draft United Nations Declaration on the Right to Peace, first session (18–21 February 2013): Canadian Position' (undated); 'Promotion of the Right to Peace' UNHRC Res 23/16 (24 June 2013) [4].

221 See 'Report of the Open-Ended Intergovernmental Working Group on a Draft United Nations Declaration on the Right to Peace' [Second Session] UN Doc A/HRC/27/63 (8 August 2014), endorsed in 'Promotion of the Right to Peace' UNHRC Res (3 October 2014) [4], the subsequent 'Promotion of the Right to Peace' UNHRC Res 30/12 (13 October 2015) [1] and ultimately the 'Declaration on the Right to Peace' UNHRC Res 32/28 (n 200) [1]–[2]. The civil society campaign called for the withdrawal of the Guillermet draft and denounced the adopted Declaration because it 'does not recognise either the human right to peace or its essential elements'. See Spanish Society for International Human Rights Law, 'Urgent Appeal to All CSOs Supporting the Human Right to Peace' (22 June 2016); 'Press Release' (30

Even apart from these unfavourable circumstances, it is certainly possible that draft article 7 could never have met a demand for consensus at Intergovernmental Working Group level. How difficult a future effort would be is not possible to gauge from this instance, however, as it does not appear from the available documentation that this proposed provision received sufficiently clear and detailed advocacy or adequate dedicated promotion.[222] Presumably, draft article 7 is among the targets of general criticism by the skeptic states, that some of the draft provisions are: based on rights that are not currently recognized and do not otherwise have a basis in international law; vague, ambiguous, or undefined as legal concepts; unenforceable, and non-justiciable insofar as they cannot be clearly applied to individuals and secured by law; potentially inconsistent with other norms of the UN Charter. All of these criticisms have been levelled at the right to resist in the past by one commentator or another, and are all answerable by a closer examination of the concept and of the law. While true that a widely agreed definition of the human right to resist as a legal concept has yet to be achieved, that fact alone does not mean that such conceptual clarification and definition is inherently impossible. Rather, a thoughtful elaboration of the right in a revised article 7 could have done much to contribute to this process. It is unfortunate that the civil society and expert submissions and reports did not present clear arguments as to how the right to resist is related to the right to peace, and why its recognition should be considered necessary for the fulfilment of a right to peace. Nor did the proposition benefit from a detailed analysis as to how the proposed codification at article 7 would have had the effect of clarifying and

January 2017). For an alternative account of the civil society response as more positive, see Guillermet-Fernández and Puyana (n 200) 41–42, 51, 52–53; Guillermet-Fernández et al (n 200) 175–177.

[222] For example, the sole in-depth presentation of the right to resist as included in the draft Declaration is a concept paper which does not assess or explain the status of the right in positive international law. See García (n 208) 175–213. The formal civil society submission identifies the international legal basis of draft article 7 as the preamble of the Universal Declaration and UNGA Res 2625 but without further explanation or argumentation to demonstrate this, and the conceptual linkage between the right to resist and the right to peace is never clearly explained. See Carlos Villán Durán, 'Artículo 7: Resistencia y oposición a la opresión' (Asociación Española para el Derecho Internacional de los Derechos Humanos, 18–21 February 2013); Carlos Villán Durán and David Fernández Puyana, 'Analysis of the First Session of the Open-ended Working Group on the Draft Declaration on the Right to Peace' (Spanish Society for International Human Rights Law, February 2013) 9–10, section I, fn 53, 54, 55; Spanish Society for International Human Rights Law-International Observatory of the Human Right to Peace-International Association of Peace Messenger Cities, 'Joint Statement on the United Nations Declaration on the Human Right to Peace' (30 June 2014) 8 [G].

advancing any customary international legal right as currently recognized in the commonly agreed source – UN General Assembly Resolution 2625 – and in particular the implied rights claimed for the Universal Declaration of Human Rights and the Nuremberg Principles. These omissions should temper any conclusions about viability of codification. Without greater legal accuracy and further explanation, it is unlikely that this proposition will ever persuade the already skeptical Member States.

7.4.3 *Legal Value of Future International Codification of the Human Right to Resist*

Draft article 7 or a similar codification improved along the lines indicated could contribute practical legal value, through an implementation provision such as those in draft articles 13 and 14. At the international level it could provide a source of regulatory guidance, even if only as a soft law standard. Had such a standard been agreed, it could have been used to assist the UN Security Council or similar regional bodies in their deliberations as to the legal basis of provision of authorized multilateral assistance to parties requesting help: either those exercising a right to resist, or alternatively to a state asserting itself against those without a valid right. Or, where the decision is to stop short of assisting resistance, taking alternative measures to ensure that the international community at least 'does not obstruct' the resistance either directly or indirectly, is another option. At the individual level, such a standard could be used to support a defence or mitigation argument in criminal proceedings, or as the basis for asserting 'protected political activity' not meeting the thresholds for criminal exclusion in refugee claims proceedings where exclusion under article 1F(b) of the Refugee Convention is a factor, or as a consideration in extradition cases. As such, at the domestic level, it could promote the adoption of a constitutional right to resist for those states still lacking such a provision, appropriate amendments to relevant laws, and allowance for related defences or mitigations, thus extending domestic recognition and thus potential for justiciability or other enforcement to more jurisdictions. A standard for this right set at international level could also help ensure that existing constitutional right to resist provisions are reformulated, interpreted, and enforced in a way that is human rights-compliant. Such are the human rights benefits lost as a result of this episode, which follows the Universal Declaration of Human Rights as another missed opportunity to increase clarity and certainty through international codification of the human right to resist.

7.5 CONCLUSION

The evidence suggests that current prospects for firmer recognition of the human right to resist in both the universal and regional treaty systems depend largely on dynamic interpretation or other construction, regardless of the presence or absence of express provision. It is true of the theorized unenumerated right in the International Covenant. It is also true of the European Convention and the American Convention, which appear to accord the right either non-recognition or disavowal, yet there is still room to ensure that even if these Conventions cannot be used to guarantee the right to resist, they also cannot be used as grounds for lawful obstruction of the customary right. Finally, it is even true of the express provisions in the African Charter and Arab Charter, which await fuller interpretive clarification. Thus, while the varying status of the right to resist has the potential to generate legal fissures between systems, the common reference point of the right's recognition in customary international law makes possible greater convergence through the mechanism of interpretation. This may yet prove a sound basis for future progressive development.

While there are some grounds for optimism regarding interpretive prospects within current legal constraints, the outlook remains bleak even for 'soft law' codification in light of the most recent failure at the UN Human Rights Council. It is nevertheless possible to identify factors that could inform and improve chances of success in future codification efforts, such as initiatives for adoption of a declaration or additional protocol. First, given the marginal status of the right in the twenty-first century, codification or other formal recognition is unlikely to advance without expanding the presently limited knowledge of the right to resist among human rights advocates and defenders. This requires a generally agreed definition and common analytical framework – such as that proposed in Chapters 2 and 4 and applied in Chapters 5–7 of this study – to guide further discussion. A shared sense of the legal concept's history and past prominent advocates, as well as the points of unresolved debate in the present – such as that presented in Part I of this study – would serve a complementary purpose. A more systematic understanding of the right's status in positive law both domestic and international – such as that presented in Part II – is essential to consolidate gains, as well as identify and fill gaps. Second, advocates will need to apply this more forensic understanding of the right to dedicated promotion efforts, since to many the idea of a human 'right to resist' as an enforceable legal right is counterintuitive or perceived as potentially contrary to the interests of peace and security. Neutrals will need to be walked through the arguments. Opponents will need to be countered with evidence such as that provided here or generated by future research. Fundamentally, however, there will be no advance in the law unless familiarity with the legal concept increases to the point where claimants and counsel use the existing law accurately in order to press claims, and adjudicators or other decision-makers treat these receptively rather than dismissively.

8

Conclusions and an Agenda for Reconsideration

8.1 THE CASE FOR REINSTATEMENT AND RECONSIDERATION

The preceding consolidation of accumulated legal scholarship, emphasizing the teachings of the most highly qualified publicists on the human right to resist, and examination of the positive law both constitutional and international, yields one principal conclusion based on the evidence. That is, the case for reinstatement of the right to resist in the human rights lexicon as a viable legal concept capable of further study, evolutive development, positivization, and enforcement has been met. This concluding chapter reprises the study's main findings on the concept and on the law which not only make this case but also help set an agenda for further reconsideration. It outlines the related theoretical role for legal scholars and practical role for other human rights defenders, whether legal practitioners or advocates more generally, in advancing our understanding of the human right to resist and enhancing its practical protective effect.

8.2 THE HUMAN RIGHT TO RESIST RECONSIDERED AS A CONTEMPORARY LEGAL CONCEPT

Part I of the book makes a series of findings that inform a definitional and conceptual theory of the human right to resist as a distinct *lex specialis*/ exceptional political right, based on its historical trajectory and comparative analysis of contemporary theories of the right as proposed by others to date. The definitional and conceptual theory advanced here arises not only from findings on what is currently agreed and not agreed between theorists, but also from further findings on what is reflected in the contemporary positive law from the Part II research. This is complemented by conclusions on the right's nature and function, and on the relationship of the right to resist with its cognate terms including their 'common core' elements, leading to a general consolidated working definition and consequent analytical framework identifying the content elements of the right.

8.2.1 A *Distinct* Lex Specialis/*Exceptional Political Right*

There is no agreed standard definition of the human right to resist, but complementary elements have been identified by various theorists that can be drawn into a useful and satisfactory composite definition, such as that proposed below. Many theorists agree that the right to resist is an exceptional political right of individuals, groups, and peoples, which belongs in the law of social contract and public law: that is, constitutional law in the domestic sphere and international human rights law in the international sphere. If it is a political right then it is related to, but also distinct from, the ordinary law on freedom of expression and assembly, association, and participation, particularly as it only applies under certain conditions that give rise to the exception. As such, the law governing the right to resist can be considered a *lex specialis* to the *lex generalis* political rights in international human rights law.

This human right to resist is in certain respects related to, but should not be confused with, other concepts in law or in political theory. It is distinct. For example, it is not the same as the doctrine of tyrannicide, its cruder ancient antecedent. Equally, it is not governed by the international humanitarian law definition of 'resistance movements', found in a different body of law for the specialized purpose of determining *jus in bello* rights and obligations, applying exclusively under conditions of armed conflict, though certain groups exercising a right to resist may become subject to that law. Nor should it be confused with the customary public international law concepts relating to 'insurgency' and 'belligerency', including the concepts of 'legitimacy' or 'effectiveness', for the purposes of recognition either during conduct of hostilities or thereafter, though those groups exercising a right to resist who have pretensions to statehood may also be evaluated under these criteria for that express purpose.

Legal scholars can generally agree that the right to resist is a secondary right, but some differences remain on detail as to the appropriate triggering conditions. Among those that have been suggested are: primary human right violations; only serious and systematic violations amounting to 'oppression'; risk of violations as sufficient, in order to prevent them; violations plus exhaustion of lawful means; violations plus no reasonable prospect of an effective remedy by any other means; those already established by the doctrine of necessity. Reaching scholarly consensus may require some further discussion.

There is also general agreement that the objectives of the resistance must be consistent with international human rights law in order to receive this exceptional authorization. To this end, there are four main conceptualizations of the right's ultimate human rights object and purpose: self-help extrajudicial fundamental rights enforcement for effective remedy, as either the superordinate or discrete purpose; otherwise as self-defence, as self-determination, or as instrumental to realizing the right to peace and human security.

There is general agreement that this right is both limited and conditional as to means, insofar as it must be exercised in a manner consistent with the relevant legal regimes: international human rights law and international criminal law, and the international prohibitions on aggression and intervention, at a minimum. Conformity with the doctrine of proportionality is generally accepted as an additional requirement. Therefore, the concept does not propose legal authorization of 'any means necessary' – as it is sometimes misconstrued, to include any form of action without limitation or condition, or a general suspension of or exemption from regulation under the laws of war. Nor does it propose unilateral or otherwise unauthorized intervention by third parties.

There is another area where agreement remains to be reached. There is no agreement as to the scope of actions covered by the right, but rather three approaches: exclusively peaceful but unlawful means are exceptionally authorized; exclusively forceful means are exceptionally authorized, as peaceful means should be otherwise protected by the *lex generalis*; inclusively unlawful means across the spectrum from peaceful to forceful are exceptionally authorized in general, but the specific means authorized in any given case would be subject to further tests, for proportionality for example. The evidence leans towards the third of these as the most appropriate.

There are also three areas of subjective assessment where consensus may not be possible. There is no agreement among proponents as to whether this right should remain exclusively moral, as a natural law or other trump regardless of the state of the positive law, or instead should be formally recognized in law, including through codification, as a way of rebalancing the law's asymmetries of power. Nor is there agreement among opponents as to whether the correct position is a doctrine of absolute denial – whether based on an aversion to violence in all its forms or on a theory of inconsistency with the rule of law – or a doctrine of either democratic or post hoc exceptionalism. Theorists also cannot agree as to the relationship of the right to resist to the rule of law, but there are three general schools of thought: that it is either incompatible or antagonistic; that it is compatible but auxiliary; that it is intrinsic and necessary as a failsafe. All these are principally matters of ideology, and therefore unlikely to ever be fully resolved.

8.2.2 *A Superordinate Right, Whose Cognates Share 'Common Core' Elements*

This study finds that there is a conceptual hierarchy in which the 'right to resist' is the broader and more inclusive superordinate containing subordinate cognate rights 'to disobey', 'to rebel', and 'to revolution'. The right to resist and its cognates are related but again distinct, neither interchangeable nor wholly severable, as they share a common legal core. This common legal core explains their frequent conflation or interchangeable usage by theorists and others – sometimes correctly and sometimes incorrectly – in the absence of definitional agreement and conceptual clarity.

The 'common core' suggests that, even while taking their differences into account, each cognate can be conceptualized as a fundamental human right:

- exercised in response to a primary trigger violation or violations;
- exercised against a state or other authority or powerful actor;
- as a self-help remedy of individuals, groups, and peoples;
- to use otherwise unlawful means – as a lawful exception;
- in pursuit of objectives that are consistent with human rights;
- when other means of enforcement or remedies prove unavailable or ineffective – that is, subject to necessity as a secondary trigger condition;
- subject to a proportionality limitation;
- subject to the constraints of international human rights law and international criminal law, and international humanitarian law as applicable;
- correlated with an obligation on state parties and other third parties to either assist within the limits of the law, or not obstruct those exercising a valid right.

8.2.3 *A General Consolidated Working Definition and Analytical Framework*

The findings clarifying the relationship between the cognates and establishing their 'common core' elements also suggest a provisional general working definition of the superordinate contemporary human right to resist as a legal concept, composited or consolidated from the prior work of the other scholars surveyed. That definition is as follows:

> *The 'human right to resist' is the exceptional, conditional, and limited secondary self-help right of individuals, groups, and peoples to use otherwise unlawful means, in pursuit of objectives that are consistent with human rights, in response to a trigger violation by a state or other powerful actor, when other means of human rights enforcement or remedies prove unavailable or ineffective. Such exceptional means may be either peaceful or forceful, subject to demonstrated necessity and proportionality, and to the relevant constraints of international human rights law, international criminal law, and international humanitarian law as applicable. The obligation this imposes at domestic level is to make legal allowances for immunity, non-prosecution, and/or exceptional defences or mitigations, and not to extradite or exclude from refugee status those with a valid right to resist where no internationally criminal conduct is shown. The obligation this imposes at international level is to either assist within the limits of the law, or not obstruct those with a valid right to resist.*

Furthermore, following Alston's analytical method, the study identifies 'conceptual dimensions' upon which any right to resist theories and legal provisions and other recognitions may be usefully compared, as follows:

- nature, function, and source – that is, whether and how is it binding in law;
- elements and content – that is, primary and secondary triggers including conditions, scope of permissible means including limits, rights-holders, duty-bearers, and nature of the consequent obligation, human rights object and purpose.

This same analytical framework can be used to compare the historical theories, the theories of the contemporary concept, and the positive legal provisions and other recognitions, both historical and contemporary, in order to – among other things – establish evidence of the 'common core' and consistency with definition indicated above, as well as to identify the most important distinctions between concepts and provisions. Establishing the human rights 'object and purpose' related to each theory or provision not only helps further distinguish and classify but also identify particular foreseeable problems associated with each type, in the form of potentially conflicting rights and norms.

8.3 RECONSIDERING THE HUMAN RIGHT TO RESIST IN CONTEMPORARY POSITIVE LAW

Part II of the book makes a series of findings that inform certain overall conclusions in relation to contemporary legal provision for the right to resist as a human right. These support the contention that constitutional law and international human rights law are the most appropriate and indeed the primary legal frameworks for codifying the right to resist. They demonstrate that the human right to resist functions as a *lex specialis* rule of exception both customary and codified domestically and internationally, and as an implicit general principle of international law. The findings also confirm there are remaining gaps in certainty, that there are both *lex lata* and *lex ferenda* options for their clarification, and that this is a potentially enforceable human right using a proposed basic claims analysis template.

8.3.1 *Constitutional Law and International Human Rights Law the Primary Legal Frameworks*

The Part II review of the positive law removes any doubt that constitutional law and international human rights law constitute the primary and most appropriate contemporary legal frameworks for the right to resist, as the location of the fundamental rights protecting individuals, groups, and peoples against abuse by their own state. Indeed, as the evidence recounted in Chapters 5–7 shows, these two bodies of law are where existing codifications may be found, or other recognitions of the right may originate, at both domestic and international levels. The research demonstrates that, as such, most reflections of the right in other areas of domestic or international law are corroborative rather than originating. Thus, while some in the past questioned whether international jurisdiction could extend to such 'domestic' matters, the research confirms that contemporary conceptualization of the right to resist as a human right arguably eliminates state sovereignty as an automatic impediment.

8.3.2 *Function as* Lex Specialis *Rule of Exception, both Customary and Codified Domestically and Internationally, and as an Implicit General Principle of International Law*

The review of the positive law likewise removes any doubt that, to the extent that it is recognized, the human right to resist functions as a *lex specialis* rule of exception that is both customary and codified as such domestically in approximately forty constitutions in Africa, Europe, and the Americas, and internationally in two human rights treaties as article 20(2) and (3) of the African Charter and article 2(4) of the Arab Charter. Moreover, it is considered an implicit general principle of international law, as set out in the fifth principle identified in UN General Assembly Resolution 2625's 'Declaration of General Principles of International Law Concerning Friendly Relations and Cooperation among States in Accordance with the Charter of the United Nations'. Some also assert that it forms a general principle of international law implicitly acknowledged in the third preambular paragraph and in articles 21 (3) and 28 of the Universal Declaration of Human Rights, which provides an interpretive framework for 'human rights' as an unelaborated overarching purpose and principle of the UN Charter, and in Nuremberg Principle VII. However, its status as such is less secure at present.

8.3.3 *Gaps Remain in Certainty*

Even if one does not accept that there are 'gaps' in the international law of the right to resist, there are definitely persisting gaps in certainty as to its full scope and applicability. The most critical of these relate to the right to resist for the enforcement of the right to internal self-determination beyond racist regime cases, and indeed the right to resist for enforcement of human rights generally, including for the purpose of effective remedy against widespread and systematic violations amounting to crimes against humanity. Uncertainty also persists about the nature of the correlated third-party duty, particularly the extent to which it exceeds the basic obligation to 'not obstruct', thus including assistance otherwise in compliance with the law on intervention. While these gaps are not fully resolved by this study, it suggests they can be considerably narrowed by further systematic consideration of the customary and conventional law.

The above findings taken together inform several general conclusions. First, they support the conclusion that international law's '*non liquet*' problem can be resolved by *lex lata* in addition to *lex ferenda* means. Second, that the 'sham law' theory is not generally proven with respect to the right to resist, but instead corroborates the contention that it is a potentially enforceable human right. In this regard, the findings also suggest a basic claims analysis template.

8.3.4 Lex Lata *and* Lex Ferenda *Options for Clarification*

The right to resist is not inherently *non liquet* in its original sense of being legally ambiguous due to provision in law that is either absent or too vague or inconsistent, and therefore *impossible* to interpret. Nor is it necessarily consigned to a fate of 'relative indeterminism' or 'fragmentation'. Instead, it has two other possible futures.

First, despite previous failures at the UN level, many states have expressly recognized the right domestically, as have two out of four regional systems, so further codification should not be entirely ruled out. However, any future international *lex ferenda* efforts would need a dedicated and more systematic approach to have any chance of success, and the most recently considered 'right to peace' framework probably should not be repeated. Yet there is a second, more immediately useful *lex lata* possibility. Dynamic or other interpretation of the existing law using the principles of integration or harmonization may, in the meantime, provide sufficient scope to deal with apparent gaps. That is, where it is not presently codified or otherwise recognized, the human right to resist may nevertheless still constitute a *lex specialis* customary rule of exception or general principle of international law requiring due consideration during the course of interpretation or evaluation of a claim.

There are two additional interpretive alternatives available, as suggested by others. The first involves using legal fictions to expand application of the existing law on the right to resist. Examples include conceptualizing resistance as 'self-defence' that may not necessarily meet all traditional elements but is nevertheless classed as if it did, or treating resistance for internal self-determination as if it were a case of external self-determination and thereby 'converted' into a recognized right. The second involves applying the theory that resistance, rebellion, and revolution are internationally permissible, or at least 'not internationally unlawful', because they are not in themselves explicitly prohibited. However, these options are less satisfactory, and not necessarily recommended.

Thus, even if one accepts that there is presently a potential '*non liquet*' problem for the right to resist in international law, it can be resolved. Whether it will be resolved remains to be seen.

8.3.5 *A Potentially Enforceable Human Right*

Few would disagree that enforceability is the crucible of any legal right. Yet assessment of the 'enforceability' of secondary enforcement rights such as the right to resist cannot be reduced to judicial enforcement alone, but rather must include its two dimensions: judicial and extrajudicial. In the latter instance, enforcement may either be direct by the rights-holders themselves as self-help, or else indirect through third-party assistance. In general, the research findings confirm that the human right to resist is at least potentially enforceable along both dimensions.

Regarding the judicial enforcement dimension of enforceability, the evidence confirms that a pronounced feature of the constitutional law landscape is the untapped justiciability potential of its right to resist provisions. It also confirms unrealized potential for justiciability and other enforcement of the limited right to resist as recognized in customary international law or otherwise provided for in treaty law. However, these facts alone are not sufficient to arrive at a conclusion that the right to resist amounts to 'sham law'. Its apparent under-utilization may equally indicate the opposite in some cases – that it is effective as a deterrent, or that its use is unnecessary where judicial and other legal remedies are available and effective. Equally, bypassing judicial enforcement where it is not available as an effective remedy, in favour of the more frequently used extrajudicial enforcement dimension, is also not necessarily an indicator of 'sham law'. Instead, it may indicate direct application of the law by its beneficiaries – an informal enforceability 'from below' such as that indicated by the cumulative works of Falk and Mégret on this subject – and the *lex specialis* functioning as intended, by rendering self-help measures lawful under exceptional circumstances. Either way, any argument that existing positive provisions for the right to resist categorically amount to little more than 'sham law' remains to be proven. This study suggests that it is not supportable as a general proposition. Therefore, which explanation is correct can only be determined on a case-by-case basis.

Thus, the right to resist is at least potentially enforceable as a human right, under some conditions, and more so in certain jurisdictions than in others. Whether it can meet its full enforcement potential in the future remains to be seen.

8.3.6 A *Basic Claim Analysis Template*

The analytical framework developed in Chapter 4 and the legal recognitions and provisions identified in Chapters 5–7 together generate a series of basic questions to be answered and elements to be identified in evaluating either a domestic claim or an international claim to a human right to resist, within the confines of the existing law.

The first step is to identify the positive law that may apply, as follows:

(a) is there an applicable domestic constitutional provision;
(b) is there an applicable regional human rights provision;
(c) if neither of these or in any case, is there a recognition in general or customary international law that may apply, in particular under UN General Assembly Resolution 2625;
(d) if none of the above or in any case, can an argument be made that it relates to an unenumerated but implied customary right, for example under the Universal Declaration of Human Rights or Nuremberg Principles.

The second step is to use the analytical framework to assess the details of the claim against the identified required elements associated with the particular source, usually in the following sequence, as to:

(a) rights-holders;
(b) primary triggers;
(c) secondary trigger conditions where applicable;
(d) object and purpose;
(e) permissible means including applicable limitations;
(f) consequent duty-bearers and the nature of the obligation.

While this very basic claims analysis template can surely be improved as the scholarship evolves, it nevertheless has the potential to assist both the interpretation and enforcement of the *lex lata* right to resist as a human right.

8.4 AN AGENDA FOR FURTHER RECONSIDERATION BY SCHOLARS, PRACTITIONERS, AND HUMAN RIGHTS ADVOCATES GENERALLY

For scholars, the conceptual findings demonstrate that there is ample scope for reintroduction of the legal concept of the human right to resist into the standard human rights lexicon for further study, debate, and coherent development. Likewise, there are sufficient grounds to prompt increased interdisciplinary dialogue on this topic between legal scholars and other specialisms already engaged in these discussions, such as within ethics and political philosophy, as well as between leading jurists and emerging scholars, consolidating this as a valid discrete human rights subfield. What is needed now is not only reinstatement of the concept within the discipline – moving it from the margins to the mainstream of discourse – but also a process of further clarification with a view to resolving the still unanswered questions identified here, with special attention to those that stand to benefit the most vulnerable, Baxi's so-called rightless persons.

For practitioners, whether judges, diplomats, advocates, or activists, the positive law findings of this study demonstrate that both making and assessing claims to a human right to resist is already possible, using the *lex lata*. Following the example of the Southern Africa Litigation Centre in S v *Okah*,[1] it remains for other practitioners to reconsider, to use, and to test the

[1] 'Written Submissions for the *Amicus Curiae* Southern Africa Litigation Centre ("SALC")', *State* v *Henry Eomotimi Okah*, Case No CCT315/16 & CCT 193/17, Constitutional Court of South Africa, 24 November 2017 [38]–[71]. This analysis appears to have been generally accepted by the Court in S v *Okah* [2018] ZACC 3 [44]–[52].

international and constitutional law of the human right to resist as it stands. Utilizing the existing right in a more systematic and well-informed way could be particularly relevant for human rights defenders on the frontlines of climate change resistance and indeed environmental defence in all its guises, particularly as our understanding of the human right to a healthy environment, the discrete analogous 'rights of nature', 'ecocide' as an international crime, and the full extent of the human rights of indigenous peoples to self-determination continues to evolve in the twenty-first century.

Finally, for human rights advocates generally, the overall findings of this study have particular implications for reconsidering the *lex ferenda* of the human right to resist. Even in jurisdictions where no constitutional right exists, and where applicable regional human rights treaty law remains 'silent', it remains open for domestic law to legislate for the exception in a manner that conforms with the human right to resist concept as set out in this study. Indeed, this has been done in Ukraine under siege in 2022, which legislated for the human right to resist Russia's aggression and unlawful occupation, providing limited immunity on a *lex specialis* basis.[2]

In short, what is needed now is not only to interpret, to use, and to test the existing law in the making and adjudication of claims – whether in strategic litigation or in campaigning – but also to imagine the possibilities for sensible codified clarifications that do not repeat the past mistakes of international codification failures. Any future codification efforts at international or regional level will need stronger well-informed advocacy that makes discrete arguments for this right, learning from prior experience at the UN Human Rights Council. If this book can make a contribution to supporting such efforts in the agenda outlined above, it will have fulfilled its purpose.

[2] Law of Ukraine No 2114-IX (9 March 2022). According to the English translation provided by *Levyy Bereg* (LB.ua), it provides for a 'right to resist armed aggression by the Russian Federation', whereby civilians in Ukraine, whether Ukrainian or foreign citizens or stateless persons legally present, can obtain and use 'against persons committing armed aggression' any 'award weapons, sporting weapons, hunting smoothbore, rifled or combined weapons, and ammunition' for this purpose, without criminal liability. However, such materiel must be relinquished 'to the National Police no later than 10 days after the martial law in Ukraine was cessed [sic] or terminated'. See 'Law That Permits Civilian Ukrainians to Kill Occupants Comes into Force (document)' *Levyy Bereg* (LB.ua) (10 March 2022).

Bibliography

Abi-Saab G, 'Wars of National Liberation and the Laws of War' [1972] 3 *Annales d'Étdues Internationales* 93.

'Preface' in Voeffray F, *L'actio popularis ou la défense de l'intérêt collectif devant les jurisdictions internationales* (Graduate Institute Publications 2004).

Agamben G, *State of Exception* (Kevin Attell tr, University of Chicago Press 2005).

Al-Midani MA, 'Arab Charter on Human Rights 2004' (2006) 24 *Boston University International Law Journal* 147.

'Statute of the Arab Court of Human Rights, Non-official English Translation' (Arab Center for International Humanitarian Law and Human Rights Education 2018).

Alfredsson G, 'Peoples' in *Max Planck Encyclopedia of Public International Law* (Oxford Public International Law online database 2007).

Alfredsson G and Eide A (eds), *The Universal Declaration of Human Rights: A Common Standard of Achievement* (Martinus Nijhoff 1999).

Alpaugh M, 'The Right of Resistance to Oppression: Protest and Authority in the French Revolutionary World' (2016) 39(3) *French Historical Studies* 567.

Alston P, 'Third Generation of Solidarity Rights: Progressive Development or Obfuscation of International Human Rights Law?' (1982) 29(3) *Netherlands International Law Review* 307.

'Conjuring Up New Human Rights: A Proposal for Quality Control' (1984) 78 *American Journal of International Law* 607.

'Peoples' Rights: Their Rise and Fall' in Alston P (ed), *Peoples' Rights* (Oxford University Press 2001).

'Against a World Court of Human Rights' (2014) 28(2) *Ethics and International Affairs* 197.

Anderson FM (ed), *The Constitutions and Other Select Documents Illustrative of the History of France 1789–1901* (HW Wilson 1904).

Anonymous, 'Resistance No Rebellion: In Answer to Doctor Johnson's Taxation No Tyranny' (J Bell 1775).

Vindiciae, Contra Tyrannos: or, Concerning the Legitimate Power of a Prince over the People, and of the People over a Prince (Garnett G ed/tr, 2003 edn, Cambridge University Press 1994).

Ansermet L, 'Manifest Illegality and the ICC Superior Orders Defense: Schuldtheorie Mistake of Law Doctrine as an Article 33(1)(c) Panacea' (2014) 47 *Vanderbilt Journal of Transnational Law* 1425.

Aquinas T, 'Commentary on the Sentences of Peter Lombard' in Entrèves AP (ed), *Aquinas: Selected Political Writings* (Dawson JG tr, Oxford University Press 1948).

De regno ad regum Cypri: On Kingship, To the King of Cyprus (Phelan GB tr, Eschmann IT rev edn, Pontifical Institute of Medieval Studies 1949).

'Summa Theologiae' in Baumgarth WP and Regan RJ (eds), *On Law, Morality and Politics* (Regan RJ tr, 2nd edn, Hackett Publishing 2002).

Treatise on Law: The Complete Text (Summa Theologiae I–II, Questions 90–108) (Freddoso AJ tr, St Augustine's Press 2009).

Archibugi D, Croce M and Salvatore A, 'Law of Nations or Perpetual Peace? Two Early International Theories on the Use of Force' in Weller M (ed), *The Oxford Handbook on the Use of Force in International Law* (Oxford University Press 2015).

Aristotle, 'Constitution of Athens' in Barnes J (ed), *The Complete Works of Aristotle* (Kenyon FG tr, Princeton University Press 1984).

The Athenian Constitution (Rhodes PJ tr, Penguin 2002).

Arnaotoglou I, *Ancient Greek Laws: A Sourcebook* (Routledge 1998).

Baldwin C and Morel C, 'Group Rights' in Evans M and Murray R (eds), *The African Charter on Human and Peoples' Rights: The System in Practice, 1986–2006* (Cambridge University Press 2008).

Bannelier K and Christakis T, 'Under the UN Security Council's Watchful Eyes: Military Intervention by Invitation in the Malian Conflict' (2013) 26(4) *Leiden Journal of International Law* 855.

Barnabas SG, 'The Legal Status of the United Nations Declaration on the Rights of Indigenous Peoples (2007) in Contemporary International Human Rights Law' (2017) 6 *International Human Rights Law Review* 242.

Bassiouni MC, 'Ideologically Motivated Offenses and the Political Offense Exception in Extradition – A Proposed Juridical Standard for an Unruly Problem' (1969) XIX *De Paul Law Review* 217.

'Final Document: Conclusions and Recommendations' in Bassiouni MC (ed), *International Terrorism and Political Crimes* (Charles C Thomas 1975).

Baumgold D, 'Pacifying Politics: Resistance, Violence and Accountability in Seventeenth-Century Contract Theory' (1993) 21(1) *Political Theory* 6.

Baxi U, 'Otonomic Prowess and Existential Impotence: Reflexions on René Marcic's Sydney Papers' (conference paper for 'René Marcic: Sydney Commemorative Symposium (54)' University of Sydney, Faculty of Law, Department of Jurisprudence and International Law, Institute for Advanced Studies in Jurisprudence, Sydney, 1972).

The Future of Human Rights (2nd edn, Oxford University Press 2008).

Beck LW, 'Kant and the Right of Revolution' (1971) 32(3) *Journal of the History of Ideas* 411.

Bedau HA, 'On Civil Disobedience' (1961) 58(21) *Journal of Philosophy* 653.

Bederman DJ, *Custom as a Source of Law* (Cambridge University Press 2010).

Bellal A and Doswald-Beck L, 'Evaluating the Use of Force during the Arab Spring' (2012) 14 *Yearbook of International Humanitarian Law* 3.

Bellamy AJ, 'The Responsibility to Protect – Five Years On' (2010) 24(2) *Ethics and International Affairs* 143.

Bentham J, 'Anarchical Fallacies; Being an Examination of the Declaration of Rights Issued during the French Revolution' reprinted in Waldron J (ed), *Nonsense upon Stilts: Bentham, Burke and Marx on the Rights of Man* (Methuen 1987).

Benvenisti E, 'Occupation, Belligerent' in *Max Planck Encyclopedia of Public International Law* (Oxford Public International Law online database May 2009).

The International Law of Occupation (2nd edn, Oxford University Press 2012).

Bielefeldt H, 'The Right to Resist' in Heitmeyer W and Hagan J (eds), *International Handbook of Violence Research* (Kluwer 2003).

Bifulco D and Golia AJ, 'The Right of Resistance as a State Law Basis for Transnational Regimes' Self-Contestation' (2018) 45 *Journal of Law and Society* 94.

Blackstone W, *Commentaries on the Laws of England*, vol 1 (1765, repr University of Chicago Press 1979).

Blunt GD, 'Is There a Human Right to Resistance?' (2017) 39(4) *Human Rights Quarterly* 860.

'Illegal Immigration as Resistance to Global Poverty' (2018) 69(1) *Raisons Politiques* 83.

Global Poverty, Injustice, and Resistance (Cambridge University Press 2019).

'Doing Nothing as Resistance', *Qrius* (6 April 2020).

Bodenheimer E, 'Significant Developments in German Legal Philosophy Since 1945' (1954) 3 *American Journal of Comparative Law* 379.

Bossuyt MJ, *Guide to the 'Travaux Préparatoires' of the International Covenant on Civil and Political Rights* (Martinus Nijhoff 1987).

Boyle A, 'Soft Law in International Law Making' in Evans MD (ed), *International Law* (3rd edn, Oxford University Press 2010).

Boyle FA, *Defending Civil Resistance under International Law* (Transnational 1988).

Protesting Power: War, Resistance, and Law (Rowman and Littlefield 2008).

Boyle FA, Hird M, Burnaby L, Clark R, Wright D, Feldman A and Dumbauld E, 'Citizen Initiatives under International Law' (1988) 82 *Proceedings of the American Society of International Law* 555.

Brennan J, *When All Else Fails: The Ethics of Resistance to State Injustice* (Princeton University Press 2019).

Brincat S, 'The Legal Philosophy of Internationally Assisted Tyrannicide' (2009) 34 *Australian Journal of Legal Philosophy* 151.

Brinkmann G, 'Militant Democracy and Radicals in the West German Civil Service' (1983) 46 *Modern Law Review* 584.

Brownlie I, *Principles of Public International Law* (7th edn, Oxford University Press 2008).

Burgess G, 'On Hobbesian Resistance Theory' (1994) XLII *Political Studies* 62.

Burgorgue-Larsen L and Torres AU, *The Inter-American Court of Human Rights: Case Law and Commentary* (Oxford University Press 2011).

Burri T and Trinidad J (eds), *The International Court of Justice and Decolonisation: New Directions from the Chagos Advisory Opinion* (Cambridge University Press 2021).

Byrnes A and Simm G (eds), *Peoples' Tribunals and International Law* (Cambridge University Press 2018).

Carter D, 'Could a Greek Oath Guarantee a Claim Right? Oaths, Contracts and the Structure of Obligation in Classical Athens' in Sommerstein AH and Fletcher J (eds), *Horkos: The Oath in Greek Society* (Bristol Phoenix Press 2007).

Cassese A, 'Human Rights and Humanitarian Law: Terrorism and Human Rights' (1982) 31 *American University Law Review* 945.

Human Rights in a Changing World (Polity Press 1990).

Self-Determination of Peoples: A Legal Reappraisal (Cambridge University Press 1995).

'Terrorism Is Also Disrupting Some Crucial Legal Categories of International Law' (2001) 12(5) *European Journal of International Law* 993.

International Criminal Law (Oxford University Press 2003).

International Law (2nd edn, Oxford University Press 2005).

'Affirmation of the Principles of International Law Recognized by the Charter of the Nürnberg Tribunal' (United Nations Audiovisual Library of International Law 2009).

'Should Rebels Be Treated as Criminals? Some Modest Proposals for Rendering Internal Armed Conflicts Less Inhumane' in Cassese A (ed), *Realizing Utopia: The Future of International Law* (Oxford University Press 2012).

Castro F, *History Will Absolve Me* (Tabío PA and Booth AP tr, Editorial de Ciencias Sociales 1975).

Chemillier-Gendreau M, 'Resistance, Right to, International Protection' in Wolfrum R (ed), *Max Planck Encyclopedia of Public International Law* (Oxford University Press 2012).

Cheng B, *General Principles of Law as Applied by International Courts and Tribunals* (2006 edn, Cambridge University Press 1953).

Chesterman S, *Just War or Just Peace? International Law and Humanitarian Intervention* (Oxford University Press 2001).

Chesterman S, Johnstone I and Malone DM (eds), *Law and Practice of the United Nations: Documents and Commentary* (Oxford University Press 2016).

Chimni BS, 'Third World Approaches to International Law: A Manifesto' (2006) 8 *International Community Law Review* 3.

Cicero, *De Officiis* (Miller W tr, GP Putnam's Sons 1913).

Clapham A, *Human Rights Obligations of Non-State Actors* (Oxford University Press 2006).

Clark JC, '"Unhand Me, Gentlemen!" The Right to Resist Unlawful Arrest in South Carolina' (2017) 69(1) *South Carolina Law Review* 247.

Claude RP and Weston BH (eds), *Human Rights in the World Community: Issues and Action* (3rd edn, University of Pennsylvania Press 2006).

Cohen D, 'Crime, Punishment and the Rule of Law in Classical Athens' in Gagarin M and Cohen D (eds), *Cambridge Companion to Ancient Greek Law* (Cambridge University Press 2005).

Cole DH, 'From Renaissance Poland to Poland's Renaissance' (1999) 97(6) *Michigan Law Review* 2062.

Cooley T, *General Principles of Constitutional Law* (Little, Brown 1880).

Corson JC, 'Resistance No Rebellion' (1930) 42 *Juridical Review* 245.

Corten O, *La rebellion et le droit international: le principe de neutralité en tension* (Adi-Poche, Académie de Droit International de la Haye 2015).

Cot JP, 'United Nations Charter' in *Max Planck Encyclopedia of Public International Law* (Oxford Public International Law online database 2011).

Cottrol RJ and Diamond RT, 'The Second Amendment: Toward an Afro-Americanist Reconsideration' (1991) 80 *Georgetown Law Journal* 309.

Crawford E, 'Levée en masse: A Nineteenth Century Concept in a Twenty-First Century World' (2011) University of Sydney Law School, Legal Studies Research Paper No 11/31 (May 2011).

Crawford J, 'The Right of Self-Determination in International Law: Its Development and Future' in Alston P (ed), *Peoples' Rights* (Oxford University Press 2001).

The International Law Commission's Articles on State Responsibility: Introduction, Text and Commentaries (Cambridge University Press 2002).

Curran E, 'Can Rights Curb the Hobbesian Sovereign? The Full Right to Self-Preservation, Duties of Sovereignty and the Limitations of Hohfeld' (2006) 25 *Law and Philosophy* 243.

D'Aspremont J, 'Le tyrannicide en droit international' in Tomuschat C, Lagrange E and Oeter S (eds), *The Right to Life* (Brill 2010).

Dannenbaum T, *The Crime of Aggression, Humanity, and the Soldier* (Cambridge University Press 2018).

'The Criminalization of Aggression and Soldiers' Rights' (2018) 29(3) *European Journal of International Law* 859.

'War Crimes and Just War Theory' in Ferzan KK and Alexander L (eds), *The Palgrave Handbook of Applied Ethics and Criminal Law* (Palgrave Macmillan 2019).

Daube D, *Civil Disobedience in Antiquity* (Edinburgh University Press 1972).

Delmas C, 'Disobedience, Civil and Otherwise' (2017) 11(1) *Criminal Law and Philosophy* 195.

A Duty to Resist: When Civil Disobedience Should Be Uncivil (Oxford University Press 2018).

Deseure B, 'From Pragmatic Conservatism to Formal Continuity: Nineteenth Century Views on the Old Regime Origins of the Belgian Constitution' (2016) 32 *Giornale di Storia Costituzionale* 257.

D'Eszlary C, 'Magna Carta and the Assises of Jerusalem' (1958) 2(3) *American Journal of Legal History* 189.

DiPiero J, 'The Common Law of Rebellion' (2017) 48(2) *Georgetown Journal of International Law* 605.

Dinstein Y, 'Aggression' in *Max Planck Encyclopedia of Public International Law* (Oxford Public International Law online database September 2015).

War, Aggression and Self-Defence (6th edn, Cambridge University Press 2017).

Dixon R and Ginsburg T (eds), *Research Handbook on Comparative Constitutional Law* (Edward Elgar 2011).

DJ, 'The Inter-American Council of Jurists' (1951) 4(4) *International Law Quarterly* 521.

Douzinas C, *The End of Human Rights* (Hart Publishing 2000).

'The "Right to the Event": The Legality and Morality of Revolution and Resistance' (2014) 2(2) *Metodo: International Studies in Phenomenology and Philosophy* 151.

Dugard J, 'Introductory Note to the Convention on the Suppression and Punishment of the Crime of Apartheid' (United Nations Audiovisual Library of International Law 2008).

Dunér B, 'Rebellion: The Ultimate Human Right?' (2005) 9(2) *International Journal of Human Rights* 247.

Durán CV, 'Artículo 7: Resistencia y oposición a la opresión' (Asociación Española para el Derecho Internacional de los Derechos Humanos, 18–21 February 2013).

Durán CV and Puyana DF, 'Analysis of the First Session of the Open-Ended Working Group on the Draft Declaration on the Right to Peace' (Spanish Society for International Human Rights Law, February 2013).

Dworkin A, 'Individual, Not Collective: Justifying the Resort to Force against Members of Non-State Armed Groups' (2017) 93 *International Law Studies* 476.

Dyzenhaus D, 'Hobbes and the Legitimacy of Law' (2001) 20 *Law and Philosophy* 461.

Eide A, 'The Right to Oppose Violations of Human Rights: Basis, Conditions and Limitations' in *Violations of Human Rights: Possible Rights of Recourse and Forms of Resistance* (UNESCO 1984).

'Article 28' in Alfredsson G and Eide A (eds), *The Universal Declaration of Human Rights: A Common Standard of Achievement* (Martinus Nijhoff 1999).

Elkins Z, Ginsburg T and Melton J, *The Endurance of National Constitutions* (Cambridge University Press 2009).

'The Comparative Constitutions Project: A Cross-National Historical Dataset of Written Constitutions' (CCP Survey Instrument May 11, 2010).

Elster J, 'Forces and Mechanisms in the Constitution-Making Process' (1995) 45 *Duke Law Journal* 364.

Evans G and Sahnoun M, *The Responsibility to Protect* (International Commission on Intervention and State Sovereignty 2001).

Evans MD, 'The Law of the Sea' in Evans MD (ed), *International Law* (3rd edn, Oxford University Press 2010).

Fabre C, 'Cosmopolitanism, Just War Theory and Legitimate Authority' (2008) 84(5) *International Affairs* 963.

'Cosmopolitanism and Wars of Self-Defence in Fabre C and Lazar S (eds), *The Morality of Defensive War* (Oxford University Press 2014).

Falk R, 'Janus Tormented: The International Law of Internal War' in Rosenau JN (ed), *International Aspects of Civil Strife* (Princeton University Press 1964).

'The Adequacy of Contemporary Theories of International Law: Gaps in Legal Thinking' (1964) 50(2) *Virginia Law Review* 231.

Legal Order in a Violent World (Princeton University Press 1968).

'Nuremberg: Past, Present and Future' (1971) 80 *Yale Law Journal* 1501.

'The Nuremberg Defense in the Pentagon Papers Case' (1974) 13 *Columbia Journal of Transnational Law* 208.

'The Algiers Declaration of the Rights of Peoples and the Struggle for Human Rights' in Cassese A (ed), *UN Law/Fundamental Rights: Two Topics in International Law* (Sijthoff and Noordhoff 1979).

'Introduction' in Boyle FA, *Defending Civil Resistance under International Law* (Transnational Publishers 1988).

'Telford Taylor and the Legacy of Nuremberg' (1998) 37 *Columbia Journal of Transnational Law* 693.

'Azmi Bishara, The Right of Resistance, and the Palestinian Ordeal' (2002) XXXI(2) *Journal of Palestine Studies* 19.

Achieving Human Rights (Routledge 2009).

Falk R and Weston BH, 'The Relevance of International Law to Palestinian Rights in the West Bank and Gaza: In Legal Defense of the Intifada' (1991) 32(1) *Harvard International Law Journal* 129.

'The Israeli-Occupied Territories, International Law, and the Boundaries of Scholarly Discourse: A Reply to Michael Curtis' (1992) 33(1) *Harvard International Law Journal* 191.

Falk R, Rajagopal B and Stevens J (eds), *International Law and the Third World: Reshaping Justice* (Routledge 2008).

Falk R and Tilley V, 'Israeli Practices towards the Palestinian People and the Question of Apartheid' (United Nations Economic and Social Commission for Western Asia 2017).

Fernandez AN, 'Derecho a la Resistencia y Justiciabilidad de los Derechos Sociales en Ecuador' (2016) 1 *Revista de Derecho Social Latinoamerica* 89.

Finch GA, 'Inter-American Academy of Comparative and International Law' (1957) 51(1) *American Journal of International Law* 97.

Finlay CJ, *Terrorism and the Right to Resist: A Theory of Just Revolutionary War* (Cambridge University Press 2015).

'The Perspective of the Rebel: A Gap in the Global Normative Architecture' (2017) 31(2) *Ethics and International Affairs* 213.

'The Deadly Serious Causes of Legitimate Rebellion: Between the Wrongs of Terrorism and the Crimes of War' (2018) 12(2) *Criminal Law and Philosophy* 271.

Fitzgibbon RH, 'The Process of Constitution-Making in Latin America' (1960) 3 *Comparative Studies in Society and History* 1.

Flikschuh K, 'Reason, Right and Revolution: Kant and Locke' (2008) 36 *Philosophy and Public Affairs* 375.

Fox JR, *Dictionary of International and Comparative Law* (Oceana Publications 1997).

Franck TM, 'The Emerging Right to Democratic Governance' (1992) 86 *American Journal of International Law* 46.

Freeman AV, 'The First Meeting of the Inter-American Council of Jurists' (1950) 44(2) *American Journal of International Law* 374.

Friedrich CJ, *The Philosophy of Law in Historical Perspective* (2nd edn, University of Chicago Press 1963).

Fritz CG, 'Recovering the Lost Worlds of America's Written Constitutions' (2004) 68 *Albany Law Review* 261.

Frowein JA, 'Ius Cogens' in *Max Planck Encyclopedia of Public International Law* (Oxford Public International Law online database 2013).

Fuller LL, *Legal Fictions* (Stanford University Press 1967).

Gaeta P, 'The Defence of Superior Orders: The Statute of the International Criminal Court versus Customary International Law' (1999) 10 *European Journal of International Law* 172.

Gagarin M, 'The Thesmothetai and the Earliest Athenian Tyranny Law' (1981) 111 *Transactions of the American Philological Association* 71.

García GMG, 'El amplio derecho a la resistencia en la Declaración de Luarca: Objeción de conciencia, desobediencia civil y resistencia contra la opresión y la barbarie' in Durán CV and Pérez CF (eds), *Contribuciones regionales para una declaración universal del derecho humano a la paz* (Asociación Española para el Derecho Internacional de los Derechos Humanos 2010).

Gardiner R, *Treaty Interpretation* (Oxford University Press 2008).

Gargarella R, 'The Last Resort: The Right of Resistance in Situations of Legal Alienation' (2003) (Yale Law School SELA [Seminario en Latinoamérica de Teoría Constitucional y Política] Papers).

'Towards a Typology of Latin American Constitutionalism 1810–60' (2004) 39 *Latin American Research Review* 141.

'The Right of Resistance in Situations of Severe Deprivation' in Pogge T (ed), *Freedom from Poverty as a Human Right: Who Owes What to the Very Poor?* (Oxford University Press and UNESCO 2007).

Latin American Constitutionalism 1810–2010 (Oxford University Press 2013).

Garner BA, *A Dictionary of Modern Legal Usage* (Oxford University Press 1987).

(ed), *Black's Law Dictionary* (7th deluxe edn, West Group 1999).

Black's Law Dictionary (2nd edn, West Group 2001).

Gasper D, 'Human Security: From Definitions to Investigating a Discourse' in Martin M and Owen T (eds), *Routledge Handbook of Human Security* (Routledge 2014).

Gebhard J, 'Apartheid' in *Max Planck Encyclopedia of Public International Law* (Oxford Public International Law online database January 2018).

Gesk G, 'Right to Resistance and Terrorism – The Example of Germany' (2012) 13 *German Law Journal* 1075.

Ginsburg T, Lansberg-Rodriguez D and Versteeg M, 'When to Overthrow Your Government: The Right to Resist in the World's Constitutions' (SSRN 2012).

'When to Overthrow Your Government: The Right to Resist in the World Constitutions' (2013) 60 *UCLA Law Review* 1184.

Glazier DW, 'Wars of National Liberation' in *Max Planck Encyclopedia of Public International Law* (Oxford Public International Law online database 2009).

Goderis B and Versteeg M, 'The Transnational Origins of Constitutions: An Empirical Analysis' (2011) (SSRN 1865724, 2011).

'The Transnational Origins of Constitutions: Evidence from a Global Data Set on Constitutional Rights' (2013) (Tilburg University CentER Discussion Paper 2013-010).

'Diffusion of Constitutional Rights' (2014) 39 *International Review of Law and Economics* 1.

Goldenbaum G, 'Sovereignty and Obedience' in Clarke DM and Wilson C (eds), *The Oxford Handbook of Philosophy in Early Modern Europe* (Oxford University Press 2011).

Goldman RK, 'History and Action: The Inter-American Human Rights System and the Role of the Inter-American Commission on Human Rights' (2009) 31 *Human Rights Quarterly* 856.

Goldstone R, 'Twenty-First Century Magna Carta' in Vincent N (ed), *Magna Carta: The Foundation of Freedom 1215–2015* (Third Millennium Publishing 2015).

Gonzalez-Bertomeu JF and Gargarella R (eds), *The Latin American Casebook: Courts, Constitutions, Rights* (Routledge 2016).

Gorelick RE, 'Wars of National Liberation: Jus Ad Bellum' (1979) 11(1) *Case Western Reserve Journal of International Law* 71.

Gourevitch A, 'The Right to Strike: A Radical View' (2018) 112(4) *American Political Science Review* 905.

Grant JP and Barker JC (eds), *Parry and Grant Encyclopaedic Dictionary of International Law* (2nd edn, Oceana Publications 2004).

Gray C, *International Law and the Use of Force* (4th edn, Oxford University Press 2018).

'The Use of Force and the International Legal Order' in Evans MD (ed), *International Law* (Oxford University Press 2010).

Greenawalt K, 'The Perplexing Borders of Justification and Excuse' (1984) 84(8) *Columbia Law Review* 1897.

Grimm D, 'The Basic Law at 60 – Identity and Change' (2010) 11(1) *German Law Journal* 33.

'Types of Constitutions' in Rosenfeld M and Sajó A (eds), *Oxford Handbook of Comparative Constitutional Law* (Oxford University Press 2012).

Grotius H, *The Rights of War and Peace* (Tuck R ed, Barbeyrac J tr, Liberty Fund 2005).

Guillermet-Fernández C and Puyana DF, 'The General Assembly Adopts the Declaration on the Right to Peace: An Opportunity to Strengthen the Linkage between Peace, Human Rights and Development in the New Millennium' (2017) 2(3) *Eruditio* 39.

Guillermet-Fernández C, Puyana DF and Bosé M, *The Right to Peace: Past, Present and Future* (UN Educational, Scientific and Cultural Organization, University for Peace 2017).

Halbert JD, 'A Responsibility to Protect or Preclude? Examining the Beneficiaries of the Responsibility to Protect' in Nollkaemper A and Hoffman J (eds), *Responsibility to Protect: From Principle to Practice* (Amsterdam University Press 2011).

Hannum H, 'The Status of the Universal Declaration of Human Rights in National and International Law' (1995–1996) 25 *Georgia Journal of International and Comparative Law* 287.

Hanlon RJ and Christie K, *Freedom from Fear, Freedom from Want: An Introduction to Human Security* (University of Toronto Press 2016).

Haque AA, *Law and Morality at War* (Oxford University Press 2017).

Hart HLA, 'Positivism and the Separation of Law and Morals' (1958) 71(4) *Harvard Law Review* 593.

Hathaway JC, 'Michigan Guidelines on the Exclusion of International Criminals' (2013) 35(4) *Michigan Journal of International Law* 5.

Hathaway JC and Foster M, *The Law of Refugee Status* (2nd edn, Cambridge University Press 2014).

Hathaway JC and Harvey CJ, 'Framing Refugee Protection in the New World Disorder' (2001) 34 *Cornell International Law Journal* 257.

Haupt CE, 'The Scope of Democratic Public Discourse: Defending Democracy, Tolerating Intolerance, and the Problem of Neo-Nazi Demonstrations in Germany' (2008) 20 *Florida Journal of International Law* 169.

Hayden P, 'Constraining War: Human Security and the Human Right to Peace' (2004) 6 *Human Rights Review* 35.

Hayes RE, 'Revolution as a Constitutional Right' (1938) 13 *Temple Law Quarterly* 18.

Hayton RD, 'Untitled Review' (1961) 55(1) *American Journal of International Law* 187.

Hehir A, 'The Responsibility to Protect: Sound and Fury Signifying Nothing?' (2010) 24(2) *International Relations* 218.

Henckaerts JM and Doswald-Beck L (eds), *Customary International Humanitarian Law* (Cambridge University Press 2005).

Hessbruegge J, 'The Right to Life as the *Jus ad Bellum* of Non-International Armed Conflict (A Reply to Lieblich)' (*JustSecurity*, 27 October 2016).

Human Rights and Personal Self-Defense in International Law (Oxford University Press 2017).

Heyns C, 'A "Struggle Approach" to Human Rights' in Soeteman A (ed), *Pluralism and Law* (Springer 2001).

'Civil and Political Rights in the African Charter' in Evans M and Murray R (eds), *The African Charter on Human and Peoples' Rights: The System in Practice, 1986–2006* (Cambridge University Press 2008).

Heyns C and Kaguongo W, 'Constitutional Human Rights Law in Africa' (2006) 22 *South African Journal of Human Rights* 673.

Higgins N, *Regulating the Use of Force in Wars of National Liberation: The Need for a New Regime* (Martinus Nijhoff 2010).

Higgins R, 'International Law and Civil Conflict' in Luard E (ed), *The International Regulation of Civil Wars* (New York University Press 1972).

Hohfeld WN, *Fundamental Legal Conceptions as Applied in Judicial Reasoning and Other Legal Essays* (Yale University Press 1919).

Hohmann J and Weller M (eds), *The UN Declaration on the Rights of Indigenous Peoples: A Commentary* (Oxford University Press 2018).

Holt JC, *Magna Carta* (Garnett G and Hudson J eds, 3rd edn, Cambridge University Press 2015).

Honoré T, 'The Right to Rebel' (1988) 8(1) *Oxford Journal of Legal Studies* 34.

Horvath B, 'Rights of Man: Due Process of Law and *Excès de Pouvoir*' (1955) 4(4) *American Journal of Comparative Law* 539.

Howard-Hassman RE, 'Human Security: Undermining Human Rights?' (2012) 34(1) *Human Rights Quarterly* 88.

Hyeran J, *Compliant Rebels: Rebel Groups and International Law in World Politics* (Cambridge University Press 2015).

Jackson VC and Tushnet M (eds), *Comparative Constitutional Law* (Foundation Press 1999).

Jägerskiöld S, 'Tyrannicide and the Right of Resistance, 1792–1809 – A Study on JJ Anckarström' (1964) 8 *Scandinavian Studies in Law* 67.

Jaski B, *Early Irish Kingship and Succession* (Four Courts Press 2000).

Jászi O and Lewis JD (eds), *Against the Tyrant: The Tradition and Theory of Tyrannicide* (The Free Press 1957).

Jellinek G, *Declaration of the Rights of Man and of Citizens: A Contribution to Modern Constitutional History* (Henry Holt 1901).

Jervey ED and Huber CH, 'The Creole Affair' (1980) 65(3) *Journal of Negro History* 196.

Jessup PJ, *A Modern Law of Nations: An Introduction* (Macmillan 1948).

Johnson MG, 'A Magna Carta for Mankind: Writing the Universal Declaration of Human Rights' in Johnson MG and Symonides J (eds), *The Universal Declaration of Human Rights: A History of Its Creation and Implementation 1948–1998* (UNESCO Publishing 1998).

Joseph S and Castan M, *The International Covenant on Civil and Political Rights: Cases, Materials and Commentary* (3rd edn, Oxford University Press 2013).

Jurdi NN, 'The Crime of Terrorism in Lebanese and International Law' in Alamuddin A, Jurdi NN and Tolbert D (eds), *The Special Tribunal for Lebanon: Law and Practice* (Oxford University Press 2014).

Kadish MR and Kadish SH, *Discretion to Disobey: A Study of Lawful Departures from Legal Rules* (Stanford University Press 1973, repr Quid Pro Books 2010).

Kälin W and Künzli J, 'Article 1F(b): Freedom Fighters, Terrorists and the Notion of Serious Non-Political Crime' (2000) 12 supp *International Journal of Refugee Law* 46.

Kämmerer JA, 'Colonialism' in *Max Planck Encyclopedia of Public International Law* (Oxford Public International Law online database January 2018).

Kapelner Z, 'Revolution against Non-Violent Oppression' (2019) 25(4) *Res Publica: A Journal of Moral, Legal and Political Philosophy* 445.

Kapferer S, 'The Interface between Extradition and Asylum' (Department of International Protection, UN High Commissioner for Refugees 2003).

Kaufmann A, 'Small Scale Right to Resist' (1985–1986) 21 *New England Law Review* 571.

Kay RS and Colón-Ríos JI, *Adjudicating Revolution: Courts and Constitutional Change* (Edward Elgar 2022).

Keller H, 'Friendly Relations Declaration (1970)' in *Max Planck Encyclopedia of Public International Law* (Oxford Public International Law online database 2009).

Kelsen H, 'Quincy Wright's A Study of War and the *Bellum Justum* Theory' (1943) 53 *Ethics* 208.

Peace through Law (University of North Carolina Press 1944).

General Theory of Law and State (Harvard University Press 1949).

'The Natural Law Doctrine before the Tribunal of Science' (1949) 2 *Western Political Quarterly* 481.

Kennedy D, *A Critique of Adjudication* (Harvard University Press 1997).

Kenny C and Butler S, 'The Legality of Intervention by Invitation in Situations of R2P Violations' (2018) 51 *New York University Journal of International Law and Politics* 135.

Kern F, *Kingship and Law in the Middle Ages: The Divine Right of Kings and the Right of Resistance in the Early Middle Ages* (Chrimes S tr, Basil Blackwell 1939).

Kesby A, *The Right to Have Rights: Citizenship, Humanity and International Law* (Oxford University Press 2012).

Khan A, 'A Legal Theory of Revolutions' (1987) 5 *Boston University International Law Journal* 1.

Khan R, 'Decolonization' in *Max Planck Encyclopedia of Public International Law* (Oxford Public International Law online database 2011).

Khoday A, 'Protecting Those Who Go beyond the Law: Contemplating Refugee Status for Individuals Who Challenge Oppression through Resistance' (2012) 25 *Georgetown Immigration Law Journal* 571.

Kittrie NN, *Rebels with a Cause: The Minds and Morality of Political Offenders* (Westview 2000).

Klabbers J, 'Some Problems Regarding the Object and Purpose of Treaties' (1997) 8 *Finnish Yearbook of International Law* 138.

Kleffner JK, 'The Scope of Crimes Triggering the Responsibility to Protect' in Nollkaemper A and Hoffman J (eds), *Responsibility to Protect: From Principle to Practice* (Amsterdam University Press 2011).

Kodjo E, 'The African Charter on Human and Peoples' Rights' (1990) 11(1–2) *Human Rights Law Journal* 271.

Kommers DP, *The Federal Constitutional Court* (American Institute for Contemporary German Studies and Johns Hopkins University 1994).

Kommers DP and Miller RA, *The Constitutional Jurisprudence of the Federal Republic of Germany* (3rd edn, Duke University Press 2012).

Kopel DB, 'The Right to Arms in the Living Constitution' (2010) *Cardozo Law Review* de novo 99.

Kopel DB, Gallant P and Eisen JD, 'Is Resisting Genocide a Human Right?' (2006) 81 (4) *Notre Dame Law Review* 1275.

'The Human Right of Self-Defense' (2008) 22 *Brigham Young University Journal of Public Law* 43.

Koskenniemi M, 'The Preamble of the Universal Declaration of Human Rights' in Alfredsson G and Eide A (eds), *The Universal Declaration of Human Rights: A Common Standard of Achievement* (Martinus Nijhoff 1999).

'Function and Scope of the *Lex Specialis* Rule and the Question of "Self-Contained Regimes", Preliminary Report' (2004) UN Doc ILC(LVI)SG/FIL/CRD 1 and Add 1.

Kozma J, Nowak M and Scheinin M, *A World Court of Human Rights: Consolidated Draft Statute and Commentary* (Neuer Wissenschaflichter Verlag 2010).

Kramer LD, *The People Themselves: Popular Constitutionalism and Judicial Review* (Oxford University Press 2004).

Kulski WW, 'Soviet Comments on International Law' (1951) 45(4) *American Journal of International Law* 762.

Kunig P, 'United Nations Charter, Interpretation of' in *Max Planck Encyclopedia of Public International Law* (Oxford Public International Law online database 2006).

'Intervention, Prohibition of' in *Max Planck Encyclopedia of Public International Law* (Oxford Public International Law online database April 2008).

Kunz JL, 'Revolutionary Creation of Norms of International Law' (1947) 41 *American Journal of International Law* 119.

Kutner L, 'A Philosophical Perspective on Rebellion' in Bassiouni MC (ed), *International Terrorism and Political Crimes* (Charles C Thomas 1975).

Lanni A and Vermeule A, 'Constitutional Design in the Ancient World' (2012) 64 *Stanford Law Review* 907.

László P, '*Ius Resistendi* in Hungary: Resistance as a Right' in László P and Lojkó M (eds), *Hungary's Long Nineteenth Century* (Brill 2012).

Lauterpacht H, 'The Law of Nations, the Law of Nature and the Rights of Man' (1943) 29 *Transactions of the Grotius Society* 1.

An International Bill of the Rights of Man (Columbia University Press 1945).

'The Grotian Tradition in International Law' (1946) 23 *British Yearbook of International Law* 1.

'Universal Declaration of Human Rights' (1948) 25 *British Yearbook of International Law* 354.

International Law and Human Rights (Stevens and Sons 1950).

Law DS and Versteeg M, 'The Evolution and Ideology of Global Constitutionalism' (2011) 99(5) *California Law Review* 1163.

'The Declining Influence of the United States Constitution' (2012) 87 *New York University Law Review* 762.

'Sham Constitutions' (2013) 101 *California Law Review* 863.

Lazar S, 'Necessity in Self-Defense and War' (2012) 40(1) *Philosophy and Public Affairs* 3.

'Authorization and the Morality of War' (2016) 94(2) *Australasian Journal of Philosophy* 211.

Lenin VI, *Critical Remarks on the National Question – The Right of Nations to Self-Determination* (1914, Foreign Languages Publishing House edn 1954).

Levi EH, *An Introduction to Legal Reasoning* (University of Chicago Press 1949).

Levinson S, 'The Embarrassing Second Amendment' (1989) 99 *Yale Law Journal* 637.

Lévitt A, 'Minority Report of Committee on Codification: A Proposed Code of International Criminal Law' (1939) 33 (27–29 April 1939) *Proceedings of the American Society of International Law at Its Annual Meeting* (1921–1969) 212.

Lewis JD, 'The Development of the Theory of Tyrannicide to 1660' in Jászi O and Lewis JD (eds), *Against the Tyrant: The Tradition and Theory of Tyrannicide* (The Free Press 1957).

Lewy G, 'Resistance to Tyranny: Treason, Right or Duty?' (1960) 13(3) *Western Political Quarterly* 581.

Lieblich E, *International Law and Civil Wars: Intervention and Consent* (Routledge 2013).

'Internal Jus Ad Bellum' (2016) 67 *Hastings Law Journal* 687.

Lieblich E and Benvenisti E, *Occupation in International Law* (Oxford University Press 2022).

Lines R, *Drug Control and Human Rights in International Law* (Cambridge University Press 2017).

Lintott A, *The Constitution of the Roman Republic* (Oxford University Press 1999).

Violence in Republican Rome (Oxford University Press 1999).

Lippman M, 'The Right of Civil Resistance under International Law and the Domestic Necessity Defense' (1990) 8 *Dickinson Journal of International Law* 349.

'Nuremberg and American Justice' (1991) 5 *Notre Dame Journal of Ethics, Law and Public Policy* 951.

Contemporary Criminal Law Concepts, Cases and Controversies (2nd edn, Sage 2010).

Liwanga RC, 'The Meaning of Gross Violation of Human Rights: A Focus on International Tribunals' Decisions over the DRC Conflicts' (2015) 44(1) *Denver Journal of International Law and Policy* 67.

Locke J, 'The Second Treatise of Government: An Essay Concerning the True Original, Extent and End of Civil Government' in *Two Treatises of Government* (Laslett P ed, rev edn, Cambridge University Press 1988).

Longobardo M, *The Use of Armed Force in Occupied Territory* (Cambridge University Press 2018).

Loughlin M, *Foundations of Public Law* (Oxford University Press 2010).

Luck E and Luck D, 'The Individual Responsibility to Protect' in Rosenberg SP, Galis T and Zucker A (eds), *Reconstructing Atrocity Prevention* (Cambridge University Press 2015).

Mačák K, 'Wars of National Liberation: The Story of One Unusual Rule I', *OUP Blog* (23 July 2018).

'Wars of National Liberation: The Story of One Unusual Rule II', *OUP Blog* (30 July 2018).

MacDowell DM, *The Law in Classical Athens* (Cornell University Press 1978).

Mackinnon ES, 'Declaration as Disavowal: The Politics of Race and Empire in the Universal Declaration of Human Rights' (2019) 47(1) *Political Theory* 57.

MacMillan C and Smith C (eds), *Challenges to Authority and the Recognition of Rights – From Magna Carta to Modernity* (Cambridge University Press 2019).

Malcolm JL, *To Keep and Bear Arms: The Origins of an Anglo-American Right* (Harvard University Press 1994).

'The Supreme Court and the Uses of History: District of Columbia v Heller' (2009) 56 *UCLA Law Review* 1377.

Manirakiza P, 'Towards a Right to Resist Gross Undemocratic Practices in Africa' (2019) 63(1) *Journal of African Law* 81.

Marcic R, 'The Persistence of Right-Law: An Inquiry into the Foundations of the Right to Resist' (1973) 59 *Archives for Philosophy of Law and Social Philosophy* 87.

Marks S and Clapham A, *International Human Rights Lexicon* (Oxford University Press 2005).

Marshall G, 'The Right to Disobey the Law' in Marshall G, *Constitutional Theory* (Clarendon Press 1971).

Mårtenson J, 'The Preamble of the Universal Declaration of Human Rights and the United Nations Human Rights Programme' in Eide A, Melander G, Rehof LA, Rosas A and Swineheart T (eds), *The Universal Declaration of Human Rights: A Commentary* (Scandinavian University Press 1992).

McGlew JF, *Tyranny and Political Culture in Ancient Greece* (Cornell University Press 1993).

'Fighting Tyranny in Fifth Century Athens: Democratic Citizenship and the Oath of Demophantus' (2012) 55(2) *Bulletin of the Institute of Classical Studies* 91.

Mead D, 'The Right to Peaceful Protest under the European Convention on Human Rights: A Content Study of Strasbourg Case Law' (2007) 4 *European Human Rights Law Review* 345.

The New Law of Peaceful Protest: Rights and Regulation in the Human Rights Act Era (Hart 2010).

Medina C, *The American Convention on Human Rights: Crucial Rights and their Theory and Practice* (Instersentia 2014).

Mégret F, '*Jus In Bello* as *Jus Ad Bellum*' (2006) 100 *Proceedings of the American Society of International Law* 121.

'Beyond "Freedom Fighters" and "Terrorists": When, If Ever, Is Non-State Violence Legitimate in International Law?' (SSRN 2009).

'Beyond the Salvation Paradigm: Responsibility to Protect (Others) vs the Power of Protecting Oneself' (2009) 40 *Security Dialogue* 575.

'Causes Worth Fighting For: Is There a Non-State *Jus ad Bellum*?' in Constantinides A and Zaikos N (eds), *The Diversity of International Law: Essays in Honour of Professor Kalliopi K Koufa* (Martinus Nijhoff 2009).

'Civil Disobedience and International Law: Sketch for a Theoretical Argument' (2009) 46 *Canadian Yearbook of International Law* 143.

'Not "Lambs to the Slaughter": A Program for Resistance to Genocidal Law' in Provost R and Akhavan P (eds), *Confronting Genocide* (Springer 2011).

'Civilian Resilience in Syria: Helping the Syrians Help Themselves? The Ambiguities of International Assistance to the Rebellion' (2014) 3(1) *Stability: International Journal of Security and Development* 1.

'Should Rebels Be Amnestied?' in Stahn C, Easterday JS and Iverson J (eds), *Jus Post Bellum: Mapping the Normative Foundations* (Oxford University Press 2014).

'International Law and Peoples' Resistance: Foreword' (2016) 1(1) *Inter Gentes* 3.

'Is the ICC Focusing Too Much on Non-State Actors?' in Amann DM and deGuzman M (eds), *Arcs of Global Justice: Essays in Honor of William A Schabas* (Oxford University Press 2017).

Meisenberg SM, 'Joint Criminal Enterprise and the Special Court for Sierra Leone' in Jalloh CC (ed), *The Sierra Leone Special Court and Its Legacy: The Impact for Africa and International Criminal Law* (Cambridge University Press 2013).

Menachery Paulose R (ed), *People's Tribunals, Human Rights and the Law: Searching for Justice* (Routledge 2020).

Meron T, *Human Rights and Humanitarian Norms as Customary Law* (Clarendon 1989).

Minh TV, 'Political and Juridical Sanctions against Violations of Human Rights' in *Violations of Human Rights: Possible Rights of Recourse and Forms of Resistance* (UNESCO 1984).

Mirow MC, *Latin American Constitutions: The Constitution of Cádiz and Its Legacy in Spanish America* (Cambridge University Press 2015).

Mommsen H, *Germans against Hitler: The Stauffenberg Plot and Resistance under the Third Reich* (Angus McGeoch tr, IB Tauris 2008).

Morsink J, 'The Philosophy of the Universal Declaration' (1984) 6(3) *Human Rights Quarterly* 309.

The Universal Declaration of Human Rights: Origins, Drafting and Intent (University of Pennsylvania Press 1999).

Inherent Human Rights: Philosophical Roots of the Universal Declaration (University of Pennsylvania Press 2009).

Muldoon J, 'The Remonstrance of the Irish Princes and the Canon Law Tradition of the Just War' (1978) 22 *American Journal of Legal History* 309.

Murphy S, 'Unique in International Human Rights Law: Article 20(2) and the Right to Resist in the African Charter on Human and Peoples' Rights' (2011) 11(2) *African Human Rights Law Journal* 465.

'The Right to Resist Reconsidered' in Keane D and McDermott Y (eds), *The Challenge of Human Rights: Past, Present and Future* (Edward Elgar 2012).

Murray AH, 'The Vindiciae Contra Tyrannos' [1958] 1 *Acta Juridica* 275.

Murray R, *The African Charter on Human and Peoples' Rights: A Commentary* (Oxford University Press 2019).

Neumann FL, 'On the Limits of Justifiable Disobedience' in Neumann FL, *The Democratic and Authoritarian State: Essays in Political and Legal Theory* (Free Press 1957).

Newton M and May L, *Proportionality in International Law* (Oxford University Press 2014).

Nguyen QTT, 'Rethinking the Legality of Intervention by Invitation: Toward Neutrality' (2019) 24(2) *Journal of Conflict and Security Law* 201.

Nicholson P, 'Kant on the Duty Never to Resist the Sovereign' (1976) 86(3) *Ethics* 214.

Nippel W, *Public Order in Ancient Rome* (Cambridge University Press 1995).
Nkansah LA, 'The Right of Resistance and the Defence of Ghana's Fourth Republican Constitution' (2014) 6 *Kwame Nkrumah University of Science and Technology Law Journal* 129.
Nowak M, *UN Covenant on Civil and Political Rights – CCPR Commentary* (NP Engel 1993).
UN Covenant on Civil and Political Rights – CCPR Commentary (2nd edn, NP Engel 2005).
Ó Néill D, 'Remonstrance of the Irish Chiefs to Pope John XXII' (1317) (Curtis E tr) in Curtis E and McDowell RB (eds), *Irish Historical Documents 1172–1922* (Barnes and Noble 1943 repr 1968).
Ober J, 'Law and Political Theory' in Gagarin M and Cohen D (eds), *Cambridge Companion to Ancient Greek Law* (Cambridge University Press 2005).
Ogato S and Cels J, 'Human Security? Protecting and Empowering the People' (2003) 9(3) *Global Governance* 273.
Ohlin JD, 'The Right to Exist and the Right to Resist' (SSRN 2014).
Ohlin JD and May L, *Necessity in International Law* (Oxford University Press 2016).
Olivier PJJ, *Legal Fictions in Practice and Legal Science* (Rotterdam University Press 1975).
Oman N, 'Hannah Arendt's "Right to Have Rights": A Philosophical Context for Human Security' (2010) 9(3) *Journal of Human Rights* 279.
Omorogbe EY, 'A Club of Incumbents? The African Union and *Coups d'État*' (2011) 44 *Vanderbilt Journal of International Law* 123.
Opsahl T and Dimitrijevic V, 'Articles 29 and 30' in Alfredsson G and Eide A (eds), *The Universal Declaration of Human Rights: A Common Standard of Achievement* (Martinus Nijhoff 1999).
Ostwald M, 'The Athenian Legislation against Tyranny and Subversion' (1955) 86 *American Philological Association* 103.
Ouguergouz F, *The African Charter on Human and Peoples' Rights: A Comprehensive Agenda for Human Dignity and Sustainable Democracy in Africa* (Martinus Nijhoff 2003).
Paine T, 'Dissertation on First Principles of Government' in Van der Weyde WM (ed), *The Life and Works of Thomas Paine* (Thomas Paine National Historical Association 1925).
Patterson C, 'Athenian Citizenship Law' in Gagarin M and Cohen D (eds), *Cambridge Companion to Ancient Greek Law* (Cambridge University Press 2005).
Paust JJ, 'Political Oppression in the Name of National Security: Authority, Participation, and the Necessity within Democratic Limits Test' (1982) 9(1) *Yale International Law Journal* 178.
'The Human Right to Participate in Armed Revolution and Related Forms of Social Violence: Testing the Limits of Permissibility' (1983) 32 *Emory Law Journal* 545.
'Aggression against Authority: The Crime of Oppression, Politicide and Other Crimes against Human Rights' (1986) 18 *Case Western Reserve Journal of International Law* 283.
'International Law, Dignity, Democracy and the Arab Spring' (2013) 46 *Cornell International Law Journal* 1.

Pauwelyn J, *Conflict of Norms in Public International Law* (Cambridge University Press 2003).

Pearsall J and Trumble B (eds), *Oxford English Reference Dictionary* (2nd edn, Oxford University Press 2002).

Plant G, 'Civilian Protest Vessels and the Law of the Sea' (1983) 14 *Netherlands Yearbook of International Law* 133.

'International Law and Direct Action Protests at Sea: Twenty Years On' (2002) 33 *Netherlands Yearbook of International Law* 75.

Plutarch, 'Solon and Publicola' in *Lives* (Perrin B tr, Harvard University Press 1914).

Portteus K, 'The Right of Revolution in the American Founding' (RealClear Public Affairs, 18 May 2021).

Pribilla M, *The Right to Resist* (Catholic Social Guild 1952).

Puyana DF, 'World Campaign on the Human Right to Peace' in Durán CV and Pérez CF (eds), *Contribuciones regionales para una declaración universal del derecho humano a la paz* (Asociación Española para el Derecho Internacional de los Derechos Humanos 2010).

Rady M, 'Hungary and the Golden Bull of 1222' (2014) 24(2) *Banatica* 87.

Rajagopal B, *International Law from Below* (Cambridge University Press 2003).

Ramcharan BG, 'The *travaux préparatoires* of the African Commission on Human and Peoples' Rights' (1992) 13 *Human Rights Law Journal* 307.

Raubitschek AE, 'The Origin of Ostracism' (1951) 55 *American Journal of Archaeology* 221.

Rawle W, *A View of the Constitution of the United States of America* (2nd edn, PH Nicklin 1829).

Rawls J, *A Theory of Justice* (Harvard University Press 1999).

Redaelli C, 'The Right to Rebel against Violations of Human Rights: A New Role for the Responsibility to Protect?' (2020) 19(1) *Palestine Yearbook of International Law* 8.

Rembe NS, *The System of Protection of Human Rights under the African Charter on Human and Peoples' Rights: Problems and Prospects* (Institute of Southern African Studies, National University of Lesotho 1991).

Remec PP, *The Position of the Individual in International Law According to Grotius and Vattel* (Martinus Nijhoff 1960).

Reynolds J, 'Third World Approaches to International Law and the Ghosts of Apartheid' in Keane D and McDermott Y (eds), *The Challenge of Human Rights: Past, Present and Future* (Edward Elgar 2012).

Rhodes PJ, *A Commentary on the Aristotelian Athenaion Politeia* (Clarendon Press 1981).

'Oaths in Political Life' in Sommerstein AH and Fletcher J (eds), *Horkos: The Oath in Greek Society* (Bristol Phoenix Press 2007).

Rishmawi M, 'The Revised Arab Charter on Human Rights: A Step Forward?' (2005) 5 (2) *Human Rights Law Review* 361.

'The Arab Charter on Human Rights and the League of Arab States: An Update' (2010) 10(1) *Human Rights Law Review* 169.

The League of Arab States Human Rights Standards and Mechanisms – Towards Further Civil Society Engagement: A Manual for Practitioners (Open Society Foundations and Cairo Institute for Human Rights Studies 2015).

Rodenhäuser T, *Organizing Rebellion: Non-State Armed Groups under International Humanitarian Law, Human Rights Law, and International Criminal Law* (Oxford University Press 2018).

Roeschke E, 'Eco-Terrorism and Piracy on the High Seas: Japanese Whaling and the Rights of Private Groups to Enforce International Conservation Law in Neutral Waters' (2009) 20(1) *Villanova Environmental Law Journal* 99.

Röling BVA, 'The Legal Status of Rebels and Rebellion' (1976) 13(2) *Journal of Peace Research* 149.

Rosanvallon P, *Counter-Democracy: Politics in an Age of Distrust* (Goldhammer A tr, Cambridge University Press 2008).

Rosas A, 'Article 21' in Alfredsson G and Eide A (eds), *The Universal Declaration of Human Rights: A Common Standard of Achievement* (Martinus Nijhoff 1999).

'Internal Self-Determination' in Tomuschat C (ed), *Modern Law of Self-Determination* (Martinus Nijhoff 1993).

Rosenfeld M and Sajó A (eds), *The Oxford Handbook of Comparative Constitutional Law* (Oxford University Press 2012).

Roşu F, 'Free from Obedience: Constitutional Expressions of the Right of Resistance in Early Modern Transylvania and Poland-Lithuania' (2017) 47(1) *European History Quarterly* 6.

Roth BR, *Governmental Illegitimacy in International Law* (Oxford University Press 2000).

Rubin E, 'Judicial Review and the Right to Resist' (2008) 97 *Georgetown Law Journal* 61.

Sager LG, 'Fair Measure: The Legal Status of Underenforced Constitutional Norms' (1978) 91(6) *Harvard Law Review* 1212.

Samnøy Å, 'The Origins of the Universal Declaration of Human Rights' in Alfredsson G and Eide A (eds), *The Universal Declaration of Human Rights: A Common Standard of Achievement* (Martinus Nijhoff 1999).

Sassòli M, 'Taking Armed Groups Seriously: Ways to Improve Their Compliance with International Humanitarian Law' (2010) 1 *International Humanitarian Legal Studies* 5.

Saul B, 'Attempts to Define "Terrorism" in International Law' (2005) LII *Netherlands International Law Review* 57.

Defining Terrorism in International Law (Oxford University Press 2006).

'Defending "Terrorism": Justifications and Excuses for Terrorism in International Criminal Law' Legal Studies Research Paper No 08/122 (University of Sydney Law School, October 2008).

Saunders JB (ed), *Words and Phrases Legally Defined* (3rd edn, Butterworths 1990).

Saxoferrato B, *On Guelfs and Ghibbellines* (Robinson J tr, Creative Commons Attribution-Non-Commercial ShareAlike 3.0 Unreported License 2014 rev 1.1a).

On the Tyrant (Robinson J tr, Creative Commons Attribution-Non-Commercial ShareAlike 3.0 Unreported License 2012 (rev 1.0a) 2016 (rev 1.2)).

Scafuro AC, 'Atimia' in *Encyclopedia of Ancient History Online* (John Wiley 2012).

Schabas WA, 'Punishment of Non-State Actors in Non-International Armed Conflict' (2002) 26(4) *Fordham International Law Journal* 907.

An Introduction to the International Criminal Court (2nd edn, Cambridge University Press 2004).

The UN International Criminal Tribunals – The Former Yugoslavia, Rwanda and Sierra Leone (Cambridge University Press 2006).

'"Complementarity" in Practice: Some Uncomplimentary Thoughts' (2008) 19 *Criminal Law Forum* 5.

'Prosecutorial Discretion v Judicial Activism at the International Criminal Court' (2008) 6 *Journal of International Criminal Justice* 731.

'State Policy as an Element of International Crimes' (2008) 98(3) *Journal of Criminal Law and Criminology* 953.

Genocide in International Law (2nd edn, Cambridge University Press 2009).

The Universal Declaration of Human Rights: Travaux Préparatoires (Cambridge University Press 2013).

The European Convention on Human Rights: A Commentary (Oxford University Press 2015).

An Introduction to the International Criminal Court (5th edn, Cambridge University Press 2017).

The Customary International Law of Human Rights (Oxford University Press 2021).

Schrijver NJ, 'Natural Resources, Permanent Sovereignty Over' in *Max Planck Encyclopedia of Public International Law* (Oxford Public International Law online database 2008).

Schwartz RE, 'Chaos, Oppression, and Rebellion: The Use of Self-Help to Secure Individual Rights under International Law' (1994) 12 *Boston University Law Journal* 255.

Schwarz W, 'The Right of Resistance' (1964) 74(2) *Ethics* 126.

Senaratne K, *Internal Self-Determination in International Law: History, Theory, and Practice* (Cambridge University Press 2021).

Shah P, 'Taking the "Political" Out of Asylum: The Legal Containment of Refugees' Political Activism' in Nicholson F and Twomey P (eds), *Refugee Rights and Realities: Evolving International Concepts and Regimes* (Cambridge University Press 1999).

Shaw MN, *International Law* (6th edn, Cambridge University Press 2008).

Shaygan F, 'Intervention by Invitation as a Tool of New Colonialism' in Crawford J, Koroma A, Mahmoudi S and Pellet A (eds), *The International Legal Order: Current Needs and Possible Responses* (Brill Nijhoff 2017).

Shear JL, 'The Oath of Demophantos and the Politics of Athenian Identity' in Sommerstein AH and Fletcher J (eds), *Horkos: The Oath in Greek Society* (Bristol Phoenix Press 2007).

Shelton D, *Remedies in International Human Rights Law* (2nd edn, Oxford University Press 2005).

'International Law and "Relative Normativity"' in Evans MD (ed), *International Law* (3rd edn, Oxford University Press 2010).

Shivji IG, *The Concept of Human Rights in Africa* (CODESRIA Book Series 1989).

Silving H, 'The Origins of the Magnae Cartae' (1965) 3 *Harvard Journal on Legislation* 117.

Simma B, Mosler H, Randelzhofer A, Tomuschat C, Wolfrum R, Paulus A and Chaitidou E (eds), *The Charter of the United Nations: A Commentary* (2nd edn, Oxford University Press 2002).

Sohn L, 'The Human Rights Law of the Charter' (1977) 12 *Texas International Law Journal* 129.

'"Generally Accepted" International Rules' (1986) 61 *Washington Law Review* 1073.

Spitz D, 'Democracy and the Problem of Civil Disobedience' (1954) 48 *American Political Science Review* 386.

Sreedhar S, *Hobbes on Resistance: Defying the Leviathan* (Cambridge University Press 2010).

Stein T, 'Extradition' in *Max Planck Encyclopedia of Public International Law* (Oxford Public International Law online database 2011).

Steinberger PJ, 'Hobbesian Resistance' (2002) 46 *American Journal of Political Science* 856.

Steinbock DJ, 'Interpreting the Refugee Definition' (1998) 45 *University of California Los Angeles Law Review* 733.

Steiner HJ, 'Political Participation as a Human Right' (1988) 1 *Harvard Human Rights Yearbook* 77.

Steiner HJ, Alston P and Goodman R (eds), *International Human Rights in Context: Law, Politics, Morals* (3rd edn, Oxford University Press 2007).

Story J, *Commentaries on the Constitution of the United States* (Hilliard, Gray and Co 1833).

Strang LJ, 'Originalism's Subject Matter: Why the Declaration of Independence is Not Part of the Constitution' (2016) 89 *Southern California Law Review* 637.

Sumida G, 'The Right to Revolution: Implications for International Law and Order' in McDougal MS and Reisman WM (eds), *International Law in Contemporary Perspective: The Public Order of the World Community – Cases and Materials* (Foundation Press 1981).

Tadjbakhsh S, 'In Defense of the Broad View of Human Security' in Martin M and Owen T (eds), *Routledge Handbook of Human Security* (Routledge 2014).

Takemura H, 'Disobeying Manifestly Illegal Orders' (2006) 18(4) *Peace Review: A Journal of Social Justice* 533.

International Human Right to Conscientious Objection to Military Service and Individual Duties to Disobey Manifestly Illegal Orders (Springer 2009).

Taulbee JL, 'Political Crimes, Human Rights and Contemporary International Practice' (1990) 4 *Emory International Law Review* 43.

Teegarden DA, *Death to Tyrants! Ancient Greek Democracy and the Struggle against Tyranny* (Princeton University Press 2014).

Thirlway H, *The Sources of International Law* (Oxford University Press 2014).

Thürer D and Burri T, 'Self-Determination' in *Max Planck Encyclopedia of Public International Law* (Oxford Public International Law online database 2008).

Tiller EH and Cross FB, 'What Is Legal Doctrine?' (2006) 100(1) *Northwestern University Law Review* 517.

Todd SC, *The Shape of Athenian Law* (Clarendon Press 1993).

Tomuschat C, 'The Right of Resistance and Human Rights' in *Violations of Human Rights: Possible Rights of Recourse and Forms of Resistance* (UNESCO 1984).

'General International Law: A New Source of International Law?' in Mazzeschi RP and De Sena P (eds), *Global Justice, Human Rights and the Modernization of International Law* (Springer 2018).

Trechsel S, 'A World Court for Human Rights?' (2004) 1(1) *Northwestern University Journal of International Human Rights* 3.

Trinidad J, *Self-Determination in Disputed Colonial Territories* (Cambridge University Press 2018).

Tucker SG, *Blackstone's Commentaries with Notes of Reference to the Constitution and Laws* (William Young Birch and Abraham Small 1803).

Tunkin G, 'Is General International Law Customary Law Only?' (1993) 4 *European Journal of International Law* 534.

Turchetti M, *Tyrannie et tyrannicide de l'Antiquité a nos jours* (Presses Universitaires de France 2001).

'"Despotism" and "Tyranny": Unmasking a Tenacious Confusion' (2008) 7(2) *European Journal of Political Theory* 159.

Tushnet M, *Taking the Constitution away from the Courts* (Princeton University Press 1999).

Umozurike UO, *The African Charter on Human and Peoples' Rights* (Martinus Nijhoff 1997).

Van Aggelen J, 'The Preamble of the United Nations Declaration of Human Rights' (2000) 28 *Denver Journal of International Law and Policy* 129.

Van Bueren G, 'Socio-economic Rights and a Bill of Rights – An Overlooked British Tradition' [2013] *Public Law* 821.

Van den Wijngaert C, *The Political Offense Exception to Extradition: The Delicate Problem of Balancing the Rights of the Individual and International Public Order* (Kluwer 1980).

'The Political Offence Exception to Extradition: Defining the Issues and Searching a Feasible Alternative' (1983) 2 *Revue Belge de Droit International* 741.

Van der Wilt H, 'Unconstitutional Change of Government: A New Crime within the Jurisdiction of the African Criminal Court' (2017) 30(4) *Leiden Journal of International Law* 967.

Vattel E, *The Law of Nations, or Principles of the Law of Nature, Applied to the Conduct and Affairs of Nations and Sovereigns* (Kapossy B and Whatmore R eds, Liberty Fund 2008).

Verdoodt A, *Naissance et Signification de la Déclaration Universelle des Droits de l'Homme* (Éditions Nauwelaerts 1964).

Viljoen F, 'The African Charter on Human and Peoples' Rights: The *travaux préparatoires* in the Light of Subsequent Practice' (2004) 25 *Human Rights Law Journal* 313.

Vincent N (ed), *Magna Carta: The Foundation of Freedom 1215–2015* (Third Millennium Publishing 2015).

Von Arnauld A, von der Decken K and Susi M, *The Cambridge Handbook of New Human Rights: Recognition, Novelty, Rhetoric* (Cambridge University Press 2020).

Wacks R, *Understanding Jurisprudence: An Introduction to Legal Theory* (2nd edn, Oxford University Press 2009).

Waite M, Hawker S, Bailey C and Cowley C (eds), *Concise Oxford Thesaurus* (2nd edn, Oxford University Press 2002).

Waldehaimanot SM, 'African Law of Coups and the Situation in Eritrea: A Test for the African Union's Commitment to Democracy' (2010) 54(2) *Journal of African Law* 232.

Waldron J, 'Jeremy Bentham's *Anarchical Fallacies*' in Waldron J (ed), *Nonsense Upon Stilts: Bentham, Burke and Marx on the Rights of Man* (Methuen and Co 1987).

'Constitutionalism: A Skeptical View' in Christiano T and Christman J (eds), *Contemporary Debates in Political Philosophy* (Wiley-Blackwell 2009).

Wegen G and Kuner C, 'Germany: Federal Constitutional Court Decision Concerning the Maastricht Treaty – Introductory Note' (1994) 33 *ILM* 388.

Williams DC, 'The Constitutional Right to "Conservative" Revolution' (1997) 32 *Harvard Civil Rights-Civil Liberties Law Review* 413.

Williams KP, *Kayanerenkó:wa – The Great Law of Peace* (University of Manitoba Press 2018).

Wilson GG, 'Insurgency and International Maritime Law' (1907) 1(1) *American Journal of International Law* 46.

Wilson HA, *International Law and the Use of Force by National Liberation Movements* (Clarendon 1988).

Winkelmann I, 'Responsibility to Protect' in *Max Planck Encyclopedia of Public International Law* (Oxford Public International Law online database 2010).

Witte JJr, 'Natural Rights, Popular Sovereignty, and Covenant Politics: Johannes Althusius and the Dutch Revolt and Republic' (2009–2010) 87 *University of Detroit Mercy Law Review* 565.

Wolff HJ, *Roman Law: An Historical Introduction* (University of Oklahoma Press 1951).

Wolfrum R, 'General International Law: Rules, Principles and Standards' in *Max Planck Encyclopedia of Public International Law* (Oxford Public International Law online database 2010).

Woocher L, 'Responsibility to Prevent: Toward a Strategy' in Knight WA and Egerton F (eds), *The Routledge Handbook of the Responsibility to Protect* (Taylor and Francis 2012).

Wood M, 'United Nations, Security Council' in *Max Planck Encyclopedia of Public International Law* (Oxford Public International Law online database 2007).

Wright Q, 'The Bombardment of Damascus' (1926) 20 *American Journal of International Law* 263.

'Recognition and Self-Determination' (1954) 48 (22–24 April 1954) *Proceedings of the American Society of International Law at its Annual Meeting* (1921–1969) 23.

'Diverse Systems of World Public Order Today – Panel I: Security Problems Among Diverse Systems of World Public Order, Discussion' (1959) 53 *Proceedings of the American Society of International Law at Its Annual Meeting* (1921–1969) 166.

'International Law and Civil Strife' (1959) 53 *Proceedings of the American Society of International Law at Its Annual Meeting* (1921–1969) 145.

'United States Intervention in the Lebanon' (1959) 53 *American Journal of International Law* 112.

'Subversive Intervention' (1960) 54 *American Journal of International Law* 521.

'Intervention and Cuba in 1961' (1961) 55 (27–29 April 1961) *Proceedings of the American Society of International Law at Its Annual Meeting* (1921–1969) 2.

'The Goa Incident' (1962) 56 *American Journal of International Law* 617.

'Towards a Universal Law for Mankind' (1963) 63 *Columbia Law Review* 435.

Yazaki M, 'Legality and the Right of Resistance' [1957] 4 *Osaka University Law Review* 26.

Zimmermann B, 'Article 1' in Sandoz Y, Swinarski C and Zimmermann B (eds), *Commentary on the Protocol Additional to the Geneva Conventions of 12 August 1949, and Relating to the Protection of Victims of International Armed Conflicts (Protocol I)* (International Committee of the Red Cross-Martinus Nijhoff 1987).

Žižek S, 'Philosophy, the "Unknown Knowns" and the Public Use of Reason' (2006) 25(1) *Topoi* 137.

Index

For EU product safety concerns, contact us at Calle de José Abascal, 56–1°, 28003 Madrid, Spain or eugpsr@cambridge.org.

www.ingramcontent.com/pod-product-compliance
Lightning Source LLC
LaVergne TN
LVHW011703200926
848484LV00004B/1051
9781108838214